T0206977

Machine Learning for Decision Makers

Cognitive Computing Fundamentals for Better Decision Making

Second Edition

Dr. Patanjali Kashyap

Apress®

Machine Learning for Decision Makers: Cognitive Computing Fundamentals for Better Decision Making, Second Edition

Dr. Patanjali Kashyap
Bangalore, Karnataka, India

ISBN-13 (pbk): 978-1-4842-9800-8   ISBN-13 (electronic): 978-1-4842-9801-5
https://doi.org/10.1007/978-1-4842-9801-5

Copyright © 2024 by Dr. Patanjali Kashyap

This work is subject to copyright. All rights are reserved by the Publisher, whether the whole or part of the material is concerned, specifically the rights of translation, reprinting, reuse of illustrations, recitation, broadcasting, reproduction on microfilms or in any other physical way, and transmission or information storage and retrieval, electronic adaptation, computer software, or by similar or dissimilar methodology now known or hereafter developed.

Trademarked names, logos, and images may appear in this book. Rather than use a trademark symbol with every occurrence of a trademarked name, logo, or image we use the names, logos, and images only in an editorial fashion and to the benefit of the trademark owner, with no intention of infringement of the trademark.

The use in this publication of trade names, trademarks, service marks, and similar terms, even if they are not identified as such, is not to be taken as an expression of opinion as to whether or not they are subject to proprietary rights.

While the advice and information in this book are believed to be true and accurate at the date of publication, neither the authors nor the editors nor the publisher can accept any legal responsibility for any errors or omissions that may be made. The publisher makes no warranty, express or implied, with respect to the material contained herein.

Managing Director, Apress Media LLC: Welmoed Spahr
Acquisitions Editor: Celestin Suresh John
Development Editor: Laura Berendson
Editorial Assistant: Gryffin Winkler
Copy Editor: Kezia Endsley

Cover designed by eStudioCalamar

Distributed to the book trade worldwide by Springer Science+Business Media New York, 1 New York Plaza, Suite 4600, New York, NY 10004-1562, USA. Phone 1-800-SPRINGER, fax (201) 348-4505, e-mail orders-ny@springer-sbm.com, or visit www.springeronline.com. Apress Media, LLC is a California LLC and the sole member (owner) is Springer Science + Business Media Finance Inc (SSBM Finance Inc). SSBM Finance Inc is a **Delaware** corporation.

For information on translations, please e-mail booktranslations@springernature.com; for reprint, paperback, or audio rights, please e-mail bookpermissions@springernature.com.

Apress titles may be purchased in bulk for academic, corporate, or promotional use. eBook versions and licenses are also available for most titles. For more information, reference our Print and eBook Bulk Sales web page at http://www.apress.com/bulk-sales.

Any source code or other supplementary material referenced by the author in this book is available to readers on GitHub. For more detailed information, please visit https://www.apress.com/gp/services/source-code.

Paper in this product is recyclable

Table of Contents

About the Author

Dr. Patanjali Kashyap PhD works as a technology manager at a leading American bank. He deals with high-impact, mission-critical financial and innovative new-generation technology projects on a day-to-day basis. Dr. Kashyap has worked with technology giants such as Infosys and Cognizant Technology Solutions. He is an expert in the Agile process, machine learning, Big Data, and cloud computing. He understands Microsoft Azure and cognitive computing platforms such as Watson and Microsoft Cognitive Services. Dr. Kashyap confesses .NET technologies to be his first love to his friends and colleagues. He has worked on a spectrum of .NET and associated technologies, such as SQL Server and component-based architectures, from their inception. He also loves to work with SharePoint (and with content management in general), knowledge management, positive technology, psychological computing, and UNIX. Dr. Kashyap is experienced in software development methodologies, application support, and maintenance. He has published several research and whitepapers on multiple topics. He is involved in organizational initiatives, such as building world-class teams and dynamic cultures across enterprises. And he is the go-to person for incorporating "positivity and enthusiasm" in enterprises.

About the Technical Reviewer

 **Krishnendu Dasgupta** is currently the head of machine learning at Mondosano GmbH, leading data science initiatives focused on clinical trial recommendations and advanced patient health profiling through disease and drug data. Prior to this role, he co-founded DOCONVID AI, a startup that leveraged applied AI and medical imaging to detect lung abnormalities and neurological disorders.

With a strong background in computer science engineering, Krishnendu has more than a decade of experience in developing solutions and platforms using applied machine learning. His professional trajectory includes key positions at prestigious organizations, such as NTT DATA, PwC, and Thoucentric.

Krishnendu's primary research interests include applied AI for graph machine learning, medical imaging, and decentralized privacy-preserving machine learning in healthcare. He also had the opportunity to participate in the esteemed Entrepreneurship and Innovation Bootcamp at the Massachusetts Institute of Technology, cohort of the 2018 batch.

Beyond his professional endeavors, Krishnendu actively dedicates his time to research, collaborating with various research NGOs and universities worldwide. His focus is on applied AI and ML.

CHAPTER 1

Let's Integrate with Machine Learning

Dr. Patanjali Kashyap[a*]

[a] Bangalore, Karnataka, India

In this chapter, I present a holistic synopsis of how machine learning (ML) works in conjunction with other technologies, including IoT, Big Data analytics, and cloud and cognitive computing. Technically, machine learning cannot and never should be understood in isolation. It is a multi-disciplinary subject. This is why you need an integrated view of the suite of concepts and technologies before you can understand the technical landscape of machine learning. Even for academic purposes, if someone wants to understand the workings of machine learning, they have to learn the nuts and bolts in detail. Hence, it is important for business leaders and managers to have a holistic and integrated understanding of machine learning to properly grasp the subject. It becomes more important if they are interested in the subject for business reasons. Because you are reading this book, I assume that you want to become acquainted with the concepts of machine learning.

During my endeavor to provide a conceptual foundation of machine learning and its associated technologies, I address multiple business questions, including these:

- What is machine learning?

- What is the business case for machine learning?

© Dr. Patanjali Kashyap 2024
P. Kashyap, *Machine Learning for Decision Makers*,
https://doi.org/10.1007/978-1-4842-9801-5_1

- How do we use machine learning?

- What are the key features of machine learning?

- Where can we implement machine learning?

- What are the major techniques/types used in machine learning?

- Why is machine learning required in business?

These questions are answered in detail in this and the following chapters. The key business benefits and values of successful machine learning implementations are also discussed in the appropriate places.

Almost the same set of questions, thoughts, and concepts are addressed for associated technologies as well. This chapter explores the core concepts behind advanced analytics and discusses how they can be leveraged in a knowledge-driven, cognitive environment. With the right level of advanced analytics, the system can gain deeper insights and predict outcomes in a more accurate and insightful manner. Hence, it is essential to study these concepts in a practical way. This chapter introduces the knowledge platform and provides you with the practical knowledge you are looking for.

Your Business, My Technology, and Our Interplay of Thoughts

My argument is very simple and you will find it conveyed throughout the book. I argue that technologies—like the cloud, Big Data analytics, machine learning, and cognitive computing—enable growth, profit, and revenue. My focus is not to explain the model and its benefits in a stepwise fashion but to explain the technologies behind it.

In any business scenario, results and outcomes have multiple dimensions. But what is important for the enterprises, business leaders, and stakeholders is to know how they impact their business strategies. The outcome depends on multiple factors, such as how quickly the infrastructure is ready, the cost per transition, the implementation time for the new applications, and even how partners, including suppliers, are integrated in the overall supply chain and decision-making processes. Another important factor is the level of automation the enterprise has (from bottom to top).

Machine learning—or, in other words, the "automation of automation"—and cognitive computing are changing the way decisions are made. Monotonous, repetitious, and less skilled human intervention is being replaced with "intelligent" automation. That's changing the dynamics of decision making. The result is increased efficiency and effectiveness of overall business processes and decision making. Its impact will be felt on enterprise profit, revenue growth, and operational efficiency. Enterprises will appreciate business value at all levels and areas of their investments, whether it's IT infrastructure, IT application, business processes, operations, or finance. If they adopt the right context-based approach to technology, benefits are bound to come.

Adopting the cloud enables companies to quickly provision their resources and reduce costs per transition and per workstation. Most of the requirements for application development are available on-demand in a cloud-based environment, so implementing a new application is fast. Suppliers have access to the robust supply chain, so integrating their services and logistics becomes easy. The cloud provides on-demand data analytics and machine learning-based, context-oriented cognitive computing functionalities in an automated fashion. This enables enterprises to enjoy high revenue growth and increased return on investment.

If you have followed the trends and direction of the IT industry in the last couple of years, one signal is clear—industries are betting heavily on this new generation of technologies. Old thoughts and technical pillars are getting destroyed and new ones are piling up rapidly. IBM, Microsoft, Google, and Facebook patents filled in recent years show the direction of the industry. Microsoft is the leader in patent filing, with over 200 artificial intelligence-related patent applications since 2009. Google is in second place, with over 150 patent filings. Patents include elements of cloud computing, cognitive computing, Big Data analytics, and machine learning. The following links provide a snapshot of the patent landscape in recent years:

- `https://www-03.ibm.com/press/us/en/presskit/42874.wss`

- `https://cbi-blog.s3.amazonaws.com/blog/wp-content/uploads/2017/01/1-ai-patents-overall.png`

The cloud, the Internet of Things (IoT), Big Data, and analytics enable effective and appropriate machine learning implementation and focused strategies. Machine learning is at the core of cognitive computing, which provides the power of real-time, evidence-based, automated decision-making capabilities to enterprises. You will be able to combine all the pieces and visualize the complete picture. This is a journey from data to wisdom. You get data through IoT systems and other sources of data, store that data in a cloud-based data store, and then apply analytics techniques to the data to make sense of it. Then you automate the analytical process by applying machine learning techniques to find patterns and make accurate predictions. You refine the results by iteratively running the models/algorithms. The options are backed by a confidence level and by evidence. An end-to-end solution!

It is worth mentioning here that this separation of technology and division of layers is logical. That is, there is no "hard" boundary defined in the standard and professional literature. For example, a lot of technical literature couples Big Data analytics and machine learning together. Some treat machine learning and cognitive computing as one. However, segregation organizes the thought process; hence, I take this approach.

By studying the five technical pillars of the current and future innovative and knowledge-based business ecosystem (the cloud, Big Data, IoT, machine learning, and cognitive computing), you will be able to draw correct inferences and make suitable business decisions for your enterprise. By the end of the chapter, you will understand what these technologies are all about, what they mean, and how they matter to the business ecosystem.

General Introduction to Machine Learning

The input-process-output model—which states that inputs enter the system, are processed, and then output is produced—forms the foundation of most information and data processing technologies. As an illustration, consider a word processing program where each keystroke results in a letter output that appears on the screen. The actions that must be taken are obvious when someone presses a letter in a word processing program. Therefore, it is simple to design a process that takes into account which input values should result in which output values.

Let's say you want to create a program that would say "This is a picture of a horse" and you have an image of a horse. The fundamental issue for computers now arises from their inferior ability to recognize patterns compared to humans. A picture is nothing more than the combination pixels composed of vectors to a computer. It is exceedingly challenging to solve if you attempt to do so using typical programming methods. However, it is a simple task with Big Data, statistics, and analytics techniques. In later sections, you'll learn about this in more detail.

Here is where ML and AI enter the picture. Artificial intelligence (AI) refers to computer programs that quickly complete tasks on their own, mimicking human intelligence. The formal concept of programmable "artificial neurons" by McCulloch and Pitts, published in 1943, is the key piece of work now typically recognized as AI. At a workshop held at Dartmouth College in 1956, the phrase "artificial intelligence" was coined. This event is frequently cited as the beginning of the field of AI.

As discussed earlier, the term "machine learning" (ML) was created three years later by a pioneer in this subject. An artificial system learns from examples and can simplify them after the learning phase is through. This process is known as machine learning, which is a broad term for the "artificial" generation of knowledge from experience. An ML algorithm creates a statistical model based on training data (more on this later). This means it does not just learn the examples by heart but identifies patterns and regularities in the learning data. In this way, the system can also measure unidentified data, although it may also fail to do so.

Machine learning is a fascinating concept these days, and nearly everyone in the business world is talking about it. It's a promising technology that has the potential to change the prevalent business environment and bring disruption in action. Decision-makers have started considering machine learning a tool to design and implement their strategies and innovative thoughts. Implementing machine learning in organizations or enterprises is not easy. One of the reasons for this is the lack of useful and reliable data. Having relevant data is essential for effective machine learning implementation. But, getting relevant and accurate data is a big challenge. Riding on recent advancements and developments in the field of IoT-enabled technologies and Big Data analytics, it is comparatively easy for enterprises to store and analyze data efficiently and effectively. This luxury of the availability of Big Data on-demand and in real time leads to the successful implementation of machine learning projects, products, applications, and services.

This also empowers decision-makers to create some great strategies. Because of this, we started seeing and realizing results and success stories regarding machine learning. The concept of machine learning is not recent and can be traced back and is linked with the artificial intelligence and expert systems. As mentioned, in recent times, it has been getting a lot of attention and traction because of some path-breaking achievements. For example, IBM Watson's capabilities to predict oncological outcome better than doctors or Facebook's success at accurately identifying the faces of humans.

In the era of machine learning and Big Data analytics, generalized prediction is at the heart of almost every scientific/business decision. The study of generalization from data is the central topic of machine learning. In current and future business scenarios, predicting outcome is the key to the organization's success. Decision-makers want to see and allow strategies to be made and implemented that not only look at historical data but also make sense of it. Optimistically, they want that to happen automatically. The expect system would "predict" the behavior of customer and their future needs. Companies can then make effective decisions based on the reports and dashboards in real time. For example, in investment banking, decision-makers want to build software that would help their credit risk officer predict most likely customer defaults. A telecom company wants to predict a customer's inclination to default on a bill based on the behavioral analysis of the customers. This would provide them with future projections of payment liabilities in real time. Based on historical payment details of a customer and machine learning, it is well possible.

In fact, decision-makers are not satisfied only with the prediction; they are more interested in understanding why someone is going to do something. Decision-makers want to explore the "why" of the story and build their strategies around that mindset or behavior. Technically as we know, machine learning learns from the data. The outcome of learning depends on the level of analytics done on the data set. Therefore, it is important to take a look at the level of learning analytics. I give a brief primer of the concept here and come back to this in the later chapters, where it needs further elaboration.

Typically, there are four levels of learning analytics associated with machine learning:

- *Descriptive*: What has happened and what is happening? This generally looks at facts, data, and figures and provides detailed analysis. It is used for preparing data for advanced analysis or for day-to-day business intelligence.

- *Diagnostic*: Why did this happen? This examines the descriptive elements and allows for critical reasoning.

- *Predictive*: What will happen? This provides different elements and focus on what the outcome would be. It proves future possibilities and trends and uses statistical techniques such as linear and logistic regression to understand trends and predict future outcomes.

- *Prescriptive*: What should I do and why should I do it? This determines how a specific result or outcome can be achieved through the use of a specific set of elements. Its focus is on decision making and efficiency improvements. Simulation is used to analyze complex system behavior and identify uses.

Recent developments in the field of cognitive computing have encouraged *cognitive analytics*, and its output is more human like, so it is more beneficial. Cognitive analytics takes perspective analytics to the next level. Companies essentially need prescriptive analytics to drive insights, recommendations, and optimizations. Cognitive analytics actually test, learn, and adapt over time and derive even greater insights. It bridges the gap among machine learning, Big Data, and practical decision making in real time with high confidence and provides contextual insights.

Based on the outcome of the level of analytics performed on the data set, companies encourage or discourage particular behavior according to their needs. This triggered a new era of human-machine collaboration, cooperation, and communication. While the machine identifies the patterns, the human responsibilities are to interpret them and put them into different micro-segments and recommend and suggest some course of action. In a nutshell, machine learning technologies are here to help humans refine and increase their potential.

The Details of Machine Learning

Machine learning is known for its multi-disciplinary nature. It includes multiple fields of study, ranging from philosophy to sociology to artificial intelligence. However, in this book, machine learning is treated as a subfield of artificial intelligence, which is explained as the ability of machines to learn, think, and solve a problem or issue in the way that humans do. It helps computers (software) act and respond without being explicitly programmed to do so.

Here are some formal definitions of machine learning:

- Machine learning is concerned with the design and development of algorithms and techniques that allow computers to learn. The major focus of ML is to extract information from data automatically, by computational and statistical methods. It is thus closely related to data mining and statistics. (Svensson and Soderberg, 2008)

- Machine learning inherited and borrowed on concepts and results from many fields; for example, artificial intelligence, probability and statistics, computational complexity theory, control theory, information theory, philosophy, psychology, neurobiology, and other fields. (Mitchell, 1997, p. 2)

Here are some important highlights about machine learning:

- Machine learning is a kind of artificial intelligence (AI) that enables computers to learn without being explicitly programmed.

- Software learns from past experiences through machine learning.

- Software can improve its performances by use of intelligent programs (machine learning) in an iterative fashion.

- Machine learning algorithms have the ability to learn, teach, adapt to the changes, and improve with experience in the data/environment.

- Machine learning is about developing code to enable the machine to learn to perform tasks.

- A computer program or algorithm is treated as a learning program if it learns from experience relative to some class of tasks and performance measure (iteratively).

- A machine learning program is successful if its performance at the tasks improves with experiences (based on data).

Machine learning is focused on using advanced computational mechanisms to develop dynamic algorithms that detect patterns in data, learn from experience, adjust programs, and improve accordingly.

The purpose of machine learning is to find meaningful simplicity and information/insights in the midst of disorderly complexity. It tries to optimize performance criteria using past experience based on its learning. It is actually data-driven science that operates through a set of data-driven algorithms. Machine learning provides power to the computers to discover and find patterns in huge warehouses of data.

Rather than using the traditional way of procedural programming (if condition A is valid then perform B set of tasks), machine learning uses advanced techniques of computational mechanism to allow computers to learn from experience and adjust and improve programs accordingly. See Figure 1-1. Traditional programming is a manual process—meaning a person (the programmer) creates the program. But without anyone programming the logic, the programmer has to manually formulate or code the rules. In machine learning, on the other hand, the algorithm automatically formulates the rules from the data.

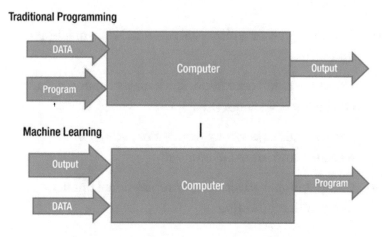

Figure 1-1. *Traditional programming compared to machine learning*

Quick Bytes

When do you apply machine learning?

- When the system needs to be dynamic, self-learning, and adaptive.

- At the time of multiple iterative and complex procedures.

- If a decision has to be made instantly and in real time.

- When you have multiple, complicated sources and a huge amount of time-series data.

- When generalization of observation is required.

Applications of machine learning:

- Machine insight and computer vision, including object recognition

- Natural language processing and syntactic pattern recognition

- Search engines, medical analysis, and brain-machine interfaces

- Detecting credit card fraud, stock market analysis, and classifying DNA sequences

- Speech and handwriting recognition, adaptive websites, and robot locomotion

- Computational advertising, computational finance, and health monitoring

- Sentiment analysis/opinion mining, affective computing, and information retrieval

- Recommender systems and optimization of systems

Machine learning fundamentally helps teach computers (through data, logic, and software) "how to learn and what to do." A machine learning program finds or discovers patterns in data and then behaves accordingly. The computation involves two phases (see Figure 1-2):

- In the first phase of computations, the specified data is recognized by machine learning algorithms or programs. On the basis of that, it will come up with a model.

- The second phase uses that model (created in the first phase) to make predictions.

This sequence continues to iterate and the user gets refined results. Learning through iterations is a basic characteristic of a machine learning algorithm and program. To achieve this, machine learning uses two main methods, called *supervised learning* and *unsupervised learning*.

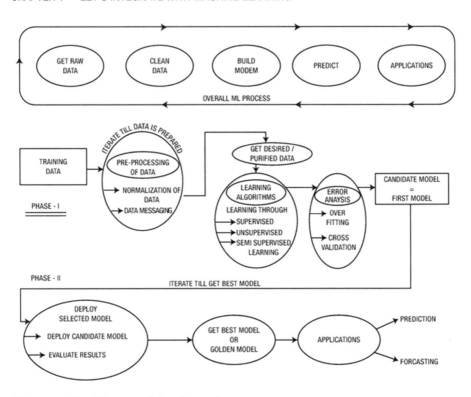

Figure 1-2. *The machine learning process*

Supervised Learning

Supervised learning is the learning process where the output variable is known. The output evidence of the variable is explicitly used in training. In supervised learning, data has "labels." In other words, you know what you're trying to predict. Actually, this algorithm contains a target or outcome variable that's to be predicted from a given set of predictors (independent variables). Using these set of variables, a function is generated that maps inputs to anticipated outcomes. The training process continues until the model attains an anticipated level of correctness on the training data (see Figure 1-3). In machine learning-related issues or problems, a train set to test set ratio of 80:20 is acceptable. In today's world of Big Data, 20 percent amounts to a huge data set. You can easily use this data for training and help your model learn better. However, this ratio changes based on the size of the data.

1. Learning or training: Models learn using training data.

2. Test the model using unseen test data, to test the accuracy of the model.

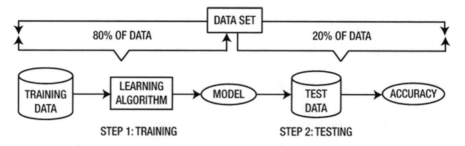

STEP 1: TRAINING   STEP 2: TESTING

* MACHINE LEARNING WOULD NOT PROVIDE AN OUT-OF-BOX SOLUTIONS GENERALLY HUMAN INPUT AND SUPERVISION IS REQUIRED.

* MODELS IN MACHINE LEARNING CONTEXT CAN BE TRAINED TO TAKE DECISIONS BASED ON EXPERIENCE. MODEL CAN BE MODIFIED BASED ON RESPONSES TO CHANGES IN DATA.

* OUT OF TOTAL AVAILABLE DATA, 20 TO 30% OF DATA IS PUT THE SIDE AND RESERVED FOR TESTING THE ACCURACY OF THE MODEL.

Figure 1-3. *Supervised learning*

Unsupervised Learning

In *unsupervised learning,* the outcomes are unknown. Clustering is happening on the available data set to revel meaningful partitions and hierarchies. Unlike supervised learning, unsupervised learning is used on data that does not have history. In unsupervised learning, the algorithm has to find the surpassed data. Also, it has to find any hidden structure in the data set. The class level of data is unknown. There is no target or outcome variable present to predict/estimate in unsupervised leaning. See Figure 1-4 for an illustration of unsupervised learning.

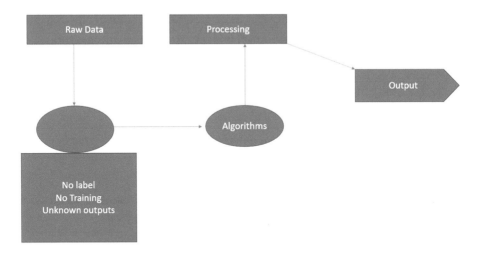

Figure 1-4. *Unsupervised learning*

Unsupervised learning is used to populate specific clusters out of different available clusters. This technique is best suited for segmenting customers into different clusters for specific involvement. Some of its areas of application are self-organizing maps, nearest neighbor mapping, singular value decomposition, and k-means clustering. E-commerce companies like Amazon use this technique for online recommendations, identification of data outliers, and segment text topics.

Machine learning changed the way data extraction and its interpretation happen. It uses automatic sets of generic methods and algorithms. Previous to this, traditional statistical techniques were used for similar types of analyses. Companies are using these new set of learning theories and practices for revenue generation. Therefore, machine learning has already started impacting many business and research organizations. Products and services are built around machine learning to achieve market leadership.

Because disruption and innovation are the mantra for success of most business strategies, machine learning and its related technologies take central stage. This is the main reason that the data-intensive machine-learning methods have been adopted in the field of science, technology, commerce, and management. This revolution is leading industry to more evidence-based decision making with the help of computers across many walks of life. The five steps of evidence-based decision making are:

1. *Ask*: Translate a practical issue into an answerable question.

2. *Acquire*: Systematically search for and retrieve the evidence.

3. *Appraise*: Critically judge the trustworthiness of the evidence.

4. *Apply*: Incorporate the evidence into the decision-making process.

5. *Assess*: Evaluate the outcome of the decision.

Machine learning has a strong scientific foundation, which includes studies of pattern reorganization, mathematical optimization, computational learning theory, self-optimizations, nature-inspired algorithms, and others. Machine learning is so pervasive that we are all using it dozens of times a day without knowing it. We are using it for online entertainment (Netflix), practical speech recognition (Apple's Siri), effective web searching, and improving our understanding of the human genome. Machine learning answered the questions of how to build intelligent computers and software that improve their capabilities by themselves through self-learning and assisting humans in all walks of life.

Characteristics of Machine Learning

Now is a good time to look at the characteristics of machine learning. Understanding these characteristics will give you a compressive outlook of the technology. Let's take a look at the characteristics:

- Ability to automatically adopt and modify behavior based on users' needs. For example, personalized email or news.

- Ability to discover new knowledge from large databases of facts.

- Ability to assist humans and replace monotonous tasks, which require some intelligence.

- Ability to generate "insight" by iteratively operating on data and learning from mistakes.

Current Business Challenges for Machine Learning

Implementing machine learning has many challenges. Its application areas and scope are wide, so the challenges are also multifaceted. Let's take a look at them.

Handling, Managing, and Using Complex and Heterogeneous Data

Huge volumes of complex data are being generated every day (every second, to be precise) from multiple heterogeneous sources of data about the customer. However, getting insight from this data is one of the challenges. Also, the availability of data makes business requirements/

decisions more complex and time consuming because the demands and expectations of customers are extraordinarily high. Fulfilling customers' expectations is a challenging task.

Typically, unknown relationships and correlations are hidden within a large amount of multi-sourced (complex, heterogeneous, dynamic, distributed, and very large) and multi-structured data (a variety of data formats and types that can be derived from interactions between people and machines, such as web applications or social networks). By running machine learning models on muti-sourced and multi-structured data sets of varying quality and availability, you can better understand the behavior of products and applications and therefore develop products/applications of a higher quality. However, developing algorithms that detect meaningful regularities from such data is another challenge. But machine learning's marriage with advanced computational, data crunching, and analytics techniques makes it possible. For instance, Microsoft Azure cloud infrastructure provides its "data factory." This is a type of cloud-based integration tool helps integrate multi-sourced and multi-structured data.

Storing, managing, and analyzing large volumes of data is another challenge. However, recent advancements in machine learning, Big Data, and storing technologies provide humans with an array of solutions to managing this challenge. The good thing is these offered solutions are scalable, custom built, quick, automated, accurate, and efficient. They also support real-time environments.

Dynamic Business Scenarios, Systems, and Methods

New knowledge and insights about tasks, activities, and business are constantly being discovered, generated, and created by humans. Hence, it is difficult to continuously redesign or re-create systems and models "by hand," which will be in synchronization if frequent changes are happening, including business environments from the organization perspective on a dynamic basis. Therefore, the complex data and changing business scenarios need some methods and techniques to teach systems (computers) to do this on their behalf. However, creating this type of dynamic system is not easy. To cope with this challenge, machine learning is one of the most important tools. The ML systems make predictions based on defined methodologies that are self-dynamic and adaptive in nature (I will discuss these in the next few chapters). Their computational efficiency can be improved, as they are dynamic and flexible systems.

Unpredictable System Behavior

System designers and technology specialists often produce machines that do not work as desired. Even when they work at their fullest capacity, they are less effective in providing real-time assistance and decision-making support. However, business typically need efficient, focused, and accurate systems that fulfill their requirements with ease and efficiency. Therefore, systems that can learn to derive conclusions and assist in making decisions with a very little or no human intervention is the need of the hour. But designing a system that potentially resolves the prevalence of unpredictability is a challenging task. With the suite of traditional technologies, this become more tedious. Machine learning technologies can accomplish this by analyzing data without any prior assumptions about the structure of the data. Hence, to encounter the challenge of unpredictable system behavior, ML is the best available technology in the pack.

The Needs and Business Drivers of Machine Learning

ML is today's fastest growing field, functionally and technically, lying at the intersection of computer science, statistics, artificial intelligence, and data science. Decision-makers, data scientists, software developers, and researchers are using machine learning to gain insights and be competitive. They are trying to achieve goals that were previously out of reach. For instance, programs/software/machine that learn from experiences and understand consumer behavior were just not possible some years back. However, system that make purchase recommendations, recognize images, and protect against fraud are now part of life.

Recent progress in machine learning has been driven by the development of new learning algorithms and innovative researches, backed by the ongoing explosion in online and offline data. Also, the availability of low-cost computation plays an important role. Here are just a few driving forces that justify the need for machine learning and look at its business drivers:

- *Diversity of data*: Data is being generated from different channels and its nature and format are different.

- *Capacity and dimension*: The increase in the number of data sources and the globalization of diversification of businesses have led to the exponential growth of the data.

- *Speed*: As data volume increases, so must the speed at which data is captured and transformed.

- *Complexity*: With the increasing complexity of data, high data quality and security is required to enable data collection, transformation, and analysis, in order to achieve expedient decision making.

- *Applicability*: These aforementioned factors can compromise the applicability of the data to the business process and improve performance.

What Are Big Data and Big Data Analytics?

Big Data offers significant assistance in overcoming obstacles and generating novel business concepts. The difficulties persist because of how much data is now being gathered by technology. Big Data technologies have the capacity to properly collect and analyze that data. New computer models that can handle distributed and parallel computations with incredibly scalable storage and performance are part of the Big Data infrastructure.

The principles of analytics and machine learning are essential to the Big Data lifecycle. Unstructured textual data is the subject of text analytics, a particular type of analysis. Text analytics has become increasingly important as social media has grown. The text data "pulled out" from various online sources, including social media, online retailing websites, and e-commerce transitions, is used to predict customer behavior and analyze consumer interests. Text analytics is now possible thanks to machine learning. By using visualization tools like Tableau, the analyzed data is graphically represented so that end users can quickly understand it and make decisions.

The compound annual growth rate of data is approaching 60 percent annually. Studies show that 70 percent of this data is unstructured. Video files, social networking data, and other types of unstructured data are examples. The difficulties are revealed by looking at the diversity of the data itself. Big Data is a hot topic in the commercial and IT worlds. Although various people have varying perspectives and thoughts, everyone concurs that

- Big Data refers to a huge amount of unstructured or semi-structured data.

- Storing this mammoth data is beyond the capacity of typical traditional database systems (relational databases).

- Legacy software tools are unable to capture, manage, and process Big Data.

Big Data is a relative term, and it depends on an organization's size. Big Data does not just refer to traditional data warehouses, but it includes operational data stores that can be used for real-time applications. Also, Big Data is about finding value from the available data, which is the key to success for businesses. Companies try to understand their customers better, so that they can create more targeted products and services for them. To do this they are increasingly adopting analytical techniques for doing analysis on larger sets of data. To perform operations on data effectively, efficiently, and accurately, they are expanding their traditional data sets. They integrate traditional data with social media data, text analytics, and sensor data to get a complete understanding of their customers' behaviors.

Data can potentially give accurate insight once analytics are performed on it. Therefore, Big Data can also be a weapon for optimizing business processes. Companies started using it to create new processes or to fine-tune existing ones. For example, retailers optimize their stock based on the recommendation of predictive model, which generates "insight" from the analysis of social media, web search trends, and weather forecast data. Leaders understand that it is just the beginning of the era of Big Data and analytics and if they are not aware or willing to take advantage of it, they will definitely be left behind and lose their competitive advantage. This is a huge risk for them!

Here are a few formal definitions and some insight about Big Data:

- Big Data refers to data sets whose size is beyond the ability of typical database software tools to capture, store, manage, and analyze.

- The analyst firm IDC defines it as follows: Big Data technologies describe a new generation of technologies and architectures, designed to economically extract value from very large volumes of a wide variety of data, by enabling high-velocity capture, discovery, and/or analysis.

- David Kellogg defines Big Data in very simple language, as "too big to be reasonably handled by current/traditional technologies," and the consulting firm McKinsey & Company agrees with this.

- Big Data technologies describe a new generation of technologies and architectures, designed to economically extract value from very large volumes of a wide variety of data, by enabling high-velocity capture, discovery, and/or analysis. Big Data plays a role in creating superior business value in today's world. These days, this includes a plethora of data generated from diverse data sources, like enterprise-wide transaction systems, machine logs, RFID systems, sensor data sources, customer call centers, web logs, and social media logs.

- Big Data is a high-volume, high-velocity data resource that mandates cost-effective, innovative ways of information processing for greater insight and effective decision making.

The Major Sources of Big Data

- *Black box data*: This is the data generated by aircraft, including jets and helicopters. Black box data contains flight staff voices, microphone recordings, and aircraft performance-related information.

- *Social media data*: The data generated by social media sites such as Twitter, Facebook, Instagram, Pinterest, and Google+.

- *Stock exchange data*: This typically contains information about share selling and buying decisions taken by traders or individual customers.

- *Power grid data*: This contains information about nodes based on usage information, power consumption details, and so on.

- *Transport data*: This contains information about possible capacity, vehicle model, availability of vehicle, and distance covered by a vehicle. Because vehicles have built-in intelligent systems and are connected through IoT, the amount of information they generate is huge.

- *Search engine data*: This is one of the major causes and sources of Big Data. Search engines have massive databases and information repositories from which they get and store this type of data.

There are a few important technologies used to realize Big Data, which I discuss in detail in the coming sections. However, one important one is Hadoop and HDFS. HDFS is used for storage, while MapReduce is used for processing. It gathers data from many sources and in different data formats. The data is preprocessed to make it appropriate for analysis before being placed in a storage platform, like HDFS or NoSQL. The analytics layer receives the preprocessed data that was previously saved in the storage platform, processes it using Big Data tools like MapReduce and YARN, and then conducts analysis on the processed data to extract any hidden knowledge.

Big Data depends on a few important pillars, known as the three Vs. Let's take a look.

The Three Vs of Big Data

Big Data for small organizations is small data for a large organization. For some enterprises, 2TB might appear big, whereas for others, 20TB might be big. Some larger enterprises consider 200GB as big. This term is qualitative and relative, and it is difficult to create a uniform guideline. Hence, it is necessary to identify Big Data by a few characteristics. The characteristics of Big Data are commonly known as three Vs:

- *Velocity*: Near-time, real-time, batch, and so on.

- *Variety*: Structured, unstructured, semi-structured, logs, sensor data, images, and so on.

- *Volume*: Terabytes, petabytes, transactions, files, records, and so on.

Velocity

Big Data is fast-growing data. The rate or the velocity at which data is growing is tremendous. Some predictions say that it would take over five years to watch the amount of video that is being created worldwide every second. Velocity indicates the speed at which the data is being created. Different applications have different latency requirements. However, in today's competitive environment, leaders and decision-makers want the essential extracted "insight" from the data/information as soon as possible. Once the data arrives at the corporate boundaries, instant analysis is the key to success. This is required because data, information, and insight are tightly integrated with decision making. Data is produced at different speeds for different business, mostly in real time or in real near time. For example, trading and stock related data, tweets on Twitter, status updates/Likes/shares on Facebook/other social media sites, and many other types of data are generated in real time/near real time.

Variety

Variety indicates the dissimilar formats in which the data is being created and stored. Different applications create and store data in dissimilar formats. In today's business environment, there are huge volumes of unstructured, structured, and semi-structured data being created and maintained in organizations and enterprises. Until the great progress happened in the field of Big Data technologies, the industry didn't have any reliable tools and technologies that could work with huge unstructured data.

Data is not only stored in traditional flat files, spreadsheets, relational databases, and so on, but a lot of unstructured data is stored in the form of images, audio files, video files, web logs, sensor data, and many other formats. This characteristic of varied data formats is denoted as *variety* in the Big Data environment. Beyond structured data like numbers, tables, and words, Big Data also includes lots of unstructured data, like video surveillance from sensors, streams, medical records, and photos posted to social network sites, and so on. We all know that even if it is unstructured it can be very useful. Because of this unstructured variety, it poses the biggest challenges. Most technologists predict that in the future, most of the Internet traffic will be video, specifically, long-form video.

In current dynamically changing business scenarios, enterprises require data from all the sources. This includes structured data that comes from enterprise databases and warehouse systems and the type of data that is being generated outside of organizations, like click stream data, social media, and so on. Integrating this data into organizations' existing systems enables them to stay in touch with their customers in real time or near to real time. This closeness with customers helps organizations remain competitive and relevant.

Volume

Volume denotes the size of the data that enterprises are using for multiple purposes. With the recent progress and development of technology and with the popularity of social media, the amount of data is rising very quickly. Data is spread across dissimilar places, in different formats, in large volumes, fluctuating from gigabytes to terabytes, petabytes, and more. Data is not only created and generated by individuals, but huge volumes of data are being created by machines.

Big Data is generally measured in terabytes (1,000 gigabytes) and even petabytes (1,000 terabytes) of data. 1,000 petabytes equals an exabyte and 1,000 exabytes equals a zettabyte, which is equivalent to 1 billion terabytes. To visualize a zettabyte, imagine this—if an 11-ounce cup of coffee represents a gigabyte of data then a zettabyte is the Great Wall of China.

What Is Analytics?

Analytics is basically the discovery and finding of communication in meaningful patterns of data sets, which can be achieved with any data set no matter big or small. Actually, Big Data is not the necessary criteria to leverage analytics and drive data-based decision making. If Big Data does not meet the three Vs, it does not qualify as Big Data.

The analytics lifecycle passed through six major standard and robust procedural phases, which were dependent on each other and were resolved until each phase met specific criteria (see Figure 1-4). The operation starts from understanding the business environment and ends in deriving results, developing recommendations, implementation, and incorporation of findings. Finally, continuous improvement of accuracy and efficiency of the model performance is being maintained through regular calibration. These steps are illustrated in Figure 1-5.

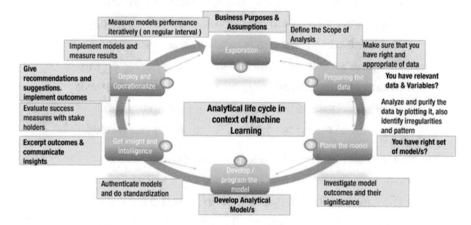

Figure 1-5. *Major steps followed in analytics*

The following list explains all the major steps involved in the analysis presented in a consolidated way:

- *Business objectives and hypothesis*: In this phase the business scenario, objectives, and availability of data in the Big Data platform are analyzed. This is also called the discovery phase.

- *Data extraction, preparation, and sampling*: In the second stage, the list of variables and tentative time period for analysis are defined. Data preprocessing is a process of preparing the raw data and making it suitable for a machine learning model. It is the first and crucial step when creating a machine learning model.

- *Model planning and development of predictive models/ algorithms*: In this phase, models are designed and efficient models based on the results are finalized.

- *Derive results and develop strategic solutions, recommendations, and operationalization*: During this stage, insights are derived from models, based on the results and their conversion to strategic solutions. Business recommendations are also made during this phase. Finally, action items are developed on the basis of the recommendations, which the company can implement based on their priorities and preferences.

Let's now examine the data lifecycle, which forms the basis for Big Data, information, and even machine learning. The data lifecycle, also known as the information lifecycle, is defined as the period of time during which data is present in your system. This lifecycle comprises each stage your data goes through, from initial capture onward. Data objects go through several stages of life at their own rates. Here is a description of a few key data lifecycle components:

- *Data generation, intake, or capture:* Whether you gather data through data entry, acquire pre-existing data from external sources, or absorb signals from machinery, you acquire information in some way. This step describes when data values enter your system's firewalls.

- *Data processing*: Encompasses a number of procedures, including cleaning and preparing raw data for further analysis. Though the precise sequence of steps may vary, data preparation frequently involves combining data from many sources, confirming the data, and carrying out the transformation. Data reformatting, summarizing, standardizing, and improving are frequent steps in the data processing pipeline.

- *Data evaluation*: This is the most important step, regardless of how you analyze and interpret your data. For studying and analyzing your data, a number of analyses might be required. This could be a reference to statistical analysis and visualization. It may also use traditional data modelling (DM) or artificial intelligence (AI).

- *Sharing or publishing data*: At this point, predictions and insights are transformed into choices and directions. Your data offers its full commercial value if the information gleaned from data analysis is shared.

- *Archiving*: Normally, data is saved for later use once it has been gathered, handled, analyzed, and shared. It's crucial to preserve metadata about each item in your records, especially regarding data provenance, if you want archives to retain any value in the future.

The data lifecycle goes from the last step back to the beginning in an endless circle. Undoubtedly, one factor has had a big impact on how people use data in the 21 century. Everyone is aware of how much data volumes have increased over the past few years and how they are still growing. Businesses are using more SaaS and web apps, and more data is being gathered from them. The number of individuals utilizing the Internet, clicking links, taking images, and completing web forms is also increasing globally. Above all, new ways to quantify data that is already known are constantly being developed through the Internet of Things

(IoT) and smart devices. Not all of the world's data must be collected, nor do you necessarily want to collect it. Even while it would seem convenient to have access to every bit of information, data-management difficulties increase with data growth. More data results in higher data storage costs.

The more data you have, the more resources you'll need for data preparation and analysis. Without a clear plan for digital transformation, businesses that just keep collecting data quickly find themselves in charge of a digital trashcan. They do really contain a wealth of knowledge. But nobody can find what they need, and what they do find is illogical, so they can't rely on it to decide how to run their firm. The majority of these procedures and techniques might be applied to large data. Implementing data lifecycle practices correctly could reduce large data problems that usually arise. For instance, excessive data collection, inefficient data handling, and the storage of out-of-date data are common problems.

To get rid of these problems, make your data collection process better by developing a strategy to identify and record only the data that is pertinent to your project. The other important factor is to make good use of data management. This means maintaining the integrity of your data and designing an architecture that combines manual and automatic monitoring and maintenance. Create a catalogue of your data to make it easy to find and utilize. In addition, get rid of any unnecessary information. Once certain data is no longer required, consider deleting it and purging old records. Finally, consider any legal requirements to keep or delete outdated records and have a clear plan in place for data deletion.

Note that in addition to velocity, volume, and verity, there are a few other "Vs" that exist.

- *Value*: Analytical techniques used throughout the data lifecycle turn raw data into knowledge that has a context and a business purpose. Corporate operations are guided by analytics and data prepared for choices.

When these steps enable a company to save money or make money, the business value of the data has finally been unlocked.

- *Visibility*: Data visibility enables you to produce data analytics with both depth and breadth. Using the most complete set of information is necessary to make the best decisions possible, because you can see how things evolve over time. Unstructured data in large quantities is like driving in terrible weather. You are unable to tell which way is up or where you need to turn. You can increase visibility by giving your data structure. In many ways, it is equal to turning on your fog lights.

- *Veracity*: In Big Data, the accuracy of the data is referred to as its veracity. In other words, how detailed and reliable the information is. It discusses data integrity. On a scale of high and low, Big Data veracity is assessed. The more authentic the data, the more beneficial it is for subsequent study.

- *Vulnerability*: This is a weakness or error in a system's or device's code that, if it is exploited, could compromise the confidentiality, accessibility, and integrity of data stored there. This happens by enabling unauthorized access, giving users more power, or withholding services.

Furthermore, be aware that at the moment, studying data and the solutions that are powered by it yields better business value than the software itself. A system's overall setup, or a collection of systems together to manage data throughout the data lifecycle, is referred to as its data architecture. This also suggests how data interoperability can be developed and maintained throughout a digital ecosystem of individuals, businesses, and systems to meet requirements for the government, society, individuals, and businesses. Data infrastructure focuses on putting the necessary design components into practical practice. For instance, the networking, virtual machines, and database for Microsoft Azure or Google Cloud explain its infrastructure, how the components communicate with one another, share data via APIs, and so on. The essential elements of a modern, unified data architecture that enables businesses to derive value from data are described by Kumar Illa (2020). The architecture consists of two major areas of focus:

- *Data engineering,* which creates the framework for organizing and preserving data.

- *Data science,* which gives businesses the ability to modify data to provide insights.

A unified data architecture provides a single, shared perspective on how diverse roles in the IT organization can use data and technological resources for advanced analytics across a cloud or collocated environment. This also helps cut down on duplicative efforts. A schematic explanation of the concept is provided in the later part of the section and in upcoming chapters.

What Is Cloud Computing?

A widely adopted definition of cloud computing comes from the U.S. National Institute of Standards and Technology:

> *Cloud computing* is a model for enabling ubiquitous, convenient, on-demand network access to a shared pool of configurable computing resources (for example, networks, servers, storage, applications, and services) that can be rapidly provisioned and released with minimal management effort or service provider interaction.

At an abstract level, cloud computing is a collection of best practices and can be one of the ways to design, implement, and use traditional and innovative technologies. The cloud computing paradigm enables business to implement solutions in simple, efficient, and reliable ways. Cloud computing is related to the technical know-how of creating a stable, robust, and secure technology base around a mix of established and evolving processes, frameworks, and best practices. The cloud computing paradigm has the following:

- Five characteristics

- Three service modes

- Four deployment modes

Let's take a detailed look at the characteristics, services, and deployment models.

Essential Characteristics of Cloud Computing

Here are the essential characteristics:

- *On-demand self-service and provisioning*: This characteristic provides power to the users to provision computing capabilities. This includes but is not limited to managing server time and storage. Provisioning services happens automatically without human interaction and intervention.

- *Wider network access*: Service and other capabilities are available over the network of networks. These services are made available to the users through multiple platforms, frameworks, devices, and equipment. Devices and equipment, like mobile phones, laptops, desktops, and wearable systems, are connected and available through wider network access to the magnitude of users. Wider network access provides high availability, which is critical in multiple business scenarios.

- *Resource pooling*: Computing resources and services are pooled to serve multiple consumers with dissimilar physical and virtual resources. The facility of dynamic resources allocation and deallocation according to consumer demand makes resource pooling very useful.

- *Speedy elasticity*: This is the ability to quickly provision computing and other resource capabilities, in most cases automatically, to rapidly scale up, release, and scale in.

- *Measured service*: Resources and service usage can be monitored, measured, controlled, and reported, mostly with the help of a dashboard or graphical user interfaces. The provider and consumer of the service appreciate how much and when they are using the services and product. This is critical for strategic decision and fine-tuning processes.

- *Dynamic pricing model*: Enables users to access services and other capabilities on a pay-per-use basis.

The combination of the characteristics, requirements, deployment, and service models creates a cloud solution. This solution is provided by many vendors, including Microsoft, Google, Amazon, and IBM. Now you will learn about the service and deployment models.

Cloud Computing Deployment Methodologies

There are three types of cloud computing deployment models, commonly known as public, private, and hybrid.

- *Public cloud*: In a public cloud deployment model, resources are shared over the Internet and used as needed by different groups, individuals, and organizations. Typical public cloud offerings are applications and services. The same is available to users in pay-per-use models. One-to-many relationships exist between the provider and consumer in this deployment model. That means that one provider serves multiple users.

- *Private cloud*: If there is one provider and one consumer, it comes under the private deployment model. In this type of service model, a one-to-one mapping between the consumer and the provider exists. The resources are not shared and are dedicated to organizations, individual users, and enterprises. Customization is easy, but there's no room for economies of scale.

- *Hybrid cloud*: A hybrid cloud refers to a mix or combination of public and private clouds. In this model, a combination of two or more deployment models (public and private) are integrated. This model is popular among users for multiple reasons. It provides flexibility and control over the resources. For instance, a banking organization may use a public cloud to store non-critical and unimportant transactional data, but use a private cloud to store and monitor critical information, such as customer bank details (sometimes they would rather use on-premise arrangements for that). For additional information related to risk and benefits, see Table 1-1.

Table 1-1. *Deployment Model Benefits and Risks*

Deployment Model	Benefits	Risks and Issues
Public	Costs	Lack of control
	Time to market	Security
	Elasticity	Regulatory and compliance
	Self-service	Data migration
	Simplicity	Application development
		Software licensing
		Vendor lock-in
		Limitations
Private	Control	Scale
	Security	Management tools
	Compliance	Charge-back
		Adoption
		ROI
Hybrid	Flexibility	Multiple points of failure
	Security	Most of the risks and issues
	Efficiencies	associated with public and private
		hosting models are applicable here
		as well

Apart from popular deployment models, such as public, private, and hybrid, another variant exists, commonly known as a *community cloud*. This is a specialized offering.

In the *community cloud model,* infrastructure is shared by several organizations. It supports a specific community that has a shared concern. So, it is a service model that provides a cloud computing solution to a limited number of individuals or organizations that are governed, managed, and secured commonly by all the participating organizations. Another possibility is that all this is managed and maintained by a third-party service provider, which provides common services to all the interested parties (in this case, the organizations).

Cloud Computing Service Models

There are three cloud service offerings—Infrastructure as a Service (IaaS), Platform as a Service (PaaS), and Software as a Service (SaaS). Apart from these there are numerous others, like function as a service, analytics as a service, machine learning as a service, and even life as a service, to everything as a service. However, only the main three are discussed here.

- *Infrastructure as a Service (IaaS)*: The providers offer highly selective computing functionality such as compute power, storage, archive, or other basic infrastructure components that are available over the Internet (or to be precise, on the cloud). They generally associate customizable utility pricing and delivery schemes with the offering. Service providers own the equipment, networking devices, and storage hardware and are responsible for hosting, coding, operation, and maintenance.

- *Platform as a Service (PaaS)*: The service provider provisions or establishes a fully functional computing solution or technology stack. Once the platform is "established," applications are deployed on that. The provider provides the network, servers, and storage for the environment or the "platform." They also take care of scalability and maintenance-related requirements.

- *Software as a Service (SaaS)*: Applications are hosted by a vendor or provider and made available to the consumers over a network (typically over the Internet). The software application functionality is delivered through a user-based pricing model. The underlying application resources are shared among a large number of users.

For a detailed view of the benefits associated with these service models, see Table 1-2.

Table 1-2. *Benefits of Service Models*

Service Models	Benefits
Software as a Service (SaaS)	<ul><li>The application is hosted centrally</li><li>Software testing takes place at a faster rate</li><li>Reduction in IT operational costs</li><li>No need to install new software or release updates</li></ul>
Platform as a Service (PaaS)	<ul><li>Facilitation of hosting capabilities</li><li>Designing and developing the application</li><li>Integrating web services and databases</li><li>Providing security, scalability, and storage</li></ul>
Infrastructure as a Service (IaaS)	<ul><li>Virtualization of desktop</li><li>Internet availability</li><li>Use of a billing model</li><li>Computerized administrative tasks</li></ul>

As the cloud computing model continues to develop quickly, the new businesses in the form of "as a service" models continue to appear. For example, integration of Big Data and the cloud now gives birth to Analytics as a Service (AaaS). Its "as a service" platform creates faster and scalable ways to integrate, analyze, transform, and visualize structured, semi-structured, and unstructured data (in real time).

Similarly, other models and services like compliance as a service, communications as a service, and human resources as a service are targeted to specific needs. In the very raw form, this model of business is described as "anything as a service," and abbreviated as "XaaS," where X denotes any service someone wants that can be obtained in the cloud.

Challenges of Cloud Computing

The following are the challenges related to cloud computing:

- *Privacy and security*: The cloud environment data is not hosted on the company's own infrastructure, so companies have concerns regarding the security and privacy.

  Possibilities for data leakage or virus attack potentially lead to critical situations in terms of security and privacy. However, all the previous concerns are handled by the providers or third parties with the help of robust architecture, intelligent backup technologies, security frameworks, appropriate deployment models, and automated processes and policies. Moreover, cloud computing is a mature technology now and is capable of handling any challenge related to security and privacy.

- *Availability*: From a cloud perspective, availability is the ratio of time a system or component is functional, to the total time it is required or expected to function. This can be articulated through direct proportion (for example, 8/10 or 0.8) or as a percentage (for example, 80 percent). Availability is typically measured by the sum of downtime your application or server has in a given period. Typically, a year is used as a standard parameter. For accurate calculation, unplanned downtime and planned downtime are both considered. Also, the cloud providers cannot ensure the uptime of their external Internet connection, which could shut all access to the cloud.

- *Reliability*: Within the cloud computing environment, reliability refers to the ability of a cloud related hardware or software component(s) to constantly achieve and perform tasks. The consistency in performance and accomplishment of tasks must synchronize according to the specifications and promises given by the service provider. In theory, a reliable product or service is completely free of errors. In practice, cloud vendors and service providers commonly express product reliability as a percentage.

  However, in real life there are instances of outages and service failure at the infrastructure or facilities of the cloud service providers. Sometime very serious events occur, which ultimately affect the business. This raises apprehensions over the trustworthiness of the cloud solutions and offerings. However, enterprises are now ready and prepared to deal with some level of failures and reliability issues in cloud-based environments.

The cloud service vendors generally guarantee 99.999 percent uptime. With the recent advent of new technologies, they are able to fulfill these promises as well. But some companies are still skeptical about the loss of control when an outage occurs.

- *Cultural change*: Enterprises desire a "culture of innovation, agility, flexibility, and quick adoption" in IT, especially in cloud-based environments because by its very nature it is agile and dynamic. It is important that IT enterprises enables new ideas, thoughts, and projects to get off the ground quickly and allow for faster iterations. Cloud computing helps to reduce the lead time to provision the environments; it reduces this from weeks to minutes. The cost of building the environments also drops significantly. The pay-as-you-go pricing model ensures that the business does not have to worry about the infrastructure and resource costs after the completion of experiments. Also, this reduces the cost of experimentation. The cloud also provides multiple out-of-the-box features, functionalities, and tools to empower agile development.

What Is IoT?

The Internet of Things (IoT) is understood as a self-configuring wireless network of sensors and devices. Its ultimate goal and purpose is to connect all "things or objects." In IoT, an object or thing is connected to other objects or things over the Internet, either as a source of data or as a consumer. Some objects may be armed with small computers or processing units, which can process the data they receive.

Most experts agree that the impact of Internet of Things on our lives will be far greater than the combined impact of computers and the Internet. With the dawn of the Internet of things (IoT), technologies like near field communication (NFC) and wearable, intelligent smartphones have become a reality and are embedded in our day-to-day lives.

IoT basically integrates the physical and digital worlds by bringing dissimilar ideas, elements, and components together. It tries to create a seamlessly interconnected network of devices (wired or wireless) that communicate over the Internet in a holistic way. The number of connected devices is in the trillions. Practically, we may visualize IoT as a networked interconnection of commonplace objects.

It is an established fact that IoT impacts almost every business and individual by its wider impact on society and commerce.

Moreover, integration of mobile, cloud, machine learning, cognitive computing, and the Internet of Things data affects a range of business operations and habits of individuals. For example, it changed the types of devices and equipment used in organizations for connection purposes. A new generation of connection devices in association with innovative services enables unique intelligent systems. These intelligent systems are powered by IoT device-generated data. Figure 1-6 summarizes IoT.

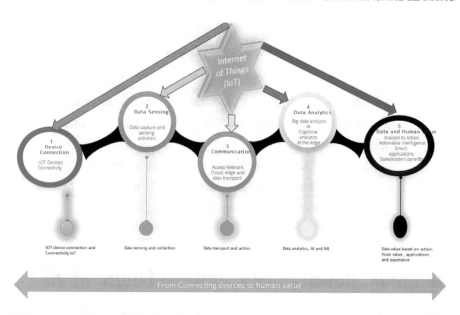

Figure 1-6. *A summary of IoT*

IoT helps businesses gain efficiencies and harness intelligence from a wide range of connected and available equipment. Overall, once an organization is powered by IoT, its operational capabilities increase. This, in turn, pays off in the form of customer satisfaction. IoT will also have a deep impact on people's lives. It is helpful in improving public safety, transportation, and healthcare with better information and quicker transportation and communication. IoT in fact affects societies, people, and organizations in multiple ways.

Some formal definitions of IoT are listed here:

- IoT is about connecting with everyday things around us using Internet technologies.

- IoT starts with connecting your things, meaning the things that matter most to your business. IoT is about making your data come together in new ways. You can tap into data with IoT enabled dashboards, uncovering

actionable intelligence. IoT helps you modernize how
you do business. (From Microsoft, on its landing page
of IoT.)

- IoT links smart objects to the Internet. It can enable an
exchange of data never available before and bring users
information in a more secure way. You can gain deeper
insight with analytics using an IoT system to enhance
productivity, create new business models, and generate
new revenue streams. (From Cisco, on its landing page
of IoT.)

Evolution, Development, and the Future of IoT

The quantum growth and universality of IoT have created multiple ways
to access heterogeneous data. IoT also boosts the analytical techniques
that extract data from desperate data sources and combines data types
that are important for decision making. The ability to accumulate, store,
and connect all this data and then make sense of it will help enterprises
differentiate themselves. The power of real-time access and analysis of
data provides an opportunity to grow fast and bring disruption to your
business models.

Jargon Buster

- *Lifelogging* is the process of tracking and maintaining
personal data that's generated by our own behavioral
activities. You can do this with the help of pen or paper
and by electronic gadgets and applications. Lifelogging
originated primarily as a way to save raw personal
data. Lifelogging tracks personal behavior data like
exercising, moving, running, sleeping, and eating.

- *Quantified self* is defined as self-knowledge through numbers. Quantified self is about analyzing lifelogged data to find correlations among the personal data sets and to draw conclusions on the basis of that.

The goal of all this is to the improve health, wellness, and lives of individuals.

Characteristics of IoT

IoT devices are connected to the Internet via wireless and wired Internet connections. These sensors and devices use many types of local area networks and connections, including RFID, NFC, WiFi, and Bluetooth, for connectivity. Sensors can also have wide area connectivity such as Global System for Mobile (GSM), General Packet Radio Service (GPRS), Third/Fourth Generation (3G/4G) mobile networks, and Long Term Evolution (LTE). The Internet of Things will handle the feats discussed in the following sections.

Connecting Non-Living and Living Things

An IoT system must be able to connect to the Internet. IoT includes almost everything from industrial machinery to homes to everyday usable objects. The types of items range from automobiles to spacecrafts to toothbrushes. It can also include living creatures, such as plants, farm animals, and people.

The Internet of Things has the potential of connecting everything through the Internet. So, based on its nature, the next step is often called the "Internet of Everything," a term that originated at Cisco. It refers to the natural extension of the Internet of Things. The vision is to connect everything—including people, places, objects, processes, and data. Basically, anything that can be potentially connected to the Internet through sensors and networks participates in these connected ecosystems.

Collecting and Transmitting Data Through Sensors

Physical objects that are being connected must contain one or more sensors. Each sensor is capable of sensing a specific condition, like location, vibration, motion, gesture, and temperature. In the IoT ecosystem, these sensors and devices connect to each other and to other systems that can understand and then present information based on the sensor's data feeds. These sensors must be capable of providing new information to an enterprise's systems, process, and people.

Communicating Over an IP Network

IoT enabled devices or equipment can communicate with each other through underlying enabling technologies. Technology provides empowerment to IoT-enabled objects through which they share data about their condition and the surrounding environment with people, software systems, and other machines. This data can be shared in real time, stored, and collected. It can maximize business benefits wherever and whenever required.

As IoT systems and ecosystem mature, everything (people, places, processes, and things) present on the network will have a digital identity and connectivity. This means that they can be identified and tracked in real time. They can communicate with objects or the system of objects according to how important the situation is in real time. It is a known fact that the volume of connected devices is very high and growing at a rapid rate. Hence, the IPv4 standard is not enough because of limited number of available IP address; therefore, using the IPv6 is encouraged.

The concept of the Internet of Things evolves with the maturity of the Internet. Intelligent devices and services are becoming smarter by the day.

Challenges with the Internet of Things

IoT technical and business ecosystems require a lot of research and expertise to establish, set up, operate, and perform, before they start paying off. Due to the complex, technical nature of incorporating processes, network diversity, and heterogeneity of data and devices, these ecosystems require a careful and thoughtful approach to decision making. Therefore, lots of challenges are associated with their implementation. Let's take a look at these challenges.

- *Working with variety of stakeholders, devices, standards, hardware, and protocols*: Establishing, building, and making sure that the IoT ecosystem is up and running is one of the biggest challenges. It involves fine tuning and synchronizing a diverse set of technologies, protocols, processes, and communication methods with multiple stakeholders. Also, it works with a diversity of devices and ensures that everything works together holistically in a desired way, which is a challenge.

- *Managing remote devices*: The IoT cloud ecosystem typically contains a huge number of sensors, gateways, equipment, and devices. Moreover, they are distributed across geographies, some of which may be in remote locations. Managing all these devices remotely in the efficient and effective way, so that they work in an integrated way, is one of the major challenges.

- *Interoperability of devices*: Seamlessly transporting data and synchronizing it is a challenge. Data flows on complex networks and sometimes on a network of networks. This demands seamless communication between sensors, equipment, and other devices.

Typically, devices are manufactured or created by different vendors and companies according to their areas of expertise. Achieving interoperability among equipment, sensors, and devices is a challenge.

- *Data integration and consolidation*: Once the IoT system or ecosystem is established and set up, the data streams from multiple sensors, mobile devices, social media networks, and from other connected resources start coming in in an ad hoc fashion. This data is continuously available. One of the biggest challenges is to handle the data by making sure that data integrity does not break and that it's available in synchronization with application logic.

- *System flexibility*: IoT is still in the nascent phase and is somewhat immature. Its standard and protocols are still evolving and are at the beginning stage of evolution. By the time it evolves fully as an established and mature system, more and more sensors and applications with increased capabilities and diversity will have popped up and been added in an unorganized and ad hoc manner. Therefore, the existing ecosystem of applications, networks, devices, and services needs to be flexible enough to accommodate future changes.

- *Data security*: In an IoT ecosystem, most of the data is collected from various devices, which are the part of the enterprise or individual's private network. They contain sensitive personal and enterprise business critical data that needs to be protected from unauthorized access.

- *Handling huge data volumes*: The IoT system deals with many devices, which results in a huge volume of data coming in at a high frequency. Managing, measuring, and effectively using that data in real time is a challenge. This is closely associated with data performance and the issue of latency.

How IoT Works

The IoT ecosystem is made or created by many components, or layers. At the device level, as mentioned earlier, it contains sensors and processing units. Then the Internet or precisely the network comes into the picture and connects those devices to the larger network. The gateways act as a secure bridge between the sensors, other tiny equipment, and devices. It also connects to the cloud through standard networking. The top layer handles overall monitoring and management of the IoT ecosystem. Also at this layer, analytics is performed on the collected and persisted data, including applications and the value the IoT ecosystem exposes.

Let's look at each part of the IoT ecosystem and broadly at the involved technologies:

- *Edge devices and sensors*: IoT is all about seamless communication and connection between devices and objects. This is achieved through edge devices and sensors. They can sense and trigger various levels of involvedness. One example in the wearables space are the biometric sensing components in wristbands and watches. In the automotive space, you'll find networks and suites of smart devices that coordinate and communicate among themselves through sensors. These "technically" connected systems provide a more pleasurable driving experience to the drivers.

- *The gateway and its communication techniques*: The gateway is an essential part of the IoT environment. An IoT gateway is an "in-between" device between the device and the network. The gateway provides power to collect and securely transport data from the devices and equipment to the network. The gateway is essentially not a singular component but rather a network of gateways that connect to all the distant devices. It is generally capable of scaling with device growth.

The gateway can be used for multiple purposes, but two of them are very important. First it can be the bridge that migrates collected edge data to the cloud and second, it can be used as a data processor. Gateways are helpful in reducing the volume of available data on its way to the cloud, because they filter out "junk data" by making decisions instantly based on the data available.

The cloud is an integral part of the IoT ecosystem. IoT gives the cloud the power of scaling and elasticity. As data grows from edge devices, the capability to scale storage and networking resources becomes very important. Compute resources in the cloud environment enable the development of the IoT ecosystems. In cloud computing environments, virtualization makes elastic compute possible. Virtualization provides flexibility to slice up a processor to represent two or more virtual processors, where each virtual processor logically time-shares the physical processor. When one processor needs less computing power and resources, and another virtual processor needs more resources, the system can logically exploit those physical resources. This enables maximum utilization of available resources.

Virtualization is not a new concept; it has matured enough to add value to almost all technology stacks available for information technology, especially to cloud computing and related areas. Virtualization means that when more IoT data flows from edge devices, physical processors can be ramped up automatically based on need to cope with the demands of these data flows. When the flow of data subsides, these resources can be reassigned to other tasks and responsibilities to save power, effort, and cost.

What Is Cognitive Computing?

The term "cognitive" refers to the mental process of knowing, including features such as awareness, conciseness, insight, reasoning ability, and judgment. Cognitive computing refers to self-learning systems that use data mining, pattern recognition and matching, and natural language processing much in the same way that the human brain works.

Cognitive computing systems can lean and interact naturally with users to extend the capability of humans or machines. Humans can do more than what they can do on their own without cognitive computing. These system(s) respond to the environment by themselves, without pre-programming. They can sense, learn, infer, and interact. In a nutshell, cognitive computing systems can sense or perceive the environment and collect data on the basis of need and situations. They can understand, interpret, and analyze the "context" based on collected data and information and make decisions based on reasoning.

Cognitive computing systems use machine learning algorithms and Big Data analytics to achieve a desired behavior, but it is not confined to just these technologies. The goal of cognitive computing is to create automated systems that are capable of not only solving problems but also can suggest better alternatives without requiring human assistance. Technically, the cognitive computing systems can access and analyze massive stores of historical data, then apply machine learning algorithms and techniques to determine the connections and correlations across all of those information pieces. It uses a knowledgebase as the apparatus for discovery of patterns, decision support, and deep learning. It decides what's right in a given situation and provides the appropriate answer at the appropriate time in the appropriate context.

Some professional definitions of cognitive computing are as follows:

- Cognitive computing is the simulation of human thought processes in a computerized model. Cognitive computing involves self-learning systems that use data mining, pattern recognition, and natural language processing to mimic the way the human brain works. The goal of cognitive computing is to create automated IT systems that are capable of solving problems without requiring human assistance. (Whatis.com)

- Cognitive computing systems are based on dialog-oriented natural language interfaces and machine learning algorithms. They have knowledge-enabled processes and mimic human like decision-making abilities to enable human and machine to interact more naturally. This extends human expertise and efficiency by intelligently analyzing volumes of data and coming up with insights and solutions in a fraction of the time it now takes. (Wipro's landing page of cognitive computing.)

Cognitive systems are different from current computing systems. They move beyond tabulation, calculation, and precompiled rules and programs. This technology allows people and enterprises to interact with computers using natural languages like English.

This enables customers to convey their thoughts, concerns, and expectations in more natural way. Hence, understanding customers and users is much easier. This "natural human-like understanding" empowers organizations and enterprises to achieve customer satisfaction of the highest degree and helps them win their trust. Moreover, they are able to get customer delight, which results in lifelong customer loyalty. The idea of interacting with computers and automated systems (robots) in a natural language is not new. It is one of the most loved topics of science fiction films and stories (including *Star Wars*).

Here are some of the use cases of cognitive computing that illustrate what these systems can achieve:

- *Application management though diagnosis in real time*: Recognize application-related problems and provide solutions to fix them before the user realizes it.

- *Service helpdesk*: Understand user problems while interacting with them through call/video/textual means and provide a solution in real time.

- *Security control and management*: Security for devices, equipment, and society, using face, voice, and body movement recognition.

- *Productivity management*: Incorporate intelligence into routine tasks to reduce/minimize human effort.

How Cognitive Computing Works

Cognitive technologies enable devices and things to sense by seeing and hearing like humans and then draw inferences by doing real-time reasoning and analysis in the context of anticipating the needs of an individual. Finally, these technologies enable devices to take action in the form of activities "intuitively," based on the context.

In the past, users had to write the text in some predefined format to perform tasks, so the system could understand and produce the result. In cognitive environment, the system understands the situation based on data analysis and produces appropriate results by applying intelligence to the data set. If a user wanted to conduct a search, they had to input the keywords manually; whereas, with the help of natural language processing, cognitive technologies allow and empower people to ask questions or speak in sentences when interacting with systems, the same way they talk to another human being to get an answer.

For example, with Apple Siri or Microsoft Cortana, you just ask a question and the software analyzes your questions based on all the available options (internally it uses machine learning and Big Data technologies to do this) and provides you with the most appropriate answer.

Cognitive computing systems use machine learning to get smarter over time, just the way humans do (see Figure 1-7). Unlike older technologies, new generation cognitive computing systems analyze vast amounts of data and generate insights. Cognitive computing offers the opportunity to resolve some of the greatest challenges humankind faces today. It's helping doctors solve health crises across the globe by fighting diseases like cancer and Parkinson's. It's allowing scientists to synthesize existing research and develop new breakthroughs. It's assisting governments and non-profits in planning for and responding to disasters. And, it's enabling businesses in nearly every industry to better serve their customers.

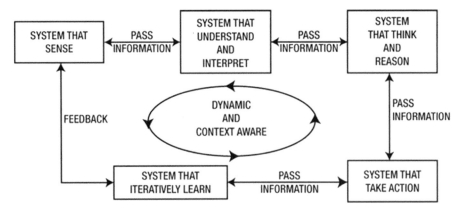

Figure 1-7. *Cognitive computing*

Cognitive computing is inspired by the human brain. It extends our abilities by serving as a natural extension of our senses. It has the potential of contextually customizing and personalizing our experiences, while creating human-like interactions with devices and things. It is capable of doing personalization. Moreover, personalization is done on the basis of where the user is, what the user is doing, and what they are planning to do. For example, when users are in a business meeting, their mobile devices will show them the relevant information about the meeting, take notes on their behalf, and even suggest a location and time for their next meeting. When users are at home, it will recognize different family members and present each of them in the appropriate content. It will help users see their work emails, while their child will see their favorite cartoon show.

Fundamentally, cognitive technologies enable computers to make sense of structured, semi-structured, and unstructured data in a given context by analyzing it to find the hidden patterns in the data. This process happens iteratively and with each iteration, cognitive computers become better at identifying patterns.

In the last few years, we have seen that devices, machines, and things (including cars, refrigerators, and other commonly used products) are becoming much more intuitive. They are helping and simplifying our daily lives. The best example is smartphones, which are becoming more aware of our preferences and surroundings. They have become "smart" and capable of anticipating our needs and providing us with relevant information at the appropriate time.

Characteristics of Cognitive Computing

Here are the characteristics of cognitive computing:

- Engage in dialogue generation and evaluation of hypotheses

- Understand and make sense of natural language

- Provide supporting evidence to the decisions

- Consume heterogeneous (big) data

- Respond with a degree of confidence and provide evidence for the same

- Learn with every interaction and improve on it with time

- Provide contextual guidance and insights to the offered actions

- Provide support for decision making

- Relate between relations

- Comprehend users at a deeper level

Nervana Systems: A Machine Learning Startup

Nervana Systems was recently acquired by Intel. They are experts in providing deep learning solutions. They are using artificial intelligence and machine learning, or more precisely "deep learning," as a computational paradigm. Nervana is building solutions augmented from algorithms to silicon to resolve machine learning problems. For the past two years, Naveen Rao (the founder) and his team of 48 at Nervana Systems have been building technology to power the next generation of intelligent and smart applications.

Nervana acquired a reputation for being one of the pioneers in developing the machine learning and cognitive technology. Recently, the U.S. chip-making giant Intel acquired the San Diego headquartered startup for a reported $408 million. Nervana's founders think that their AI expertise combined with Intel's capabilities and huge market reach (Intel has the best semiconductor technology in the world) will allow Nervana to realize its vision and create something truly special. Rao assured his team that they'll maintain their "startup mentality "while scaling up with the pace of the big company like Intel. Nervana Systems was cofounded by Naveen Rao, Arjun Bansal, and Amir Khosrowshahi.

Nervana helps users in multiple ways. For instance, for the foreseeable future, the Nervana Cloud will continue to be the fastest machine learning/deep learning platform in the world, because the Nervana Engine includes everything you need for deep learning and nothing you don't!

How the Cloud, IoT, Machine Learning, Big Data Analytics, and Cognitive Computing Work Together

The complexity of the nexus between these technologies makes cognitive computing and machine learning vital in realizing the true value of the Internet of Things and Big Data. This becomes more relevant in dynamic and Agile ecosystems of technologies and business processes that demand innovation and disruption on a continuous basis. The motive of the Internet of Things is to connect enterprise, data, and people more closely. The utility of that data is limited by its own complications until useful inferences are drawn from it. Without sense or inference, IoT data is of no use.

Machine learning, with its association of analytics, refines the data through models and algorithms by continuously processing it (new data) in real time. This trains the system to adapt to changing patterns and associations in the data. Also, wider analytical processes and tools help to discover patterns and anomalies in large volumes of data that can anticipate and predict business outcomes.

In this complete process, data is very important. To provide action steps, a cognitive system requires large, effective, and a sufficient amount of data. Based on the quality of the available data set, the cognitive system can discover patterns within it (with the help of the machine learning algorithm). If the data is not large, the result is not consistent and accurate. This can lead to wrong and useless patterns, which will be hazardous to the enterprises and defeat the overall purpose. A cognitive system also requires the ingestion and mapping of data so that the system can begin to discover connections between data sources to get insights.

To accomplish the goal of finding insights and value, a cognitive system uses almost all forms of data, including structured, semi-structured, and unstructured data. Machine learning algorithms are the heart and backbone of all this. They enable the complete process and play a big role in providing value-added IoT and Big Data services by finding the patterns, correlations, and anomalies in in the data.

Now you come to the technology and implementation component. You get data through IoT systems and other sources like log files and archives. IoT acts as a limitless data generator (because IoT is connecting virtual and physical objects to the Internet) and creator. The cloud could play the role of organizer and resource provider for IoT and other data sources. Also, the cloud in general serves as an abstraction for hiding complexity and implementation functionality. Data is stored in the cloud on a continuous and real-time basis and then data analytics are applied on that data to make sense of it. Machine learning techniques find patterns to make predictions in order to get better business results.

Let's put this in a systematic way. For the benefit of understanding, I divided the complete flow into multiple layers. However, this is not the standard segregation and depends on the implementation. Also, this varies from enterprise to enterprise based on the strategies around it. For example, in some implementations, the machine learning layer is paired with the data analytics layer, whereas in other cognitive computing implementations, the layer is merged with machine learning, data analytics, and Big Data layers. But overall, all experts agree that layers/technologies are part and parcel of any machine learning or cognitive computing implementation strategy. Here is a glimpse of the complete story (see Figure 1-8).

1. *Cloud infrastructure*: This layer provides all the basic infrastructure in the cloud, including software and hardware resources. The hosting model provides options about which model to select based on need. After that, the service model can be selected according to need. Once that's done, you are ready for the next step. If you already have this layer ready, proceed directly to the next layer. You don't have to purchase services offered by cloud provider. You can skip this and go to the available services offered in other layers.

2. *Big Data layer*: This layer receives, stores, and provides you all types of data (structured, unstructured, and semi-structured, including IoT and real-time streaming chunks) for further analysis.

3. *Big Data analytics layer*: In this layer, analytics are performed on the Big Data layer. This layer is very important for all cognitive or machine learning platforms, architectures, or frameworks.

4. *Machine learning layer*: In this layer, machine learning activities are performed on the data in collaboration and close communication with the data analytics layer. Available algorithms of machine

learning (supervised, unsupervised, and semi-supervised) come into play here and they repeatedly run algorithms in an iterative manner on the data sets. On the basis of this, prescriptive, predictive, and diagnostic predictions are performed.

5. *Cognitive computing layer*: In this layer, cognitive computing activities are performed. Like suggesting the best action based on the available list of action items. This layer provides a natural language "real-life" interface for human/machine collaboration and communication.

6. *Presentation and reporting layer*: This is the layer where the end user interacts with the system by either providing input or getting output. For example, if someone want to see a report that contains trends in a particular region of the country, they would get that information through the tools involved in this layer, like Microsoft BI.

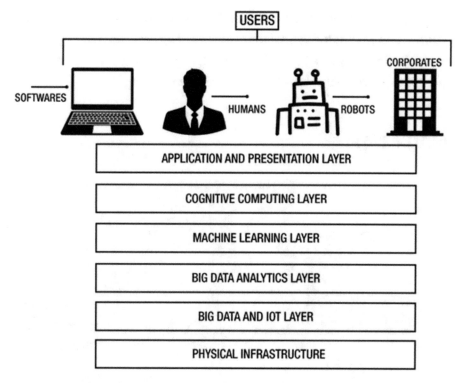

Figure 1-8. *Comprehensive model*

Video Link

http://pages.skytree.net/webinar-od-machine-learning-how-to-make-it-work-watch.html?aliId=7353129

Summary

This chapter set the stage for machine learning and its associated technologies for business users. It also provided a brief look at technical details and business cases, and their importance in the present business ecosystem. It discussed the cloud, Big Data, Big Data analytics, machine learning, and cognitive computing. At the end of chapter, you read about a holistic and integrated model that consists of all associated technologies of machine learning in a layered manner. It explained how they work together to provide solutions to solve business challenges.

Mind Map

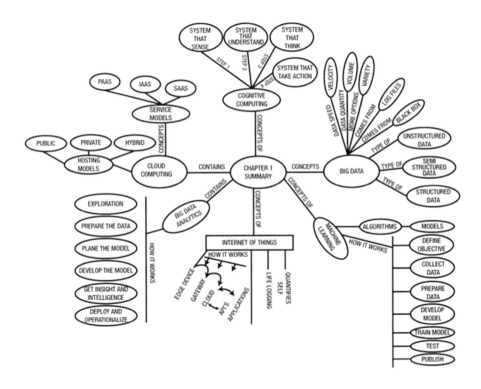

CHAPTER 2

The Practical Concepts of Machine Learning

Dr. Patanjali Kashyap[a*]

[a] Bangalore, Karnataka, India

This is an important chapter because it discusses the basic and practical concepts of machine learning (ML). I do not take an academic approach to explain these concepts. I have directed my thoughts and energy to provide you with the concepts that are useful during practical decision making. Hence, while explaining the concepts, terminologies, and technical details, I use examples and case studies that are be helpful in extracting relevant insight from the chapter.

The chapter starts with the evolution and history of machine learning and with the notion of finding links between different schools of thought and philosophies. It takes you to the world of artificial intelligence by traveling through the last few decades of progress. After that, it provides glimpses of future applications of ML. This chapter contains a section on business opportunities that machine learning is generating. This provides you with insight into business opportunities that are coming up or already exist in machine learning-enabled fields. Again, for tools like this, relevant examples and case studies are used extensively.

© Dr. Patanjali Kashyap 2024
P. Kashyap, *Machine Learning for Decision Makers*,
https://doi.org/10.1007/978-1-4842-9801-5_2

There is a thin line between application areas and business opportunities. Application areas of a technology might be the area of opportunity as well. For example, machine learning is widely applied in the retail industries for doing different types of predictions and recommendations. At the same time, enormous business opportunities exist to enhance existing products and services using ML technologies and create new markets. They can do this by engaging customers based on recommendations from habits/behavioral analyses. So, parallel discussions on application areas and business opportunities provide the most contemporary and futuristic vision of the subject.

I also discuss some important models, algorithms, tools, frameworks, and programming languages involved in machine learning. There is a section on machine learning architecture that gives you a holistic and integrative view of the "generalized" architecture of machine learning. In a nutshell, this chapter provides you with overall insight into the technologies under discussion.

Linking History, Evolution, Machine Learning, and Artificial Intelligence

The field of artificial intelligence is based on the possibility of automating human thoughts and their cognitive abilities. Broadly, AI technologies try to simulate and reproduce human thoughts and behavior. These thoughts and behavior can be further categorized into thinking, speaking, feeling, and reasoning. The science of designing programs makes computers smarter and this includes the goal of "making computers do things at which humans are better."

Historically, Greek, Indian, and Chinese scholars had a firm belief of the concept of the "thinking machine." They believe that the "thinking machine" is possible and building one is achievable. Their philosophers, psychologists, and mathematicians were engaged in this approach with their thoughts, inventions, and discoveries. However, they mostly worked in isolation in their confined geographical boundaries. Because they did not have the "luxury" to be always connected as we are now, a consolidated thought never emerged that could be accepted by everyone.

For example, during the 17th century, Gottfried Leibniz, Thomas Hobbes, and René Descartes explored the possibilities of explaining thoughts simply by using mathematical symbols. But their ideas were not connected and existed in isolation. Explaining thoughts in the form of symbols and logical steps is part of algorithmic study. Algorithm development is a branch of mathematics. Algorithms played a crucial part in the evolution of artificial intelligence and machine learning. Hence, it's not possible to discuss history, evolution, and the development of AI and machine learning without considering algorithms.

Representing, explaining, and splitting the facts and figures of a complex problem into symbols and rational/logical steps is the central theme of algorithms. Algorithms established themselves as a primary tool for problem solving due to their simplicity and effectiveness of explaining a problem. Development and uses of algorithms can be linked to the Babylonians and they get credit for inventing the first devised factorization and square roots in 1600 BC (which can be achieved through logical steps). However, Euclid's finding of the Greatest Common Divider in 300 BC and Aryabhata's discovery of 0 are some of the earliest examples of development and impact of algorithms in human history.

Ada Lovelace's derivation of the first algorithm intended to be carried out by machines in 1843 would be taken as a benchmark for algorithmic development. Ada's work laid the foundations, but she never talked about or wrote about anything close to artificial intelligence. Formally, AI is born with Alan Turing's paper entitled "Computing Machinery and Intelligence." This interesting research paper was published in 1950. In the paper, Turing invented, explained, and theoretically tried to established the idea of whether machines could think or not. The paper explained and conveyed some very important concepts, but with limitations. On the downside, the paper was not very generic and mostly was confined to conceptual boundaries.

The Turing paper explained the concept of AI with the help of game-based hypotheses. The games involved three players. Player A is a computer and Player B is a human. Each must prove to Player C (a human who can't see either Player A or Player B) whether they are human or computer. If Player C can't determine who is human and who isn't on a consistent basis, the computer wins. We may agree or disagree with this hypothesis, but it definitely laid the foundation for artificial intelligence.

The term *artificial intelligence* was first mentioned by John McCarthy in 1955. He thought and explained it as the "discipline of science and engineering of intelligent machine." He also emphasized the computer's working ability of knowledge "without being explicitly programmed." This idea was novel at that time. He explained the concepts of "explicit programming" while he was trying to explain artificial intelligence.

AI is incredibly complex because of its multi-disciplinary nature and expectations of solving some of the biggest problems of human kind. There was a lot of optimism associated with AI during its inception and progress in the 1950s and 1960s. In its initial days, it was believed that, by riding the potential and power of AI, the world would produce intelligent machines in just 20 years.

As mentioned earlier, AI includes and is influenced by many other disciplines. One example of this is the concept of shallow and deep learning, which originally come from psychology. The main reason behind this influence is the goal of AI itself. Mainly, it was thought, documented, explained, and imagined as a machine that has the capability of processing the "simulation of thought process". Hence, it was expected that AI-enabled systems would mimic human physical and cognitive behavior. Likewise, human thought processes are influenced and affected by multiple factors, including sociological, psychological, and biological aspects. Therefore, it was natural that AI would be developed by considering multiple areas of human endeavor under its umbrella.

In the last few decades, machine learning has evolved as a separate science. If we trace back the history, we can find the genes of machine learning in computer science and statistics. In its early days, ML took inspiration from computer-assisted tutoring systems. Over the years, ML has, in turn, encouraged growth in this field to produce intelligent tutoring systems based on AI techniques. However, machine learning actually originated from pattern recognition and neural networks. These are the sub-fields of artificial intelligence. The notion backed by the theory that computers can learn without being programmed to perform specific sets of tasks is the main motive behind machine learning development.

The method of viewing and treating machine learning these days is different from its original form. In its early days, ML was seen as a computation, processing, and storage hungry endeavor, whereas now it is visualized as a data-driven technology. This change in mindset forced enterprises and researchers alike to carry out experiments and validate a computer's learning ability from data (or Big Data). Here, the iterative aspect of machine learning becomes important because as models are exposed to new data sets, they are able to independently adapt patterns from the data lake (see the section called "Jargon Buster"). They learn from previous computations or iterations to produce reliable, efficient, and effective decisions, results, and actions.

Jargon Buster

- *Machine intelligence*: Artificial intelligence related capabilities such as machine learning, deep learning, cognitive analytics, robotics process automation (RPA), and bots collectively make up machine intelligence. Algorithmic capabilities that can augment employee performance, automate increasingly complex workloads, and develop "cognitive agents" (a term used for machine learning-based intelligent personal assistance) that simulate human thinking and engagement fall under the machine intelligence umbrella.

- *Robotic Process Automation (RPA)*: This is a type of software robot, also commonly known as a "bot." These are used to accomplish monotonous business processes by imitating the ways people interact with software applications.

- *Data lake*: A gigantic but easily accessible, centralized source of huge volumes of structured, semi-structured, and unstructured data. A typical data lake is thought of as a data store that's capable of storing everything in terms of Big Data. Data lakes are mainly "storage" sites for Big Data and do not provide any significant classification or segregation of the stored data. Hence, the data lake is less structured compared to a data warehouse. Data lakes serve as a data source for multiple intelligent systems. Once they have the data they processed, analyzed, and optimized, they use it for different purposes. Any type of analytics or machine learning activities are generally preformed on the "assessed" data of the data lake.

- *Data island*: A data store that resides on devices like PDAs (personal digital assistants) or other computing devices, which have nonexistent or limited external connectivity. Therefore, this limits the ability of the user to synchronize with or copy the data to other devices. Hence, when new data is added to the system, the ability to move the "newly added data" elsewhere becomes difficult or impossible. From a database perspective, a data island is like a related group of tables. For example, a database has 15 tables, 10 are related to one group called group1 and 5 are related to group2. A condition notes that group1 and group2 are not linked to each other. In such situations, your database or model has two data islands—group1 and group2—and they work in isolation.

References:

- http://labs.sogeti.com/wp-content/uploads/2015/01/machineintell-en.pdf

- https://www2.deloitte.com/content/dam/Deloitte/global/Documents/Technology/gx-tech-trends-the-kinetic-enterprise.pdf

IBM's Arthur Samuel was the first person who used the term "machine learning" while he was developing the first self-learning computer program called a game checker. Previous to Samuel's work, nobody formally provided the idea that computers could be self-programmed. The general thought and assumption was that, for computers to perform any task, "pre-programming" would be required.

A more formal definition of machine learning came in the late 90s by Tom Mitchell (1998). He stated that "A computer program is said to learn from experience (E) with respect to some class of tasks (T) and performance measure (P), if its performance in task (T), as measured by (P), improves with experience (E)". In simplified form, a computer program is said to be self-learning if it has the ability to predict a definite result with increasing accuracy over time (in an iterative manner) when it operates on a data set.

Machine Learning, AI, the Brain, and the Business of Intelligence

According to John von Neumann (a pioneer in computer science who derived the first formal structure of computer), neurons can learn from "patterns" based on their inputs. Neuroscientists now call this *neurotransmitter concentrations*. However, von Neumann was not aware of how neurological learning works. It is a recent advancement in neuroscience that tells us that learning takes place through the generation/creation and destruction of connections between available neurons in the brain.

Jargon Buster

- *Neurons*: The human brain contains approximately 100 billion nerve cells, also called *neurons*. Neurons have the incredible skills to gather and communicate electrochemical signals. Gates and wires in a computer can be thought of as neurons. Neurons have the same characteristics and similar makeup as other cells. However, the built-in electrochemical properties let them transmit signals over long distances. They have fantastic capabilities to connect to each other and send messages among themselves.

von Neumann notes that the speed of neural processing is extremely slow, on the order of a hundred calculations per second, but the brain compensates this through massive parallel processing. Neurons connect and create new pathways and circuits in a "parallel" computation fashion. Likewise, modern day computers carry out parallel processing to perform/learn tasks. As mentioned, brain-like artificial intelligence isn't a new idea.

The concept of neural networks, which would be capable of mimicking the basic structure of the brain, was extremely popular in the 1980s in the scientific community. But during that time, the field of artificial intelligence lacked the computing power and availability of huge quality training data. Both the computing power and the data are mandatory for the models powered by algorithms to become really effective.

Recent advancements in computer hardware have contributed to cheaper processing power (in terms of speed and memory). Hence, one section of the scientific and industrial community is trying hard to achieve human intelligence through computers. The result of this effort is seen in the form of multiple robots and huge machines coming out of the labs. One of the goals of achieving "human intelligence" is to get business and commercial advantages over competitors. One example of this is IBM Watson. The scientific and industrial community (mainly the business community, including startups) is trying to cash in on recent advancements in technologies through several "quick" products and services. They are creating the chatbot (automated user query replying machines/software) types of products/services by leveraging already available platforms, services, and frameworks. Technologies like deep learning and natural language processing enable these platforms.

A new breed of entrepreneurs is reaching out to "targeted and focused" customers using the "me first" approach. What this means is that they are portraying themselves as the real innovator and provider of breakthrough machine learning-enabled products, applications, and services. They are appearing for the "first time" in the market and potentially have the capability to disrupt the market/industry dynamics. To make their point, they create quick prototypes and convert them into the products in an Agile fashion. They avoid having to perform extensive research from scratch.

However, both are betting on "data" now and most of the achievements in these areas are guided by the data itself.

The actual learning capabilities of machine learning are achieved by learning algorithms, which are representative of neural networks in the human brain (as ultimately it tries to simulate the brain's behavior). The basic "intent" of the machine learning algorithm is to find patterns similar to the brain. The model of simulation of artificial neural networks helps the system gather and process information about the given data sets. Then, with its self-learning ability, it extrapolates the data to predict future events and occurrences. The end result of this overall process comes in the form of logical decisions made by machine and humans together.

Humans learn and understand through trial and error with a continuous process of successive approximations. Humans frame a theory about a specific task, and based on the result of the first trial or approximation, they regulate their theory. This process continues iteratively until the optimal result is achieved. Machine learning algorithms work in a similar fashion. As the machine learning system gathers and processes more and more data, their results get better and better. This happens because it provides them with the ability to refine output and helps them predict the relationship between existing variables with increasing accuracy. To understand it better, imagine, when a child is born, their brain is a clean slate. They start learning by different means, which include a variety of data sources including observation, book-based learning, voices, and so on... The same is applicable to the machine as well. It learns from data that it receives from different data sources and algorithms.

General Architecture of Machine Learning

Figure 2-1 presents the general architecture of a machine learning system. Typically, it has six parts. However, it can be customized based on the need of the project, the system to be created, and the requirements.

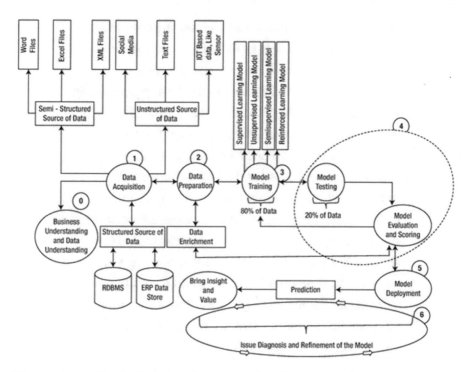

Figure 2-1. *Block diagram for general technical architecture of machine learning*

This list includes descriptions of each part:

- *Data acquisition* (collect and gather the data set):
  To create a machine learning system, you need two
  important things to work on—the data and the models.
  When acquiring/gathering the data, you must have
  enough quality data. As a general rule of thumb, the
  more data you have, the better the possibility of having
  an accurate prediction. Therefore, you have to be very
  selective with your data sources (Step 1).

- *Data preparation* (join, filter, cleanse the data sets):
  Once you have the data available for your machine
  learning system, you have to prepare it. You are
  enabling your ML systems to do the further processing
  by providing data in an appropriate format. The
  learning system takes data in a particular format,
  not in a crude and ad hoc format. Also, multiple
  transformational operations need to happen on
  data sets, which includes filtering, manipulation,
  sampling, and scaling. Once these steps are performed
  successfully, the data is reduced (converted) to the
  desired format. For example, while preparing a data set,
  you have to scrub missing values, edit the columns in
  a particular format, and split your data set for training
  followed by validation. This enables you to feed data to
  your selected training model (Step 2).

- The initial phase in data analysis is called *data
  exploration,* and it involves looking at and visualizing
  data to find insights right away or point out regions or
  trends that need more investigation. Users may quickly
  gain insights by using interactive dashboards and
  point-and-click data exploration to better comprehend
  the broader picture. *Data granularity* is the amount of
  information your data can describe. Therefore the more
  granularity it has, the more detail it can convey. People
  can rapidly and effectively analyze data, especially
  massive amounts of data, by using data visualization.
  It enables employees to base choices more accurately
  on data by offering clear visual representations of
  that data.

- All of that granular data can be transformed into valuable, aesthetically appealing, and easily understandable business information with the use of data visualization.

- *Train the model* (use machine learning to generalize): While you are in the process of creating an accurate machine learning model for your work, the one thing you have to discover is what type of analysis will help you achieve your goal. Accordingly, you have to train your model.

A program that uses a data set that has never been seen before to detect patterns or make choices is known as a machine learning model. A machine learning model is also a representation of an algorithm that searches through vast amounts of data to look for patterns or forecast future outcomes. ML models are the mathematical powerhouses of artificial intelligence, powered by data. You can also think of a model as an experienced algorithm. Machine learning algorithms, for instance, can analyze and accurately identify the intent underlying previously unheard utterances or word combinations in natural language processing. A model can ingest the data in a two-step process. That can be further used for multiple purposes, including training the model.

- Data collection entails acquiring information from a variety of sources, including databases, APIs, sensors, and external data sets.

- Before ingesting, the data mistakes, inconsistencies, and missing values data must be found and fixed.

It may be a classification analysis (a typical example is finding spam vs. non-spam in the system), a clustering analysis (is an automatic classification required?), or a regression analysis (is my model going to do prediction and forecasting?). Once this is done, you have to compare the results of multiple available models. This exercise enables you to know which model is the most efficient for your data set (Step 3).

Let's look at this in a more systematic way:

- *Evaluate/test the model* (simulate and cross-validate): Before going into the details, I define cross-validation. Basically, cross-validation is a machine learning approach that is frequently used to evaluate a data set's variability as well as the dependability of any model developed using that data set. A labeled data set is provided as input to the cross-validation model component. Additionally, cross-validation may be used to test several machine learning models by training them on different subsets of the input data and then comparing the results. Cross-validation might be used to spot overfitting, which is when a pattern fails to generalize.

  The performance of a machine learning model is a very important stage. It gives you an idea how successful the predictions of a data set have been by a trained model. Also, evaluation and cross-validation are established and standard methods measure the performance of the model under consideration. Both provide you with evaluation metrics, which allow you to evaluate and judge the preference of another model so that you can make the best choice (Step 4).

- *Deployment* (run in the score; track the concept drift): Assuming the previous steps are completed successfully and you are satisfied with the outcome of the model (basically values), this is a strong indicator that your evaluation is successful and your model is ready for the next step. As you tried multiple models during evaluation, you have to clean up everything and make sure that only one model is left, with the optimum performance. You assess machine learning models to make sure they are functioning as anticipated and are adequate for the purpose they were designed for. After the model training phase is complete, the assessment phase is carried out. The evaluation aids in the analysis of a model's main flaws. Machine learning algorithms look for various patterns and trends. Not all data sets or use cases lend themselves to the same algorithm. You must run several tests, assess machine learning algorithms, and fine-tune their hyperparameters in order to discover the optimal answer. *Hyperparameters* are variables whose values influence the learning process and define the model parameter values that a learning algorithm ultimately learns.

- *Finally, publish/deploy your model* (in Azure ML, you have to define an input and output and then run and publish it as a web service): Refer to Step 5 for more details.

- *Diagnose issues and refine the system:* In the (usual) case, if system does not meet the success criteria the first time, you diagnose the issues and refine the system. If the corrective action is not taken at the time, this will lead to reduction of prediction accuracy. Visualization is a powerful tool for identifying and showcasing the problems with data, models, or algorithms. However, issues can also be diagnosed by using synthetic data sampled from the model (Step 6). Information that has been created intentionally rather than as a result of actual occurrences is known as *synthetic data*. It is produced algorithmically and used to train ML models and serve as a stand-in for test data sets of production or operational data.

Note   Refining the system means decontaminating the data, models, visualizations, inferences, and evaluations. This is an ongoing activity to make model perfect. Diagnosing issues and refining the system must be repeated until the system is performing at a level necessary for the intended application. Model-based machine learning can make this repeated refinement process much quicker. The refinement suggestions need to be immediately applied to the model. This allows for rapid exploration of a number of models.

Machine Learning: You and Your Data

Machine learning is an old science, but it is gaining momentum due to generation of huge amounts of data from heterogeneous sources at a rapid pace. While many machine learning algorithms have been around for a long time and carry a legacy from statistics, the ability to automatically apply complex mathematical calculations and logic to Big Data with the help of sophisticated analytics over and over, faster and faster, is a recent development.

Technology Related to Machine Learning

This section presents some common machine learning and associated technologies and their relationship. It will help you understand some important concepts.

- *Data science*: At broader level, data science is an integrative discipline of mathematical science, statistics, and programming. However, it must not be confined to only these areas of studies and extended to artificial intelligence, statistical behavioral science, database technologies, psychology, sociology, cognition, and neuro-science.

- *Data analysis*: An investigative activity. In data analysis, after scanning the available data set, the analyst gets insights hidden in the data sets.

- *Data analytics*: When you apply mathematics, statistics, and algorithms on the available data set to find insight and meaningful correlations between them, the process is called data analytics. Analytics is the outcome of analysis. Whereas analysis is the method or group of methods that can be used to analyze the data.

- *Predictive analytics*: Conceptualizing and generating a quantitative model that permits an outcome or result to be predicted based on considerable historical data/ information can be a complicated and technologically intensive task. Input data contains numerous variables and they all need to be considered simultaneously. Some of these variables are relevant and others may not be that significant in determining the outcome. The predictive model governs what insights from the data can be extracted and used to make an accurate and relevant prediction in a given scenario. A good model allows and is open to changes so that it can accommodate the change in the variables. At times changes are required in order to increase predictability. The right change may increase the chances of a desired outcome.

- *Data mining*: Finds patterns in the available data set. This term became popular in the late 90s and early 2000s when organizations realized the power of consolidating data and its uses. With the use of this technology, data from heterogeneous sources is brought together to discover previously unknown trends, anomalies, and correlations. Data mining permits searching through massive amounts of data without having a precise idea what you're looking for. It helps identify correlations in available data sets through the use of the techniques like brute force analysis and neural networks.

Note   Data mining can be thought of as a superset of many methods and techniques to extract insights from available data. The technology may involve traditional statistical methods or techniques or the advanced concepts, like machine learning. A few techniques that come under the data mining umbrella include statistical algorithms, machine learning, text analytics, time-series analysis, and other areas of analytics. Data mining also includes the study and practice of data storage and data manipulation.

- *Deep learning*: Techniques and algorithms are being used to identify specific objects in images and carry out natural language processing. With the help of the combined power of computing resources, large amounts of data and special types of neural networks, deep learning can identify complicated patterns in large data sets. Researchers, institutions, and enterprises are now looking to apply deep learning's pattern-recognition capabilities to more complex tasks. For example, it is applied in automatic language translation, medical analyses, and other significant social and business problems areas.

- *Shallow learning*: The concepts of shallow and deep learning originally come from psychology. Broadly, shallow learning refers to superficial understanding of the subject "without knowing the deeper concepts". For example, you memorize your reading, without trying to understand its underlying meaning or implication. Whereas deep learning is about exploring the subject/ reading in greater detail. It involves your wish to comprehend the basic principles. Also, it is about your ability to put forward your own arguments. In a nutshell, shallow learning is about memorizing facts, whereas deep learning is about formulating logical and deep arguments.

The field of artificial intelligence associates deep learning algorithms with neural networks, which contain two or more layers of neurons. These algorithms are mainly used for pattern recognition related tasks. However, they are also used for image, video, and speech recognition activities. Broadly, machine learning algorithms that are not categorized as deep learning are known as shallow machine learning algorithms. For tasks that involve large volumes of training data and greater computational power, deep machine learning algorithms are a good pick. Also, deep learning is always a better choice for data sets that have no clear features. Hence in the areas such as image and voice recognition, it is widely used. If the data is already characterized by powerful features, shallow machine learning algorithms are a good choice because they are effective and more efficient.

Machine learning is born from artificial intelligence, so their relationship is very intimate. On the broader level, deep learning, pattern recognition, and shallow learning all are related. Machine learning is a group or collection of algorithms and set of techniques used to design a responsive automated system that can learn from data. The algorithms of ML usually have a strong mathematical and statistical basis. These are not tightly coupled with domain knowledge and data preprocessing. Therefore, ML can also defined as a field of computer science that uses statistical methods to create programs that improve over time and detect patterns in huge quantities of data that humans would be unlikely to find manually. Like artificial intelligence, machine learning attempts to replace explicit programming with automatic detection of parameters. However, machine learning works on non-aggregated data that contains discrete samples, which include positive and negative cases. For example, if someone wants to find/detect fraud in a financial data set, they need individual transaction records that show examples of valid transactions specific to fraud.

The Need for Machine Learning

Most of us think that the world is messy and chaotic at times, which leads to a lot of problems because of uncertainty. However, some people visualize this "problem" as a business opportunity. They start finding solutions that would transform this uncertainty or unpredictability to predictability using data and technology. They start providing solutions to new enterprises around predictions. The old and established enterprises hone their skill sets and come up with products and services or hire/purchase them from providers to sustain and accelerate the market.

IBM Watson, Microsoft cognitive services, and a lot of other products created a new set of offerings. Success stories, like Netflix's adoption of machine learning technology to predict customer behavior and offer them "personalized" services, which ultimately improved their revenue and customer satisfaction, has given new insight to businesses and customers alike. Also, it showed the potential of recommendation-based services, applications, and products. We can see that software/applications/ machines are accurately predicting customer behavior, which was historically known for its unpredictability.

Mining, compiling, and using adequate data and thoroughly evaluating all the variables involved may not produce accurate predictions of upcoming events. But they definitely take you adjacent to that goal. Machine learning provides algorithms that can measure many variables. For example, how does a group or individual perform under certain climatic conditions? How many points would a certain sports team score/ generate when a superstar player is expelled from the team? What is the best team composition of the team in certain given conditions?

With the help of mathematics (more accurately, statistics), trained humans can shuffle and play with the mathematical variables and get the desired results. But they cannot tackle thousands of variables at a time. Neurologically, the human brain is weak at handling so much information. This is a fact proved by numerous studies in neuroscience and neuroplasticity. But a machine can do this very easily with the help of effective and efficient algorithms. Welcome to the fantastic world of machine learning—it is here to rescue you from problems and serve your needs.

Prediction involves effectively and efficiently recognizing patterns in the available data and using the available, appropriate variables in the proper manner. Once the software recognizes those patterns, it uses them to anticipate future events. Apart from this, these programs can do a lot of other things much more effectively, like helping you make decisions and providing a list of action items. Prediction, automated decision making, and action planning are the need of the hour and the reality of tomorrow.

When it comes to making money and profit, "sufficient" is an alien word. Business and enterprises must always find new markets and develop innovative products. They have to be informed about new market trends and new competitors, and align their thoughts according to the changing needs of the time and market. In the current business and commercial world, machine learning has emerged to help in this regard. Almost all the industries are affected by ML, mostly in a positive way.

Machine Learning Business Opportunities

These technologies—machine learning, Big Data analytics, and cloud and cognitive computing—are transforming the business models of almost all industries across the globe. The old ways of doing business are changing rapidly. Enterprises across all the vertical and horizontal markets are finding novel ways to operate and innovate their businesses. This creates new business opportunities and avenues for digital and physical enterprises. Entrepreneurship is on the rise; innovative minds are creating new business models around the new generation of technologies. The result of this traction is showcased in the form of optimized operations, reduced costs, improved services, and/or launching new products. Lots of companies are using ML to their financial benefit and achieving great results:

- AOL uses machine learning to provide shopping recommendations.

- Booz Allen Hamilton uses machine learning (Mahout's clustering algorithms) for its business purposes.

- Cull.tv uses machine learning for its content recommendations system.

- DataMine Lab uses the machine learning cluster classification algorithm to improve its clients ad targeting.

- Drupal is betting on machine learning algorithms for providing its open-source content recommendation solutions and systems.

- Evolv is using machine learning-based platforms for predicting its workforce-related activities.

- Foursquare and Idealo uses Mahout (a machine learning framework) for its recommendation engine.

- Google uses machine learning for computing the probabilities of clicks for its AdSense and other advertising networks.

- Machine learning algorithms and models are used for automated algorithmic trading (AAT). Money market-based companies set and train models and use them to place trades in nanoseconds. A large percentage of today's trades are made by computers and lots of big FinTech enterprises are involved in this.

- Retailers use machine learning to optimize and recommend their inventory, marketing activities, product placement, pricing, and targeting. Some examples are Walmart, Apple, and Flipchart.

- Pharmaceutical companies like Rose Pharmaceuticals use machine learning for data mining related activities.

- India is home to the third largest cluster of AI startups in world. These startups are involved in development of bots, recognition tools, and machine learning enabled virtual assistance (Source: KPMG).

- India is also ranked third in implementing robotic automation on in its core business process. Finance professionals are ready to adopt machine learning-based automation to save time and get help in decision-making processes (Source: KPMG).

- Companies like Microsoft, IBM, Google, and Amazon are providing "off-the-self" platforms. Startups are using these platforms to find their own solutions. Also, the big giants launched several ML products and applications to solve and enhance a number of industry specific challenges in recent times.

As machine learning is everywhere, the business opportunity is tremendous in almost all these areas. New generations of machine learning have several innovative capabilities that serve as catalysts for business opportunities. Apart from technical areas, machine learning is creating new opportunities in these functional areas:

- Research and development

- Production and operations

- Sales and marketing

- Customer support

- Financial, human resource, and administrative functions

- Agriculture, healthcare, utilities, and oil and gas

- Retail

- Mining, construction, wearable tread, wholesale, arts, entertainment and recreation, and real estate

- Educational services, accommodation and food service, warehousing, and manufacturing

Apart from all this, industry-specific opportunities are also being generated. Some new areas have popped up in recent times with the growth of machine learning, some of them being emotion-based products and services, intuitive learning, intelligent drones and robots, chatbots, and many more. Today's consumer wants applications, products, and services that are more intuitive. Consumers are now closer to applications than ever, owing to the wide exposure to personal assistance devices like mobile phones and smart watches. Their expectation from the applications and products is to "understand" their way of working and behavior.

This introduces a new horizon of "transformable" business opportunities. Also, there has been a shift in the mindset of decision-makers from creating "data" to "insight-oriented and intuitive" products and services that generate tremendous business prospects. This thought process is unique to the industries and enterprises. However, it is a different story that this "thought process" is guided by market dynamics and competition. Machine learning-based digitization is enabling multiple types of innovations. The digital universe is growing with unexpected speed and creating lot of opportunities.

It is worth having a look at the "WISDOM" pyramid (or data hierarchy) now, because the next section focuses on its individual components. The lower layer of the pyramid refers to the large amount of data produced by the unstructured (including IoT devices), semi-structured, and structured sources of data (see Figure 2-2). These devices generate data in petabytes or even more. The layer above the data is "information," which provides filtered, structured, and machine-understandable information from the data. Also, it works as a layer of abstraction and summarizes the available data. However, what humans and high-level sophisticated applications need are services, not information.

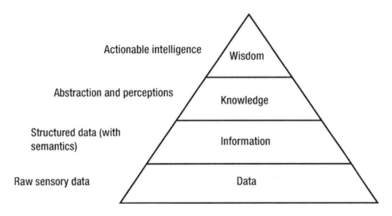

Figure 2-2. *The wisdom pyramid*

The unseen knowledge (third layer) above the information layer provides a better understanding of the data and information. It also presents information in a machine-understandable format, which can be used by machines to generate insight after analyzing the "refined" information. The knowledge layer is further refined to an upper level known as the *wisdom* layer. It does the refinement on the knowledge layer by finding wisdom from the hidden "sea" of knowledge. With the hidden knowledge, a machine can conclude something called *wisdom* that can be used for forecasting (which essentially predicts what will happen in the future) and then provide insights and action steps. This kind of wisdom can be used to develop end-to-end intuitive, smart, and intelligent products and services. This organization of data narrowing down from cluttered, mere facts to wisdom can be visualized in multiple ways. For example, if you think of these layers from the technical perspective, they can be linked in the following manner:

- The data layer is associated with IoT, which includes structured, unstructured, and semi-structured data or Big Data in a nutshell.

- The information and knowledge layers are associated with Big Data analytics.

- The wisdom layer is associated with machine learning and cognitive computing.

For enterprises, business and commerce opportunities exist all around and are related to machine learning. Leaders have to grab them. However, to harness the enormous potential of the machine learning ecosystem, business leaders and decision-makers have to invest in technology. At the same time, they have to work toward transforming their organization. Therefore, the mindset becomes critical. Some of the thoughts that can help in creating and exploiting breakthrough opportunities are as follows:

- Leaders have to work for an integrative approach of machine, software, process, and data.

- Adoption of a very fast experimenting, testing, learning, and scaling approach.

- Quickly reimaging, reinventing, and innovating the business model whenever required.

- Adopting digitalization and building capabilities. This is different from land, labor, and machine models of business.

- Adopting and implementing technology-specific and less bureaucratic processes across the organization.

- Adopting polices and frameworks that encourage investment in processes, people, and technologies.

Business opportunity is a general term that's used in multiple areas. Machine learning helps create jobs and open avenues for generating profit and streamlining the labor market. Advancements in robotic process automation, robotics, artificial intelligence, deep learning, and machine learning lead to breakthroughs, innovation, and opportunities. Connecting these evolving technologies will solve complex business problems and provide benefits to companies. There are numerous ways to exploit the opportunities in these areas, starting from sensing new avenues of business to creating, maintaining, and transforming the existing business ecosystem.

For instance, ML enables businesses to improve their performance, efficiency, and effectiveness. This can be attained by reducing errors, improving quality, and improving speed of operations. Businesses are moving away from a reactive approach to operation to a proactive approach. For example, businesses previously had to wait for a machine to fail and then call or ask for maintenance, but now they can determine the condition of specific equipment to predict when to perform maintenance. This is possible due to extraordinary advancements in the execution of machine learning techniques and algorithms.

Uses of machine learning can be found in almost all areas of human endeavor. The following areas list use cases and applications. Detailed application areas are described in the form of applications, products, and services (APS). The next sections present APS use cases in the form of products, services, and applications.

All the areas contain huge business opportunities. Here are the five areas of APS:

- Customer Experience Enrichment

- Autonomous and Intuitive Systems Prediction

- Digital Assistance and Recommendation APS

- Domains Specific APS

- Science and Technology

Customer Experience Enrichment

Within this category are the applications, products, and services (APS) that can make decisions on their own, with minimal intervention from humans. They are self-sufficient and can extract insight from systems automatically. I confine myself to the customer space because of the scope of the book. However, its boundaries are almost endless and the dimensions are infinite. There are enormous business opportunities in this area. The following sections explain the broader segregation of APS of this type.

Automated Machine Learning Based Customer Support Systems

Companies like Wise.io use machine learning to provide "wise and intelligent" customer support. For example, they provide quicker responses to customer service tickets. As a result, their client's customer care agents can focus on solving more critical customer issues, instead of routine work.

Here is how this can help businesses:

- Machine learning enables the support engine to predict which group or individual agent should receive the new customer ticket based on the skill set of the support representative. After that, the engine will automatically put the ticket in the correct queue.

- Machine learning enables the support interface (engine) to show the agents the best response template to be used based on the content and history of the ticket.

- If a machine learning-enabled system finds a solution to the customer raised ticket/issue in the knowledge repository, the system automatically picks the resolution, fixes the issue, and responds to the ticket. A Wipro machine learning and artificial intelligence-based system is working on the same philosophies. Wipro is using this approach to achieve customer delight and to enhance the agent's productivity.

A Tale of Customer Support and Automation

Automation is about consuming or using technology to permit processes to run flawlessly without manual/human intervention. This thought is the opposite of the hypothesis that anticipates that business automation will replace human resources and knowledge workers. Automation facilitates knowledge workers by freeing them to concentrate on more intuitive tasks. It frees them from the responsibility of administrative and repetitive tasks. It allows human intervention only when it's indispensable. Automation is possible almost everywhere, but it plays a greater role in organizations where the resources and their knowledge are very precious. Here are four ways customer support teams can reap the benefits of automation:

- *No repetitive work*: Support teams are generally flooded with repetitive requests. Most of the time, they are forced to answer the same question again and again. At times, it becomes frustrating and demotivating. Automation helps the support teams in these situations. The automated system handles situations like these in multiple ways. For example, based on the severity or priority of the tickets, the system will route the tickets to the appropriate support executive, who has the proper skill set and expertise for solving a particular issue. For example, say the support team receives a ticket with a specific class of issue. Based on the classification of the ticket, the system can go to the available knowledgebase, find the solution, and fix the issue. Once the issue is fixed, the system can close the ticket and notify the requestor that the issue has been fixed.

- *Consistency*: Automation permits grouping or centralization of knowledge and enables its proper storing and recording. Once the process of knowledge capturing is automated, it is easily optimized and easily referenced across any organization. This helps "centralize" the knowledge, as teams (support and development) often work in isolation and there are situations when communication gaps cause damages. Also, teams have a tendency to make create support documents for their work and not share that information.

- *Robust scaling*: Many support teams start out small. They use key artifacts (like documents), speak to their colleagues and SMEs to fix issues which come their way, educate customers, and inform the rest of the organization about their latest progress. All this is easily feasible unless the customer base is small and the number of incoming tickets is also small. But once the customer base starts growing and tickets start piling up, the ticket queue starts growing and the real problem appears. As time-intensive, manual processes deliver less than perfect results, automation becomes critical for companies. They have to utilize and protect their hard-earned knowledge. As any company grows, employee attrition becomes critical. Automation safeguards against knowledge loss in this situation as well.

- *Better job satisfaction*: The work of agents and customer service representatives is monotonous and demanding. They have to work on the same set of activities during their working hours. Providing agents with the power of auto-knowledgebases and personalized issue resolution guidance increases their satisfaction. Automatically routing tickets to agents with certain skill sets, personality traits, and performance indicators shows that you value their individuality and that you are equipped with the proper data sources to ensure their success. In short, customer support automation recognizes individuality and empowers teams with the resources to be proactive rather than reactive.

Machine Learning Customer Retention Systems

Product and marketing teams often face continuous challenges in retaining customers. Generally, customer behavior is unpredictable. For example, businesses often don't know why a customer cancelled an order that they placed earlier. Now, with the help of machine learning-based retention applications, which are powered by innovative ML algorithms, companies can analyze various touchpoints of customer interactions. This enables them to take corrective actions to retain customers. This helps enterprises in multiple ways. A few of them are mentioned here:

- Predicting customer behavior deviations during the initial stage of engagement to take action

- Showing reasons for customer behavior deviations for each individual customer

- Recommending and suggesting the most suitable marketing strategies

- Personalized and individualized content to improve customer retention

- Helping to ensure customer's "professional" health is known to each customer-facing team in every interaction

With a more intuitive, innovative, and data-driven approach to customer success and retention, organizations can be more efficient and effective in prioritizing. They can serve the most critical customers while continuing to drive satisfaction across the entire customer base.

Business Success, Customer Engagement, and Machine Learning

Customer success begins with finding and locating the right customer for the business. Selecting customers must be based on the portfolio of the product and the services available. This enables businesses to provide appropriate services and products to the targeted customer. If a business is not able to locate and select the right customer for their offerings, their profits will suffer. Also, selecting the wrong customer will lead to customer disengagement and damage to brand damage. Ideal customers actually help businesses get the maximum return on their marketing spend and achieve improved ROI. To find the "right" customer, businesses have to know and understand a few important things:

- Who the customers are

- How the business team will approach and acquire them based on their needs and wants

- How to position or present products or service offerings to deliver maximum value

- How to predict what a particular customer is likely to buy in the coming days and months

- Which customers are going to be the largest spenders

- What marketing content is most appropriate for the targeted customers

- Which sales representatives are the best match for handling a specific type of customer

Machine learning technologies are enormously helpful in finding the answers to these questions. With the proper application of analytics techniques on historical, structured, and semi-structured data related to the customers, business get insight about the customers' behavior. Also, based on insight, business can generate strategies that provide them multiple benefits. Some of those benefits are described next.

Appropriate Customer Acquisition

Machine learning enabled applications and products help the sales team focus on leads that result in appropriate customers. These products also help the marketing team present the best content based on the customer's personality and their buying patterns. Other benefits of appropriate customer acquisition are:

- Higher sales and win percentage

- Better promotion and marketing translation rates

- Higher ROI on marketing and promotion spend

- More appropriate campaigns through personalization

Better Customer Support

Machine learning-based applications, products, and services help business provide better support to their customers. For instance, product support is generally achieved using ticket-based systems (systems that provide logging of issues). If a machine learning-based ticketing tool or system is used for the purpose of providing customer support, it automatically routes tickets to the most appropriate agent or generate auto-response messages by the intelligent use of an existing knowledgebase. Benefits of machine learning-based customer support include the following:

- Quick channelization of service or customer ticket to the appropriate agent or executive

- More reliable support because the system is automated and less human intervention is required

- Greater productivity for customer service representatives, as monotonous work is taken care of by the system and they take more valuable tasks

- Efficient customer self-help

Customer Base Expands

Machine learning-based systems, applications, and products help businesses identify, track, and analyze usage patterns and messaging of their customers. It helps them find the potential "suitable" customers who will help them expand their business. Adding more customers to the business ecosystem means additional revenue. Also, if the customer is engaged with the business, it helps them in many ways, including word of mouth publicity. Other benefits of machine learning enabled customer expansion include:

- Greater product assignation

- More revenue and cost benefits from cross-sell

- Increase in upsell opportunities

Customer Retention

Machine learning-based applications can identify the at-risk customers and the signals they are demonstrating, while predicting what content or approach will most likely re-engage them. This strategy, powered by machine learning, helps businesses retain their customers. Customer retention is important for businesses, because it is cheaper and takes fewer resources to retain a customer than to get a new one. Some of the benefits of customer retention include:

- Reduction in customer churn

- Greater dependable approach for account managers

- More productive account managers

Customer Segmentation Applications and Products

Getting a new customer in this competitive business environment is difficult. A lot of hard work and effort is invested in doing so. Also, getting a new customer is only half the battle. Retaining customers by delivering ongoing value and satisfaction is the key to success. The question of how a company should continuously deliver value to each customer, so that the customer engages more intensely, is a challenge. But once a business achieves this, it can sell customers more products and services. By offering wise and intelligent machine learning enabled revenue growth and finance (FinTech) applications to the customer, they realize the value of their money. The new generation of machine learning APS is capable of enhancing economic, financial, and revenue streams from customers. Also, organizations benefit by doing this because it enables them to achieve effective and efficient customer segmentation.

It can potentially help businesses in many ways:

- Matching the right product or service with the right customer

- Recommending or suggesting the best price available to determine upsell

- Providing personalized marketing messaging to the individual customer

Integrating customer data with past outcomes presents a holistic predictive roadmap for delivering additional value to customers and expanding revenue.

Intelligent Customer Prioritization and Classification Products, Applications, and Services (APS)

Often, businesses try to find their customers from the sea of available databases of customers. Machine learning helps businesses classify, prioritize, and rank the most suitable customers. This enables teams not only to target ideal customers but also to provide them with their desired product or service quickly.

Here's how this can help businesses:

- Improving the close rate for the sales pipeline

- Increasing the return on your marketing spend

- Making the best of your sales team

Using a data-driven approach to uncover the patterns of the target market, sales teams can develop an efficiently led prioritization process and focus on the best opportunities. Here is as glimpse of the technological and process operations of predictive APS:

1. The machine learning technology analyzes historical data (for example, closed tickets) and identifies the patterns and correlations in them. Based on this analysis, it determines how the tickets were classified, routed, and resolved.

2. When a new event happens (new support tickets arrive), the machine learning-based engine immediately verifies the content, predicts attributes, and recommends an appropriate response.

3. Based on the predictions, a trigger can route rules or response macros to automate the process.

4. Once a resolution is found, the system learns and adapts its predictions so that it is always up-to-date with current the needs and processes.

Autonomous and Intuitive Systems

The applications, products, and services (APS) that fall under this category generally have the capability to "think" like humans. This is an evolving area. Basically, these APS try to mimic the human brain. They create artificial neural circuits and pathways, exactly the way the human brain generates biological neurons. They are potentially capable of making decisions based on situations and have can adjust in dynamically changing environments. There are enormous business opportunities in this area and multiple types of applications and services exist. The following sections describe a broader segregation of APS of this type.

Autonomous Systems

Machine learning plays a crucial role in the development of intuitive applications, products, and services. The data is the building blocks of APS. This data can help statistical procedures recognize institutive patterns in a sea of data through data mining. Machine learning processes, algorithms, and methods use artificial neural networks to generate predictions. In turn, this leads to automated decision-making and action planning. For example, Siemens created a software simulation environment with the help of neural networks (SENN) that can be used to provide answers to various questions. Siemens is using SENN to predict raw material prices.

Autonomous systems are the best examples of intuitive products and services. An altogether new market is emerging around them, and this will become an interesting business soon. Apart from Siemens, other companies are introducing autonomous system products. These companies are offering individualized and personalized products. As the market is gaining momentum, cost is also becoming competitive. In all the cases ranging from industrial and service robots to cars and drones, the common thread is the ability to perform general tasks. They can also make "small" decisions (as of now) based on their ability to sense and process information in a dynamically changing environment.

The Latest Trends

The human-free interview (technology enabled) is picking up. HireVue is a pioneer in making video interview software. They work with around 600 organizations/enterprises. Their list of clients includes Deloitte, JPMorgan

Chase, Under Armour, and some key U.S. airlines. In 2016, HireVue is planning to conduct 2.5 million interviews for their clients. This is a significant growth in volume, up from 13,000 five years ago. Most of the interviews that HireVue conducts (90 percent) are on-demand interviews. In this type of scenario, nobody exists at the other end.

Human-free video interviews are efficient for hiring managers. Also, companies can get to know more about the people whom they are interviewing. In the process of the video interview, human involvement is only required when reviewing the answers provided by the interviewees (in the future, this will also be automated with the more advanced use of machine learning and cognitive computing). Humans can do this at their convenience. For example, they can align their schedule, tasks, and availability and make time for the review during their downtime. Also, they need not travel to the location to interview. Using HireVue, a lot of enterprises are seeing tangible benefits. For example, Hilton is able to reduce its hiring cycle to 4.5 days, which is almost 20 days shorter than their previous hiring period. Cigna was able to bring down its requirement travel expenses for its recruiters from $1 million a year to under $1,00,000 per year.

Candidates are also seeing benefits from robot-based recruitment, mainly in the form of convenience. Candidates/interviewees can give on-demand interviews at their convenience. These robot-based interviews will not replace human interaction completely (at least in the shorter term). Most companies are using it for first-round screening interviews, after which the traditional one-on-one sort of interview happens.

Self-Learning Machines Products, Applications, and Services

A new breed of machine learning systems like AlphaGo is evolving to fulfill the demand of hyper-intelligence systems. Enterprises like Google achieved a milestone in the creation and development of self-learning machines.

In March 2016, AlphaGo defeated the world's best Go player: Lee Sedol. Lee Sedol is the second-highest ranking professional Go player. Go is an Asian game considered very complex for computers to understand and interpret. Because the game has an almost infinite number of possible positions, someone who plays it has to bet on intuition and not just be confined to calculating moves.

AlphaGo was developed by Google's DeepMind, which is focused on solving complex tasks. AlphaGo uses reinforcement learning algorithm (a type of machine learning algorithm). In the reinforcement algorithm, the system learns to use a value function that rates game positions by analyzing millions of past games (data set) and then playing against itself.

AlphaGo is fundamentally a computer program that integrates tree algorithms with deep neural networks. These neural networks take in the details of the Go board as input and process it through different network layers composed of millions of neuron-like networks. One neural network, the "policy network," chooses the next move to play. The fresh neural network, the "value network," forecasts the victor of the game. Alphabate (by Google) presented AlphaGo to numerous amateur games to develop an understanding of rational mortal play. AlphaGo becomes better at literacy and decision-making over time.

The same type of algorithm is used by Siemens to optimize its wind and gas turbines, which is again an example of a successful self-learning machine. Computer systems that can learn from various types of data and draw their own inferences work based on machine learning. For example, Siemens is working on enabling wind turbines to automatically regulate themselves according to changing environmental conditions like wind and weather. It will boost their electricity output. The foundational logic for self-optimizing wind turbines is the ability to drive wind characteristics from the turbines based on operating data. The associated parameters, which are measured by sensors and outside wind power facilities, include wind direction and force, air temperature, current and voltage, and vibrations in large components such as generators and rotor blades.

Ericsson showcased a 6G use case wherein thousands of sensors were combined into a T-shirt that could help track vital parameters like blood pressure and oxygen levels. In fact, it is also possible to implant the chipset into the clothes without being visible, because it is so small that it can only be observed under a microscope. The exceptional feature is that it does not have batteries but can still communicate data, as it yokes energy from radio frequencies.

With 5G services rolling in, one can remotely drive a car sitting at home. This is to some extent similar from driverless cars as one can essentially control and drive a vehicle while sitting remotely. What's astonishing is the fact that the car will come to a halt if it loses connectivity, thereby decreasing the odds of an accident.

ChatGPT is an artificial intelligence model advanced by OpenAI that can produce human-like answers to textbook inputs. It usages innovative machine literacy styles to comprehend and understand natural languages, permitting it to have exchanges with people. It's popular due to its human-like responses and ease of use. Its use cases are set up in multiple areas. For instance, India's two top IT enterprises—Tata Consultancy Services (TCS) and Infosys, along with global tech advisers such as Accenture—are counting on training and skilling modules for beginners on ChatGPT and other machine literacy/artificial intelligence technologies.

Generative AI models like ChatGTP may disrupt Indian IT enterprises. TCS will create generative-AI themed courses for professional staff development. ChatGPT is useful for operations like adding information and content from multiple sources to address a precise question contextually. ChatGPT could become necessary for people who are going to write, which would be a "step change" in terms of writing laws.

Some tasks that ChatGPT fulfilled include these:

- ChatGPT scored over 50 on the U.S. medical licensing test

- It got an unobstructed Wharton Business School test for the final test of the MBA program's operations operation

- It helped to author a novel in a weekend, which was then placed online

And much more...

The rush to develop AI advancements, particularly in the area of generative AI, has accelerated as AI technology improves, raising both hopes and worries. Therefore, let's look at some of its innovative features, like the Reinforcement Learning from Human Feedback (RLHF) technology.

These technologies have the potential to transform our world, but there are also hazards involved. The RLHF technology helps guarantee that AI models are in line with human values and provide beneficial, truthful, and harmless answers. It is more crucial than ever to include a continuous, effective human feedback loop given the worries over the pace and extent of generative AI.

RLHF uses both reinforcement learning and human input to train AI models. Through trial-and-error training, known as reinforcement learning, an AI model is taught new skills while being rewarded for making wise choices and punished for bad ones.

Reinforcement learning does have certain restrictions, though. For instance, it may be difficult to verify that the model adheres to human values since it is difficult to define a reward function that encompasses all facets of human preferences and values. By incorporating human feedback into the training process, RLHF overcomes this difficulty and increases the effectiveness of the model's alignment with human values.

Humans can assist the model in learning more quickly and precisely and can also decrease the likelihood of mistakes by providing comments about the model's output. People can give feedback about a model's output—for instance, when they see instances of the model responding in an inappropriate, biased, or harmful way—and offer corrective input to help the model learn.

Additionally, the problem of sample inefficiency in reinforcement learning may be resolved with the use of RLHF. When reinforcement learning is used to learn a task, sample inefficiency occurs, making the process time-consuming and costly. However, by incorporating human feedback, the model may learn more effectively and require fewer iterations to master a job.

How Are Big Language Models Like ChatGPT Using RLHF?

With their outstanding performance in a variety of language tasks, including language modeling, machine translation, and question-answering, large language models (LLMs) have established themselves as a key tool in Natural Language Processing (NLP). Despite their great powers, LLMs also have drawbacks, such as a propensity to produce subpar, irrelevant, or even objectionable content.

Obtaining high-quality training data is one of the biggest issues because LLMs require a lot of data to work well. Additionally, supervised learning requires human annotators to classify the data, which is a time-consuming and expensive operation.

In order to address these issues, RLHF was presented as a framework that can produce superior labels for training data. To produce high-quality, pertinent, cohesive text in this framework, the LLM is first pretrained using unsupervised learning and then tweaked using RLHF.

LLMs may learn from user preferences and produce outputs that are more in line with user objectives and intentions, thanks to RLHF, which can have a big impact on a variety of NLP applications. LLMs may be effectively trained with less labelled data and perform better on certain tasks using RLHF, which combines reinforcement learning and human feedback. As a result, RLHF is an effective framework for boosting LLMs' capacities and strengthening their capacity to comprehend and produce natural language.

In RLHF, a sizable corpus of text data is used to teach the LLM, which is then pretrained. In order to produce coherent and intelligible outputs, the model has to learn the underlying patterns and structures of the language. RLHF may be used to fine-tune the LLM after pretraining, which is computationally costly but offers a strong basis.

The development of a reward model, a machine learning model that assesses the caliber of the text produced by the LLM, is the second stage. The reward model creates a scalar number that indicates the output quality from the LLM's output as its input. Another LLM that has been changed to produce a single scalar value rather than a series of text tokens might serve as the reward model.

A data set of LLM-generated text is labelled for quality by human raters in order to train the reward model. When given a cue, the LLM produces a number of outputs that human judges score from excellent to worst. The quality of the text produced by the LLM is then predicted by the reward model. By learning from the LLM's output and the ranking scores given by human assessors, the reward model develops a mathematical description of human preferences.

The LLM becomes the RL agent in the last stage, establishing a reinforcement learning loop. In each training episode, the LLM creates text using a number of cues from a training data set. The reward model then receives its output and assigns a score based on how well it matches the human preferences.

The LLM is then updated to generate outputs that score higher on the reward model.

Deep Learning and Simulated Neuron Based APS

Deep learning techniques in association with machine learning are generating a lot of business opportunities, for example, enabling a new application to use automated image recognition. APS around these technologies use simulated neuron techniques to link multiple levels of results based on available data to give desired results. They actually recognize images on the basis of associate pixels of an image to another pixel. Most of us already unknowingly carry an artificial neural network enabled device or application with us. For example, voice command systems in Android smartphones use artificial neural network techniques to take the voice commands from users.

Emotions and Sentiment Analysis Based APS

Emotions are an essential part of human endeavor, which influence cognition, perception, and other day-to-day activities such as learning, managing oneself, and communicating with oneself and others. Also, emotions contribute to rational decision making. Traditionally, technologists have largely ignored emotions in the workplace. Also, only a few services and products are available in this space, which integrate verticals, horizontals, and other business areas with emotions. After the boom in the Big Data analytics and machine learning technologies, enterprises dealing with retail, healthcare, marketing, banking, and financial services have started adopting "emotion-based APS." Because enterprises realized that humans are emotional beings it is an integral part of their decision making. When someone wants to purchase a product, their emotions play a role in this decision-making process. Hence, integrating emotions into APS would give businesses new opportunities to explore. Some of the pioneers of this area are Emotient, RealEyes, and Affectiva. They all use facial expressions to infer emotion, largely (it appears) for marketing purposes. Companies like CogitoCorp and BeyondVerbal concentrate on understanding emotional cues in voice to conduct market research and deliver better customer experiences.

Other Intuitive Applications, Products, and Services

Other applications include personalized and individualized care and education. Systems that deal with conflict resolution and negotiation provide customized training. There is a separate category of games that monitor and learn your habits and customize games for you, called adaptive games. There are enormous business opportunities in this area.

Prediction, Digital Assistance, and Recommendation APS

Predicting and forecasting APS falls under this category. Machine learning, in collaboration with cognitive computing, potentially offers a lot of smart products and services that the world only imagined just a few years back. This type of APS was recently limited to science fiction books, films, and research labs. For example, your phone could offer you suggestions and recommendations for things even before you think of doing them or suggest that you need a new wardrobe that would suit your job profile and personality type.

As mentioned, "smart" systems are capable of making predictions, providing suggestions, and giving digital assistance. For example, assume you are planning to host a party for some happy occasion.

Cognitive computing systems powered by machine learning algorithms could generate a guest list based on the people you've been interacting, communicating, and collaborating with. It would also factor the guest list based on the intensity of your relationships. The demand for this type of APS is increasing day by day. Hence, enormous business opportunities exist in this area. The following sections describe the broader segregation of APS of this type.

Recommendations Based Applications, Products, and Services

Smart APS are heavily used for recommendations. Its uses are diverse. For example, when you visit an e-commerce site (like Amazon), look up an ice cream parlor on your phone, or see a film on Netflix or YouTube, chances are that you see recommendations based on your tastes. Actually, machine learning algorithms embedded in this APS pick up "appropriate" recommendations for you on the basis of your visit history and other parameters (factors used by the model to group patterns or make decisions).

Virtual Digital Assistance

These applications work as an intelligent and smart digital assistance for individuals. For example, you have an urgent meeting scheduled at 9:30 in the morning or your flight is scheduled at midnight and you are a forgetful person. You generally miss these types of assignments. No need to worry; your digital assistant (such as Goggle's Allo/Now or Apple's Siri) can help. It can read through your email and SMS and calculate the time needed to reach the office or airport. It then compares this with the ideal time taken to reach office or board flight. After that, it can send you notifications about when you should leave for the office or airport.

Advertising

Machine learning algorithms also work as technically smart virtual salespeople and advertisers. For example, a woman who buys maternity clothes online receives a discount for buying diapers in bulk. Machine learning algorithms are running in background of this overall buying process; they gather and process the purchasing behavior of the customer and advertise relevant content.

Phototagging

Social media giant Facebook/Meta analyzes and uses facial features for its marketing, suggestions, and recommendations. It determines the distance between the eyes and nose to identify faces. It also uses profile pictures and photos that you have tagged to narrow down to an identifiable face. All the areas are ripe for business opportunities. Prospects are growing with the speed of thoughts for creating APS.

Domain-Specific APS

It is evident that the developments in Big Data analytics and machine learning affect almost all the areas of our lives. These areas offer strong business opportunities for enterprises in the different vertical and horizontal sectors. Companies can streamline their processes, reduce costs, increase efficiencies, and provide better and/or new products and services. This ends up providing tremendous business opportunities and avenues for all. The following sections show the broader segregation of APS of this type.

Financial and Insurance Services

Consider these business opportunities that exist in these areas:

- Algorithmic-enabled trading and management of stocks for better profitability. Opportunity for dynamic tracking of funds and their flow.

- BFSI (banking, financial services, and insurance industries) related fraud anticipation and discovery. BFSI maintenance and prediction applications.

- Customer segmentation-based applications.

- Predictive injury assessments and valuation in insurance and related industries.

- Automated claims authentication, validation, and verification for the insurance industries.

- Customer understanding generation (insight) and relationship management from the integration of transactional and other data.

- Sentiment analysis-based APS.

- Portfolio, risk exposure assessment, and management-based APS.

- Real-time customer profiling, locating, targeting, and optimization of offers and services for cross-selling.

- Data-based customer and call center efficiency optimization and management.

- Predictive brand reputation and valuation APS.

Telecom Network, Products, and Services

Business opportunities exist in the following areas:

- Dynamic and predictive network optimization for customer and network service providers.

- Customer preservation or retention to the native company based on call data records and predictive machine learning analytics (machine learning analytics = machine learning + analytics).

- Customer activity optimization in subscriber's networks though smart APS.

- Customer scoring, churn identification, and mitigation-based APS.

- Optimization of offers made to customers for cross-selling to improve efficiencies and effectiveness.

- Real-time customer and call center improvement and management.

- Fraud analysis, prevention, and management.

- Location-based services improvements through the use of GPS data and analytics.

- Customer center and call center efficiency.

- Bandwidth allocation based on use patterns.

Professional Services

Business opportunities exist in the following areas:

- Advertisement target analysis through deep and machine learning algorithms.

- Social media attending, real-time sentiment/emotion analysis, and targeted marketing on the basis of machine learning analytics.

- Effective and efficient campaign management and injection of on-time loyalty programs based on predictive analytics. There are enormous opportunities in this space to create APS.

- Real-time crime identification, detection, and prevention for providers of security.

- Personalized pricing for travel based on the behavior analysis of individual/groups.

- Real-time IT infrastructure monitoring and management. Provisioning of self-healing services, predictive maintenance, and management in IT.

- Real-time security breach pattern detection through machine learning to create customized rules in IT.

Public Sector and Government Initiatives

Business opportunities exist in the following areas:

- Enhancement of citizens lifestyles and quality of life. For example, enhancements in patient services and highway management based on machine learning.

- Improvement in weapon and war intelligence systems to counter terrorism with the help of machine learning (predictive analytics)-based APS.

- Smart taxing systems through machine learning-based APS.

- Fraud identification, detection, and prevention in the public domain and government.

- Enhanced cyber security of public network and government organizations and departments.

- Enhanced surveillance and response programs for public and government organizations.

- Efficient, effective, and optimized health informatics, bioinformatics, and pharmacogenomics with the proper use of analytics.

- Real-time treatment assessment and prediction based on the population density.

- Enhanced clinical decision support systems.

- Intelligent and smart pollution control and management through machine learning enabled APS.

Retail and Wholesale

Business opportunities exist in the following areas:

- Real-time store location and layout management through the use of machine learning APS.

- Supply and value chain enhancement and optimization.

- Real-time RFID tracking and management.

- Price and cost optimizations. For example, providing dynamic suggestive pricing based on Big Data analytics and machine learning.

- Customer behavior, social media persona mapping, and sentiment and emotion analysis based on social media feeds.

- Generating actionable customer insight and feedback based on analysis of heterogeneous data. For example, providing micro-segmentation of customers' behavioral data.

- Customer loyalty and promotions analysis and prediction.

- Real-time discount optimization based on customer buying patterns and behavior.

- Real-time marketplace cart analysis and prediction based on demographics cultural orientation.

- Fraud detection, identification, and prevention in e-commerce to physical shops.

Transport

Business opportunities exist in these areas:

- Real-time logistics, passenger, goods tracking, management, and optimization.

- Location-based analytics for improving transportation services and assets using GPS data.

- Customer loyalty identification through relevant analytics and marketing.

- Predictive maintenance and management of transport services.

- Real-time capacity, efficiency, and pricing optimizations for public and private transport systems.

- Intelligent and smart taxi-management systems.

- Chauffer behavioral analytics.

Utilities, Oil, and Gas

Business opportunities exist in the following areas:

- Smart and intelligent meter monitoring. Identification of real-time usage patterns through analysis and optimization of energy consumption, which are then used for pricing.

- Prediction of load and forecasting use by using predictive analytics.

- Real-time sensor monitoring for condition-based and predictive maintenance.

- Smart and intelligent energy grid optimization, weather pattern forecasting in real time, and real-time usage and distribution of resources.

- Effective and efficient operational modeling.

- Real-time distribution load forecasting and optimized scheduling.

- Targeted customer offerings.

- Real-time and effective disasters and outages management.

- Effective and efficient compliance checks and audits.

- Real-time customer feedback gathering and call detail record analysis though the use of machine learning technologies.

- Effective and efficient natural resource identification and exploration in the oil and gas industry.

- Real-time seismic data processing.

- Efficient and effective drilling surveillance and optimization.

Manufacturing

Business opportunities exist in the following areas:

- Predictive maintenance

- Process and quality analysis

- Effective warranty and policy management

- Optimized factory automation

- Effective automatic detection and prevention of adverse drug effects in the pharmaceutical industry

- Intelligent real-time sensor monitoring for the maintenance of automobiles, buildings, and machinery

- Real-time smart meter monitoring for optimized energy consumption and management

- Smart and effective location-based analytics through GPS data analytics

- Predictive analysis of social media comments, feedback, and sentiment for vehicle quality and efficiency management in the automotive industry

- Social media listening for marketing in consumer industries

- Effective and need-based concurrent and effective engineering and product lifecycle management

- Design-to-value-based product implementation

- Smart analytics-based crowd sourcing

- Demand forecasting and supply planning

- Digital factories for lean manufacturing

- Distribution optimizations

- Quality management based on social media feeds

The next sections discus three specific areas of business opportunities.

Machine Learning for Legal Activities

Legal documents are generally too complicated to comprehend. Large organizations have their team of lawyers check the legalities of any issues or deals. However, new and evolving enterprises do not have this luxury. Machine learning plays a role in both scenarios. It can help organizations decode the legal documents, with or without assistance. Machine learning systems use deep learning algorithms. For example, Legal Robot built a legal language model that translates "legal language" into a big string of numbers, which in turn is translated into plain language. This enables decision-makers to understand the legalities quickly. Legal

Robot also helps their customers establish what's missing from a contract or SOW. Also, it helps them determine if there are missing elements/information in the document. For example, the system can determine if a royalty fee section is present in the non-disclosure agreement or not. If not, it would suggest the action steps to be taken to cope with such a situation.

Machine Learning to Prevent Money Laundering

For government organizations, banks, and other financial institutions, money laundering is a big issue. Traditional instruments are not usually successful at preventing it. However, by the combined power of deep and machine learning, companies are successfully distinguishing between legitimate and fraudulent buyers and sellers. Ultimately it is all about anomaly detection. PayPal is using deep learning to avoid fraud and money laundering. There are big opportunities in this area.

Improving Cybersecurity

For organizations, security is a very important area of concern. Machine learning systems handle this concern effectively. The machine learning-based systems monitor and measure traffic coming from and being exchanged between workstations and servers. If any anomalous behavior is identified, it circulates automatic notification to the stakeholders and tries to remove the anomalies based on its knowledge repositories. For example, Israeli communication services provider Orange is using machine learning applications to protect its business and customer data. Recently, the system detected malicious code in a video file that an employee had downloaded. The security team instantly notified the employee.

Science and Technology

This section covers business opportunities in science, from human psychology to space science and cosmology.

Because science affects almost everything, it is natural that mashups of technology, sciences, and social studies have created new business avenues. Science is a broad term. At the same time, it provides a glimpse into present human successes, struggles, and failures.

Science is a big business as well. A couple of decades back, stories like space travel and trips to the moon were confined to scientific communities and government agencies like NASA and ISRO. But now companies like SpaceX are trying to make this possible for average people. The vision to enable people to live on other planets was alien just a few years back. With the advent of a new generation of entrepreneurs and companies, this is becoming a reality.

Similarly, medicine and medical science is a huge business now. The new generation of pharma companies are incorporating inputs from multiple sciences while creating/modifying drugs. They are trying to come with holistic personalized treatment strategies to help their customers fight a disease. This is a paradigm shift in the way that traditional medicine used to operate. For example, allopathy is known for a way to treat patients with diseases. Doctors are now referring it as modern medical science because it covers wider thought processes and a mixture of multiple sciences like psychology, physics, and chemistry. Likewise, treating cancer is not the subject matter of allopathy only. The treatment combines nuclear physics (radiation/chemotherapy) followed by rehabilitation (psychology).

Machine learning has enormous business and commercial implications for science and ideally is subject matter for a separate book. It is not possible to cover all the opportunities in one small section of a chapter.

Medical Science

Machine learning has the capability to become an excellent and powerful tool in surgery. This could enable surgeons and physicians to use complex clinical data (with the help of analytics) to make critical decisions. For example, machine learning and Big Data analytics could potentially contribute heavily to progress in plastic and reconstructive surgery. Machine learning fundamentally could analyze historical data and develop algorithms/models that could provide insight to doctors through knowledge acquisition. This is not news, as machine learning has already been applied to process huge chunks of complicated data in medicine and surgery with a great success. IBM Watson is an excellent example of integrating machine learning with medical science; it is capable of providing real-time diagnoses and suggesting treatment.

Here are the areas of plastic surgery where the business opportunities are explored, and where machine learning is already playing a role:

- *Burn surgery*: A machine learning approach has been generated to analyze and predict the therapeutic time of burns. It can provide exact healing time based on the depth of the burn.

- *Microsurgery*: Monitoring and predictive devices monitor blood perfusion of tissue flaps, based on smartphone photographs and by using deep learning algorithms. Individualized suggestions for surgery based on the patient history is another area where a lot of opportunity exists.

- *Craniofacial surgery*: Future algorithms may be useful for identifying known and unknown genes responsible for cleft lip and palate.

- *Radiology*: When applied to radiology data such as traditional radiography, CT, MRI, and PET scans as well as radiology reports, machine learning automatically recognizes complicated patterns and aids doctors in making informed judgments. According to research published in radiology, an AI tool can reliably distinguish between normal and pathological chest X-rays in a clinical context. Deep learning may be used to automate a variety of time-consuming operations carried out by radiologists, such as lesion identification, segmentation, classification, monitoring, and treatment response prediction, which are typically not possible without software. AI-powered image analysis might potentially be used to track changes in blood flow through the heart and its accompanying arteries or detect the thickening of certain muscle components. Cancerous lesions can also be found using AI.

Machine learning would not only help in the decision-making processes but also in finding patterns and correlations that might not be visible by analysis of smaller data sets or anecdotal experience. ML might help stop diseases before their symptoms pop up.

Space Science

There are terabytes of data analyzed every second by companies like SpaceX and organizations like NASA of galaxies and stars. For example, to catalog stars in our galaxy and find their position, NASA uses evolving machine learning techniques to speed up this overall process. To make its analysis perfect, the organization has been using machine learning to "teach" computers how to spot patterns in new stars and galaxies based on data. Machine learning is used by space-based companies for multiple purposes, including the following:

- They are developing machine learning algorithms and models to automate manually intensive processes and tasks.

- They are developing new tools, frameworks, capabilities, and automated infrastructure to improve propulsion-based data crunching, analysis, and review.

Physics

At times, physics deals with complicated problems and with lots of data. For example, in the Large Hadron Collider (LHC) experiments at CERN, machine learning became very useful in understanding the impact of collisions. It analyzed every collision and provided useful insights to the scientists. Machine learning algorithms beat physicists in regression or classification-related tasks by 25 to 30 percent.

- Machine learning algorithms and models are used to process satellite data. Also in atmospheric physics, machine learning is used for weather forecasts and predictions.

- Machine learning is routinely used in astrophysics to classify and organize huge amounts of data. For example, clustering algorithms are used on Kepler data to sort, locate, and identify star systems that have steady surroundings possibly suitable for occupancy.

Biology

Machine learning algorithms and models like Markov models, support vector machines, neural networks, and graphical models are used frequently to handle and manage randomness and uncertainty of data. These are the key techniques for the analysis of the human genome. They are specifically used for forecasting coding or non-coding areas of the genome; other uses include RNA prediction. There are a number of new and established companies in this arena.

For example, DuPont Industrial Biosciences is doing extensive work in protein engineering of enzymes and metabolic engineering of microbes to protect our environment. They are analyzing the proteins and enzymes and extracting insight with the help of machine learning algorithms and models. A few other areas where business opportunities exist include the following:

- *Gene-finding algorithms*: By using Markov models, Hidden Markov models (HMM), Viterbi algorithms, and parameter estimations, companies can provide personalized and individualized genetic information.

- *Finding miRNA sites*: Companies like Rose pharmaceutical use Hidden Markov models to enable research in areas like hepatitis C research.

- *Classification and prediction*: This involves integrating various biological data and selecting the best model for doing classification of the data and prediction.

Business opportunities not only exist in these areas, but they span other disciplines as well, including astro-biology, environmental science, socio-biology, psychology, and so on. The point here is to highlight the spectrum of opportunities of machine learning in the scientific field.

Types of Machine Learning

There are multiple types of machine learning algorithms in the world of data science. This chapter concentrates primarily on three types of algorithms—supervised, unsupervised, and reinforced. Chapter 1 covers the basic concepts and workings of supervised and unsupervised learning. Here, I elaborate a bit on reinforcement learning.

Reinforcement Learning

Reinforcement learning is a category of machine learning that trains the system by rewards and penalties. In other words, it trains a system just like humans train a pet. For example, if your dog obeys and acts according to your instructions, you encourage them by giving them rewards and maybe punish them when they disobey. Similarly, if the system does well, the trainer gives it positive rewards (positive points). When the system does not perform well, the trainer punishes it (negative points). The learning system that receives negative points has to improve itself exactly like the dog does.

This is a trial-and-error mechanism/process. The reinforcement learning algorithms selectively retain the outputs that exploit the acknowledged reward over a period of time. Broadly, reinforcement learning algorithm tries to mimic how the human brain acts regarding punishment and reward. They select actions that provide them with the greatest reward. Reinforcement learning is also used to select the best possible option from a set of available actions. They select the best option, based on their understanding, and get feedback after each action in an iterative manner. The feedback mechanism enables reinforcement learning to identify that the action was good, neutral, or a huge mistake.

Typically, reinforcement learning algorithms are best for automated systems. They make small decisions without a human's guidance through self-learning programs. Automated elevators, escalators, heating systems, cooling equipment, and lighting systems are excellent candidates for implementing reinforcement learning algorithms. Reinforcement learning algorithms were originally developed to control robots (automated systems). Anything that moves on its own without human intervention, ranging from automated drones to vacuum cleaners, probably runs on a reinforcement learning algorithm. Reinforcement learning algorithm-based programs and systems always answer the question of what action should be taken, although the action is usually taken by a machine.

Reinforcement systems typically answer questions like these:

- What are the appropriate places in a web page for a particular advertisement to be placed, so that it has the best chance of being noticed by the user?

- Should I increase the temperature of the air conditioner or lower it based on the current environmental conditions?

- Is this the right time to purchase shares; if yes, how many shares of ABC stock should I buy now?

- Should I remain driving my car at the same speed or apply brakes or accelerate through this traffic signal?

Reinforcement learning algorithms typically take more effort to make them functional than other algorithm types. The reason behind this is that they are tightly integrated and bound with the overall of the logic of the system. The upside of reinforcement learning algorithms is that they can start working without any data. They accumulate data as they go. In Figure 2-3, the general workings of reinforcement learning are explained. In this type of learning algorithm, the learner collects information by interacting with the environment. This is unlike supervised learning, where predefined labeled data sets exist.

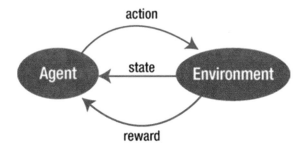

Figure 2-3. *Reinforcement learning*

In reinforcement learning, the reward relates to the tasks and their associated goals. The objective of the agent is to maximize its rewards. Hence, it is natural that it would determine the best course of action or policy to achieve the maximum reward (the same way that rats/monkeys/ humans work). The information the agent receives from the environment is the immediate reward (related to the action just taken). No futuristic or long-term reward feedback is provided by the environment.

Two scenarios are important for reinforcement learning:

- The case where the agent knows the environment model. In this case, the objective is to maximize the reward received.

- In the other case, the agent is not exposed to the environment model and it is unknown to them. Obviously, in this case, they face a learning problem.

In the second case, the agent has to learn from the state and optimize the information gathered. This can be used to gain information about the environment and determine the best action. The Markov Decision Processes (MDPs) model of the environment and interactions with the environment is widely adopted in reinforcement learning. For completeness, let's take a quick look at supervised, unsupervised, and semi-supervised learning (I keep them short as they are covered in Chapter 1).

Supervised Learning

In supervised learning, input is called training data and has a known label and a known result/output. A model is generated or created by training data in a two-step process (model and prediction). The model is used to make predictions and is corrected when predictions are incorrect. The training process (of model) continues until the model achieves a desired level of accuracy (in iterative manner) on the training data.

Unsupervised Learning

Input data is not labeled in unsupervised learning and in this type of learning algorithm, the target data is not known. In unsupervised learning, the model would be prepared by inferring structures and patterns present in the input data. It can be done through a mathematical process of systematically reducing redundancy, through rules, or by organizing data by resemblance.

Semi-Supervised Learning: A Quick Look

I have not covered this type of learning algorithm in this book. However, it would be helpful for you to know about this. In semi-supervised learning, input data is a combination of labeled and unlabeled data. Here, the model learns from the structures based on organizing the data and must be capable of doing predictions. In semi-supervised learning, a few data sets are labeled, but most of them exist in unlabeled formats. A combination of supervised and unsupervised modeling and other techniques are used.

All the learning algorithms have subtypes. I do not explain these subtypes here, because they are the subject matter of Chapter 3. However, it is worth having a look at the different subtypes available in each learning algorithm (see Table 2-1).

Table 2-1. *Categories of Machine Learning Algorithms*

Supervised Learning	Unsupervised Learning	Reinforcement Learning
Artificial neural network	Artificial neural network	
Bayesian statistics	Association rule learning	Q-learning
Case-based reasoning	Hierarchical clustering	Learning automata
Decision trees	Partitional clustering	
Learning automata		
Instance-based learning		
Regression analysis		
Linear classifiers		
Decision trees		
Bayesian networks		
Hidden Markov models		

Machine Learning Models

The machine learning model is created during the training process. The training process contains the following steps:

1. Provide the input training data sources.

2. Provide the name of the data attribute that contains the target to be predicted.

3. Provide the required data transformation instructions.

4. Provide the training parameters (factors used by the model to group patterns or make decisions) to control the machine learning algorithm.

Training ML Models

The process of training a machine learning model includes providing an ML algorithm (that is, the learning algorithm) with training data. The training data is supposed to contain the correct answer. This is commonly known as the *target attribute* or for short, the *target*. The machine learning algorithm finds the patterns in the available training data set. After that, it maps it to input data attributes to the target (the answer or result that you want to predict), and it outputs an ML model that gathers these patterns.

At this point, it is necessary to clearly understand the difference between machine learning algorithm and the model. The learning algorithm gives the model as its output. Consider an example to understand this better. Linear regression is a technique that fits points to a line: y = mx+b. Once the fitting happens, you get the result—in this case for example, y = 12x + 6.

Different Types of Algorithm-Based Models for Machine Learning

Your model will run iteratively and give you the result. So technically you can create multiple models based on the algorithms. A few famous models are discussed next. These section provide insight into how these models work based on algorithms. The rest of the models and their algorithmic association are discussed in detail in the next chapter.

Binary Classification Model

The binary classification model predicts a binary outcome. Amazon machine learning uses the industry-standard learning algorithm, logistic regression, to train binary classification models. The next sections list some examples of binary classification problems.

This model enables the system to answer these questions:

- Is this email message spam or not?

- Will the stock price go up?

- Was this file review written by a customer or a robot?

Multiclass Classification Model

This model permits you to produce predictions for many classes (it can predict one out of more than two outcomes). To provide training to multiclass models, organizations generally consume learning algorithms like multinomial logistic regression. Multiclass problems enable systems to answer these questions:

- Is this product a car, a bicycle, or a bag of chips?

- Is this book an action, thriller, or a love story?

Regression Model

These models are generally used to predict a numeric value. To train regression models, enterprises use the learning algorithm called linear regression. The basic assumption in this model is that the output variable can be articulated in the form of linear amalgamation (weighted sum) of a group of input variables. Here are examples of regression problems:

- What will Delhi's temperature be tomorrow?

- For this share of this company, how many units should be sold?

As mentioned, multiple important models do exist apart from these, and they are covered in the next chapter.

Tools for Machine Learning

Google, Microsoft, IBM, Amazon, and a lot of other innovative companies are offering machine learning APIs and tools via their respective cloud platforms. This makes life easier and APS (applications, products, and services) are built quickly. Tools are one of the most important parts of the machine learning ecosystem. Choosing the right tool depends on multiple factors, including the requirements. Machine learning-related tools equip you with capabilities to deliver results smoothly. In the current scenario, where deadlines are stringent and stiff, the appropriate selection of tools serves as an integral weapon. Also, they are the important part of architectural decisions and strategies. At the project level, selecting the appropriate tool plays a very important role.

Jargon Buster

- *API (Application Programming Interface)*: A list of instructions as well as the setup of those instructions that one application can send to another. Also, it is a description of how a software application/component may intermingle or communicate with other software applications/components. It is used in a way so that an individual program can interconnect with another directly and they can use each other's functions in a well-defined way.

- *Platform*: A complete all-in-one solution for a very extensive range of problems. For example, Microsoft .NET and Windows platforms provide a solution for multiple problems. Multiple vendors are providing cloud-based platforms, commonly known as Platform-as-a-Service (PaaS) solutions. A platform may include a number of tools and components. In turn, tools and components may be helpful in solving wider ranges of problems, like persistence, security, concurrency, and so on. Generally, a good platform would fulfill all your needs. A platform comes with a preselected set of technologies, tools, components, and libraries and you have to choose among them what you want to use for your system (which you are going to develop/ modify). A platform is a fundamental entity; think of it as a service provider. The platform provides services to run/install tools and frameworks; once that is done, programs run on top of that.

- *Framework*: Uses the features and functionality provided by the underlying platform(s) to achieve the job. For example, a framework may serve as a tool for the developers to access the various parts and sections of the logic. A framework offers a layer of abstraction over multiple parts of the underlying platform. You can run multiple frameworks on top of a platform. For example, based on your project requirements, you might run the same framework on dissimilar platforms. For example, you can run the .NET core framework on Windows and Linux (platforms), whereas the .NET framework 4.5 will run only on the Windows platform.

- *Tool*: An apparatus for doing specific functions in software programs when coding or when performing specialized tasks. It has predefined inputs which deliver predefined outputs. A toolkit is like a software development kit—it is a collection of tools that includes code libraries and components, and it generally saves coding efforts because it has complied and organized tools and libraries.

- *Library*: A portion of code that you can call from your program to perform tasks more quickly and easily. For example, an input and output (I/O) library will provide facilities for loading and manipulating input, output, and files (in the form of precoded and compiled code chunks). This enables you to complete your tasks faster and saves time because you need not write all the code/programs by yourself.

Tools can be helpful in automating tasks and steps in machine learning processes so that human intervention is less necessary during the overall process. Also, this makes development faster. The time you save by using tools can be invested in more productive tasks. In both the cases, either you choose to complete your tasks by tool or on your own—you have to research and invest the time.

Before selecting a machine learning tool, it is always good to evaluate the tool based on tested parameters. These parameters are applicable to almost any tool selection and not limited to only machine learning tools.

- *Intuitive and intelligent interface*: Machine learning involves a lot of complex activities. For example, mapping subtasks to the main tasks, creating and executing models, associating training data sets with the selected model and algorithm, and monitoring the progress. Hence, intuitive and intelligent interfaces are very important. So, while selecting a tool, keep this in mind.

- *Alignment with best practices and standards*: Tools must be aligned with the best practices, standards, policies, and the prevailing patterns and practices. Without these, the output generated by the tool is of no standard value.

- *Updated and supported by the community*: While selecting tools for machine learning projects, it is important to ensure that it is well-supported by the community, contains good documentation, and is updated on a frequent basis by the vendor/open-source community. All this is the bare minimum for a good tool. As machine learning itself is an evolving and dynamically changing technology, selecting an tool that's frequently updated is critical.

A machine learning tool generally provides the following:

- *Application Programming Interface (API)*: Machine learning-based tools generally provide an application programming interface, which gives you the flexibility to decide which elements to use and exactly how to use them in your own programs/code/software.

- *Graphical User Interface (GUI)*: Machine learning tools generally provide a GUI, which simplifies the tasks you are doing by allowing you to interact with windows, access timely alerts, see the data visually, associate, integrate, and map, provide information and facts in visual form, and so on.

- *Command-line interface*: Apart from a GUI, there are scenarios when you need a lighter version of productive tools that enable you to perform your tasks quickly. Hence, a good machine learning tool generally provides an interactive command-line interface. You can execute programs and commands through the command line and enable command-line parameterization.

Frameworks for Machine Learning

A large volume of data and computational power is required to create, perform, and execute machine learning-based systems. The cloud is an ideal environment for developing and hosting machine learning applications. Several companies are already offering these applications and services. For example, Microsoft is doing this through its Azure ML frameworks in a pay-as-you-go mode. To perform tasks in the cloud environments, you need good frameworks and toolsets apart from other important ingredients, like libraries, API, and SDKs from the technical side and good working business models and strategies from the business side.

Having a good framework that's up and running is one of the "bare" minimum requirements for your machine learning-related endeavors. Machine learning frameworks allow you to create and train models. Once the model is created and trained, it provides functionality to turn those frameworks into APIs that can be used or consumed by other services. New generations of machine learning frameworks offer a wide range of facilities to transform algorithms to models.

The following list presents a snapshot of machine learning tools, libraries, frameworks, and APIs.

- *Caffe*: It is a deep learning and machine learning framework. It was developed by keeping expression, speed, and modularity in mind. Companies who use this: Flicker, Yahoo, and Adobe.

- *Google TensorFlow*: Implements data flow graphs, where batches of data ("tensors") can be processed by a series of algorithms described by a graph. Companies who use this: Arm, Google, Uber, and Airbus.

- *MatLab*: A high-level technical computing language and interactive environment. It is commonly used for algorithm development, data visualization, and data and numerical analysis. Companies who use this: Shell, Netflix.

- *Microsoft Azure ML Studio*: Allows users to create and train models in real time. It also enables users to turn the models into APIs, so that they can be consumed by other services. Companies who use this: ESSAR GROUP, CloudMunch, and ICICI Lombard General Insurance Company Ltd.

- *Spark*: A fast and general-purpose engine for large-scale data processing and analysis. Spark exposes its APIs in Java, Scala, Python, and R. Spark also provides batch and streaming APIs. Companies who use this: IBM, Google.

- *H 2 O*: A math library that's open-source. It is written in Java and provides support for native Java API drivers for R, Python, Excel, and Tableau REST APIs. Companies who use this: IBM, Google.

- *Sprinkling Water*: A framework that is generally used for integrating Spark and H2O. It provides flexibility of transparent use of H2O data structures and algorithms with Spark API and vice versa. Companies who use this: Netflix, IBM.

- PyTorch: Deep learning models, a kind of machine learning frequently used in applications like image recognition and language processing, may be built using PyTorch, a fully featured framework. Most machine learning engineers find it reasonably simple to understand and use because it is written in Python. This Torch-based open-source machine learning toolkit was created to boost deep neural network installation speed and flexibility. In both academia and business, PyTorch is now the most widely used library for AI researchers and practitioners.

Distributed Machine Learning

Modern machine learning algorithms work with any type of data. But when the data is large, it takes a lot of time to process it and make predictions. However, there are a few techniques available to make algorithms run faster.

- Reduce the algorithm's complexity

- Implement optimization techniques

- Reduce the amount of data, whenever possible

- Write distributed algorithms that run on different machines and "distribute" data and processing load on multiple machines

- Use efficient tools to reduce the processed chunks of data

Of all these techniques, applying distributed algorithms is most practical because you are not compromising on anything. Also after commoditization of hardware, the price of hardware will come down, so the cost will be minimal. In fact, this way of processing allows you to use your resources most effectively and efficiently. This processing paradigm is known as *distributed machine learning*. Here are a few characteristics of distributed machine learning:

- Data-centric because it enables you to train the model over large data sets and split the data over multiple machines in the distributed environment.

- Model-centric because a large number of models are involved in data crunching and training.

- Distributes models split over multiple machines. However, a single training iteration spans over multiple machines.

- Graph-centric because mapping (of different machines) is done in a graphical way.

Large-Scale Machine Learning

Training data sets are growing in size as machine learning models become more complicated over time. Language models are learned across millions or billions of phrases, whereas embedding models are taught using web-scale sets of text and graphs. It is acceptable to conclude that during the past several years, training machine learning models across huge data sets has greatly benefited downstream tasks but has also proven to be computationally expensive. A strong machine learning system with models that can handle millions to billions of parameters effectively and efficiently is necessary given the enormous growth in Big Data. The system must be able to process extremely large quantities of data and provide precise predictive analytics. Traditional machine learning systems are unable at processing large amounts of data since they process the data sequentially in commercial or academic ways, using standard iterative ML algorithms. Therefore, it makes sense that the need for large-scale machine learning

(ML) systems is increasing given that these systems are able to meet the processing requirements of machine learning algorithms at this huge scale. They do this by learning from complicated models with millions to billions of parameters. The system requires dispersed clusters made of tens to thousands of machines to function.

Because it includes enormous volumes of data, large-scale machine learning differs greatly from typical machine learning. A large number of training/test instances, characteristics, or classes are manipulated. For instance, such machine learning algorithms are used by Facebook, Instagram, and Flickr, which each have tens of billions of photographs available at any given moment. These are all present in large-scale machine learning data sets:

- More than 100 billion training examples

- More than 100 billion features

- Around 100 features per training example (sparse data)

The development of large-scale machine learning systems that would offer scalable, effective, fault-tolerant, parallel systems that carry out learning tasks on enormous volumes of data is receiving a lot of attention from businesses and academia. For companies and organizations that depend on n data to make choices, large-scale machine learning is a vital tool. Quickly processing enormous amounts of data can produce insightful information and improve decision-making.

Predictive analytics, customer segmentation, risk management, and fraud detection are a few applications of large-scale machine learning. Large-scale machine learning can identify relationships, trends, and connections that would be difficult to see without gigantic data sets. As a result, corporations may be able to get smarter and produce more effective plans.

Fundamentally, algorithms are utilized in the large-scale machine learning process to discover patterns in the data. The algorithms are frequently used to predict or position trends after being trained on a data set. One method trains a machine learning algorithm to find trends in customer data and then predict customer behavior.

Variants of ML, such as natural language processing, also use large-scale machine learning. Algorithms for natural language processing are used to examine material written in natural languages and find textual patterns. This can be used to decipher a text's meaning, pinpoint topics, and form predictions.

Large-scale machine learning is a useful tool for companies and organizations. It can be beneficial to swiftly process vast amounts of data and find insightful information. Organizations can create more successful strategies by utilizing large-scale machine Learning.

Programming Languages for Machine Learning

Selecting a programming language to program "critical tasks" is a difficult and intelligent decision. It depends on multiple factors, based on the requirements and relevance of a particular business scenario. It becomes more challenging when it is associated with machine learning and cognitive computing, because the process of programming involves embedding intelligence into the raw program and a lot of data manipulation and crunching capabilities. However, the factors described in the following list help make these decisions, as they provide insights and guidelines for choosing the appropriate language. Parameters like speed, programmability, library support, built-in functionality of the language, open-source support, and scalability are discussed in brief.

- *Speed of developing the program*: Speed is very important, whether programs are developed individually or by a team. Factors like how long it takes you to write code become crucial with tight deadlines. However, other associated factors, such as how long it takes you to find a solution to the problem and the facility of finding bugs quickly, are also important.

- *Ease of programming, learning, and understanding*: The easier the programming language is to learn and understand, the faster they become productive. For example, Java is an easier programming language to learn than C++, and C is probably even easier (however, this is subjective and depends on the coder's exposure to the particular programming language), as almost all the programs are written once and read multiple times. Thus, it is important to be able to interpret and understand the essence of the program and understand what's happening. Another important factor is the syntax of the programming language, which is generally overlooked, but it can make a huge difference in how easy it is to use the language.

- *Library support*: For machine learning programming languages, good software library support is very important. This must include support for data structures, interfacing with the operating system, and statistical and data crunching capabilities. The Perl programming language has a huge number of third-party libraries, which makes it a suitable choice for developing machine learning systems.

- *Built-in functionality languages differ in terms of the primitives*: While choosing a programming language to perform a task, it is important to determine its built-in functionality to support that task. For example, to accomplish machine learning related requirements, the language must support statistical, predictive analytics and graphics. Good built-in capabilities are mandatory.

- *Scalability*: This is where otherwise higher-level languages are often genuinely tested. While choosing a language for coding, be careful about the scalability part of the language.

Apart from these parameters, portability, performance, and fit-for-purpose are some additional factors that you need to consider before making your choice. The sections that follow present a snapshot of the main programming languages used in machine learning, covering the benefits and salient features. The following sections can serve as a handy toolkit for making decisions.

R

R is a free software development environment for statistical computing, graphics, data mining, and machine learning-based computing. It compiles and runs on a wide variety of available platforms, including UNIX, Linux, Windows, and macOS. R is one of the most popular software packages and programming languages. It is popular among statisticians and researchers because it provides excellent and elegant statistical coding/programming features. R provides more than 4,000 specialized packages, which are primarily targeted to leverage statistical features. In a nutshell:

- R is a data analysis software package.

- R is also used as a programming language.

- R is an environment for statistical analysis and data crunching.

- R is an open-source software project.

- R is popular within the community of statisticians, data analysts, and data scientists across the globe.

Why use R?

- *Data manipulation capabilities*: R allows the data scientist to form the data set into a format that can be easily retrieved and analyzed by dividing large multivariate data sets.

- *Data analysis functionality*: A huge variety of statistical data analysis features are available in R. R is an open-source development tool/environment/programming language. It is supported by a large community of statisticians, programmers, hobbyists, and computer scientists. One of the reasons for its popularity is that it provides multiple efficient functions for hypothesis testing, statistical model creation, and fitting. It also provides several robust clustering techniques for efficient and effective implementation of machine learning algorithms.

- *Data visualization*: R is established as the "statistical package of choice" for data representation, analysis, and visualization. As a programming language, R provides a lot of ready-to-use functions for visualizing data in the form of graphs and charts. R allows developers to implement any visualization idea for any data set. R data representation is not limited to static representations of data; it also provides capabilities for implementing animations and other innovative interactive visual techniques.

- *Excellent usability*: R programs have explicit capabilities to document the steps involved in the analysis. Hence, it makes it easy to imitate and/or update analyses. This functionality enables developers to quickly test multiple ideas and, if required, correct issues instantly.

- *Integration facility*: R provides great integration features with other popular languages, like C/C++, Java, and Python. It has native support for ODBC, which enables it to talk with multiple data sources, like Excel, Access, and other ODBC-compliant databases (Oracle, SQL Server parallel databases). It integrates well with statistical packages as well (such as SAS, Stata, SPSS, and Minitab).

R is not only free, but is open-source as well. This practically signifies that anybody can inspect the available source code to see which code is implemented to perform a task and get insight out of it.

Scala

The Scala programming language is a combination of a functional and an object-oriented programming language. It runs on the Java Virtual Machine (JVM). Its .NET version is also available, which empowers it to run on the .NET environment as well. Scala is based on the idea that there are a lot of commonalities between functional and object-oriented programming languages. As a functional programming language, Scala provides pattern matching capabilities (which are useful for machine learning bound programming). Whereas as an object-oriented programming language, it adopts the object-orientation like facilities of using classes and polymorphism. Scala inherited a lot of features from Java, along with many features that are not in Java. In a nutshell:

- It uses revolutionary and innovative frameworks (for example, AKKA and Finagle). These were developed in Scala and allow developers to develop reactive systems.

- Scala provides excellent pattern-matching capabilities, which is very useful in machine learning-based programming.

- Scala uses functions as first-class objects.

- Scala has great support for higher order functions. That means that developing higher order functions in Scala is easy.

- Scala runs on top of the Java Virtual Machine. Hence, it provides seamless integration of the Scala code with code written in Java.

- Scala is easily integrated with the .NET framework. The code written in Scala can be compiled into CLR byte code.

Why use Scala?

- *Functional language*: Most of the functional languages provide a toolset to developers, programmers, and data scientists to implement iterative computations and do predictive program development. Scala is not an exception; it too provides a rich toolset of functionalities and capabilities to the developer community. Scala is an extension of the MapReduce programming model for distributed computation.

Scala handles large amounts of data very efficiently. Scala provides most of the vital elements, components, APIs, and tools required for machine learning programming. It is also a good choice for doing statistical analysis.

- *General-purpose programming language*: Scala is designed for rapid development of common programming patterns in a concise, sophisticated, and type-safe way. Scala effortlessly integrates features of object-oriented programming (OOP) and functional languages. Hence, it makes developers productive to their fullest. As it is fully compatible with Java, it effortlessly retains full interoperability with Java and benefits from modern multicore hardware features. Scala fundamentally avoids a shared state, so calculations and computations can be readily available to be distributed across centers (cores) on a multicore server, and across servers in a data center. This makes Scala a good fit for contemporary multicore-based CPUs. Also, it has excellent support for distributed computing architectures, so it best suits cloud-computing workloads. Cloud-computing workloads require concurrency and parallelism, which are easily achievable through Scala.

- *Compact*: Scala type inference and other compact and timely features make it a concise and elegant language. For example, it typically enables developers to reduce the size of the source code by a factor of two or three compared to Java. Scala comes with a rich set of development and productivity enhancement tools. Therefore, developer productivity is much better in comparison to the developer of the languages like Ruby and Python (if they use the features correctly).

- *Scalability*: Whether it is a large development team, large codebases, or large numbers of CPU cores, Scala scalability is never compromised. Also, for multicore and distributed computing models, the pairing of Scala with platforms like Light Bend reactive platforms enable it to develop an industrial-strength implementation. A concurrency model called Akka combined with Scala provides special power for handling large-scale machine learning-based project implementations.

- *Interoperable with Java*: Since Scala is a JVM-targeted language, all the existing Java libraries and tools can be used seamlessly with it. It ensures that previous investments of effort, money, and intelligence are fully protected.

- *Programmability*: Scala programs are compiled directly to Java bytecode. In turn, bytecode runs on the JVM. The JVM is very mature and stable. Scala leverages the JVM's great features, like just-in-time compilation, automatic garbage collection capabilities, and excellent deployment techniques. These features make it a very efficient programming language. The learning curve for developers in Scala is not steep, as developers work with familiar tools and learn them in parallel without much effort. Scala enables developers to start writing code that's more concise, faster, scalable, and even more fun.

Additionally with Scala, you use something called Apache Spark. This is not a language but is used along with Scala and Python very frequently.

As associations produce different and more concentrated data products and services, there's a growing need for machine literacy, which can be used to develop personalization, recommendations, and prophetic perceptivity. The Apache Spark machine learning library (called MLlib) allows data scientists to concentrate on their data problems and models rather than working on the complications girding distributed data (similar as structure, configurations, and so on). Spark allows data scientists to address multiple data problems in addition to their machine literacy problems.

Additionally, the Spark ecosystem supports streaming (real-time computations), real-time interactive query processing with Spark SQL and data frames, and graph calculations (through GraphX). Spark is written in Java, and Scala leverages the JVM.

Numerous programming languages, including Scala, Hive, and Pig, are supported by Spark. For Spark operations, Scala is one of the most well-known programming languages created. With built-in modules for streaming, SQL, machine learning, and graph processing, Apache Spark is renowned as a quick, simple-to-use, all-purpose tool for Big Data processing. Machine learning activities can be carried out utilizing the Spark frame and the MLlib library that is included with Apache Spark.

You can use the Spark ML module in PySpark since PySpark is the Python API for Apache Spark. Numerous algorithms and machine learning serviceability are available in MLlib. With support from the greatest open-source community in Big Data, Apache Spark is a super-fast open-source data processing device for operations involving machine learning and AI. Spark is excellent at iterative calculation, which makes MLlib run quickly. In parallel, we monitor algorithmic performance. The high-quality algorithms in MLlib can replicate and produce results that are superior to the sporadic one-pass approximations utilized in MapReduce.

The framework to improve ETL is provided by Apache Spark. Through robotization, data conduits allow associations to form faster data-driven opinions. They're an integral piece of an effective ETL process because they allow for effective and accurate aggregating of data from multiple sources.

Python

Python is an interpreted and interactive object-oriented, high-level programming language. It is called a strong general-purpose programming language. Python places strong emphasis on code reliability and simplicity so that programmers can develop applications rapidly. It is a multi-paradigm programming language, which allows users to code in several different programming styles. In a nutshell:

- Python supports cross-platform development and is available through open-source.

- Python can be easily integrated with C/C++, .Net, and Java.

- Most programs in Python require considerably less code to achieve the same functionality, which requires less effort and lines of codes.

Why use Python?

- *Readability*: Python has good code readability for fast software development. A high level of readability is at the heart of the Python language. Python uses a complete set of code style guidelines and "Pythonic" idioms. These increase readability of code written in Python.

- *Less coding effort*: Python uses less code and provides more productivity.

- *Good support for mathematics and statistics*: Python's applications span across multiple areas, including web, GUI, OS, science, and statistics.

- *Fast growing*: It is a fast-growing programming language among open-source communities.

- *Flexibility*: Python is extremely flexible.

- *Good numeric and symbolic features*: It provides numeric and symbolic computation features.

- *Good plotting features*: 2D/3D plotting is easy in Python.

- *Machine learning compatible*: Python is useful for scientific and machine learning related tasks.

- *User interface support*: t has great support for user interfaces.

- *Support for advance computing*: It supports parallel and distributed computing.

- *Excellent pre-built libraries*: It has special libraries for machine learning and image processing.

- *Developer friendly*: It includes game and web development functionality, which attracts all type of developers.

- *It is here to stay*: Python is not going away any time soon.

- *Easy*: Python is easy to set up and use.

Some valuable insight is provided by Adam Geitgey, director of software engineering at Groupon:

```
https://jaxenter.com/python-popular-programming-language-
today-machine-learning-128942.html
```

The Latest Advancements in Machine Learning

Until now in this chapter, I have discussed breakthroughs in machine learning that happened in the last few decades. I also described how Big Data streams affect technologies like high-speed Internet and cloud computing. However, there is a lot of innovation happening in areas closely associated with machine learning, like deep learning. Deep learning keeps machine learning at its core, but its implication is wide. It spans across recommendation systems (Netflix and Amazon), face recognition technology (Facebook), email spam filters (Google and Microsoft), and speech recognition systems (Apple's Siri).

The depth of advancement is generally unknown to general users until it becomes public. But based on the speed of progress, we can say with high certainty that developments that happened in the past five years will be almost nothing compared to what we're going to see in the five years to come. Based on the current state of machine learning's technical development and traction, the following sections discuss a few areas that could lead to exceptional progress.

Image-Based Recognition

With the help of deep learning, the current state of image-based recognition will take a quantum leap, as a lot of research is happening in this area. For example, machine learning-based systems/applications will recognize images and identify people and their actions in pictures, with high accuracy. The best part of this is that the application will be able to do this based on the image alone, with less dependence on external data. Modern deep learning algorithms and models will not only be able to recognize new pictures, but they also will gather insight from pictures of the entire human history and video footage. This will transform the way these assets are organized, located, viewed, and shared. For example, YouTube might soon be able to intelligently find content related to parts of a clip or video footage that you watched and liked. This will be done only on the basis of visual content of the video.

Case Study: Face Recognition

Challenge

Design a face detection and recognition algorithm for applications across multiple domains.

Approach

Created a databases of faces and performed face detection using the Haar Cascades algorithm. Matched captured face images in the existing database of facial images of people. Used face recognition algorithms with the principle component analysis.

Result

Achieved accuracy close to 60 percent for face recognition and 70 percent for face detection. This can be applied to strengthen security measures in organizations or identify and provide offers to repeat customers in retail stores.

Source: *BlueOcean AI website*

Healthcare

The ability of machine learning to analyze and store massive amounts of data (in association with Big Data technologies) will provide doctors and patients much-needed second opinions in real time. This will enable them to diagnose and provide treatment of medical illnesses in an on-demand fashion. These IoT enabled smart, wearable computing devices and personal health monitoring systems can detect various health and fitness conditions in real time and send notifications to the patients, to make them less prone to diseases. The latest advancements in this area will make these technologies widespread in the next five years. Wearing these devices might become as ubiquitous as having a mobile phones today is. Machine learning is leading a silent revolution in the field of healthcare by fueling breakthroughs.

Travel and Communications

Real-time translation technology is the area on which a lot of industries and enterprises are betting. In the near future, we will see applications on our phones that will instantly translate voice and texts (all types of conversations) to the listener's native language. The applications will do this so flawlessly that the listener will not know the difference. After the shaping of the globalized world, the language lines have become blurred. Businesses/enterprises are in continuous pursuit of a global market. Tech giants such as Google and Microsoft sensed the demand of the market and started taking the necessary steps to build such tools. A few early offerings from them are Google Personal Assistance and Microsoft Cortana. However, these are just the beginning. Based on the current state of the research, be ready to be flooded with these applications/products and services in the near future.

Advertising

Recent advancements in machine learning enable advertising firms to integrate augmented reality technology with branding. This will allow advertisers to seamlessly place products and service information into existing content by appropriately recognizing the depth, comparative and quantifiable size, and lighting and shading of the products and services.

Also, this will not be limited to just new content; it can be extended to any content. Hence, this will enable advertising firms to integrate any historical video property with new technology. The computer vision technology firm Mirriad has already tried this. This advancement in technology will revolutionize the capabilities of advertising firms.

Jargon Buster

Virtual reality provides for the creation of real-life simulations and reproductions. It generates an immersive environment to make users feel as if they are interacting with the digital environment in real life.

Augmented reality provides digital enhancements that supplement the prevailing real-life situation by appealing to the senses. The fundamental elements of virtual reality are through a headset or other VR devices worn by the user. Typically, these virtual reality devices display or project a simulation of a real-life environment. The surroundings provided by the devices are immersive, interactive, and give the feeling of a real-life environment. As virtual reality devices are available in a variety of price ranges and styles, it is easy for companies and users to use this technology. For example, real estate industries can use these technologies to provide their prospective customers with the real-life feel of a property for sale. Augmented reality is a powerful, sophisticated, portable, and cost-effective technology. It enables consumers to have an interactive, rich, and meaningful experience with a company or brand.

Machine learning-based products, applications, and services are commercializing at a very fast speed due to this innovation-driven market. These areas are only a few of many. Almost all sectors (verticals and horizontals) of the economy are affected enormously by the efficiencies and effectiveness of this new era of machine learning. We are already witnessing an increase in consumer demand for predictive applications and products that essentially require machine learning. At the moment, we are just at the surface of what is possible. If things continue on the trajectory we expect, the golden age of machine learning might very well make the next five years in technology the most exciting yet.

More Case Studies

This section contains two final case studies.

Case Study: Machine Learning Text Analytics

Challenges

The client is capturing consumer conversations from multiple sources (tech forums, call center agent transcripts, email, and chat). They are currently categorizing the customer experience (text data) manually on a minimalized sample basis, which does not provide a holistic view of customer experience insights.

The goal is to automate text classification on the entire data population, which will enable them to gather detailed insights about the customer experience.

Approach

The data they received had a breadth of topics and had six levels of classification for each row. Level 5 has the highest number of distinct nodes at 4277, followed by Level 3 at 616 nodes.

The merged and cleaned the forum, agent transcript, chat, and email data to create 130,000 rows of training data. The initial focus of the work was to simplify the complex hierarchical structure to ensure appropriate classification as per business requirements.

They designed a comprehensive natural language processing-based rule set and developed a machine learning algorithm to build an auto-code engine to ensure most categories would be captured. The business rules were created and combined with the synonym sets to build the model.

Result

Achieved accuracy close to 70 percent.

Source: *BlueOcean AI website*

Case Study: Automation Reduces Resolution Time by 50 Percent

Challenges

With nearly half a million support cases and over 900,000 emails coming in over a seven-month period, a leader in the gaming industry needed to improve the efficiency of their customer support process. The support team relied heavily on response templates, but there were more than 8,500 response templates available. Also, there is no effective auto-response mechanism or template selection process available for representatives to help them quickly choose the best one. Although their support software recorded how often each response template was used, it didn't provide information about which template was used on which cases, leaving support technicians starting from scratch every time a ticket came in.

Approach

Wise.io worked hand-in-hand with this company to help make their template library much more usable and useful. By applying sophisticated natural language processing (NLP) techniques, Wise.io was able to identify duplicate templates that could be removed from the library. Wise.io then developed an application that recommended the most appropriate templates based on responses to similar cases in the past. Recommended responses were shown directly in the agent view so that customer service representatives could take advantage of the suggested templates without learning a new workflow.

Results

Using this automated identification approach, this gaming company was able to reduce their library of templates by over 90 percent, making agent training and usability much easier to manage. In addition, by presenting their customer service representatives with recommended responses, median resolution time decreased by over 50 percent, indicating that agents could resolve twice as many tickets in the same amount of time or could engage more deeply on the customer issues that really needed more attention.

Source: *Wise.io website*

Audio and Video Links

Watch these talks about some really interesting applications of data mining and machine learning:

- ```
  https://www.ted.com/playlists/56/making_sense_
  of_too_much_data
  ```
- ```
  http://iasaglobal.org/3-iasa-august-esummit-
  machine-learning-101/
  ```

Summary

This chapter presented a thesis of basic practical machine learning concepts in brief. At the same time, it discussed the evolution and history of ML in the context of artificial intelligence and brain science. The chapter provided a snapshot of concepts like generalized machine learning architecture and discussed its associated components. It also presented details of business opportunities in the context of machine learning that exist in multiple areas. With the help of the innovative "WISDOM" umbrella of prospects, the chapter took a futuristic look at the possible seen and unseen opportunities. This chapter also provided a glimpse of the tools, frameworks, libraries, languages, and APIs within the machine learning ecosystem.

Mind Map

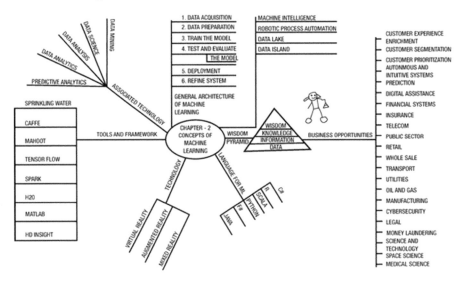

Reference, Web Links, Notes, and Bibliography

1. Kodratoff, Yves et al. (1990), Yves et al. *Machine Learning: An Artificial Intelligence Approach,* (Vol. 3).

2. Hastie, Trevor; Toshigami, R.; Friedman, J. (February 2009).

3. *The Elements of Statistical Learning: Data Mining, Inference, and Prediction.* http://www-stat. stanford.edu/~tibs/ElemStatLearn/Christopher M. Bishop (2006). Pattern Recognition and Machine Learning, Springer ISBN 0-387-31073-8.

4. Werneck, Yang et al. (July 2010). *Machine Learning in Medical Imaging,* IEEE Signal Processing Magazine, vol. 27, no. Good code readability for fast development. 4, pp. 25-38.

5. Yahoo Research (Machine learning group). Current research on Machine Learning Applications at Yahoo. http://research.yahoo.com/Machine_ Learning.

6. Pieter Abbeel (October 2012). Machine learning for Robotics, a video lecture. http://videolectures. net/ecmlpkdd2012_abbeel_learning_robotics/

7. Klingspor V.; Demiris, J. Human-Robot communication and Machine Learning, *Applied Artificial Intelligence Journal,* Vol. 11, pp. 719-746, 1997. http://www.iis.ee.ic.ac.uk/yiannis/ KlingsporDemirisKaiser97.pdf

8. [MacDonald14]. Scott MacDonald Whitney Rockley, "The Industrial Internet of Things," McRockCapital, 2014. http://www.mcrockcapital.com/ uploads/1/0/9/6/10961847/mcrock_industrial_ internet_of_things_report_2014.pdf

9. Bryan Catanzaro Senior Researcher, Baidu "Speech: The Next Generation," 05/28/2015, Talk given at GPUTech conference 2015.

10. Dhruv Batra CloudCV: "Large-Scale Distributed Computer Vision as a Cloud Service," 05/28/2015, Talk given at GPUTech conference 2015.

11. Dilip Patolla. "A GPU Based Satellite Image Analysis Tool," 05/28/2015, Talk given at GPUTech conference 2015.

12. Franco Mana. "A High-Density GPU Solution for DNN Training," 05/28/2015, Talk given at GPUTech conference 2015</aHailin Jin. "Collaborative Feature Learning from Social Media" 05/28/2015 Talk given at GPUTech conference 2015

CHAPTER 3

Machine Learning Algorithms and Their Relationship with Modern Technologies

Dr. Patanjali Kashyap[a*]

ª Bangalore, Karnataka, India

This chapter provides an executive summary of machine learning algorithms. It's important that decision-makers understand, analyze, and evaluate the ground level reality of the business and the technological landscape. This is equally critical for managers, because proper understanding of algorithms and associated technologies will make them more confident in managing their projects better. It becomes crucial when it comes to machine learning-based project implementations and strategies because of the highly technical aspects of the subject. Hence, having a practical overview of the algorithms and their behaviors in real-time business scenarios will help you make accurate decisions and define thoughtful roadmaps for your teams and organizations.

© Dr. Patanjali Kashyap 2024
P. Kashyap, *Machine Learning for Decision Makers*,
https://doi.org/10.1007/978-1-4842-9801-5_3

Algorithms are the soul of machine learning processes and technologies. But they are complex and difficult to understand. In this chapter, I bridge the gap between complexity and understanding. I explain these algorithms in plain English with the help of examples, success stories, and practical scenarios, so that anyone can decode the underlying wisdom and use them.

Algorithms, Algorithms, Everywhere

An *algorithm* is sequence of steps that solves a problem. People generally associate them with computers. But why? To perform a task, computers need accurate instructions and steps. Thus, if you want a computer to solve a particular problem, you have to provide appropriate accurate instructions in the form of steps. In other words, algorithms are important for computers because they are the building blocks of their intelligence. More precisely, without algorithms, computers are just dumb boxes of materials and plastic. As a cell plays its role in a biological system, algorithms have similar significance in software. You could even draw parallels between cells and algorithms for better understanding.

In the last few decades, hardware has increasingly become cheaper, more powerful, and more efficient. This advancement enabled mobile devices to run powerful machine learning, artificial, and deep learning algorithms locally as well as in the cloud. This progression in hardware will bring deeper and more integrated machine learning algorithms to all the devices. However, to get the maximum benefit of ML, the cloud model is advisable. There is no hard, set rule of separation between local and cloud implementation of product and services. They work in conjunction.

Algorithms have become a pervasive and indispensable part of business. For example, Shell uses algorithms for oil exploration and achieving market competitiveness, while Microsoft and IBM use them to provide innovative products to their customers. In these changing times, companies have started using machine learning algorithms for internal efficiency as well as to deepen consumer loyalty and trust. For example, viewers of Netflix trust algorithms to get personalized content for their enjoyment. Similarly, Amazon's customers believe in the algorithms to get some useful products and recommendations for their customized purchases.

The fact is that the algorithms of today are extraordinary echelons of productivity and intelligence. Those that don't get on board soon with algorithms are at risk. Metaphorically, it is similar to working on typewriters in the age of computer processors and keyboards. To reach this point of wining the confidence of the masses, algorithms have traveled an extraordinary journey (see Figure 3-1). It is good to consider the evolution of ML algorithms. But before that, take a look at some widely used terms.

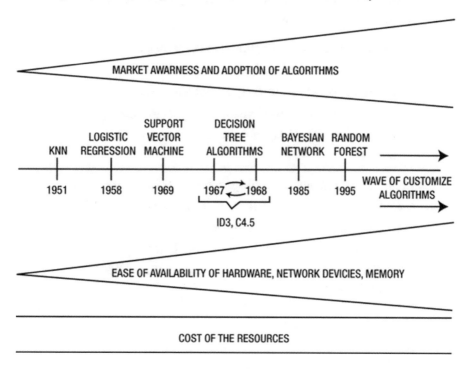

Figure 3-1. *The evolution of machine learning algorithms and their adoption*

Jargon Buster

- *Neurons and artificial neurons*: Nerve cells that transmit signals throughout your body to enable activities like breathing, talking, eating, walking, and even thinking. Most neuroscientists, or scientists who study the brain, believe that humans were born with all the neurons we would ever need. A link in a synthetic neural network is referred to as an artificial neuron. Similar to the biological brain network of the human body, artificial neural networks have a layered design and each network node (connection point) is capable of processing input and transmitting output to other nodes in the network.

- *Overfitting*: When a machine learning model predicts outcomes accurately for training data but not for new data. This is an undesired behavior. When data scientists use machine learning models to make predictions, they first train the model on a known data set.

- *Inference*: The act of feeding data points into a machine learning model to produce an output, such as a single numerical score. Other terms for this procedure include "operationalizing a machine learning model" and "putting a machine learning model into production."

Machine Learning Algorithm Classifications

Data science or statistical algorithms are further classified into multiple machine learning specific algorithmic categories:

- Supervised learning algorithms (label and output are both known)

- Unsupervised learning algorithms (label and output are not known)

- Reinforced learning algorithms (reward-based agent action)

- Semi-supervised learning algorithms (mix of supervised and unsupervised learning)

These algorithms in turn contain multiple sub-algorithms and types (see Table 3-1). For example, a few algorithms fall in the category of parametric, whereas others are nonparametric. In parametric algorithms, information about the population is completely known, which is not the case with nonparametric algorithms. Typically, parametric models deal with a finite number of parameters, whereas nonparametric learning models are capable of dealing with an infinite number of parameters. Therefore, when the training data grows, the complexity of nonparametric models increases. Linear regression, logistic regression, and support vector machines are examples of parametric algorithms. K-nearest neighbor and decision trees are nonparametric learning algorithms. These algorithms are computationally faster in comparison to their nonparametric companions.

As Table 3-1 depicts, there are many machine learning algorithms.

Table 3-1. *Machine Learning Algorithms*

Supervised Learning	Unsupervised Learning	Reinforcement Learning
Artificial neural network	Artificial neural network	
Bayesian statistics	Association rule learning	Q-learning
Case-based reasoning	Hierarchical clustering	Learning automata
Decision trees	Partitional clustering	
Learning automata		
Instance-based learning		
Regression analysis		
Linear classifiers		
Decision trees		
Bayesian networks		
Hidden Markov models		

Algorithms can be further grouped into four categories for convenience and practical reasons:

- Clustering

- Regression

- Classification

- Anomaly detection

This grouping is helpful in understanding the algorithms and providing clarity. You can find additional classifications and categorizations in the literature available for machine learning. However, I follow the previously mentioned categorization throughout the book. So, let's start the journey of exploring the wonderful world of algorithms with clustering.

Clustering

Clustering is the activity of collecting samples into groups according to some predefined similarity or dissimilarity. In simple words, in clustering, data in a particular cluster must be similar to the other members of that particular cluster (see Figure 3-2). Due to the peculiar properties of grouping similar samples, for example, it can be used to bundle customers into different market segments.

Figure 3-2. *Clustered data*

Some clustering types are mentioned here:

- *Hierarchical clustering*: Produces a tree of groups/clusters in which each node is a subgroup of its mother. It is a form of a parent-child relationship between clusters.

  - *Pros*: Preferable for detailed data analysis

  - *Cons*: Less efficient than non-hierarchical clustering

- *Non-hierarchical clustering*: The relationship between clusters is often left unsettled. Most non-hierarchical clustering algorithms are repetitive. They start with a set of original clusters and then repeatedly improve them using a reallocation arrangement.

  - *Pros*: Preferable when data sets are very large

- *Exclusive clustering*: An item belongs to only one cluster.

- *Overlapping cluster*: One item belongs to many clusters.

K-means is one of the most widely used clustering algorithms.

Applications and Use Cases for Clustering

Here are some use cases:

- Does grouping based on similar functionalities.

- Used for summarizing or reducing the size of large data sets.

- Customer segmentation.

- Image and video processing to identify objects in a video.

- Classification of plants, animals, and humans based on specific categories.

- Identify probable areas of oil exploration based on the type of seismic data.

When to Use Clustering

When you need to discover structure in the data sets, clustering is a good approach.

Regression

Regression is used to predict values. For example, this category of algorithms provides you with answers to questions such as, "what will the temperature be tomorrow" or "what was the final score of the soccer match." Regression algorithms fall under supervised learning. Regression analysis is used to estimate the connection among two or more variables.

There are hundreds of regression types. The main ones are
discussed here:

- *Linear regression*: A statistical modeling technique used
  to examine the relationship between a dependent and
  independent variable. It is one of the oldest types of
  regression.

- *Logistic regression*: A statistical modeling technique
  extensively used in industries for multiple purposes,
  including fraud detection.

- *Polynomial regression*: A type of regression analysis that
  deals with the association between the independent
  variable x and the dependent variable y, which is
  modeled as an nth degree polynomial in x. In turn, the
  polynomial is defined as an appearance of more than
  two arithmetical terms, particularly the summation of
  numerous terms that comprise dissimilar powers of the
  same variables. It is used for cross-validation.

- *Ridge regression*: A modeling technique used to deal
  with multiple independent variables that are highly
  correlated.

Here are the pros:

- Prediction and forecasting

- Used to find outliers

- Ease of use

- Uses data efficiently

- Provides support to business decisions based on data
  analysis

- Discovers hidden and new insights

Now the cons:

- Sometime outputs lie outside of the range

- On long ranges, assumptions are required

- Very sensitive to outliers

Applications and Use Cases of Regression

Some use cases:

- Forecasting

- Optimization

- Assessing risk in the financial services and insurance domains

- Analyzing the marketing effectiveness

- Demand forecasting in business and in government organizations

- Analyzing the effect of proposed radiation on tumors for reducing their size

When to Use Regression

When you need to predict and forecast values, regression is a good fit.

Classification

Classification is used to predict a category. For example, when an image needs to be classified as a picture of a human or a machine, the algorithm to do so falls under this category. It contains supervised types of algorithms. When you have only two choices, the classification is known as two-class or binomial classification. When more than two categories are available, the set of algorithms used for their classification is known as multi-class classification. For example, while answering the questions such as, "which car needs service most urgently"? Or "which flight goes from Delhi to Atlanta"? To answer these questions, multiple choices are available. These types of scenarios are subject to multi-class classification.

Differences Between Classification and Regression

Classification	Regression
Classification algorithms group the output into classes. For example, they are used to find the answers of the questions such as, "is this identified tumor cancerous or not."	Regression algorithms are used to predict the values using the training data. For example, it would be used in predicting the share price of a particular share of a company.
Disconnected and categorical variables are used in a classification problem.	Number and continuous variables are used in a regression problem.

The broader categories of classification algorithms are as follows:

- *Artificial neural networks (ANNs)*: Computational models that mimic human brain functionality. They are created on the basis of the structure of biological neural networks.

- *Decision trees*: Broadly, a decision tree is a support instrument. They provide tree-like graphs or models for decisions. They also explain the various probable significances of the decisions, which includes but is not limited to chance event outcomes, resource outlays, and usefulness. They are one of the ways to present an algorithm.

- *Ensemble learning*: A machine learning-based model where various learners are trained to solve the same problem.

Some examples of classification algorithms are as follows:

- Linear classifiers

- Support vector machines

- Quadratic classifiers

- Kernel estimations

- Boosting

- Decision trees

- Neural networks

- Random forests

- Naïve Bayes

Classification algorithms contain multiple sub-categories and therefore lots of algorithms. All the algorithms and categories have their own pros and cons. Here are some general pros:

- Super simple and easy to interpret and explain

- High accuracy

- Strong theoretical foundation regarding overfitting

- Easy correlation between data sets

Now the cons:

- Not very effective with huge data sets

- Easily over fit

- Hard to tune the parameters

- Takes time to build the model

Applications and Use Case for Classification

Some use cases:

- Video, image, and audio classification

- Web page classification

- Product categorization

- Forecast likely bank loan defaulters based on behavioral and financial history of the customers

- Identify customer churn

When to Use Classification

When you need to predict and forecast categories, classification is a good tool.

Anomaly Detection

An *anomaly* is defined as something that diverges or deviates from what is standard, normal, or expected. There are times when you need to find anomalies in an available data set. That "identified unusual" data point could help detect unique behavior (see Figure 3-3). For example, you could detect a change in employee behavior that points to a potential security breach committed by an employee. This activity would alert your employer to take corrective action before the damage happens. Anomaly detection is also helpful with fraud detection. For example, any exceedingly uncommon credit card expenditure patterns are flagged.

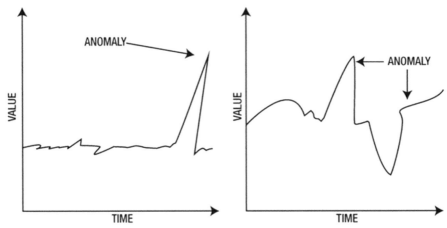

Figure 3-3. *Anomaly detection*

The method that anomaly detection takes is to learn from normal
actions or activities. In the previous examples, algorithms analyzed
historical data of non-fraudulent transactions and recognize anything that
is significantly different.

The broader categories of classification algorithms are the following:

- *Supervised anomaly detection*: A set of techniques
  that detect outliers in the labeled data sets. Labels are
  available for normal data and outliers.

- *Unsupervised anomaly detection*: A set of techniques
  that detect outliers in the unlabeled data sets. Labels
  are available only for normal data.

- *Semi-supervised anomaly detection*: A set of techniques
  that detect outliers in the unlabeled data sets. No
  labeled data set exists.

As anomaly detection algorithm contains multiple sub-categories and therefore lots of algorithms. All the algorithms and categories have their own pros and cons. Here are some general pros:

- No need to be supervised

- Easily adaptable in online mode

- Suitable for anomaly detection from temporal data

Now the cons:

- Computationally expensive

- Clusters data into groups of different densities, which leads to easy manageability

Applications and Use Cases of Anomaly Detection

- Detecting credit card and other financial fraud

- Detecting telecommunication and retail fraud

- Detecting faults

- Discovering unusual instances

- Identifying incorrect data

- Detecting network intrusions

When to Use Anomaly Detection

When you need to find unusual data points, anomaly detection is the tool to use.

Building a Machine Learning Model

Constructing a machine learning model can seem like an intimidating task, but with the correct tools and resources, it's a lot easier than you might think. I started by doing research on the best algorithms and techniques for data, then collected and prepared the data to guarantee its accuracy. At that point, tools like Python libraries like scikit-learn and TensorFlow, which build and train models, are very useful. The process is generally challenging, but also extremely satisfying. This approach helps explain machine learning, and also allows you to create something that could potentially have a real-world impact.

If you want to build a machine learning model of your own, don't be frightened to dive in and give it a try! If you need any guidance along the way, there are plenty of resources along with this book to help you out.

Selecting the Right Algorithm/Model for Your Requirements

Typically, model development and maintenance include multiple stages, starting from collecting data to preparing and staging it. Applying different machine learning techniques and algorithms to find the most suitable model for the given need is very important. Continuously tweaking the parameters of the algorithms based on changes in the data set and refining the outcome is foremost important. Traditionally, to accomplish all this, data scientists had to do lots of work. They had to code the model and select the appropriate parameters, including the runtime environment. Data scientists also have to train the model on data (including batch), monitor the process, and troubleshoot errors wherever required. Keeping track of all the steps in a complete cycle is monotonous, as the flow repeats itself iteratively.

Finally, data scientists, in collaboration with other teams, compare multiple models. They do so on the basis of parameters like accuracy and performance. Best performing models are selected and deployed. Multiple teams and individuals are involved, from validation to deployment. In a nutshell:

1. Business experts define the problems.

2. Based on that data, experts identify the sources of data and provide a mechanism to gather and store the data using processes, intelligence, experience, and technology.

3. Data scientists create actual models through the help of algorithms and then test and deploy the application or product. They do this using processes, intelligence, experience, and technology.

4. Business experts determine whether everything is working okay.

5. This complete flow happens in an iterative manner.

6. Iterative execution of the flow helps remove any errors and refine the model.

Using the right algorithm at the right place, time, condition, and scenario is very important. Also, associating algorithms with specific requirements that fulfill them effectively and efficiently is an art and a science. The following sections present the summary of the algorithms.

Approaching the Problem

To implement any machine learning algorithm, there are many well written, tested, flexible, robust, and efficient libraries available in the new generation of programming languages. They are also customizable.

Therefore, you can tailor them according to your needs. However, picking the best machine learning algorithm is a very subjective endeavor. It mostly depends on your requirements, tasks, domain, business needs, and available technical situations.

Moreover, selecting an algorithm is based on the problem someone is confronting. For example, if the requirements are to work on a text classification problem, then a support vector machine is probably a good choice because it provides accuracy and efficiency. Whereas for recommendation-based situations, decision tree algorithms would be good candidates for selection and proceeding. Thus, finding the best algorithm and method is a relative decision that's based on the domain and situation related to your specific requirements and it depends on the problem and business need.

Choosing the Correct Algorithm

When you have fewer options, making a decision is easy. For example, if you have continuous problem you need to solve, using the regression model is a straightforward choice, whereas if you have to select from binary options, using the logistic regression algorithm is advisable. However, the decision is not always this easy. We encounter multiple complex problems and requirements that we are supposed to resolve. Generally, the standard algorithm or customized/modified versions of them are applied to solve problems. Here are some best practices, guidelines, and standards that can definitely help you choose the right algorithm or model.

1. Data investigation and finding relationship between variables.

2. Rational choice and efficient comparison of algorithms and models.

3. Cross-validation.

4. Properly researched, carefully studied, purified data.

5. Tool selection, ease of use, and availability of infrastructure, talent, and other resources.

6. Determining appropriate objectives and business value.

7. Learning and developing flexibility, adaptability, innovation, and out-of-the-box thinking.

Step 1: Data Investigation and Finding Relationships Between Variables

While selecting an algorithm, knowing the nature of the data is very important, so that the appropriate algorithm can be attached to the data set. For example, if the business requirement is to analyze unstructured data available in the form of video and image files, the associating algorithms would have to efficiently handle unstructured and semi-structured data, such as text, time-series data, spatial data, graphs, and images. Appropriate selection of algorithms will never be possible if you do not know the nature of your data.

Data investigation is an unavoidable part of building a correct, effective, and efficient predictive model. To choose the right algorithm and model for your requirements, identifying the relationship and assessing the impact of the variables on each other and on the overall environment is required. To get a prefect model, the method and the parameters pertaining to that method must be selected appropriately.

Finding the best values in order to get the highest possible accuracy in a given data set leads to intensive data investigation and finding the relationship between the variables. Intuition and experience help in getting the best results. Typically, a data scientist trains a large number of models, looking at their cross-validated scores and putting some thought into deciding which parameters to try next. They also do proper clustering or grouping for best results. Multiple tools are available in the market that can be used for doing data investigation, including Microsoft Azure. However, manual methods and processes are also effective, provided the data set is less bulky.

Step 2: Rational Choice and Efficient Comparison of Algorithms and Models

One algorithm cannot fit all the requirements, so a logical, rational, and statistically supported (mathematics-driven) comparison is required. The analysis of different metrics like the statistical significance of parameters plays an important role. For example, decision trees are a popular learning algorithm for doing predictions and suggesting recommendations. Hence, they are widely used by enterprise practitioners due to their accuracy. However, despite their popularity and adoption across industries, decision trees should not thoughtlessly be pickled as the algorithm for every problem. Instead, you should always use the algorithm that best fits according to the characteristics of the data and the problem type.

Step 3: Cross-Validation

Cross-validation evaluates ML models by training multiple machine learning models on subcategories of the input data and assessing them on the matching subcategories of the data. Dividing data sets into two clusters or groups and cross-validating them is an excellent way to get the right model and algorithm. Cross-validation splits the training data into a number of partitions, commonly known as *folds*. Folds subcategories of data. After splitting, all the subcategories are trained except one (all-1).

The next step is to evaluate the model on the subcategories that were not used for training. This process is repeated multiple times (equal to the total numbers of folds), with a different subcategory kept for evaluation (and excluded from training) each time. Finally, the best performing model is selected. Cross-validation can take a long time to run if lots of data is used. Therefore, using the cross-validate model in the initial phase of building and testing is advisable. Cross-validation is often used to detect overfitting. Cross-validation is also one of the best ways to assess models that are used for prediction and forecasting.

Step 4: Properly Researched, Carefully Studied, Purified Data

A study of the historical performance of a model and algorithm in a similar situation is helpful. The performance of machine learning algorithms depends on the quality of the data; they are only as good as the data. Hence, improper data collection and cleaning methods will have a negative impact on your ability to build a good predictive, generalizable machine learning model. On the other hand, when carefully studied data is integrated with automated tools, this can provide excellent insights. Data cleaning can be helpful in identifying data quality issues related to records, features, values, and sampling.

Step 5: Tool Selection, Ease of Use, and Availability of Infrastructure, Talent, and Other Resources

Selecting a tool to implement an algorithm is a very important step. Also, ease of implementation, availability of proper talent, and infrastructure/ resources need to be considered before choosing an algorithm for a particular project. For example, the more data you have in an algorithm processes, the more accurate, efficient, and effective it becomes. So, selecting a tool that's capable of handling huge data sets becomes the most critical aspect. However, if you do not have the proper talent to use that tool, effectively the tool is of no use. Therefore, these interlinked aspects must be considered before making any decisions.

Step 6: Determining Appropriate Objectives and Business Value

Understanding the hidden features in the data and then improving on them by creating new features and eliminating irrelevant ones has a high effect on predictability. Machine learning algorithms and methods are meant to handle raw data and convert it into a rich feature space that can be effectively and efficiently exploited by companies for appropriate business purposes. Hence, finding the collection of features used to characterize the data that would better capture various complex characteristics of it, such as nonlinearity and interaction/interdependence between multiple features, is required. These are also important for the learning processes. Selecting an algorithm to determine how the objectives affect the business value is very important. Hence, while selecting an algorithm or model, this aspect must be also considered.

Machine learning algorithms must be selected based on business problems. For example, some business problems—like fraud detection, product suggestion/recommendation, spam email detection, and ad targeting—have "standard" machine learning formulations and algorithms with a proven track record in those specific situations. However, even for these well-known problems, there are lesser-known but more powerful formulations available that can lead to higher predictive accuracy. So, selecting the algorithm based on that knowledge, the business objectives, and research is key.

Step 7: Learning and Developing Flexibility, Adaptability, Innovation, and Out-of-the-Box Thinking

Some important business problems of our time—like fraud detection, product recommendation/suggestion, and advertisement targeting— are typically associated with standard machine learning algorithmic formulations. They are associated with specific formulations because

186

those formulations are reasonably successful. However, there are lesser-known but more powerful methods that have capabilities that could lead to higher predictive accuracy. Therefore, an innovative approach and out-of-the-box thinking is very important. Machine learning by nature is a very creative and experiment-oriented field, so flexibility and adaptability is an important parameter for success. Lastly, translating business requirements to implementation is an art and science, and it is the by-product of these qualities (flexibilities, adaptability, innovation, and out-of-the-box thinking).

Expert Opinion

"When a new technology is as pervasive and game changing as machine learning, it's not wise to let it remain in a black box. Opacity opens the door to error and misuse. Amazon's algorithm, more than any one person, determines what books are read in the world today. The NSA's algorithms decide whether you're a potential terrorist. Climate models decide what's a safe level of carbon dioxide in the atmosphere. Stock-picking models drive the economy more than most of us do. You can't control what you don't understand, and that's why you need to understand machine learning—as a citizen, a professional, and a human being engaged in the pursuit of happiness."

—Pedro Domingos, a professor at The University of Washington, and a leading researcher in machine learning. He authored a book called *The Master Algorithm: How the Quest for the Ultimate Learning Machine Will Remake Our World.*

A Review of Some Important Machine Learning Algorithms

When an algorithm is considered for business or project requirements, a few aspects always need to be considered. This includes usefulness of the algorithm in different critical business scenarios, frequency of its uses, and so on. Finding the answers to questions like, "how is this algorithm used in a specific project,?" "how efficient and effective is it?," "how easily would it be to implement it?," and "does this algorithm help achieve business competitiveness?" becomes very important.

I picked a few algorithms on the basis of their popularity and on their prospects. In the process of coming to a final conclusion, I asked multiple questions from the decision-makers, developers, data scientists, and business analysts. I collected opinions of data scientists, business leaders, and project managers from varied sources, including market research, technical and process document crunching, company news analysis, market projections, financial insights, and so on. This data is then analyzed before coming to a final conclusion. A couple of questions I asked of them include these:

1. Intensity of use in the industry and at different enterprises

    a) Poor

    b) Average

    c) Good

    d) Very Good

    e) Excellent

2. Future prospects

a) Dull

b) OK

c) High

d) Very High

e) Bright

The basis of my analysis is the primary source of data. The secondary sources were data available on the Internet, from university libraries, and from enterprise repositories. Some other sources included industry interviews, vendor briefings, insights from conferences, and product demonstrations given by companies. The case studies, whitepapers, research papers, technical articles, and historical performance of these algorithms in specific situations were also important sources of my research. In a nutshell, almost all the available quantitative and qualitative data was used for this purpose. My research is supplemented by the review and analysis of all secondary information available on the topic, which includes available technology specifications information, product attributes, governmental economic data and technical vision documents, and industry reports and databases from third-party sources.

User responses to these questions were recorded. This was validated by the other sources of the information. Also, insight was generated by the use of careful studies of reports, case studies, product documentations, and so on. On the basis of all this information, the future prospects of these algorithms was calculated.

The following sections discuss advantages, disadvantages, and applications of nine algorithms, along with other details, such as their history and creator. To provide practical insight, whenever possible, I include success stories. The top nine algorithms commonly used across industries are discussed.

The Random Forest Algorithm

The random forest algorithm uses a "catching" approach to create a group of decision trees with random subsets of data. Once the trees are created, their outputs are combined to make final predictions. The final prediction of the random forest algorithm is derived by either polling the results of all decision trees or by going with a prediction that appears most of the time in the decision trees. A random forest is essentially a group of a specific type of decision tree.

- Developed by: Tin Kam Ho in 1995. Its extension was developed by Leo Breiman and Adele Cutler.

- Type of algorithm: Classification/Supervised

- Intensity of use in the industry and enterprises: Good

- Future prospects in industries: Bright

- Why use this algorithm: Random forests algorithm can be used for classification and regression types of problems and requirements.

- When to use: When accuracy is important.

- Who would use the Random forest algorithm: Teams/enterprises/organizations who of online businesses and when categorization is important.

- How do you implement the Random forest algorithm: You can implement it multiple ways, and many tools are available. However, Apache Mahout and Microsoft Azure ML are popular choices.

- Applications: Click stream analysis: e-commerce companies are using random forest algorithms to analyze and predict customer purchases based on the users' click history and current patterns. It is also used for voice classification and identification. For example, Google used it for Siri.

Advantages of Random Forest

- It is good at maintaining accuracy when there is missing data and for resisting outliers.

- It is efficient at saving data preparation time, as it does not require any input preparation.

- It provides benefits of implicit feature selection, as it estimates which variables are important in the classifier.

- It is generally effective at operating on large data sets. When the data set is large, random forest algorithms are advisable, because it is difficult to build bad random forest algorithms.

- It has a higher classification accuracy.

- Multiple random forest algorithms can be grown in parallel.

- It can handle thousands of variables without variable deletion.

Disadvantages of Random Forest

- It is easy to use this method practically, but its theoretical analysis is difficult.

- It often tends to underestimate the high values and overestimate lower values. Also, it does not predict beyond the range of response values in the training data.

Success Stories of Random Forest

Baidu is a Chinese web company. Their artificial intelligence software called WRAP-CTC is used to improve speech recognition capability in their E2E speech recognition program called Deep Speech 2. The software recognizes English and Mandarin. In some cases, the software performed better than humans. It is very difficult to say exactly which algorithm they use internally for achieving these functionalities in the software program. However, for classification and speech recognition related functionalities, random forest algorithms are one of the choices along with other machine learning algorithms. The software is available to the open-source community on GitHub. Source: Baidu research website (`http://research.baidu.com/institute-of-deep-learning/`)

Netflix is one of the pioneers in adopting machine learning technologies. They took a holistic and integrated approach toward ML. Netflix is using multiple algorithms for their business. Netflix is applying these algorithms to improve their customer experience.

The Decision Tree Algorithm

The decision tree algorithm is a decision support tool/algorithm that uses tree-like graphs to provide decisions. It is a branching methodology that demonstrates possible outcomes of a decision based on some condition. A decision tree is a simple depiction of classifying instances. Decision tree machine learning algorithms are one of the most widely used techniques for supervised machine learning.

A decision tree creates a type of flow chart, which consists of a node (known as a leaf) and a set of decisions to be made based on the node, known as branches. The internal node (non-leaf) represents the attribute (labeled with input features). The arcs coming from a node are marked with a feature and used to represent each of the possible values or outcomes of the feature. Each leaf of the decision tree is marked with a

class or a probability distribution over the classes. The classification rules
are represented through the path from root to the leaf node. The leaf and
branch structure form a hierarchal representation that mimics the form of
a tree. Decision tree is one of the most widely used algorithms for machine
learning. It mirrors human decision making more closely than other
algorithms. The three basic algorithms that are widely used in decision
tree ecosystems are ID3, C4.5, and CART.

- History and development: Decision tree was developed
  by J. Ross Quinlan while he was associated with the
  University of Sydney. His first algorithm for decision
  tree creation was called the Iterative Dichotomiser
  3 (ID3).

- Type of algorithm: Classification/supervised.

- Intensity of use in industry: Good.

- Why use this algorithm: Decision trees can be the
  best candidates for linear decision boundary types of
  problems.

- When to use: When accuracy and speed are important.

- Who would use the decision tree algorithm: Teams/
  enterprises/organizations of online businesses and
  when categorization/grouping is important.

- How do you implement the decision tree algorithm:
  You can implement it in multiple ways, as there are
  many tools available. However, Apache Mahout and
  Microsoft Azure ML are popular tools that implement
  this algorithm. However, it depends on the project
  scenario and its requirements.

Advantages of Decision Trees

- It is fast, accurate (compared to other classification techniques), simple, and inexpensive to construct and classify unknown records.

- Generates understandable and easily interpretable rules.

- Gives a clear picture of which fields are most important for classification and predictions.

- C4.5, which is a decision tree and extension of ID3, is used in multiple industries for its ability to provide quick qualification and high precision.

- CART, another important decision tree algorithm, is very efficient in generating a regression tree, which is used in many industries where quick decision making is required, like the e-commerce industry.

- It can handle numerical and categorical data. This quality gives it an edge over the other algorithms because most of them are specialized in analyzing data sets that have only one type of variable. For example, relationship rules can be used only with nominal variables, while neural networks can be used only with numerical variables.

Disadvantages of Decision Trees

- Performance is not good if there are lots of uncorrelated variables in the data set.

- Computationally expensive to train, as it forms many subtrees, which are compared.

- Generally easy to use, but making them, particularly huge ones with numerous divisions or branches, is complex. It is a time-intensive endeavor.

Applications of Decision Trees

- Used for multiple purposes during decision making. For example, widely used for risk identification and analysis.

- Used for process optimization. For example, Shell uses it for their oil and gas-based process optimization.

- Efficient and effective in classifying objects, products, and goods, therefore many e-commerce organizations use it. Some of the leading organizations that use these algorithms are Amazon and Flipkart.

- Used in the financial domain for options pricing. Also, financial institutions like banks use these algorithms for classifying loan applicants to separate good risks from bad ones.

- Used in remote sensing-based applications for pattern recognition.

Success Stories

The stock market is based on supply, demand, and economy growth. In the stock market, prediction is very important and several mathematical and statistical techniques are typically applied to stock market data to get better results and insights. Traders and analysts use an array of different approaches for predictions based on financial and customer landscapes, which are derived from fundamental technical and psychological analyses.

In the era of machine learning, multiple decision tree machine learning
algorithms are used for price and share prediction. Typically, the traders
and brokers use software powered by a combination of algorithms, such
as LR and SVR, along with decision tree algorithms to get effective and
efficient results.

Logistic (Classification) and Linear Regression

Logistic regression algorithms are used to model the relationship between
dependent and independent variables. They also look at the fitness of the
model as well as at the significance of the relationship of the dependent
and independent variables being modeled. In linear regression, the
relationship between the dependent and independent variables is linear,
and this assumption is not made in logistic regression.

Regression models are developed and built on the basis of historical
data that contains dependent as well as independent variables.
Typically, a dependent variable is a feature or quality that's measured
using independent variables. Once this (generalization of dependent/
independent variables) is done, this information can be used for future
predictions using new cases.

Linear regression is used when the response is a continuous variable.
Determining a figure of product sales or finding/predicting company
revenue are examples. Logistic regression is used when prediction of
categories is required (for two or more levels), such as predicting the
gender of a person or the outcome of a cricket match on the basis of
historical data. There are multiple types of regression algorithms, apart
from logistic and linear. A few of them are:

- Polynomial regression

- Stepwise regression

- Ridge regression

- Lasso regression

- Elastic-net regression

However, logistic and linear are general-purpose algorithms and the most common ones used in the industry. Others are specialized and used for specific purposes.

- History and development: Regression techniques originate from the method of least squares, which was proposed by Legendre in 1805 and by Gauss in 1809. However, the term "regression" was used by Francis Galton in the 19th century to explain a biological phenomenon. Later, Udny Yule and Karl Pearson extended his work to a more general statistical context.

- Type of algorithm: Classification/supervised.

- Intensity of use in industry: Good.

- Future prospects in industry: Bright.

- Why use this algorithm: Regression algorithm is best suited when prediction of the continuous values is desired and classification is not that important. Also, it is used for optimization of the result.

- When to use: When you need to determine factors that influence output. Regression algorithms can be used for impermanence studies as well.

- Who would use the regression algorithm: Any individual/team/enterprise that is interested in establishing relationships among data types. Logical regression is used by anyone who wants to generate insight from large, but simple, data sets.

- How do you implement the regression algorithm: You can implement it multiple ways. For example, all major statistical packages and libraries provided by machine learning programming languages can do regression, including F# (Microsoft), R, and Python. Also, Classias, which is a collection of machine learning algorithms for classification, is used for its implementation apart from Apache Mahout and Microsoft Azure ML.

Advantages of Logistic Regression

- Regression-based forecasting techniques are used for research and analysis, to predict what will happen in future. Thus, a lot of companies are using these algorithms to forecast what will happen in the next quarter, year, or even farther into the future. Regression-based analysis serves as a forecasting tool that can provide insight into how higher taxes, for example, would be managed.

- Regression and forecasting algorithms are also used as decision support tools. They bring a scientific and statistical angle to businesses management by reducing large amounts of raw data into actionable information.

- Forecasting and regression can lend experimental support to management intuition. These algorithms can potentially correct management decisions when the evidence indicates otherwise. For example, a retail store manager may believe that extending shopping hours will greatly increase sales. A regression analysis, however, may demonstrate that longer hours do not significantly increase sales to justify the increased operating costs, such as additional employee labor.

- Large data sets have the potential to uncover valuable new information and provide wisdom about businesses. However, the data does not speak for itself, making analysis necessary. Regression and forecasting techniques can yield new insight by uncovering patterns and relationships that managers had not previously noticed or considered.

Disadvantages of Logistic Regression

- While solving problems, sometimes models become complicated, due to the complexity of the mathematical equations. When creating models, multiple equations are required.

- Linear regression is only concerned about the linear associations between dependent and independent variables. It accepts in theory that there is a straight-line association among variables. However, this is not always the case and proves to be incorrect in many scenarios. For example, it would not be accurate to apply linear regression between the income and the age of an employee.

- Linear regression assumes that data is independent, which is not always true. So, a careful approach and strategy would be needed when this algorithm is considered for implementing critical requirements. For example, assuming a group of students in a class are similar in multiple ways—for instance they may come from the same area, they have the same teachers, and so on. However, they may also have differences, such as culture, religion, level of intelligence, and financial

status of their parents, which could affect their overall
behavior. Hence, they are not completely independent.
In the situation like this, regression algorithms-based
prediction can be wrong.

Applications of Logistic Regression

- Used for multiple purposes during decision making.
  For example, it is widely used for risk identification and
  analysis.

- Used for process optimization. For example, Shell uses
  this for their oil and gas-based process optimization.

- Efficient and effective in classifying objects, products,
  and goods; therefore many e-commerce organizations
  are using these algorithms. Some of the leading
  organizations that are using these algorithms are
  Amazon and Flipkart.

- Used in the financial domain for options pricing. Also,
  financial institutions like banks use these algorithms to
  classify loan applicants and separate good risks from
  bad ones.

- Used in the remote sensing-based applications for
  pattern recognition.

Success Stories

PayPal is a respected financial company that provides third-party services
for financial transactions. It is necessary for them to come up with fraud
prevention technologies on a regular basis and then continue to refine
and advance their use of complex algorithms to manage extraordinary

amounts of data efficiently and effectively. PayPal uses a combination of linear and neural network machine learning algorithms to collate and analyze huge amounts of data intelligently. Also, they extract insights about buyers and sellers from available data mountains with the help of intelligent algorithms. Their collected data contains network information, machine-based information, and transactional data. They use all this data to safeguard their customer's financial identity and transactions. In a nutshell, the smart way of using algorithms equips them in their pursuit of the ultimate brand objective, trust. PayPal also uses neural net machine learning algorithms to implement deep learning techniques in their organizations.

Source: Extracted from 2015 article from *InfoWorld*. Based on the option of Dr. Hui Wang, Senior Director of Risk Sciences for PayPal.

Support Vector Machine Algorithms

Support vector machine algorithms analyze data and find patterns. For example, given a set of training examples, each marked in one of two categories, the SVM training algorithm builds a model that assigns new examples in one category or the other, making it a non-probabilistic binary linear classifier. SVM creates a representation of the examples as a point in space, which is mapped in a way so that the examples of the separate categories are divided by a clear gap that is as wide as possible. New examples are then mapped to the same space and predicted to belong to a category based on which side of the gap they fall.

- History and development: Developed by Vladimir N. Vapnik and Alexey Ya Chervonenkis in 1963 in its original form. However, using nonlinear classifiers by applying the kernel trick to maximum-margin hyperplanes, which is more specific to machine learning, was developed by Bernhard E. Boser, Isabelle M. Guyon, and Vladimir N. Vapnik in 1992.

- Intensity of use in the industry and enterprises: High, as it is among the best performers for classification related tasks. Works equally well with text and genomic data.

- Type of algorithm: Classification/supervised.

- Industry prospects: Bright.

- Why use this algorithm: It's good for binary classification types of problems.

- When to use: For simple classification and when speed is a priority.

- Who would use the SVM algorithms: When the practice sets are exposed well before the decision. E-commerce companies use it for classification.

- How do you implement these algorithms: You can implement them multiple ways, as many tools are available. However, SVMlight and its associated tools/ algorithms/methods are specific to SVM (for academic and scientific purposes) implementations. For commercial purposes, you can use Microsoft Azure ML, Apache Mahout, and so on.

Advantages of SVM

- Flexibility in the choice of the threshold form.

- Robustness toward a small number of data points.

- You can do almost anything with the right kernel (tricky!).

- SVM works very well when the structure is not known.

- Performs better when the number of dimensions is higher than the number of available samples.

Disadvantages of SVM

- Although SVMs have good generalization performance, they may be terribly slow during the test phase. This problem needs to be addressed in a proper manner to get good, optimized solutions. By using clean and accurate data, this would be optimized.

- The most serious problem with SVMs is the high algorithmic complexity and extensive memory requirements of the required quadratic programming in large-scale tasks.

- If the points on the boundaries are not informative (e.g., due to noise), SVMs does not do well.

- Can be computationally expensive.

Applications of SVM

- Handwritten character recognition.

- Facial recognition.

- Applied in multiple scientific fields for categorization purposes. For example, protein and genome classification.

- Applied in the field of medicine for classification of tumors. For example, grouping cancerous cells of a particular type.

- Text and hypertext classifications.

- Used by e-commerce companies to compare shopping sites. For example, extracting product and pricing information from many sites.

Success Stories

Netflix uses multiple machine learning algorithms for many purposes—popularity and rating prediction are a couple of them. By using these algorithms, they improve rankings. Typical choices include logistic regression, support vector machines, neural networks, decision tree-based algorithms, and gradient boosted decision trees (GBDT). Netflix uses its wealth of source data, innovative measurement techniques, and experiments to create a culture of a data-driven organization. Data has been part of Netflix's culture since the company was conceptualized. They call it consumer (data) science. Broadly, their prime goal is to provide a consumer science approach in an innovative way to their members (customers) effectively and efficiently.

Naïve Bayes Algorithms

Naïve Bayes falls under the classification category of algorithms. It is not a single algorithm and signifies a group of algorithms. All the algorithms of this group share the same set of properties and principles. A Bayesian network is a graphical model that encodes probabilistic relationships among variables of interest. Naïve Bayes algorithms are one of the most commonly used groups of algorithms in the machine learning world. Although Naive Bayes is based on the simple principles of the Bayes theorem, it is very effective in scenarios like spam detection.

For example, a vegetable may be considered to be a carrot if it is orange, short, and about 5 inches in length. A Naive Bayes classifier considers these features (orange, short, 5 inches in length) to contribute individually to the probability that the vegetable is a carrot, regardless of any correlations between features. But generally, features are not always independent. Treating problems in this way is often considered a shortcoming of the Naive Bayes algorithm. This is one of the prominent reasons that it's called naïve. In short, the Naïve Bayes algorithm allows you to predict a class, given a set of features using the theory of probability.

- History and development: The Bayes theorem was named after the mathematician Reverend Thomas Bayes, who lived between 1702 and 1761. Bayes work is a landmark in binomial distribution. After Bayes' death, his friend Richard Price edited and presented his work in 1763. However, in machine learning, Naive Bayes classifiers are a family of simple probabilistic classifiers based on applying Bayes theorem with strong (naive) independence assumptions between the features.

- Intensity of use in the industry and enterprises: High, as it is among best performers for classification-related tasks. Works equally well for text and genomic data.

- Type of algorithm: Classification/supervised.

- Industry prospects: Bright.

- Why use this algorithm: When the features and variables are conditionally independent of each other, Naive Bayes is a good choice. Also, it is simple to implement.

- When to use: For simple filtering and classification through machine and algorithms.

- Who would use Naive Bayes: E-commerce, software products, and manufacturing companies.

- How do you implement Naive Bayes: You can
  implement it multiple ways, as many tools are
  available. However, implementing it through Apache
  Mahout is common. Other tools include Microsoft
  Azure ML, Weka, jBNC, and so on.

Advantages of Naïve Bayes

- It's comparatively simple to comprehend and build.

- It's effortlessly trainable, even with a small data set.

- It's fast.

- It's not sensitive to irrelevant features.

Naïve Bayes algorithms are especially effective in the following
conditions:

- If you have a moderate or large training data set.

- If the instances have several attributes.

- Given the classification parameter, attributes that
  describe the instances should be conditionally
  independent.

- Equally effective in text classification and spam
  filtering.

- Recommender systems apply machine learning and
  data mining techniques to filter unseen information
  and can predict whether a user will like a given
  resource.

- Online applications.

- Simple emotion modeling.

Disadvantages of Naïve Bayes

- They assume every feature is independent, which isn't always the case. Dependency often exists among variables.

- Computation intensive.

Applications of Naïve Bayes

- Sentiment analysis: Used at Facebook to analyze status updates expressing positive or negative emotions.

- Document categorization: Google uses document classification to index documents and find relevancy scores, that is, the PageRank. The PageRank mechanism considers the pages marked as important in the databases that were parsed and classified using a document classification technique.

- Also used for classifying news articles about technology, entertainment, sports, politics, and so on.

- Email spam filtering: Google Mail uses Naïve Bayes algorithm to classify emails as spam or not spam.

- Credit approval and target marketing.

- Medical diagnosis and treatment effectiveness analysis.

Success Stories

Microsoft SQL server 2005 uses the Naive Bayes algorithm for classification in analysis services (SSAS). It is used for predictive modeling there. The main reason behind that is the algorithm is good at computing the conditional probability between input and predictable columns. In doing so, the algorithm assumes that the columns are independent . However, the downside of this is that the algorithm does not consider any dependencies between the different columns, even if they exist.

The algorithm is used in analysis services to achieve data mining capabilities because of its lower computational qualities in comparison to other available algorithms. SQL Server 2005 uses this algorithm in its "analysis services" engine along with other algorithms to do initial explorations of data. The algorithm provides the results of initial stages to another set of algorithms, which they use to create additional accurate mining models. In the later stages of analysis of data mining, more computationally intense processing is required (where Naive Bayes is weak) to provide more accurate results. Apart from this, it is used by several e-commerce companies to do classifications, including Amazon, Tesco, and so on.

k-Means Clustering Algorithms

k-means clustering algorithms are used to discover categories. k-means clustering is an investigative data analysis technique/algorithm. It is a non-hierarchical way of grouping different objects. By definition, cluster analysis is the technique of grouping a set of objects. In general, clustering allows you to put objects in the like groups (known as a cluster). For example, retail stores categorize or cluster similar objects or things in their stores, such as women's wear and men's wear. Also, online e-commerce sites like Amazon groups and showcases personalized products to their customers by combining personal information with purchase histories.

k-means clustering performs clustering tasks using direct logic. First, it randomly selects the k (the number of partitions) points in the available data set. After that, it maps every outstanding sample in the data to the closest "mean." After that, for each cluster or group, a different mean is calculated by taking the midpoints mapped to that cluster. These different new means will lead to an altogether different mapping of the data to the clusters. This process continues iteratively until it reaches a reasonable partitioning of the data.

- History and development: James MacQueen developed it in 1967. It is also referred to as Lloyd's algorithm, because Stuart Lloyd in 1957 used it for pulse-code modulation at Bell Labs.

- Type of algorithm: Clustering/unsupervised.

- Intensity of use in industry: Average.

- Future prospects in industry: Normal.

- Why use this algorithm: k-means clustering algorithms are useful when data grouping is required.

- When to use: When a large number of groups are present for classification.

- Who would use the k-means: Groups or individuals that have a good understanding of algorithms.

- How do you implement the k-means: You can implement it multiple ways, as many tools are available. However, implementing this using Apache Mahout is one of the common ways. Other tools include Microsoft Azure, IDL Cluster, MATLAB k-means, and so on.

Advantages of k-Means

- Generally, k-means provides faster results when the order of time complexity is linear for the given data set. It works great if clusters are spherical. It does not work well with non-circular cluster shapes. Spherical k-means is an unsupervised clustering approach in which all vector lengths are normalized to 1, resulting in differences in direction but not in magnitude between the vectors being compared. The opposite is true for non-circular cluster shapes.

Also, to get better results, the number of cluster and initial seed values need to be specified beforehand.

- Provides easily interpretable clustering results.

- Fast and efficient in terms of computational cost.

- Excellent for pre-clustering in comparison to other clustering algorithms.

- Typically, faster than hierarchical clustering (if k is small).

- Items are automatically assigned in the k-means algorithms.

- The simplest algorithm and easy to analyze and implement. All you need to do is identify k and run it a number of times.

Disadvantages of k-Means

- Strong sensitivity to outliers and noise. Sometimes it is difficult to predict the k value.

- Doesn't work well with non-circular cluster shapes. Also, the number of clusters and initial seed values need to be specified beforehand.

- Low capability to pass the local optimum.

- For global clusters (wider and distributed), it doesn't work well.

- Different initial partitions can result in different final clusters.

- It does not work well with the original raw clusters of different density and size. Reorganization of data according to need and then separating it into logical groups is required for better results.

- A fixed number of clusters can make it difficult to predict the k number.

Applications of k-Means

- Used in search engines like Bing and Google to cluster similar web pages to make searches relevant.

- It can be applicable to any scenario whereby someone wants to make groups of similar things from a randomly spread collection of things. For example, in enterprises, document clusters are required as they have to categorize a lot of documents on various different topics (Java, ERP, and ETL) for several purposes.

- Applying k-means algorithms to a group of pictures and categorizing them based on similar tests of the user.

Success Stories

Salesforce, through its Salesforce1 Platform, uses the k-means algorithm to cluster records of customers and users. For example, one of their clients, Acme Inc., sells different cooling and heating equipment and has over 100,000 customers. They use the Salesforce1 Platform, which in turn uses k-means for splitting their customers into groups and profiling them. They can better market and sell their products to each group. This algorithm also helps them understand profiles of the group members.

    Source: `https://developer.salesforce.com/page/Machine_`
`Learning_With_Apex`

Apriori

Apriori is a "separate and concur" class of algorithm used for unsupervised learning. It helps you determine recurrent item sets in a given data set. Apriori works well when big transitional data is available. For example, Amazon uses it to provide recommendations to their customers based on the crunching of huge data done by Apriori algorithms. This class of algorithms actually tries to find patterns in the data set. It takes historical transitional data of users (typically stored in the data stores) and identifies frequently occurring items or sets of items that can then be formulated to some meaningful rule.

For example, if someone purchases a laptop, there is high possibility that they will also purchase a carry bag. Apriori algorithms are the best candidates for identifying and predicting these type of transactions.

- History and development: Developed by Agrawal and Srikant in 1994. Apriori is basically designed to function on database stores comprised of transactional records.

- Intensity of use in the industry: High, as it is among the best performers for classification related tasks. Works equally well for text and genomic data.

- Type of algorithm: Classification/supervised.

- Industry prospects: Bright.

Advantages of Apriori

- Efficient and effective when dealing with large item sets.

- Easy to implement.

- Provides real insight on affinity promotion (which product customers may purchase based on analysis of their previous purchase behavior).

Disadvantages of Apriori

- Assumes transitional database is memory resident.

- Requires many database scans.

- Slow.

- Higher runtime for execution.

Applications of Apriori

- For generating insight about which products are likely to be purchased together and providing suggestions to the customers.

- For IntelliSense/suggestion for auto completion of text (search).

- To carry out customer analysis by applying empirical analysis on consumer purchase behavior. Also, applied to identify the frequency of consumer behavior or inclination of particular purchases.

- Used for market basket analysis and grouping sets of products. Also, used for finding regularities in shopping behavior.

- For predicting crime behavior by doing network forensic analysis.

Success Stories

Apriori is a typical traditional predictive analysis machine learning algorithm that finds association rules through association analysis techniques. Association analysis is a technique to uncover the unseen patterns and correlations. For example, through association analysis, you can understand which products and services customers are looking to purchase and then can predict future behavior of the customers.

SAP HANA is using this algorithm for their predictive analysis by processing large chunks of in-memory data in real time. Also, companies like BestBuy, Amazon, and eBay are using the Apriori algorithm for multiple purposes. For example, to give personalized recommendations and suggestions based on clicks.

Markov and Hidden Markov Models

In Markov models, the state of the model is directly visible to the viewer or observer, so the state change probabilities are considered as the only parameters. However, in the Hidden Markov model (HMM), the observer cannot observe the state directly. In HMM, the output dependent on the state is visible.

Markov models are probabilistic sequence models. A Markov model runs through a sequence of states emitting signals. If the state sequence cannot be determined from the single sequence, the model is said to be hidden. Hidden Markov models are used to recognize patterns, for example, in handwriting and in speech analysis. In a Markov model, the system being modeled is assumed to be a Markov process with hidden (unobserved) stats.

- History and development: Andrey Markov developed the model in 1906 in the form of a Markov chain. The Hidden Markov model was developed by L. E. Baum and coworkers in the second half of the 1960s. Speech recognition may be considered the first application of HMM.

- Type of algorithm: Classification/regression.

- Intensity of use in industry: Good.

- Future prospects in industry: Bright.

Advantages of Markov Models

- Fairly readable and understandable.

- Well studied and established algorithm.

- Useful in problems having sequential steps.

- Can handle variations in record structure like the following:

  - Optional fields

  - Varying field ordering

Disadvantages of Markov Models

- Can only observe the output from states, not the states themselves.

- Not completely automatic.

- May require manual mark-up.

- Size of training data may be an issue.

Success Stories

Absolutdata works on lawsuit-recommendation problems, which provide solutions to common questions such as, how much time a particular case will take, the overall cost of a case, and several other questions like this. Around 15 million lawsuits are filed in the United States on a yearly basis (2016 Data, Source: Common Good). Lawyers face the problem of taking the appropriate case that suits their credentials and determining which ones they can win. Absolutdata is developing an analytic system for categorizing the characteristics of lawsuits based on data from 20+ years of cases and lawsuits, which the company pulled from public repositories, such as PACER. The enterprise then applies text analytic techniques to digitize the words into major concepts. After that, it uses machine learning algorithms, such as Hidden Markov models, to find correlations in the data.

Bayesian Networks and Artificial Neural Networks (ANNs)

Bayesian network is based on the theory of probability, precisely on the Bayes theorem. Bayesian networks establish relationships between events in the context of probability. In a nutshell, they map the existence of certain events' influence over the probability of different events occurring.

Whereas neural networks are a computational method, Bayesian networks are based on a huge assembly of neural elements roughly modeling the way a biological brain works and resolves problems. The artificial network of connected electronic components works the same way the large clusters of biological neurons work in the human brain.

216

In general, artificial neural network (ANN)-based algorithms are a machine learning approach that models human brain and consists of a number of artificial neurons. Artificial neurons in ANNs tend to have fewer connections than biological neurons. Each neuron in ANN receives a number of inputs. An activation function is applied to these inputs, which results in an activation level of a neuron (output value of the neuron). Knowledge about the learning task is given in the form of examples, called training examples.

An artificial neural network is specified by three things—the neuron model, which is the information processing unit of the NN, an architecture, which is a set of neurons and links connecting neurons, and a learning algorithm, which is used to train the NN by modifying the weights in order to model a particular learning task correctly on the training examples.

- History and development: Named after Thomas Bayes, who proposed the Bayes Theorem. His friend Frank Rosenblatt in 1958 proposed this name.

- Intensity of use in industry: High, as it can solve problems involving categorical and continuous valued attributes.

- Type of algorithm: Supervised.

- Future prospects: Bright.

- Why use this algorithm: ANN algorithms are good for multi-class classification problems. They also perform well when non-linear boundaries are encountered. For achieving human-like decision making, neural networks have been a good choice. They are also used in chatbots and robotics. For achieving data classifiers functionality, neural networks are a good choice.

- When to use: When you have sufficient time, processing power, and technology to simulate parallel processing, neural networks are a good choice. You can use an artificial neural network when you have the time to train the system. Additionally, if you have a sufficient array of processors with which you can go significantly parallel, neural networks make a great deal of sense.

- Who would use the artificial neural network: Industries, enterprises, and organizations that need to do forecasting, data analysis holography, and apply neuro-dynamic factors.

- How do you implement the artificial neural network: You can implement it multiple ways, as many tools are available. Most of the machine language targeted programming languages support it. However, many specific tools are also available in the market, including NeuralWorks, NeuroShell Predictor, Xerion, and so on.

Advantages of ANN

- Neural networks are quite simple to implement.

- Neural networks often exhibit patterns similar to those exhibited by humans. Therefore, it is appropriate to use these algorithms to mimic human tasks.

- Artificial neural networks provide effective and efficient solutions in feature selection, density estimation, classification, and anomaly detection.

- ANN is good for online learning, as it is capable of reflecting the information of new instances on a model very efficiently by just changing the weight values.

- ANN methodology proves itself superior as a modeling technique, in comparison to classical statistical modeling methods, especially for data sets showing non-linear relationships.

Disadvantages of ANN

- Takes a long time to be trained. Neural networks cannot be retrained. If you add data later, it is almost impossible to add to an existing network.

- Handling time-series data in neural networks is a very complicated.

- Generally needs a large data set due to the training time being significant.

Applications of ANN

- Speech, face, and image recognition.

- Natural language processing.

- Recommendation systems.

- Classification and clustering.

- Pattern association and forecasting.

- Optical character recognition.

- Stock-market prediction.

- Navigating a car.

- Applied in intelligent security systems.

Success Stories

Baidu uses Hierarchical Recurrent Neural Networks for their video paragraph captioning program. It generates one or multiple sentences (based on the situation and demand) to label a realistic video with appropriate caption.

Also, for their "conditional focused neural question answering with large-scale knowledge bases program," which is commonly known as CFO, different variants of neural network algorithms are used. Compology uses neural networks for waste removal. Netflix and Amazon also use it.

Machine Learning Application Building

As machine learning becomes an integral part of our life (knowingly or unknowingly), creating the application around the technology is not an easy task. From getting to know the requirements of stakeholders or deciding on the purpose of the application, to deploying it, the application goes through various stages. Here are the various stages of application building:

1. *Understanding the requirements*: This involves breaking down the business perspective into workable realities. Basically, this step is all about understanding the end users and what they expect from the application when the application is in their hands. For example, is the application meant for kids, teenagers, and adults, or is it broader, like Facebook or Netflix?

2. *Doing user research*: As part of the practical research, about 5 or 10 percent of people who could potentially be users of the product or application must be interviewed before starting the work. This provides insight about what they need, how the application/product must feel, and so on.

3. *Coming up with the basic flow*: At this stage, a user's journey is planned. The first step is to sign up, the next can be introduction of the application, then searching the products, and finally completing the task.

4. *Creating an informational architecture*: How should the application look? What information should be most visible? What can come next? Where should a certain task be placed and why?

5. *Getting stakeholder feedback*: After each major step, the designer, developer, and architects (through a coordinator check with the stakeholder) check if any course correction is required.

6. *Creating a design prototype*: A prototype of the end product is created to get approval from the stakeholders.

7. *Developing the application*: At this stage, the application is created.

8. *Testing*: The application is tested so that the developers can be sure that it works on all sorts of environments with the same efficiency. The best practice is to do testing after each major step.

9.   *Deploying and releasing*: The application is finally
     released into the market.

10. *Maintaining the application*: Maintenance of the
     application takes place here. This is an ongoing
     process.

Following the Agile methodology is one effective way to implement
effective machine learning projects. Let's take a look at this methodology.

Agility, Machine Learning, and Analytics

Traditionally, analytics and analytics-based data visualization are created
using a waterfall approach. In a waterfall approach, a client/team/expert
gives the requirements to the IT team in the so-called *requirement phases*
of the process and verifies the final outcomes with the requirements at
the end of the phase, called *implementation*. In Big Data, however, the
Agile approach is much more suitable, whereby the stakeholders and the
IT team work together to build a solution in a more collaborative fashion.
An Agile process is dynamic and time-boxed in nature. Also, visibility
and overall transparency is critical to this process. The following sections
provide a brief summary of the Agile approach and its comparison to the
waterfall approach.

Agile methodologies are an iterative, incremental, and evolutionary
way of developing project. Agile works in short iterations that are typically
one to three weeks long. The goal of every iteration is to provide user-
valued features (what actually matters to the users). Each developed
feature must be fully tested during the development of a specific iteration.
The Agile development methodology is not about creating dull examples
that have no value in the real world. Also, one of the expectations when
implementing the Agile methodology is to automate routine processes
whenever possible. Test automation is possibly the most important among

idea. Agile exists in multiple variants and types, like extreme programming,
Scrum, LeanUX, Kanban, ScrumBan, and so on. All these approaches have
their own benefits, suitability, and drawbacks. Scrum, Kanban, and XP are
the most common.

Why Do You Need Agile?

Analytics and machine learning projects are complex in nature, and if
you track them well you could potentially develop them better. If not, you
could experience the following drawbacks:

- The project is overbudget.

- The schedule has slipped.

- Some expected functionality was not implemented.

- Users are unhappy.

- Performance is unacceptable.

- Availability of the warehouse applications is poor.

- There is no ability to expand.

- The data and/or reports are poor.

- The project is not cost-justified.

- Management does not recognize the benefits of the
project.

These happen because of:

- Lack of experience.

- Ambitious and unrealistic goals.

- Domain knowledge and subject matter expertise
don't exist.

- Unrealistic expectations from the project.

- A focus only on technology not on business.

- A lack of collaboration.

- A lack of specialized skills.

- A lack of multiple skills in the project/organization.

- Difficulties in implementing the Agile approach.

- Tool support: There aren't many tools that support technical practices such as test-driven machine learning development.

- Data volume: It takes creative thinking to use lightweight development practices to build high-volume data warehouses and BI systems. You need to use small, representative data samples to quickly build and test your work.

- Lack of knowledge: Not enough knowledge of the end-to-end Agile development practice.

Show Me Some Water Please

The waterfall software development lifecycle, or SDLC, is a traditional methodology. In the waterfall development methodology, every stage of a product's lifecycle takes place sequentially. It is known as waterfall because progress flows steadily downward through these phases like a waterfall. The waterfall software development model operates in a phased manner and is often rigid. Typically, it contains phases like Define, Develop, Test, and Implement.

Making changes to waterfall projects is comparatively costly. Whereas in Agile, the changes to requirements can be generally incorporated at any point in the process. Even at the advanced stage of development, Agile is willing to accept and accommodate changes. Therefore, this is less costly.

Agile's Disadvantages

- It requires stakeholders' availability, involvement, and cooperation on a continuous basis.

- It requires customers to have clear priorities and visions, which sometimes is not possible. Noncompliance sometimes leads to going off-tracking and the failure of the project.

- Senior and experienced programmers with decision-making capabilities are required during the implementation process. Hence sometimes, inexperienced programmers may feel uncomfortable if experienced resources are not available to help.

- It is hard to quantify the total effort, estimation, and cost due to the qualitative nature of the process.

- It's difficult to execute in distributed teams.

Agile Usage

- Best suited when the deadlines are aggressive.

- Good for a project with ambiguous requirements. It is excellent in accommodating changes during the latter part of a project.

- Good for complex projects.

- Good for innovative projects.

Some Machine Learning Algorithm-Based Products and Applications

With the help of machine learning, Artificial intelligence (AI) is attaining a status where chatbots like ChatGPT-4 (see Table 3-2) are using large language models with supervised and reinforced learning techniques to clear medical and legal examinations. This sounds threatening—until it becomes clear how human and machine intelligence cooperate. For instance, take the chess grandmaster Garry Kasparov. His loss to the IBM supercomputer Deep Blue altered his game. In a match with an opponent he had earlier beaten hands down, Kasparov drew when they both played using computers. Kasparov's takeaway was, that for humans and machines to team up successfully, the quality of the dealings is key. This is distinctly borne out by the results of an online chess tournament where a couple of laypeople won against grandmasters, all of them playing using computers.

The process of interacting with AI offers scope for the most transformative productivity improvements by producing augmented intelligence for business.

Machine supervision of human action works better in closed systems dealing with duplication. The reverse holds true in systems open to dynamic, outside conditions involving out-of-box thinking. Machines don't have the human competence to visualize, anticipate, feel, and judge, all of which are vital. Businesses will naturally seek to influence the human ability to decode insight into data-driven processes that feed machine learning.

Some jobs will, of course, go as they have been doing since the Industrial Revolution. Manufacturing and services can, however, be brought at far lower costs if human engagement with AI changes from skepticism to acceptance. Economies will become accustomed to the efficiency improvements if there is no robust political pushback. That is where lawmakers need to step in to educate electorates that AI is not a zero-sum game when it comes to working. Governments also need to be proactive in producing pathways for labor redeployment. The end of work is nowhere in sight.

There are multiple applications and products available that use machine learning and artificial intelligence technologies to assist humans. Their spread is everywhere, from our daily life to the workplace, from spaceships to the chessboard. Table 3-2 shows a snapshot of some products.

Table 3-2. *Products That Use Machine Learning and Artificial Intelligence*

Product	Company	Description
Bard	Alphabet	An AI chatbot and ChatGPT competitor that uses LaMDA, or the Language Model for Dialogue Applications.
		Google Bard was introduced in response to rival AI systems like ChatGPT. It employs a combination of machine learning and natural language processing to provide precise, beneficial answers to users' inquiries while simulating interactions with a human. These technologies may be most helpful for smaller businesses who want to provide their clients with natural language support without recruiting large teams of support or for improving Google's search tools.

(continued)

Table 3-2. (*continued*)

Product	Company	Description
		Microsoft announced that ChatGPT, sponsored by OpenAI, would power the upcoming iteration of the Bing search engine. Google/Alphabet has not integrated Bard into their newly released solutions. LaMDA is not used in its place. The current set of Google solutions will employ the Pathways Language Model API, which was introduced in 2022. Developers may access Google's foundation models through this, train or fine-tune them using their own data collection, and then scale up apps from there.
		AI for Developers with Maker Suite is another service provided by Google. This low-code tool will help you write code based on developer-provided examples.
		Selected users will be able to access these solutions during a special opening.
		Additionally, Google has announced the launch of AI-driven solutions in its Workspaces productivity package, which includes Gmail, Google Meet, Docs, Sheets, and Slides. These solutions will enable users to summarize, interpret, proofread, collaborate, and quickly create text, audio, and visual material.
		Furthermore, using the Generative AI App Builder, organizations and governments may design their own chat interfaces and digital aids driven by AI. They will be able to complete transactions as well. By doing this, Google will give businesses the know-how to deploy the fundamental AI models on their own data sets, a corporate search engine solution that can work with those data sets, and conversational AI skills to generate content from the data.

(*continued*)

Table 3-2. (*continued*)

Product	Company	Description
ChatGPT	OpenAI	ChatGPT is an artificial intelligence chatbot developed by OpenAI and launched in November 2022. It is built on top of OpenAI's GPT-3 family of large language models and has been fine-tuned using both supervised and reinforcement learning techniques. ChatGPT is a sisterly model to InstructGPT, which is trained to follow an instruction in a prompt and offer a comprehensive response. The same techniques are used in InstructGPT. Microsoft integrated OpenAI's models into its Bing search engine
Siri	Apple	The voice/personal assistance application from Apple. The application got its name from a Norwegian woman who was the co-creator of Siri known as Dag Kittlaus. Apple also introduced a male voice option a year after Siri's launch. Siri launched in October 2011.
Cortana	Microsoft	Microsoft's personal assistant application. It was launched in April 2014. Cortana is named after the 26th-century female artificial intelligent character in the hugely popular Halo videogame franchise.
Deep Blue	IBM	Deep Blue is an AI chess playing machine. IBM's Deep Blue is known for its chess fight with Chess grandmaster Garry Kasparov. In February 1996, Deep Blue became the first machine to win against the ruling winner. This grand chess-playing machine is heavily dependent on massive parallel processing and artificial intelligence-based technologies and was named on the basis of a naming contest conducted by IBM.

(*continued*)

Table 3-2.   (*continued*)

Product	Company	Description
Jarvis	Facebook (Mark Zuckerberg)	This is newest on the block. As a new year's resolution, Mark Zuckerberg embarked on a personal challenge and built this simple artificial intelligence application to control different things around his house. The home assistant took its name from the science-fiction film *Iron Man*'s assistant. It is powered by the voices of Morgan Freeman and Arnold Schwarzenegger.
Alexa	Amazon	Echo is an Amazon product. It is a combination of wireless speaker and voice-command device. It uses a woman's voice for communication, named Alexa. Amazon was trying to replicate the concept of an all-knowing computer on the TV series *Star Trek,* which was activated with a single voice-based command. The name Alexa was chosen out of respect for the Library of Alexander, which was one of the largest libraries in the ancient world.
Watson	IBM	Watson is a cognitive system from IBM. It took its name from the first CEO, Thomas J. Watson. Watson as a cognitive system took part in the popular quiz show *Jeopardy* and won. This advanced software/system is being used in the treatment of lung cancer, and is doing predictions for multiple other areas using machine learning algorithms. Companies like Capgemini use it to provide efficient solutions to their clients. Now, the cut version of Watson, called "Baby Watson," is also available.

(*continued*)

Table 3-2. (*continued*)

Product	Company	Description
Donna	Incredible Labs	Donna took its name from the fictional character Donna Moss. Donna Moss works as a White House assistant in the TV show *West Wing*. Incredible Labs was acquired by Yahoo in 2013. Yahoo decided to shut down its services in February 2014.
Google Home	Alphabet	Google Home highlights the fact that it's intended for the home. It is a voice-activated WiFi speaker powered by the Google Assistant. It also works as a smart home control center. The philosophy behind it is to provide an assistant to the whole family. Google Home will be used to provide entertainment to the entire house. This voice assistance can smoothly manage everyday tasks. Google Home is different from Amazon's Alexa, as it is virtually a Google in your hand.

Algorithm-Based Themes and Trends for Businesses

Change is a reality. Society, technology, process, business, and, moreover, life is changing at a rapid speed. New thoughts are accepted and old thoughts are debunked. For example, just a few years back, no one thought that driverless cars and intelligent clothing could become a reality. The stories related to them were in science fiction movies and novels. However, driverless cars are a reality and are all set to hit the road. These real examples of breakthrough technologies are making their way from the laboratory to the real world very quickly. Also, business leaders and consumers are ready to rapidly adapt to these fast changes. The following sections give some realistic insights and business themes and trends that could impact the way we do business and live our lives in the coming years.

The Economy of Wearables

The inclination toward intelligent Internet of Things (IoT) wearables started with smart watches and wrist bands. Now they have grown to a level where they have become part and parcel of one's life. Now we have smart eyewear, smart clothes, clip-on devices, and helmets. Clothing brands and electronics companies are coming up with the more intuitive smart clothing that connects to the cellular network to access or transmit enormous amounts of data generated by humans. IDC reported that the worldwide wearable devices market would reach 101.9 million units by the end of 2016 and around 214 million units in 2020. IoT, Big Data analytics, and machine learning algorithms create and continue to generate a huge opportunity for businesses across sectors related to consumer products.

New Shared Economy-Based Business Models

Businesses no longer have to own assets (for example, Uber does not own a single taxi). AirBnB has not a single owned hotel, but they changed the economics of the market like no other. Lyft, a company that provides application-based ride-sharing facilities in over 200 cities in the United States, is working in the model that would change the philosophies of car ownership. They are providing car polling services and encourage people to use them instead of owning a car. This is becoming a major transportation trend.

In a thought-provoking article written by John Zimmer, cofounder of Lyft, he projected that by 2025, private car ownership in main U.S. metropolitan areas will end. These trends are not limited to the United States. Across the world, businesses, people, and entrepreneurs are adopting these ideas. For example, in India, people are opening up their homes to vacationers through Oyo (an Internet-based hotel and property booking platform). They provide a facility to convert your property to a holiday destination. This strategy is compelling hostels and private guesthouses to rework their business strategies.

Connectivity-Based Economies

The dynamic and anytime-anywhere connectivity between devices, machines, and other resources across the globe is the backbone of today's businesses. In comming times more and more devices are connected to each other intelligently. And, further it would create an intelligent network among devices to communicate. This intelligent network is a recent development. Now a new economy is created around this, as doing business anywhere in the world is as simple as doing it in your neighborhood. For example, Practo, a Bengaluru (India)-based company, is now known as the world's largest appointment booking platform. It handles roughly over 40 million appointments annually.

New Ways to Manage in the Era of the Always-On Economy

Technology-enabled services are evolving and taking place in our life so quickly that we actually take them for granted. For example, standing in the queue to book railway tickets or withdraw money from a bank was the reality sometime back. Things have changed so rapidly that people have started believing that "net-banking" and "online booking" have always been part of our lives.

Online banking, withdrawing money from ATMs, mobile banking, and digital wallets have changed the traditional ways of money transactions. The driving forces behind this digital economy are transaction cost, speed, ease of use, time savings, and security. In-app payment solutions like Paytm, Apple

Pay, Android Pay, and proprietary multiple retailer-based payment solutions are invading our economy at the speed of light. Retailers provide innovative solutions that are integrated with robust backend processes to permit customers to do safe and seamless transactions.

Macro-Level Changes and Disrupted Economies

In the past few years, we have seen that businesses and their policies have been impacted by changes in geopolitical environments such as Brexit and the crisis in the Middle East and their impact on the world (for example, fuel prices). Regulatory changes also affect businesses. Examples include changes regarding Sarbanes-Oxley, Solvency II, the demonetization in India, as well as the proposed diesel cab ban in Delhi. Natural disasters and diseases and illness such as tsunamis, earthquakes, and the spread of Ebola in Africa or Zika in South America also affect businesses.

These macro-level deviations are beyond anyone's control and disrupt the world and businesses. Enterprises, companies, organizations, and governments are working on multiple strategies to mitigate these problems and provide effective solutions. As most of these require manipulating data in effective ways, machine learning plays a central role. Machine learning, (algorithm-based), along with Big Data analytics technologies, are at the heart of these macro-level solutions and can heal disrupted economies.

The Marriage of IoT, Big Data Analytics, Machine Learning, and Industrial Security

IoT's marriage with machine learning and cognitive computing is evolving and is interesting to watch. The duo (IoT and machine learning) already started driving innovation across businesses. The amalgamation of machine learning, IoT, and Big Data is slowly becoming an integral part of IT infrastructure and innovation.

Businesses, as well as general users, are extensively adopting intelligent algorithm-based connected devices. This is one of the biggest driving forces behind increased collaboration and productivity. This hyper-intelligent connectivity across levels will potentially expose everything that's connected to the Internet in an enterprise, so security becomes very important. Also, this forces enterprises to adopt severe safety protocols. They understood that if the required security measures are not followed, disaster will ensue. Examples such as Dyn DDoS attacks have showcased to the world and, hence to enterprises, that unsecured IoT can be manipulated and breached.

The automobile industry also promises to become a security battleground between manufacturers, users, and developers. As a greater number of smart parts become affiliated with vehicles, they can easily be manipulated and hacked. Moreover, with driverless cars also poised to hit the roads soon, security breaches in this case could eventually end up causing physical damage. As self-driven cars become a near-time reality, automobile hacks also have become the talk of the market. Examples of this includes cars being held for ransom, which could be done by obtaining the location of the car for hijacking. This could also lead to a question of liability between the software vendor and automobile manufacturer, which will have long-term implications on the future of connected cars. Having mentioned all this, it is definitely worth watching the future in this regard. In today's globalized world, businesses anywhere can be affected and need to stay attuned to market changes and align their models accordingly.

Startup Case Study: Belong

Traditionally, most hiring happens through job portals. The candidate-selection process goes like this: The candidate needs to be active on the job portal and then recruiters fetch their CV from there and supply them to the appropriate companies based on their understanding of the candidate's profile. They organize the candidate's interview with interested companies. Finally, based on the interview results, the candidate is selected or rejected. This is a time-consuming process and does not guarantee the candidate's trustworthiness. It does not provide any insight into the behavioral traits of the candidate. Companies and recruiters want to know that the candidate is being truthful about their records. But mostly they have no clue. The current process is unable to answer these questions/concerns. Now machine learning is changing everything.

Companies are also facing lots of challenges to select the right candidate from the market because of the limited availability in competitively talented markets. Recruiting costs and the time to hire is a big concern as well. Therefore, recruitment firms are facing increasing pressure to overcome these roadblocks. Hence, they are looking for a new set of technologies, processes, and capabilities to overcome these challenges and establish themselves as market leaders.

Bengaluru-based startup Belong chose machine learning and Big Data technologies to make a difference in this space. Their innovative way of using machine learning is helping companies achieve what they want. They connect an employer with a potential employee. They are enabling this connection to the next step, which is beyond skills and experience. They are trying to synchronize the values and culture of the employee and employer.

To make this happen, Belong, through Big Data and machine learning technologies, analyzes the behavior and responses of the candidate, which are available on platforms such as Facebook, Twitter, Quora, GitHub, blogs, and more. To analyze the candidate's likes and dislikes, they use that information for employment, to fit them in the perspective culture. This helps create a more holistic profile of a candidate, which is then matched using machine-learning algorithms to relevant companies and jobs. Belong's proprietary predictive analytics platform identifies the "DNA" of each candidate's profile—the most suited ones are featured on the first page of results, much like a ranking. The company's algorithm ensures that no two companies see the same set of candidate profiles for the same role.

For the complete story, see Subramanian Senthamarai Kannan/ December 3, 2016, published on LinkedIn.

Industry 4.0: IoT and Machine Learning Algorithms

Wikipedia defines industry 4.0 as the current trend of automation and data exchange in manufacturing technologies. It includes cyber-physical systems, the Internet of Things, and cloud computing. Industry 4.0 is all about connecting everything centrally and using it in a better way through algorithms. This includes services, products, and matters that a company might not provide itself or outsource. In Industry 4.0, computers and generally intelligent processing and automation will be integrated in an entirely new way. The systems (including robotics) connected remotely to information systems powered by machine learning algorithms would learn and control the automated system with very little input from human operators.

This section considers the bigger ecosystem of Industry 4.0 from a technical perspective, which includes but is not limited to machine learning technologies, analytics, and IoT. These technologies complement each other. For example, IoT-based technologies are used to share simple information with third parties and connected systems. Whereas through cloud-based portals, end users can access all the data of collaborating parties and systems. Analytics and machine learning is used to make sense of this data. Ultimately, with the use of IoT, analytics, and machine intelligence, many previously unavoidable production processes, stepping stones as they were, can now be skipped. This has created space for the company to review their existing business models and tune them to deliver customer service at the price of a mass product.

Implementing Industry 4.0 systems will require a robust information
technology system that must have the capacity to process and analyze
a huge amount of data. Also, a technical infrastructure and process is
needed to record the transmission of the data and information exchange
24/7. The Industry 4.0 model is very useful in dangerous working
environments, where the health and safety of human workers is at stake—
their quality of life will be improved dramatically with the use of it.

With the Industry 4.0 model-based techniques and procedures,
manufacturing companies can control their supply chain more efficiently
because data is collected, analyzed, and processed at every level though
automated connected systems. This will enhance the manufacturing and
delivery processes. Computer control could produce much more reliable
and consistent productivity and output. Proper implementation of the
industry 4.0 technical ecosystem helps businesses increase revenues,
market share, and profits. From agriculture to retail, the Industry 4.0
models and IoT are changing the way companies in many industries do
business. Here are the areas where the Industry 4.0 model has showcased
its potential:

- *Agriculture*: One of the impacts of implementing the
  Industry 4.0 model in agriculture is installations of
  automated and IoT-based devices in agriculture-
  based products (tractors and cropping machines).
  Through automated systems, farmers can collect data
  about their crops in real time. With cloud, analytics,
  and machine learning techniques, that information is
  converted into insight. The results are used in multiple
  ways to optimize yields.

- *Healthcare*: Connecting the healthcare industry
  through automated systems means not only more
  efficient businesses, but it also means better service
  for the patient. For example, by connecting an MRI
  machine to the Internet and the information systems,
  hospital employees get notifications when their help
  is needed.

- *Manufacturing*: This is the biggest industry being
  impacted by Industry 4.0. Manufacturers across the
  world invest around $70 billion on IoT and Industry 4.0
  solutions. This enables factory workers to not only see
  when a part of equipment needs repair or modification,
  but it also provides insight on how to make the entire
  system work more efficiently.

- *Energy*: The combo of Industry 4.0, IoT, and machine
  learning technologies is changing the way energy
  companies do business. Energy and utility companies
  across the world, for example PG&E, are beginning
  to use smart technologies. Because of the smart and
  effective communication through the devices, energy
  and utility companies can better predict demand, spot
  outages, and schedule repairs.

- *Transportation*: From supply-chain logistics to public
  transit, the combination of Industry 4.0 and IoT
  solutions is being used to augment transportation
  in many ways. For example, by connecting shipping
  vehicles with sensors to monitor temperature,
  enterprises can help deliver goods, especially food, in a
  safe condition. Sensors and machine learning-enabled
  software can be used to collect data in an automated

fashion, which can help the driver handle the vehicle in a manner that helps save fuel. In the future, connected, efficient, effective, and smart infrastructure will also work with other connected systems to help reduce traffic and prevent accidents and other harmful incidents.

Review: Generative AI: A Miracle Lead by Machine Learning Technologies

OpenAI owns ChatGPT, the generative artificial intelligence-based chatbot that has already taken the world by storm. However, ChatGPT is only one example of how generative AI is being utilized to enhance results and productivity. ChatGPT provides accurate responses to queries in a conversational language that is human-like. Additionally, both the technology and use cases are rapidly developing. Simply defined, generative AI employs algorithms to process data and produce fresh results. Several tech firms have begun incorporating generative AI into their internal workings or client products. Fundamentally, generative AI offers a completely new way to communicate with artificial intelligence. It enables users to produce original text, graphics, and other content from text-based prompts and is based on pretrained, big language models.

One of the common ways to use ChatGPT is to incorporate it into Chatbots. Hence, a lot of innovations are happening around this area. These innovative chatbots are currently being used for internal inquiries as well as customer support, distilling product or HR policy manuals into clear, short responses. For instance, Einstein GPT, created by Salesforce, enables customers to create customized content throughout the Salesforce ecosystem. It may generate personalized emails, targeted content for marketers, customized customer service responses, and even auto-generated code for developers. As another example, high-level discussions with Indian clients about using generative AI for end-user interaction across industries have begun at SAP, a German business software corporation.

The market for generative AI is worth $7.9 billion globally. According to a survey by Acumen Research and Consulting, it is anticipated to increase by more than a third annually on average, to $110.8 billion by 2030. According to Gartner research, generative AI is expected to produce 10 percent of all data by 2025 and 20 percent of test data for consumer-facing use cases.

ChatGPT in the Corporation

In 2019, Microsoft made a billion-dollar investment in OpenAI, becoming one of the company's earliest sponsors. After ChatGPT was introduced, it followed this up with a $10 billion investment that was more significant. The technique would find applications across industries, from insurance assessments and financial analyses to medicine development and fashion design, because of the nature of generative AI. Basically, generative AI begins generating productivity and many more application cases in practically every industry imaginable. For instance, in a hybrid mode of work, productivity tools with generative AI integration, like Teams, can assist in summarizing, transcribing, and tracking meeting outcomes. Or AI on papers can create summaries and articles using your own data.

The broader technology and developer communities see generative AI as having enormous promise. In order to grasp the syntax algorithms that are used with generative AI, it is necessary to build new competencies and skills in fields like content moderation, security, development, coding, and contextual knowledge. A boatbuilder tool was recently released by conversational chatbot provider Gupshup, which integrates GPT-3 (version three of the generative pretrained transformer model) to create sophisticated enterprise chatbots. These chatbots are a lot tougher. Because queries have to be phrased a certain way in order for the bot to comprehend and react, its method of operation is slightly different and easier. Additionally, responses are much more articulate and written in well-formed English, making it nearly seem as though you are speaking to a human. This not only improves the client experience but also helps establish trust.

The adoption of ChatGPT technology is super-fast. Recently Pegasystems also introduced generative AI capabilities through its Pega Infinity low-code platform. Pega is creating these features so that users can execute activities using straightforward natural language prompts, such as "generate a report," "refine this offer copy," or "build an application," using generative AI in conjunction with organizational governance. Improving platform engineering's speed, intelligence, and usability will boost user productivity.

Risks with ChatGPT

Businesses need to make sure that their generative AI models are trustworthy and transparent, and that they adhere to or challenge legal constraints. As these models must be regulated at the application level, businesses must also invest in creating the required infrastructure and hiring trained staff to support their development and upkeep. Large volumes of data, including potentially sensitive personal and corporate data that needs to be protected, are a key component of generative AI. Enterprises must also make sure that the models can be seamlessly integrated with their current systems and solutions. Businesses can gain from using this technology in three ways: automation, augmentation, and acceleration. It does, however, present a unique set of difficulties.

There may not be enough room for error in generative AI models for use cases demanding accurate calculations. Training these models on data sets that are copyright-protected can provide a number of problems, including the exposure of private information to outsiders. Additionally, enterprise use cases demand governance of generative AI to include constantly updating and changing enterprise-specific information. Additionally, there are issues with the possible production of offensive or hateful content.

One possible response to these issues is to implement generative AI with "humans in the loop" as part of the deployment process. For instance, in call centers, human agents can use AI-generated outputs instead of end consumers who consume them directly. Utilizing AI-generated code advice, which utilizes a "pair programming model with the generative AI in the navigator seat," is another intriguing application.

Trustworthy AI

The standard of the input that is fed into the system is crucial for ensuring that generative AI produces the proper kind of outcomes. When it comes to generative AI, the essential decision may depend on what it generates, making the industry's discussions about trustworthy AI and responsible AI even more important. Of course, the data is the most important factor. The data set doesn't lack anything in terms of algorithms. In other words, even the most brilliant algorithm won't work without the necessary data set.

In fact, the requirement to preserve corporate data has fortified Google to unveil a Generative AI app builder that will permit businesses and governments to run searches.

The Audio and Video Links

1. Pedro Domingo's talks at Google, "The Master Algorithm."

   Source: https://www.youtube.com/watch?v=B8J4uefCQMc

2. How to read the genome and build a human being.

    Source: `https://www.ted.com/talks/riccardo_`
    `sabatini_how_to_read_the_genome_and_build_a_`
    `human_being`

Before Winding Up

There are two final things for you to consider:

- Tesla makes a car that's 100 percent auto-pilot
  ready. Self-driving cars can improve our lives in the
  following ways:

  – Reduced carbon emissions

  – Lives would be saved as thousands of people die every year in
    car accidents (1.24 million) because of driver error

  – Reduced traffic congestion

  – More free time due to reduced traffic

  – Increased productivity

  – Mobility of people will improve

  – No more hunting for parking spaces

- The market for artificial intelligence and virtual reality
  will grow as adoption of smart technologies accelerates,
  but people also risk being cocooned in silos, unaware
  of opposing ideas and a diversified view of the world,
  says an Ericsson report on future consumer trends.

Summary

This chapter discussed some important algorithms and their uses. It also
provided some guidelines for using algorithms and machine learning
models in effective and efficient ways. While discussing the important
aspects of algorithms, the chapter provided success stories associated with
particular algorithms/models/techniques. The end of the chapter included
some vital machine learning-based trends and their impact on businesses.

Mind Map

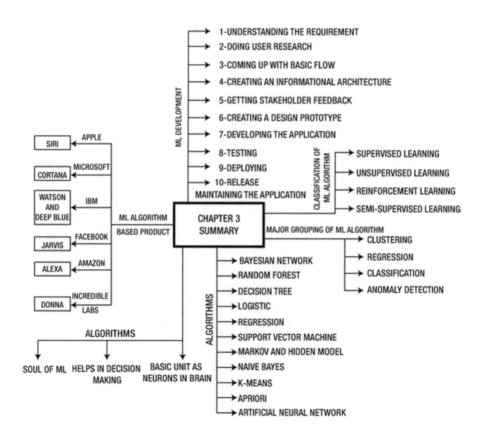

CHAPTER 4

Technology Stack for Machine Learning and Associated Technologies

Dr. Patanjali Kashyap[a*]

[a] Bangalore, Karnataka, India

Machine learning is a large and evolving field. It is full of potential and there are enormous possibilities to exploit it. The last few chapters explored some of the important and relevant aspects of machine learning.

At all levels, technology plays a crucial role because, without it, (almost) nothing is possible. Business strategies are made in the boardroom but when it comes to realization, technology is the enabler. Technology contributes to making a product or application and helps with its marketing, including physical or virtual supply chains. The lion's share of technology happens throughout the lifecycle of the product or application, during the development, maintenance, and support phases.

Due to the nature of the technologies involved in machine learning ecosystems, such as IoT, Big Data analytics, and cloud and cognitive computing, there is a natural overlap of technologies and technical

© Dr. Patanjali Kashyap 2024
P. Kashyap, *Machine Learning for Decision Makers*,
https://doi.org/10.1007/978-1-4842-9801-5_4

discussion. For example, if someone wants to discuss data analytics, this subject is appropriate in all discussions of its associated technologies. The IoT technology stack and Big Data analytics are both part of it all.

Before adopting or developing IoT and machine learning-based products, platforms, or services, industries must assess, create, or revisit their company's strategy. Planning and strategies must be the top-most priorities. There is a reason for this, as it relates to almost everything, from product conceptualization and design to sourcing and production (manufacturing). It is also very important when implementing effective sales and services. Industries must fine-tune their virtual and physical logistics and supply chain management systems, so that they can securely collect and respond to data from customers and suppliers. We are in an era where even the products themselves collect the data and transmit it to places where it is required in an automated way.

Going from traditional to data-first strategies is difficult initially, but it is required to stay competitive in the market. Also, it necessitates the development of advanced analytic capabilities. Netflix is the most commonly cited example in this case. To capture, explore, and exploit the significantly available economic opportunity that exists in the fields of IoT, Big Data, and machine learning, a new technology infrastructure and mindset are required. They allow companies to fast-track the time to market for smart, connected products and operations. IoT enables a range of capabilities and components that will empower industries to achieve the following:

- Deploy applications that monitor, manage, and control connected devices.

- Collect, process (via Big Data analytics), and analyze (via machine learning techniques) machine and sensor data in a business context.

- Secure connectivity between devices and real-time data streams.

- Provide effective device/sensor management and enable remote device updates.

- Create an application environment that supports rapid, fast, continuous, iterative IoT-based solution creation.

- Integrate with third-party systems efficiently.

- Use augmented reality (AR) for next-generation marketing, selling, servicing, and training in dynamic industrial environments.

Let's accept the fact: the technology stack is key.

Software Stacks

Any software application can be developed with the use of a technology stack, as it is the foundation for any engineering work. When selecting a technology stack for building an application/product, a careful approach is required, because revising the technology stack is generally difficult. This chapter discusses multiple technology stacks available for machine learning and their associated fields. It includes a comprehensive view of the machine learning technology stack. This chapter is confined to information technology specific details only, due to the scope of the book and the chapter.

This chapter also discusses the technology offerings from multiple vendors, including Apache, IBM, Microsoft, and others whenever relevant. Additionally, the mapping between different layers and technologies is described. Technology stacks are generally linked to specific concepts and their associated ecosystems. For example, IoT is associated with one kind of technology suite, whereas machine learning and Big Data are associated with another. However, for practical reasons, such as overlap of technology (the same set of technologies are applicable to realize multiple concepts on the ground level), business need, implementation, financial dependencies, and client demand, most of the time, the reality is different. Therefore, this chapter provides a holistic and integrative view of technology stacks. Having said that, wherever possible, it also provides technology-specific information. Some generic technical concepts are also described. For example, MapReduce is described in detail in this chapter.

Chapter Map

The comprehensive model discussed in Chapter 1 contains multiple layers and each layer is somewhat dependent on the other layers for input and output. Hence, overall the model is a layer of layers. Each layer or sublayer deals with a specific technology. However, most of the time overlap among technologies exists. In this chapter, I extend that model and provide a detailed view of it. I go to the level of "technical mapping" and describe the technical detail of each layer. For example, IoT is mostly about getting data from multiple devices and sensors and transmitting it to the cloud or to an on-premise infrastructure for further utilization and processing. After that, Big Data technologies take control and, with the help of a specific technology stack, deal with the challenge of storing, managing, processing, and making sense of that data. If required, they present the processed data in a proper way to the wider audience. Also, the Big Data analytics technology stack passes its inputs to the machine learning frameworks to achieve intelligence from the processed data. However, you can associate Big Data technologies to part of a specific IoT stack. The same is true with machine learning, Big Data analytics, and cognitive computing.

A few important points about the structure and content of the chapter.

- *Technical discussion*: There is overlap of the technical discussions. However, this happens only when it is required. For example, data gathering and networking technologies are discussed during the explanation of Big Data and the IoT technology stack. Processing technologies are discussed under the Big Data technology stack. For completeness, these concepts are again touched on under the connector layer of machine learning. The same is true with processing/store technologies under data processors and store layers of machine learning.

- *Rule of thumb*: If a concept is discussed in detail earlier, the chapter does not go into the details again. Recall that brief descriptions of some important machine learning frameworks, libraries, and tools are provided in Chapter 2. If you are interested in knowing about the technologies go back to the Big Data section while reading the machine learning technology stack.

- *The purpose of discussion and the structure of the content*: The technology stack discussed in this chapter can be visualized in two ways.

  – *Layer-specific disconnected view*: Layer-specific technologies are discussed. For example, Big Data analytics is treated as one layer. Technologies related to Big Data analytics are mentioned in that section. So, if you just want to know the about the Big Data technology stack, you can refer to that section only, by following the Data Acquisitions ➤ Analytics ➤ Machine Learning ➤ Presentation Layer hierarchy. Similarly, if you want to learn about the ML technology stack, follow the Connector ➤ Storage ➤ Data Processing ➤ Model and Runtime ➤ Presentation Layer hierarchy.

  – *Composite-connected view*: This provides a
    connected view. It does not go into the details of
    the sublayers and treats layers as components of
    the comprehensive model.

Before going into the details of the technology stack, let's look at
the concepts and technology map shown in Table 4-1. This is a tabular
representation of which concepts appear where in this chapter.

Table 4-1. *Concepts and Technology Map*

Technology Stack	Layer Name	Layer Discussed in Detail	Technology and Concepts Discussed
Internet of Things (IoT)	• Device and sensor layer • Communication, protocol, and transportation layer • Data processing layer • Presentation and application layer	• Device and sensor layer • Communication, protocol, and transportation layer	Sensors, devices, gateways, and communication technologies

(*continued*)

Table 4-1. (*continued*)

Technology Stack	Layer Name	Layer Discussed in Detail	Technology and Concepts Discussed
Big Data analytics	<ul><li>Data acquisition and storage layer</li><li>Analytics layer</li><li>Machine learning layer</li><li>Presentation and application layer</li></ul>	<ul><li>Data acquisition and storage layer</li><li>Analytics layer</li><li>Presentation and application layer</li></ul>	OBIEE, Cognos, Infographics, HDInsight, Apache Spark, Apache Solr, Apache Storm, MangoDB, NoSQL, HBase, YARN, MapReduce, Hive, Pig, HiveMall, Amazon Simple Storage Service (S3), HDFS, HCatalog, Oozle, Avro, Ambari, and ZooKeeper
Machine learning	<ul><li>Connector layer</li><li>Storage layer</li><li>Processing layer</li><li>Model and runtime layer</li><li>Presentation and application layer</li></ul>	<ul><li>Connector layer</li><li>Model and runtime layer</li></ul>	Logic App, Apache Flume, MQTT, Apache Kafka, Apache Sqoop, Apache Mahout, Amazon's Deep Scalable Sparse Tensor Network Engine (DSSTNE), Google TensorFlow, Microsoft Cognitive Toolkit, and Video analytics

(*continued*)

Table 4-1. (*continued*)

Technology Stack	Layer Name	Layer Discussed in Detail	Technology and Concepts Discussed
Cognitive computing	• NData gathering layer • Data preparation, extraction, and conversion layer • Data processing layer • Analytics, machine learning, and cognitive layer • Presentation and application layer	Most of the layers are discussed in the IoT, Big Data analytics, and machine learning sections. Therefore, as the concepts and functionality of layers remain the same, they are not discussed in this section.	Anticipative computing
Cloud computing	• Infrastructure-as-a-Service layer • Platform-as-a-Service layer • Machine Learning-as-a-Service • Software-as-a-Service	These layers are mainly discussed in Chapter 1. They are not mentioned here again.	Infrastructure-as-a-Service, Platform-as-a-Service, Machine Learning-as-a-Service, and Software-as-a-Service

The next sections discuss the main technologies and technology stacks (wherever required) of the machine learning ecosystem, which I called "pillars" in the first chapter.

The Internet of Things Technology Stack

It is very difficult to come up with the generic technology stack for IoT, because diverse industries have their own requirements and require different applications, products, and services to fulfill their needs. However, this section provides a generic snapshot of the main ingredients of implementing IoT technologies across industries and provides a technical level of details for an IoT technology stack. Further customization may be done on the specific requirements of the individual/ users/enterprises. But, the basic structure of the stack remains the same. The Internet of Things (IoT) brings enormous possibilities and promises a bright future; it is here to stay.

The volume of sensor-based devices and equipment is growing at breakneck speed and the developments in this field are enormous. Therefore, the existing business model is expected to align itself with this rapidly changing technology. Hence, the business world needs to educate its workforce in this regard, which includes but is not limited to projects, products, and technology managers. They are involved in collecting information to provide the input to the higher levels of management. On the basis of data and insight provided by middle management (project/ product and technology managers), the top layer of the organization (CTO/CFO/COO) can make decisions.

Middle management is an integral part of the overall ecosystem of the organization, and they ensure the success of products/applications or service of IoT-based systems. In these changing times, it is clear that managers who are equipped with technical capabilities will provide better direction to their organizations. Therefore, roles and responsibilities of managers have also changed. More technical alignment and innovative mindsets are mandatory for success. The technical journey of a manager starts by understanding the technology stack. Therefore, only those who understand the stack can evaluate the complexity of the requirements and the project. As managers are the targeted audience of this book, let's start this knowledge-gathering exercise with the IoT technology stack.

IoT's technology stack is divided into layers:

- Device and sensor layer

- Communication, protocol, and transportation layer

- Data processing layer

- Presentation and application layer

Tiers represent the physical separation of the presentation, business, services, and data functionality of design across separate computers and systems. *Layers* are the logical groupings of the software or hardware components that make up the application. They segregate the variety of tasks performed by the components in a logical way. This makes it easier to create a robust and reliable design that supports reusability of existing components. Also, each logical layer can contain a number of separate component types. The component types are grouped into sublayers, where each sublayer performs a specific type of task to achieve a certain functionality.

IoT, You, and Your Organization

Building a complete IoT system or solution is a costly and business-critical decision. It requires modern technical skills, expertise, time, and money. It needs to be planned properly before being implemented. If the resources are not utilized in the proper manner, the solution may go through long IT project cycles and end up with a low return on investment. Therefore, identifying an effective IoT platform is mandatory. An effective IoT platform equipped with the proper technology stack will simplify the development of IoT solutions. Hence, factors like scalability, robustness, and performance are essential for a good platform. Whenever needed, the platform should be able to easily accommodate continual growth and change.

These must-have features enable enterprises to develop systems and solutions (on top of platform) that help industries/organizations/ enterprises develop robust IoT solutions that have capabilities to easily connect to a diverse set of devices and sensors. They can benefit from the seamless information flow between systems and operational assets and deliver solid business value to their customers through IoT/IOE/IIoT (Internet of Everything/Industrial Internet of Things). Today's customers are well educated about technologies, their future, and use cases. Therefore, having a good platform provides confidence to users about fulfillment of their requirements.

The Device and Sensor Layer

This is the starting point of an IoT system. From here, things start their journey (technically). The device and sensor layer originates from one device and is passed to multiple other connected "things" or to a larger network (or to a network of networks). Also, this layer is responsible for interacting with the physical world. The following list explains some important highlights about this layer from a technical perspective. This section belongs to IoT and specifically to devices, things, and gateways.

With the changing times, edge computing has become very important, which is the practice of physically moving computing services closer to either the user or the data source. These computing services are available on what are called *edge devices,* which are computers that enable real-time raw data collection and processing for quicker, more accurate analysis. IoT and other edge devices can now execute machine learning models locally, thanks to machine learning at the edge.

This section provides a glimpse of the technical landscape, technology frameworks, and other details of IoT devices and sensors.

- Objects or things are generally small in size and capacity. Hence, these objects and things are programmed using microcontrollers because they are lightweight and less resource-hungry. Microcontrollers are specialized for performing particular sets of technical tasks.

- The software running on the IoT-enabled devices typically consists of a very lightweight operating system; it's a software layer that enables objects to access the feature of hardware (MCU).

- The device or objects support wired or wireless protocols, such as Bluetooth, Z-wave, Thered, CANBus, CoAP, and MQTT. Typically, these are used for connecting devices.

- The IoT devices generally have remote management capability. This functionality comes in handy when "things" are required to be managed remotely. Examples include software upgrades and correcting minor issues remotely.

Facts for You

Google's operating system for IoT is called Android Things. It is built for connected devices and used for the Internet of Things. It is tuned to take advantage of Intel's innovative architecture. IoT application development on Android Things is fast and robust.

Windows 10 IoT Core is a cut down version of Windows 10. Windows 10 IoT Core targets and is optimized for smaller devices. It runs on devices like the Raspberry Pi 2 and 3, Arrow DragonBoard 410c, and MinnowBoard MAX. Windows 10 IoT Core can be extended to use the features of Universal Windows Platform (UWP) through the uses of their API for building next generation solutions. Windows 10 IoT Core also supports Arduino Wiring API, which is used in Arduino sketches and libraries for direct hardware access. The Window 10 IoT application is developed using Visual Studio Community Edition. Visual Studio Community Edition comes with quality development tools that include universal app templates, a code editor, a powerful debugger, and rich language support. With the help of frameworks like Connect-the-Dots, the Windows 10 IoT Core targeted devices can be integrated with the Microsoft Azure cloud platform. Microsoft Azure allows you to leverage advanced cloud-based analytics services.

While choosing the technology stack, you need a focused, thought-based practical strategic direction, mainly in terms of what kind of data needs to be collected and the type of hardware required. Business models and requirements clearly need to be charted out for this technology stack. Also, the support models and execution plan must be defined and validated well in advance.

This type of planning is helpful throughout the lifecycle of creating, modifying, maintaining, and phasing out the stack. This approach works as an enabler to keep the IoT technology stack in synchronization with the creation of any solution. If these factors are considered, the technology stack can handle any type of practical requirements. Either it uses a simple data collection through a single smart sensor or it uses a more complex scenario, like gathering data from industrial computers and processing systems that host many sensors, powerful processors, advance storage systems, and gateway systems.

Sensors measure values and send raw data while consuming very little power. Sensors can be embedded in any device or object. This includes smartphones, watches, wristbands, coffee machines, cars, satellites, toothbrushes, contact lenses, fabric, and so on. They can be worn or implanted in the body or skin. For example, Nokia recently patented a system for creating magnetic tattoos embedded in the skin. The tattoos vibrate upon incoming calls or when a message arrived. Their method description says that the patented technology sprays a ferromagnetic material onto the user's skin. Once this is done, the tattoo can be paired with any mobile device to do the communication.

Another example is Fitbit's new advanced sleep tracking device, which uses sensors to measure how much time during the night the user is restless, in deep sleep, or awake. It has a built-in heart rate monitor that can break and analyze data into clinically defined stages. (For more information, visit `www.fitbit.com/global/in/technology/sleep`.)

The Indian institute of technology, Bombay team, developed a prototype of a wearable baby wellness monitor. It helps parents track their kid's clinical and general well-being with the help of multiple sensors. The team created an IoT-enabled device that is easily embeddable/attachable to a diaper. This is an innovative way of monitoring a baby's movements, including their body temperature, blood pressure, and so on.

Microsoft, in association with the University of Washington, came up with an innovative contact lens to analyze and provide real-time updates on biochemical instabilities in the human body. With the advancement in the microelectromechanical systems, which is commonly known as microelectromechanical systems (MEMS), the size and cost of these sensors has dropped significantly. Therefore, MEMS-based devices are becoming part of the mainstream. MEMS work on a tiny level of electronics. They use the combined power of electronics, physics, chemistry, and mechanical engineering to integrate sensors and actuators. Sensing information and sharing and transporting that information over a network was traditionally tackled by separate components in a device.

However, recent technical advancements make it possible to integrate sensing, networking, and power into one unit. Thus, they can be used easily and in many environments, as they work as a single unit.

Huge power source requirements and networking capability are no longer constraints. For example, a lot of devices and sensors equipped with global positioning capabilities are available in the market and have excellent networking abilities. They can track an individual's location and help them find a missing pet, their car, a nearby hospital, shopping malls, or a parking spot in real time.

The nature and type of sensors and the basic communication technique is almost the same in all devices. They communicate with each other via a wireless mesh network protocol. This capability of devices fueled some very ambitious plans of multiple companies. For example, a project from Hewlett-Packard called Central Nervous System for the Earth (CeNSE) combines advances in materials, nanotechnology, and MEMS to develop a planet-wide sensing network. They are using tons of inexpensive sensors to get a holistic view of the world by integrating the physical and digital worlds. These "nerves of silicon" basically map the whole Earth. In turn, this mapping is used to monitor the conditions of bridges, highways, rivers, forests, and the air people breathe.

IoT-enabled devices use a computing processing unit, but they are not general-purpose computers. The main purpose of these devices is to serve as the eyes and ears of the targeted IoT system. Low power consumption, mobility, ease of use, working in adverse conditions, good in using low throughput communication channels, and communicating with the network through radio interface are some of the salient features of these IoT devices. Sensors and gateways and their interplay create some very useful use cases.

The following sections discuss some main technologies that are used in IoT.

The Communication, Protocol, and Transportation Layer

The communication and transportation layers share the sensor information (incorporated in devices, things, or objects). In plain English, this refers to all the different ways of exchanging information/data. When it comes to the technical world, it broadly implies "exchanging" information through devices. However, in IoT terminology, it refers to exchanging information through "things" with the rest of the world. This exchange of information happens over a network, which includes physical and virtual networks, and uses different types of protocols.

The communications mechanisms consist of an interplay of devices or things, including hardware and software. Hence, selecting the right communication mechanisms, which include all types of transportation and protocol requirements, is very important while you are conceptualizing and thinking about constructing an IoT stack. This layer signifies and determines how to interact with the underlying infrastructure. This in turn provides answers to questions such as, which type of platform would be best for your solution, a third-party platform or on-premises or cloud infrastructure? If you want to go with cloud-based solutions, this layer is responsible for data management. For example, how do you put data in and take it out from the cloud infrastructure? It does this with the help of a wide area network, a local area network, WiFi, and other related technologies.

The gateway is an essential part of the IoT environment. An IoT gateway is "in-between" equipment and it connects sensors, devices, systems, and applications. It provides tremendous value, as it filters and passes data gathered form sensors and devices. The gateway enables the IoT ecosystem to efficiently collect and securely transport data from devices and equipment to destination systems or infrastructure. The gateway is not a singular component. It may be designed as a network/

combination of gateways that can connect all the distant devices and is capable of scaling with growth. The gateways, in combination with IoT sensors and devices, play an important role in the IoT ecosystem, as they provide abilities to achieve, secure, manage, and maintain the overall system. The gateway can be used for multiple purposes, but a couple of them are very important:

- It is used to migrate meaningful data to the cloud and reduce the volume of available data on its way to the cloud by filtering out junk data.

- It is used as a data processor.

A few highlights of the communication, protocol, and transportation layer are mentioned here:

- IoT gateways are integration points for the sensors.

- Acts as an actuator to connect things or devices to each other or to the external networks.

- An IoT gateway can be a physical piece of hardware or functionality that can be incorporated, built, and attached to the devices.

- An IoT gateway is used to gather data from sensors.

- Some important protocols for gateways include:

  – CoAP

  – MQTT

  – HTTP

  – XMPP

- An IoT gateway is capable of processing data at the edge and can have storage capacity for dealing with network latency.

263

Now is a good time to look at some of the popular communication and networking terminologies. Proper understanding of these terminologies is helpful in understanding IoT technologies. A few of them are used today, and others are emerging at rapid speed (see Table 4-2).

Table 4-2. *Wireless Networking Options*

Type of Network	Description
Cellular mobile network	Available in multiple variants, including 2G, 3G, 4G, and 5G (the newest addition), where "G" stands for generation.
Bluetooth and Bluetooth low energy	Wireless personal area network (WPAN). A standard for transferring data short distances.
ZigBee	A wireless mesh networking protocol. Excellent for low data rate and high battery life.
Z-Wave	Wireless protocol for home automation.
MAN	A metropolitan area network is similar to a LAN. However, its reach extends to a city or large campus or multiple campuses. Typically, it is designed for a city or town.
PAN	A personal area network is a network that revolves or organizes around an individual or person. It can potentially enable wearable computer devices to communicate with other nearby computers or smart devices and exchange data digitally.
WAN	A wide area network spans across large or big geographies. It potentially connects smaller networks, including LANs or MANs.
6LoWPAN	IPv6 over low power wireless personal area networks.
WiFi	A wireless technology used for local area networks. It is an integral part of most of the devices available now, including mobile, tablets, and PCs. However, it is not limited to devices only and extends its reach to electronic goods as well (refrigerators, washing machines, etc.).

The Data Processing Layer

The cloud platform is the backbone of modern IoT solutions. It is one of the biggest enablers of the boom in data science and machine learning. As per principles of data processing, data can theoretically be processed anywhere, provided the technical infrastructure is available. However, companies prefer to process data over the cloud for obvious reasons. Here are some of the critical aspects related to this:

- *Data collection and management*: Smart devices can stream data to the cloud easily, including junky and noisy data, with the help of modern data streaming technologies. Data can come from a variety of sources with fluctuating internal arrangements, formats, and structures. Also, the data might need to be preprocessed to handle or find lost and unwanted data. Additionally, the data needs to be assimilated with different data sets that come from different sources to come up with an amalgamated representation before being directed and stored in the data store. Therefore, while defining the requirements of the IoT-based stack, having a good idea about the type and volume of data is important. An unambiguous acquaintance of daily, monthly, and yearly data requirements is one of the important steps for designing and creating a robust, effective, and efficient stack. Defining scalability parameters properly and well in advance helps the architects, data scientists, and data administrators define the appropriate data management solution and associated ecosystem.

- *Analytics*: Analytics is one of the key components of any IoT solution. Analytics, in the context of IoT, refers to the ability to crunch data in meaningful ways, find hidden patterns, and generate insights. In order to perform business-critical forecasts, the technical interplay of machine learning and Big Data analytics comes into the picture. Also, it equips the overall ecosystem with the ability to extract cognitive insights (understanding the way humans interpret data in an automated way) from the available data. This stage also incorporates the constant reclamation and investigation of actions performed and deposited to archived data in order to understand past data and forecast upcoming movements, or to perceive irregularities in the data that may prompt additional examination or action. Remember, raw data alone cannot provide business solutions. It is analytics-based insight powered by modern data-driven technologies and machine learning that turns soil into gold. Therefore, the IoT technical stack must be capable of incorporating analytical capabilities and facilitate building effective and efficient solutions.

- *Cloud APIs:* IoT is all about connecting multiple devices or objects to each other, to the network, or to a network of networks. The purpose of creating this network of devices is to share data for different needs, including business and personal requirements of enterprises and individuals. In and around the IoT solution, data is universally available. It travels from things/objects/devices to the cloud infrastructure from the cloud to backend systems, from multiple handlers or users to their objects or devices. At the heart of this process are the APIs that enable all the communication and collaboration among the devices. This seamless communication among multiple objects, things, devices, and networks is usually done by consuming exposed APIs at either the cloud level or at the device level. These APIs are exposed by the vendors and providers as one of basic elements of the cloud offering. APIs allow users to interact with devices or to exchange data. Remember that opening an API to a target audience is not a technical decision, it's a business decision. Proper API administration enables the movement of data securely, which helps guard sensitive data.

The Presentation and Application Layer

This layer provides a means of interacting with the users of applications. Software installed on devices/objects works as an interface for communication. The layer also contains applications and interactive products through which end users communicate. This layer sits on the top of the technology stack and most of the technical complexity is underlying. Hence, this layer is easily interpretable by almost everyone. To people who are exposed to a bit of technology or even to the layperson, this is the "layer of use," because it contains applications and products that they use without knowing the hidden complications.

Enterprises earn most of their revenue in this layer. Technical and product managers easily relate to this layer. The applications, products, and services that sit here are generally web-based. However, this is not the mandatory criteria and it depends on the user's needs. The APSs (applications, products, and services) are meant to target the desktop, mobile, and wearables. Also, many applications or apps are made available to fulfill customer needs and demands. In changing times, customers are more inclined toward cloud-enabled applications or products, because they provide flexibility to access information from smart IoT-enabled objects in an "anytime anywhere" manner. This "anytime anywhere" access aligns with the ultimate goal of IoT to provide the users with freedom and agility.

Industry-specific applications also sit at this layer. Consumers use this layer to fulfill home, lifestyle, and health related needs. Business and industries are using this layer for their professional needs.

IoT Solution Availability

Microsoft is one of the end-to-end solution providers of IoT-based technologies, products, and solutions (there are multiple others, including IBM). IoT is in demand. Many companies are helping their clients and stakeholders in this area. They are continuously innovating and introducing breakthroughs in the market. In today's world, doing only research and innovation will not work. Proper positioning of products, branding, and marketing and articulation of research, innovations, and associated offerings to the right people is all equally important. These factors help customers make informed decisions about products and applications for a particular purpose that serve their needs.

For a better understanding, look at the Azure IoT ecosystem, which will help you decode this layer better.

The Internet of Things (IoT), which connects gadgets and enables data-driven decision-making across businesses, has changed how people engage with technology. Strong development tools are necessary for creating complex IoT applications, as organizations use IoT to improve operations and spur innovation. As a complete response to these needs, Microsoft's Azure IoT Software Development Kit (SDK) enables developers to build cutting-edge IoT applications on the Azure platform. This section digs into the realm of the Azure IoT SDK, examines its essential components, and explains how crucial it is to the development of IoT.

Real-Life Scenarios

Nanotechnology Sensors

Nanotechnology is a field of study where particles are studied at the nano scale (a very small scale). It has been widely used in medical science to treat illnesses in early stages. When nanotechnology is integrated with IoT, Big Data analytics, and machine learning, it becomes very effective.

1. Injections of nanoparticles are given to the patient to be released into the bloodstream. The nanoparticles identify biological or chemical changes. This activity monitors the chemical and physical changes in the patient's body to detect illnesses in the early stages. This is based on the simple principle that unexpected changes in the internal biological, chemical, and physiological mechanisms of the body can be a sign of disease.

2. The nanoparticles interact with wearable devices to indicate changes made by foreign particles interfering with the normal flow in the body. Wearable devices receive data on an ongoing basis from the nanoparticles.

3. The wearable devices use this data for disease diagnoses, which in turn use predictive and prescriptive analytics.

4. Machine learning, in combination with cognitive modeling and computational algorithms, learns the process of change and the behaviors of the internal bodily mechanisms and diagnoses any disease effectively and proactively.

This overall process increases the effectiveness and efficiency of disease diagnoses. Therefore, it helps reduce hospitalization time and costs. It also generates intuitive and effective reports.

Monitoring

Machine learning takes monitoring to the level of cognitive intelligence. Machine learning provides these benefits to the IoT system:

- The wearables provide alarms and notifications on health around the clock. They are generally not as effective at tracking the actions for these alarms and notification and properly recording them.

- Machine learning, with the support of neural networks, can track activities based on human actions and record the responses.

- The recorded data will be forwarded to the doctor.

Here are the steps in an interesting future use case:

1. The patient gets out of bed and the sensors in the floor and bed record this event.

2. The sensor-enabled toilet examines the patient's stool and urine, before uploading the details to the cloud. A sensor-enabled toothbrush examines the oral health of the patient.

3. Important health indicators such as pulse, blood sugar levels, and blood pressure are recorded and uploaded to the cloud.

4. Sensors in the wall and floor assess the risk of a fall based on the patient's movements.

5. Diuretic medicine contains tiny transmitters that sends signals to the wearables that the patient has taken their medicine.

Let's look at a couple more healthcare use cases. These use cases highlight the importance of technologies and apps as well.

- *Modification of patient behavior.* Many common ailments can be controlled or even prevented. For instance, leading a better lifestyle can help you prevent conditions like Type 2 diabetes, obesity, and heart disease. However, altering one's lifestyle necessitates altering one's behavior, which calls for ongoing reminders. In order to accomplish this, machine learning algorithms can compile data originating from linked health devices and sensors used by patients in order to produce insights into their behavior and direct them during this transformative journey.

- *Using SmokeBeat to change smoking habits.* Innovative software called SmokeBeat collects information on a user's smoking habits without their knowledge. Hand-to-mouth movements are detected by the program using the accelerometer on a wristwatch or smart band. This data is processed by SmokeBeat, which provides real-time CBT incentives. In order to increase efficacy, user reactions to such incentives are continuously monitored and recorded. SmokeBeat also makes comparisons between user smoking data and that of their preferred peer group, developing a type of encouraging social network.

- *Virtual nursing.* In today's hectic hospital setting, nurses can become overwhelmed and struggle to provide each patient with enough individualized care. Virtual nurses are used by healthcare facilities to address this problem. Computer-generated virtual nurses converse with patients the same way that real nurses do. They are sociable, kind, and educational.

  In between medical appointments, virtual nurses engage with patients more frequently than real nurses and provide information. They are readily available around the clock and provide prompt responses (faster than waiting for a real nurse).

The Big Data Analytics Technology Stack

Creating a Big Data technology stack depends on the requirements and specific needs of the business. Also, while making decisions about a Big Data technology stack, you must consider the three Vs (velocity, variety, and volume; for further details refer to Chapter 1) as well as the availability of the analytics infrastructure. The technology stack for Big Data creates value. However, data cleanliness is guided by the requirements, rules, business logic, and analytical capabilities as well.

Typically, Big Data technologies are divided into layers to separate concerns and logic (see Figure 4-1). Logical subdivisions of complexity in the form of layers serve as the building blocks for the Big Data technology suite. Some redundancy exists across layers, because isolated layers cannot serve this purpose.

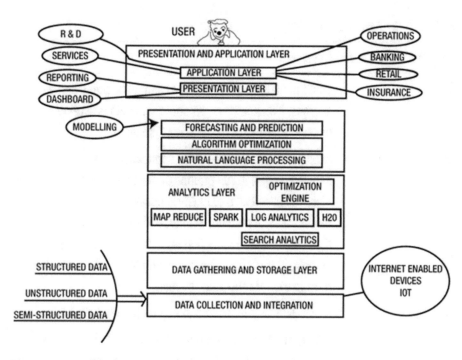

Figure 4-1. *Big Data analytics stack*

Note   Data processing and analytics are an important step during "insight" generation and are tightly associated with machine learning. Machine learning and data analytics can be treated as one layer. However, for clear segregation, it is always good to keep them separate (at least logically). Machine learning, including its workings and relationships with the technologies, is discussed in the greater detail in the "Machine Learning" section. Figure 4-1 shows one way that machine learning and Big Data analytics are tightly bound.

Table 4-3 shows the Big Data analytics technology and process suite in a nutshell. The next section explains some important software, frameworks, and libraries that are closely associated with the Big Data technology suite.

Table 4-3. *Main Technologies of Big Data*

Name of Technology	Description
Hadoop	Implementation of MapReduce. Can work with diverse data sources. Also known as an enterprise data operating system (for details, refer to the "Hadoop" section).
Hive	Allows traditional data-driven applications like business intelligence (BI) to run queries against a Hadoop cluster. Also, visualized as a data warehousing service that provides the facilities of reading, writing, and managing large data sets. It's an abstraction layer (which hides internal complexities of the technologies) on MapReduce (for details, refer to the "MapReduce" section).
Hive QL	A SQL-like language used to submit MapReduce jobs.
Pig	Allows applications to run queries on the Hadoop cluster. However, it is a Pearl-like language instead of a SQL-like language (Hive).
	For details, refer to the "Pig" section.
HDFS	A distributed filesystem technology. Generally used to store unstructured data (for details, refer to the "HDFS" section).
MapReduce	A distributed computation framework. However, it is slow in computation in comparison to newly evolving frameworks (for details, refer to the "MapReduce" section).
HBase	Column-based storage service that stores data in a tabular format.
ZooKeeper	Distributed coordination service.

(continued)

Table 4-3. (*continued*)

Name of Technology	Description
Yarn	Yarn stands for yet another resource navigator. In Big Data analytics systems, its role is to act as a central operating system that provides and manages resource and application lifecycle management to the technology stack.
Ambari	Used for provisioning, managing, and monitoring the Hadoop cluster.
Avro	A data serialization system. Its .NET flavor also exists in one offering from Microsoft, called HDInsight, which is a Hadoop distribution from Hortonworks. It is also visualized as Apache Hadoop running on Microsoft Azure (a Cloud Platform-as-a-Service offering from Microsoft).
HCatalog	Provides a relational view of the data on a Hadoop cluster. Tools like Pig and Hive run on top of HCatalog and it serves as a layer of abstraction.
Oozle	An application used for coordination of the workflow of Hadoop jobs.
Tez	An application framework for doing high-performance batch and interactive data processing. It makes the Hadoop job faster and maintains MapReduce scalability and robustness. It generally operates on petabytes of data.

(*continued*)

Table 4-3. (*continued*)

Name of Technology	Description
Azure Data Factory	The most prominent ETL service in Azure is Azure Data Factory. It defines incoming data (in terms of its format and schema), transforms data in accordance with business rules and filters, expands on the data that already exists, and then transfers data to a destination store that is easily accessed by other downstream services. It can execute SQL Server Integration Services packages, custom infrastructure, and pipelines (which contain ETL logic) on Azure.
Azure Data Lake Storage Gen 2	Enterprise-level Big Data storage that is resilient, highly available, and secure right out of the box. It can scale to petabytes of data storage and is Hadoop compatible. Because it is built on top of Azure storage accounts, it benefits directly from all of their features. After the features of Data Lake Storage Gen1 and Azure Storage were integrated, the most recent version, known as Gen2, was created.
Databricks	The foundation of Databricks is Apache Spark. Users can access a managed Spark cluster through this Platform-as-a-Service. It offers a ton of extra features, including a comprehensive gateway to manage the Spark cluster and its nodes, as well as assistance with notebook creation, job scheduling and execution, and security and support for multiple users.

The Data Acquisition Integration and Storage Layer

This is the bottom or the lowest layer in the Big Data technology stack. This layer is responsible for the collection of all types of data (structured/unstructured and semi-structured) and storage. The data comes from multiple sources, including IoT-enabled devices, social media, and RSS feeds. Because of the volume, velocity, and variety of data received at this layer, some firms are use data lakes as a source of their Big Data repository. A *data lake* is a data acquisition and storage approach. It stores and embraces raw data in its natural setup, form, and format. Its main purpose is to store data and not to apply any type of intelligence and sophisticated operations to it. For example, the how/why/where the data is stored data is not an area of concern for data lakes. Its technology also does not care about the governance and security aspects of the data.

Providing a solution for Big Data technologies is a huge, open, and evolving market. Many companies are offering their solutions in this space. The major players are Apache, Hortonworks, IBM, Amazon, and Microsoft. Hortonworks and others provide a compressive set of tools and technologies for Big Data, Big Data analytics, and machine learning. Refer to these links for more details:

- Technology offerings from Apache (Source: `https://hortonworks.com/products/data-center/hdp/`)

- Technology innovations at Apache (Source: `https://hortonworks.com/products/data-center/hdp/`)

Once data is collected from multiple sources, it is integrated as one source. Data generation and availability have increased dramatically over the past ten years, which has led to a spike in data integration. There is data practically everywhere, and its amount, variety, and velocity have all dramatically grown.

Every organization uses a wide range of programs, and many produce data in a unique format that is proprietary. Data is frequently also bought on the open market.

Data must be moved and combined, even during organizational mergers. The practice of combining data from several sources to create new output with more significance is known as *data integration*.

There are multiple technical offerings in this space from a variety of companies. A brief look at the main ones will give you a good understanding of data acquisition, integration and storage.

Hadoop Distributed Filesystem (HDFS)

A distributed filesystem (DFS) is any filesystem that allows access to files from multiple hosts shared via a computer network. A distributed filesystem may include facilities for transparent replication, capabilities to deal with large data sets, write once/read many times, and fault tolerance. It is used to store large volumes of data in inexpensive commodity hardware. The Hadoop distributed filesystem (HDFS) is used as the main data storage system by the Hadoop suite of applications/ecosystem.

HDFS is a scalable, robust, fault-tolerant Java-based distributed filesystem. HDFS creates multiple replicas of data blocks and distributes them on compute nodes throughout a cluster of reliable, extremely rapid computations. HDFS stores system metadata and application data separately. It stores metadata on a dedicated server, called the *NameNode*, and application data on other servers, called *DataNodes*. All servers in HDFS are fully connected and they communicate with each other using TCP-based protocols. File content in HDFS is replicated on multiple DataNodes for reliability, and it has the advantage that data transfer bandwidth is multiplied, so there are more opportunities for locating computations near the needed data.

The Core Hadoop Architecture

A Hadoop cluster is based on a masters and slaves (see Figure 4-2) architecture. However, the terminologies are different in comparison to the traditional master/slave architecture. In Hadoop terminologies, the NameNode is the master of a Hadoop cluster and it is responsible for the filesystem namespace and access control for clients. A JobTracker distributes jobs to waiting nodes. NameNode and JobTracker are the masters of the Hadoop architecture. The slaves contain the TaskTracker, which manages the job execution. It takes complete responsibility, from starting, monitoring, and capturing the output of the job. It also notifies the master about the job completion. The DataNode is the storage node in a Hadoop cluster and represents the distributed filesystem. The TaskTracker and the DataNode work as slaves in the Hadoop cluster.

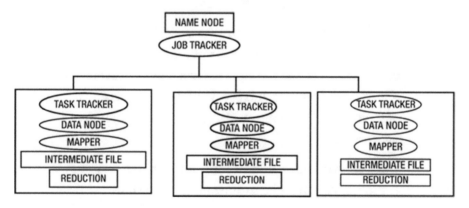

Figure 4-2. *Elements of a Hadoop cluster*

Hadoop has a flexible, efficient, and robust architecture. Hence, it is equally effective in supporting a single node cluster, where all objects exist on a single node, and a multi-node cluster. That way, JobTracker and NameNode are distributed across thousands of nodes.

Salient Features of HDFS

Here are the most interesting features of HDFS:

- *Reliability and fault tolerance*: It is designed to store very large data sets reliably (fault tolerance), because of data replication in the cluster or in multiple clusters. Typically, one set of data is dependably deposited on the machine cluster. Therefore, if one machine is down, the data is still available on the other machine. It also streams data sets at high bandwidth to user applications to achieve high performance.

- *High availability*: Even if some of the machines or hardware are not working or have crashed, the data can be accessed through another path.

- *Distributed storage*: HDFS provides excellent results in the distributed storage environment and performs computation across multiple heterogeneous servers. Its effectiveness remains intact even if the resource grows with demand (scalability). Also, it remains economical at every size.

- *Open-source*: It is an open-source project, so it enables the modification and customization of the code according to need.

- *Scalable*: It is highly scalable, which means adding new hardware is easy. Hardware can be added to the nodes effortlessly. It can be horizontally scaled, which enables addition of the new nodes on the fly without any downtime.

- *Flexible*: Hadoop enables accessing new data sources without effort and taps into dissimilar kinds of data, including structured, semi-structured, and unstructured data to produce value from that data.

- *Fast*: Hadoop's inimitable storing technique is based on a distributed filesystem that fundamentally maps data wherever it is positioned on a cluster.

- *Economical*: Hadoop provides cost-effective storing solutions for the huge data sets. Hadoop-based solutions are cheap because it runs on clusters that are installed on the commodity hardware. It does not need a dedicated machine. Therefore, Hadoop offers enormous price savings.

Amazon Simple Storage Service (S3)

S3 is a cloud-based scalable, robust, and file-tolerant system. It is a distributed filesystem offering from Amazon. It can be exploited as the data layer in Big Data and analytics-based applications to build the architecture. However, it may require additional components. Amazon S3 provides a simple web service-based interface. It can be used to store and retrieve any amount of data, at any time, from anywhere on the web. It also provides a highly scalable, reliable, fast, inexpensive data storage infrastructure. Amazon S3 is used by Amazon to run its own global network of websites.

The Analytics Layer

This layer typically organizes and prepares data for analysis. It processes huge and diverse sets of data that it gets from the data acquisition layer, with the help of different processes, technologies, and algorithms. There are a variety of analytical tools, frameworks, technologies, and robust algorithms available with varying capabilities. Depending on the requirements and market demand, any one or combination of technologies is used. This layer converts raw data into actionable insights. This is the layer that deals with multiple types of analytics, including descriptive, diagnostic, predictive, and prescriptive. Technically, many authors consider machine learning as one of the ingredients of this layer. However, this chapter discusses those concepts in the machine learning section because machine learning libraries, frameworks, and tools sit on the top of the analytics layer.

Apache is no doubt the leader in providing Hadoop-based Big Data solutions. Figure 4-3 presents the Hadoop stack, which shows the positioning of HDFS and MapReduce in the overall stack.

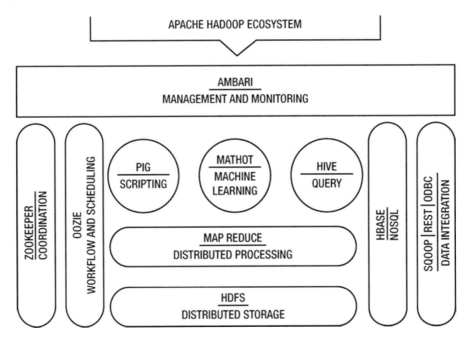

Figure 4-3. *Positioning of HDFS and MapReduce in the overall Hadoop stack (which covers all layers of Big Data analytics)*

Multiple vendors are providing their solutions in the Big Data space, starting with gathering data to presenting it, which includes offerings from Apache, IBM, and Microsoft. However, it is difficult to cover all the offerings of these vendors. Therefore, this chapter confines its discussion to Apache/Hadoop-based products and touches on the products of other vendors in a few places. Let's start with the revolutionary technology called MapReduce.

Hadoop MapReduce

Hadoop MapReduce is an excellent software framework for processing large data sets in a distributed computing environment. MapReduce is the heart and soul of the Hadoop framework. It is a programming model that facilitates massive scalability across hundreds or thousands of servers in a Hadoop cluster. It works on compute clusters of commodity hardware. The framework is used by organizations, enterprises, and companies to schedule tasks, as well as monitor and re-execute any failed tasks. Because it's a sub-project of HDFS, its working style has inherited the basic philosophy of HDFS.

The term *MapReduce* refers to two separate and different actions that a typical Hadoop program performs. A MapReduce job usually splits the input data set into independent groups of data, which is processed by the map tasks in a parallel way. The "map" job takes a chunk of data from the available data store and converts it into another set of data, where individual elements are broken into key/value pairs. The framework categorizes the results of the maps, which become input to the reduce tasks.

Then, the "reduce" job takes the output from a map step as input and combines those data key/value pairs into a smaller set of *tuples* (a commonly used synonym for the key/value pair). As the name MapReduce implies, the reduce job is always performed after the map job. Typically, the input and output of the job are warehoused in a distributed filesystem. (Figure 4-4 shows the overall architecture of MapReduce.)

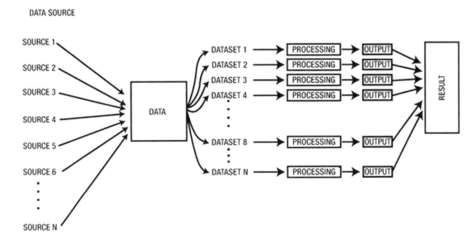

Figure 4-4. *MapReduce architecture*

MapReduce Word Count Example

Challenge: Count the number of different words in a provided document.

The Map() and Reduce() functions run in parallel on the Hadoop cluster machines to solve this challenge in a parallel manner. Input to and output from these functions are key/value pairs. The following steps are involved:

1. Mapping

2. Reducing

3. Overall computation

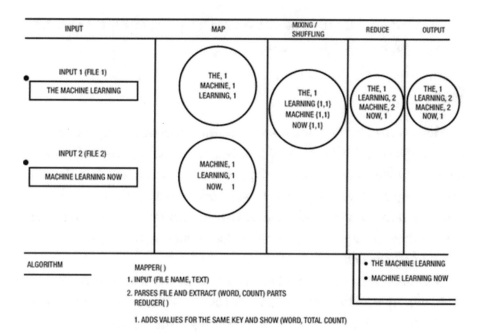

Figure 4-5. *Machine learning*

Quick Facts About MapReduce

MapReduce is the main algorithm that changed the way Big Data is processed.

Google was a pioneer in MapReduce. The two main papers are:

- The first paper was Sanjay Ghemawat et al., (2003), titled "The Google File System." It describes how the files are processed on Google clusters in a distributed manner.

- In 2004, Jeff Dean et al. (2004) also discussed details about MapReduce in their paper: "MapReduce: Simplified Data Processing on Large Clusters." It describes the programming model used on Google clusters.

MapReduce is the framework used by Google internally to index the WWW to support Google searching.

Pig

Pig sits on top of the Hadoop framework and processes large data sets without the users having to write Java-based MapReduce code. Pig is a high-level platform for creating MapReduce programs used with Hadoop. Apache Pig allows Hadoop users to write complex MapReduce code by using Pig script, which is a simple, easy-to-understand scripting language. Pig translates the Pig Latin script into MapReduce, so that it can be executed on the data.

Various coding approaches and technologies exist to solve Big Data problems. Apache Pig can be thought of as one of the options of Hadoop MapReduce. Every coding approach and programming language has some advantages and disadvantages. Pig is not an exception. It is up to the developers to evaluate and choose which coding approach or programming language will best fulfill their needs and requirements.

However, based on the general guidelines, programmers who are not well-versed in the technicalities of Hadoop MapReduce will find Pig easy. It is easy to start with and less chaotic. Pig can be potentially extended by following UDFs (user-defined functions). UDFs enable users to write code or program in the language of their choice, including Java, Python, JavaScript, and Ruby. These can be called directly from the programming languages.

Apache Hive

Hadoop was developed to organize and store massive amounts of data of all types and formats. Data analysts, enterprises, and companies uses Hive to query, summarize, explore, and analyze data, which can potentially be converted into actionable business insights. Table 4-4 shows the features of Hive.

286

Table 4-4. *Features of Hive*

Benefits and Features of Hive	Details
SQL-like scripting	Provides flexibility to query though SQL scripting. Users can use:
	*Subqueries like IN/NOT IN
	*Permanent-user defined functions
	*Stream data from Flume. Apache Flume is a distributed service for gathering, integrating, and moving huge volumes of streaming data into the HDFS.
	*The JOIN keyword in a WHERE clause
Speed	Provides:
	*Faster query planning features and cost-based optimization
	*Interactive queries through Hive
Integration	Easily integrated with the traditional data source and ETL (Extract Transform and Load) tools
Supports scalable and extensible architecture	Easily extensible and scalable. This feature comes in handy when the data volume grows in a heterogeneous environment

One of the important extensions of Hive is HiveMall, which is an open-source scalable machine learning library that provides a collection of machine learning algorithms as Hive UDFs. UDFs permit you to modify how Hive assesses data and manipulates queries. HiveMall makes machine learning easy for developers by providing interactive and stable APIs w/SQL abstraction. It supports regression, classification, recommendation, anomaly detection, k-nearest neighbor, and feature engineering algorithms. Also, HiveMall runs on top of Hive and does not need programming to perform machine learning-based development activities. It is based on Hive so it is easy for Hive users to learn.

Table 4-5 presents a comparative study of MapReduce, Pig, and Hive.

Table 4-5. *Summary of the MapReduce, Pig, and Hive Technologies*

Pig	Hive	MapReduce
Scripting language	SQL-like query language	Complied language
Higher level of abstraction	Higher level of abstraction	Low level of abstraction
Fewer lines of code in comparison to MapReduce	Fewest lines of code in comparison to Pig	More lines of code in comparison to Pig and Hive
		Lines of code: MapReduce ➤ Pig ➤ Hive
Less development effort in comparison to MapReduce	Least development effort in comparison to Pig and MapReduce	Development effort: MapReduce ➤ Pig ➤ Hive
Less exposure to bugs	Least amount of bugs	More exposed to bugs
Less efficient in handling unstructured data, such as images, videos, audio, and text that is vaguely delimited, as well as log data	Efficient at handling unstructured data, such as images, videos, audio, and text	Effectively handles unstructured data, such as images, videos, audio, and text
Code efficiency	Code efficiency	Higher code efficiency in comparison to Pig and Hive

HBase

HBase is a non-relational NoSQL database that runs on top of the Hadoop distributed filesystem. NoSQL database technology is designed to support the changing requirements of cloud-based applications, which contain and deal with a very large volume of unstructured data. HBase is designed to take care of those requirements. It can overcome the existing problems of traditional databases, such as poor scaling, slow performance, ineffective data models, and data distribution of the large volume of data.

The parameters and bottlenecks mentioned previously are the typical limitations of relational databases. HBase provides real-time read/write access to large data sets. HBase scales if required to handle huge data sets in a linear fashion. It efficiently deals with a large number of rows and columns. When it comes to combining multiple data sources that use a wide variety of different structures, formats, types, and schemas, HBase is very handy. HBase has native support to integrate multiple data formats with the Hadoop framework and technical ecosystem.

It works flawlessly with other data access engines through YARN, which is commonly known as the operating system of the Big Data system. YARN and HDFS are the foundational components of the Hortonworks Data Platform (HDP). While HDFS provides scalable, fault-tolerant, cost-efficient storage for Big Data stores, YARN is designed to provide a centralized flexible, robust, and scalable architecture. It enables users and automated applications to process multiple jobs at the same time. YARN also takes care of resource management activities. YARN's plug-and-play architectural design facilitates a wide variety of data access methods. Table 4-6 lists interesting information about NoSQL and relational databases. It is good to take a brief look at the comparisons between NoSQL and RDBMS.

Table 4-6. *Multiple Aspects of NoSQL Database, RDBMS, and MangoDB*

RDBMS vs NoSQL	
Benefits	
RDBMS	**NoSQL**
Structured and transitional. Efficient at handling high-performance workloads.	Semi-structured, schema-less architecture allows for frequent change and provides features of varied addition of data to the system.
Good for relational data.	Object-oriented and good for non-relational data.
Constraint-based.	Eventfully constraints.
Rigid, mature, and stable.	Flexible, emerging, and scalable.
Drawbacks	
Rigid schema defined for the organization of data. Difficult to scale.	Not mature. Hence, difficult installation and toolset availability.
Cannot handle very high volumes of data, pictures, or videos efficiently.	Slower response time.
Examples: SQL server, Oracle, and MySQL.	Examples: MangoDB and Amazon Dynamic DB.

Table 4-7 shows a summary of NoSQL databases.

Table 4-7. *Types of NoSQL Databases, Vendors, and Uses*

NoSQL Database	Properties	Uses	Example and Vendors
Graph-based	• Highlights connections between data elements. • Stores data in related node.	• Spatial data storages • Recommendation engine	• Infinite graph • NodeJS
Column-based	• Deals with a large number of columns. • Good for Internet-based searches. • Good for large, web-based applications.	• Read and write extension • Effective in storing large data • Efficient with distributed environments	• HBase • SampleDB • Hypertable • Cassandra
Key/value-based	• Uses key/value concept to store data. • Typically associates one key with one value. • Excellent for click-stream types of applications.	• Efficient and effective in small read and write operations • Good for high availability systems • Good for large database requirements	• Riak • Oracle BDB • RADIS

(continued)

Table 4-7. (*continued*)

NoSQL Database	Properties	Uses	Example and Vendors
Document-based	• Stores data in document-like structures. • Typically uses JSON formats. • Good for content management. • Excellent for web-based applications.	• Used for consistent data • Efficient and effective at storing unstructured data	• Couchbase • MangoDB

Graph database is a type of NoSQL database. Fundamentally, it is a specialized, single-purpose platform for building and modifying graphs. In a way that relational databases are unable to, graphs' nodes, edges, and attributes are utilized to represent and store data.

The theory of graphs serves as the foundation for the idea of a graph database. It was released in 2000. Because nodes, relationships, and properties are used to store data instead of conventional databases, they are also known as NoSQL databases. A graph database is especially helpful for data that is highly related. The main categories of Hadoop and Neo4j are "databases" and "graph databases," respectively. The graph's arcs (arrows) show relationships between the nodes. As a tree, an XML document is a particular sort of directed graph.

The capacity to collect vast volumes of data, contextualize it, analyze it, and make it searchable with meaning is essential given the fast use of AI and the innovation occurring around big language models.

The ability to access *vector embeddings*, a data type that offers the semantics required for AI to have a similar long-term memory processing, is a prerequisite for Generative AI processes and applications that are being built to natively incorporate Generative AI functionality.

When making complicated judgements, AI models (such large language models) build and utilize vector embeddings as their data representation.

Complexity, depth, patterns, and linkages all need to be stored and represented as parts of the underlying structures, much like memories do in the human brain, which makes managing all of this challenging.

Another important database in the context of NoSQL is the vector database. It is a purpose-built database (or brain) for AI workloads that is created for highly scalable access and is especially made for storing and accessing these vector embeddings. For embeddings especially, vector databases like DataStax Astra DB (based on Apache Cassandra) are intended to offer optimized storage and data access capabilities.

A database type known as a vector database is made expressly to store and query high-dimensional vectors. In a multidimensional space, where each dimension represents a distinct characteristic, which are mathematical representations of objects or data points called vectors.

A vector database's strength and power ultimately lie in this area. Vector search—which is what AI processes use to provide the correlation of data by comparing the mathematical embedding, or encoding, of the data with the search parameters and returning a result that is on the same path with the same trajectory as the query—is ultimately enabled by the ability to store and retrieve large volumes of data as vectors in a multi-dimensional space. Compared to standard keyword searches, this enables a much larger scope result and can account for a lot more data when new data is added.

Most people are probably familiar with recommendation engines, which analyze a user's search and suggest other items they might find interesting. For example, consider a viewer who is binge-watching a sci-fi western-themed show on their preferred streaming provider. Without having to tag every piece of media with a theme, Netflix can quickly and easily recommend other shows or films that are nearest neighbors using vector search on the entire media library. In addition, the viewers will probably receive other nearest neighbor results for other themes that they may not have been specifically querying but have relevance to their viewing patterns based on the shows they are interested in.

Providing NoSQL-based solutions is a big business. Thus, multiple vendors have offerings in this area, apart from Apache. For example, Cassandra is an open-source distributed NoSQL database that's highly scalable, fault tolerant, and used to manage huge volumes of data. It is based on Amazon's Dynamo. Deciding on relational database systems or on the NoSQL system is guided by multiple factors and requirements. Table 4-8 shows some conditions that play a critical role in that decision-making process.

Table 4-8. *Specific Business Uses of RDBMS and NoSQL Systems*

Use an RDBMS When You Need/Have	Use NoSQL When You Need/Have
Centralized applications (e.g., ERP)	Decentralized applications (e.g., web, mobile, and IoT)
Reasonable to high availability	Continuous availability; no downtime
Reasonable velocity data	High velocity data (devices, sensors, etc.)
Data coming in from one or a few locations	Data coming in from many locations
When data is primarily available in a structured form	When data is structured or semi/unstructured
Complex/nested transactions	Simple transactions
Primary concern is scaling reads	Concern is to scale both writes and reads
Philosophy of scaling up for more users/data	Philosophy of scaling out for more users/data
To maintain moderate data volumes with purge ability	To maintain high data volumes; retain forever

MangoDB

The other popular NoSQL database is MangoDB. It is fundamentally a distributed database. However, MongoDB is also used as a document database because of its excellent features like scalability and flexibility. It also provides querying and indexing features. Here are some interesting features of MangoDB:

- Great for general purpose uses

- Excellent as a document database

- An open-source product

MangoDB is great for dealing with time-series data (sets of values detected at different timestamps), including sensor data. This feature makes MangoDB one of the main choices for applications targeted to:

- Financial market prices

- Sensors (temperature, pressure, and proximity)

- Industrial fleets (location, velocity, and operations)

- Social networks

- Mobile devices

In the era of cloud computing, MangoDB as a company came up with its "cloud specific offering" known as MongoDB Atlas. It is a cloud targeted and hosted Database-as-a-Service offering. The package works in a pay-as-you-go mode and primarily permits users to deploy their applications on Amazon Web Services (AWS). It also has support for the Microsoft Azure and Google Cloud Platform. Recently, MongoDB came up a connector for Spark, which gives the users an analytics processing engine that enables them to query live MongoDB data.

Apache Storm

Storm is a distributed real-time computation system for processing large volumes of high-velocity data. Storm is a free and open-source distributed computation system. It is fault-tolerant and effective in real-time environments. Its real-time capabilities make it easy to process unbounded streams of data. It is different from traditional batch systems. Traditional system work in store and process fashion, whereas Storm uses an unbounded sequence of tuples (core unit of data). Storm makes it easy to reliably process unbounded streams of data, doing for real-time processing what Hadoop did for batch processing.

An application is defined and identified in Storm through a topology. The topology explains its logic as a DAG (directed acyclic graph) of operators and data streams. In Storm terminologies/context, a graph is an assemblage of nodes that are linked by edges. The nodes denote executable tasks and the edges are task dependencies. In the most simplistic form, the DAG can be visualized as a flow chart that tells the system which tasks to perform and in which order. Let's look at the two most important components of Storm—spouts and bolts.

- *Spouts*: Sources of data streams. Their role is to read data from external sources (e.g., Twitter or the Facebook API) or from physical/virtual disks and emit or pass the data into the topology.

- *Bolts*: Process input streams and (eventually) produce output streams. They represent the application logic.

Apache Solr

Apache Solr is the open-source enterprise search platform that is based on Java search servers. It is used for multiple purposes and applications related to search. Typically, it is used for searches of data stored in HDFS on a Hadoop cluster. It is one of the prime applications of Solr in the enterprises. Solr is popular because it's flexible and easy to integrate into machine learning and Big Data technologies. It is a scalable, fault tolerant, mature, and reliable open-source enterprise search platform. Solr is built on Apache Lucene, which is an information retrieval software library.

Solr is widely used with enterprise content management systems to provide full-text and near real-time indexing to big Internet sites. For example, Alfresco and Drupal use Apache Solr to incorporate search capabilities and provide benefits to end users. It is excellent in finding tabular, text, geo-location, or sensor data stored in Hadoop and is optimized for handling high volumes of web traffic.

Apache Spark

Apache Spark is an open-source cluster computing-based processing framework for large-scale data processing. It is built on in-memory compute engines. Spark can run up to 100 times faster than the older technologies like Hadoop MapReduce in memory. Also, it can be ten times faster on disk for program execution.

Spark provides in-memory computations (processing happens in local memory), which means it achieves increased speed and data processing over MapReduce. Spark empowers high-performance querying on Big Data. It takes advantage of a parallel data processing framework that persists data in-memory and disks if needed. It runs on top of the existing Hadoop cluster and can access HDFS, and it also processes structured data from Hive. It streamlines data from HDFS, Flume, Kafka, Twitter, and other sources (Flume and Kafka are explained later in this chapter). Spark is mostly supported by the Big Data vendors and open-source community. However, the Microsoft Azure implementation of Spark is easy and cost effective. One of the prime reasons to deploy Spark and Spark-based solutions on Microsoft Azure is that no hardware needs to be procured and no software needs to be configured, due to its cloud-based nature. Azure also facilitates third-party integration of Spark with business intelligence tools.

Azure HDInsight

Microsoft and Hortonworks are working together to help companies realize the advantages of Big Data analytics through HDInsight. HDInsight is an Apache Hadoop distribution powered by the enormous potential and efficiencies of the cloud. It scales horizontally and vertically, based on dynamic demand. This capability allows HDInsight to deal with any volume of data. It also natively integrates with Azure Data Lake Store. Azure HDInsight is intended to make Hadoop and Spark simple with lower manageability costs. It provides higher developer productivity for making Big Data-based solutions. It provides 63 percent lower total cost of ownership (TCO) to the customers. Practically speaking, HDInsight is offered as Hadoop-as-a-Service, hence no additional hardware is required.

Azure HDInsight uses the Hortonworks data platform and easily integrates between on-premise and cloud solutions. It also makes hybrid deployments easy over on-premises and the cloud. By addressing both environments with a common platform, Microsoft is guiding users on a path that delivers the advantages of the public cloud while respecting the complexities of today's on-premises large data initiatives

When customers want to move code or projects from on-premises to the cloud, it's done with a few clicks and within a few minutes, without buying hardware or hiring specialized operations teams typically associated with Big Data infrastructure. It is a managed Hadoop service and it has the most Apache projects in the cloud. It benefits from core Hadoop offerings like HDFS, YARN, MapReduce, Hive, Tez, Pig, Sqoop, Oozie, Mahout, and Zookeeper and advanced workloads, including Spark, Storm, HBase, and R Server.

The practice of combining data from several sources to create new output with more significance and usefulness is known as data integration. In the following situations, data integration is unquestionably required:

- Moving data from a source or collection of sources to a desired location. This is required to make data accessible to various stakeholders and consumers in various formats.

- Gaining knowledge from data. Organizations seek to gain insights from data, which is now readily available. They need to combine, purge, enrich, and store data from various sources in a data warehouse in order to develop solutions that offer insights.

- Producing reports and dashboards in real-time.

- Developing analytics-based solutions.

Microsoft Azure HDInsight is an integral part of the Cortana intelligence suite, which is a Microsoft machine learning solution that provides an end-to-end solution, from information management to machine learning, dashboards, and cognitive services. Azure HDInsight is based on architecture that supports redundancy. This provides it with high availability. It is available 99.9 percent of the time and provides support 24*7 to the enterprise.

The Presentation and Application Layer

This layer is integrative, which means it combines multiple layers. However, segregation is still possible. I discuss the presentation and application layers separately here.

- *Application layer*: This layer provides user interfaces for using Big Data applications. Applications from different areas—like transportation, retail, healthcare, manufacturing supply chain, and governments—all sit here.

- *Presentation layer*: This layer presents the insights and intelligence generated with the help of machine learning and the data analytics layer to the targeted audience, including users and decision-makers. Clear, brief, visual, understandable presentations are available through this layer. Also, critical communication to the decision-makers is provided through this layer. Data and facts without proper presentation and articulation have no meaning, especially for people who do not have a background in statistics. The communication and presentations are done through interactive reports, charts, figures, key recommendations, and suggestions.

The major technologies associated with this layer are described in the following list. Apart from them, there are multiple other offerings that you can consider for specific needs.

- *SQL Server Reporting Services (SSRS)*: This tool is an offering from Microsoft. SSRS provides a platform for creating and delivering reports that can be viewed in a wide range of electronic document formats, including Excel, Word, PDF, image, and XML. It can also be integrated through HDInsight to Hive tables to fetch and display data.

- *Excel/Excel BI/Power BI*: Facts and data can be represented in multiple ways to the users, managers, and decision-makers. Microsoft Excel, Excel BI, and Power BI offer many features, including:

  - Bar graphs

  - Line graphs

  - Pie charts (multiple options)

  - Scatter plots

- *Oracle Business Intelligence Enterprise Edition (OBIEE)*: An excellent offering from Oracle. It can be easily integrated to a Big Data store like Hive to fetch and showcase data. OBIEE works seamlessly with traditional data stores as well. Therefore, it can be used as one data visualization tool for both types of data, structured and unstructured. It also provides Hadoop access to users without programming knowledge. It is good at doing federated queries across Hadoop and Oracle to avoid constant data movement. If required, it can be tiered together with the other data stores like SQL Server.

- *IBM Cognos*: IBM created a group of Big Data and analytics tools on top of the Hadoop architecture. They call it BigInsights. It contains tools for scaling and managing the Big Data and machine learning platforms. Cognos is the part of that suite and it uses Hadoop as a data source. Cognos connects to Hadoop using Hive.

- *New data visualization tools*: Good presentation of
  the data is not enough if it makes no sense. Therefore,
  presenting data in a meaningful way is equally
  important. With the evolution of Big Data, multiple new
  data visualization tools emerged that can be used for
  this purpose. The only criteria is that they effectively
  display maps, text, data connections, behaviors, and
  emotions.

Google Maps, Earth, and Places are a few options used to present
maps in several ways. D3.js, which is a JavaScript library, can be used to
display data in multiple formats and types, including box plots, bubble
charts, bullet charts, non-contiguous cartograms, chord diagrams, contour
plots, dispatching events, spline interpolations, and dendrograms. Tools
like Crazy Egg are used for multiple purposes to capture and present
user behaviors and emotions, like tracking visitors' clicks on a website.
It also generates heat maps that indicate which part of site/page gets the
most attention. Multiple tools and their online versions are available for
displaying connections, including Microsoft Knowledge map and Ayadsi.
Connection tools typically help establish relationships between different
available data sets, so that holistic insights can be developed.

- *Infographics*: Infographics is one of the new ways
  of presenting Big Data. As the name suggests, it
  is a combination of information and graphics. In
  infographics, the facts are presented in the form of
  charts, texts, or graphics, which provide a snapshot
  of facts to the users. Typically, this is a one-pager to
  provide the user with instant information.

  Data is scattered in multiple places and in multiple
  forms. For example, it resides in Excel sheets, several
  reports, emails, charts, and databases. Busy managers

and decision-makers cannot go through it to get insights. Infographics become handy here, as they provide the desired information on one page. Therefore, a good infographic must be visually attractive and include useful content.

- *Many other tools on a dashboard*: This is one way to present information visually to management. Strategic decision making becomes easy for management with the help of a dashboard, because all the desired information is available to the users/decision-makers in a consolidated format. Dashboards need not be associated with strategies. They can be extended to the operational level or present operational information. KPIs (key performance indicators) can be integrated into it, to provide a snapshot to the users.

This layer is very useful, as it provides the freedom, flexibility, and opportunity to see and analyze a holistic picture quickly in a graphical format. Therefore, it enables quick decision making. All this is useful only if it is targeted to the right audience.

Offerings from Vendors in the Big Data Space

While discussing Big Data and Big Data analytics-based technologies, the Apache offering is the focus. Apart from Apache, there are other companies that provide end-to-end solutions. This includes IBM, Google, and many more. Discussing offerings and solutions from all vendors is not possible here due to space constraints. However, you will take a quick look at a couple of big offerings. This will help you when making decisions.

CHAPTER 4 TECHNOLOGY STACK FOR MACHINE LEARNING AND ASSOCIATED TECHNOLOGIES

An excellent decision tree available at `https://biz-excellence.com/2016/09/13/machine-learning-dt/` provides an overview of decisions related to Big Data implementation. The graph depicts the situations and provides suggestions from the Microsoft perspective.

Real-Life Scenarios

Big Data has a role in many areas. A few use cases are provided here:

- *Anti-money laundering and Big Data*: Anti-money laundering is one of the important areas of financial institutions. By using effective transition monitoring, anti-money laundering solutions and systems are enhanced and work well with Big Data analytics solutions. They are used to develop complex detection models by leveraging additional transaction data using structured and semi-structured data. This type of developed model can effectively handle data that exists in inconsistent formats. Along with machine learning technologies, the models are tuned based on need. Unsupervised machine learning is applied to find undiscovered new attributes, which may be related to the anti-money laundering related risks. Also, behavioral model creation is possible due to Big Data analytics, which ultimately helps discover uncommon behaviors. This further extends to notification and alerts based on anomalies.

- *Smart reporting for decision-makers*: Decision-makers need intelligent and insightful reports because raw data is of no use. Also, to explain company performance and offer forecasts, they need good reports. Machine learning, along with Big Data, did the quantum shift to reporting. By connecting multiple processes in an end-to-end fashion and using the right digital technologies and analytics, organizations can start delivering quicker, more insightful outcomes. This results in increased market confidence. On the ground level, they present the forecast of the company's performance in a confident way by using intuitive and smart reports. Machine learning analytics-based reporting solutions provide a new style to data organization, authentication, and understanding. This happens because of automating annotations and report generation using cutting-edge digital technologies and analytics.

The integration of Big Data and machine learning makes the cloud-based reporting solution an excellent option to pull and integrate structured, unstructured financial and non-financial data from in-house and exterior data sources. It also automates reporting using innovative process-centric technologies, like natural language processing, machine learning, and cognitive and predictive analytics. The machine learning reporting solution presents influential insights to decision-makers with the help of the following key components of the technology stack:

- *Data sourcing*: The solution identifies and extracts data from the relevant internal sources.

- *Data preparation*: Data is prepared for analysis using machine learning. This permits automated report creation with personalized reporting views.

- *Data analytics*: At this layer, business rules are defined and the analytics happens. Also, hundreds of "what if" scenarios and trend analysis capabilities are incorporated here.

- *Commentary generation*: Using natural language processing and generation, the solution automates variance analysis and commentary scripting in a methodical and organized way.

Machine learning enables better-quality predictions and forecasting by reimagining reporting results and implanting the intelligence reporting solution into finance and other support functions. Using Big Data and machine learning enables reporting enterprises to influence:

- *Investor confidence*: Understanding that business act with additional information helps increase the faith of stakeholders.

- *Quickness and dynamism*: Support functions can produce actionable insights by reporting data quicker to allow real-time decision making. Automation also helps decision-makers become accustomed quickly to fluctuating business requirements and demand, which would significantly increase quickness in the decision.

- *Proficiency*: Enterprises, especially decision-makers, take advantage of efficient and real-time reporting in multiple ways, including the quick reaction time to the market sentiment and aligning their business functions and decisions accordingly.

The Machine Learning Technology Stack

The primary ingredient for building machine learning solutions is data. The source of that data is obviously the IoT devices, social medial, and so on. The data gathered from sensors is stored in the cloud or on-premise or a mix of both. Typically, these systems are designed so that they scale and handle huge amounts of data of all types. Then machine learning-specific algorithms and models, which are capable of learning from the data, make implications about the new data. After that, mathematical and machine learning libraries, frameworks, and programming languages like R, Python, and C# are used to realize requirements through code. There are many technologies, frameworks, processes, and skills involved in building effective machine learning solutions and they are discussed in detail in this chapter. However, it is good idea to take a look at the overall flow of machine learning from a technical perspective first.

The success of machine learning projects, applications, and products is based on multiple aspects. Therefore, selecting the best technical stack, including hardware and software, becomes critical. A good choice leads to extraordinary results, whereas a bad choice can lead to disastrous situations. For example, from a technical perspective, machine learning projects require massive computational capabilities to crunch and process data in real time, which would shorten the time needed to train the system and make the overall response time faster. Parallel processing of vast amounts of unstructured data, like video streams and sensor data feeds in real time, enables machine learning systems to provide just-in-time reliable results.

Speed, agility, and using underlying hardware are important criteria for building a good machine learning platform. Hence, while you are considering building a technology stack for a machine learning system, you need to think about the development systems (hardware and software) equipped with processors with multiple integrated cores and faster memory subsystems. They must process good architecture that can parallelize processing and contain excellent concurrent multi-threading abilities. The platform must have built-in flexibility to support scalable clusters (if the complex solution needs to be built) that you would use to train complex machine learning models.

Selecting specialized hardware is critical. Betting on offerings like Intel® Xeon Phi™ is an excellent choice because it's the first bootable host processor specifically designed for highly parallel workloads. It is also the first of its type to integrate memory and fabric technologies. Machine learning applications developed on frameworks like Caffe and Theano are good choices. Then, selecting the software framework that would be in tune with the underlying hardware is important.

The selection of the software, libraries, frameworks, and hardware must be based on need, ease of use, and requirements. For example, selecting the tools that provide good drag-and-drop interfaces to enable data scientists and programmers to create high-performance machine learning applications is a prime factor of the success of your machine learning projects. Microsoft Azure ML is easy to use and fast. If the requirements, infrastructure, and cost permits, Azure ML is a good choice. Lastly, but most importantly, people are an important factor of success. Ultimately, people are the real resource who realize the vision of an enterprise and serve the stakeholders. Therefore, their well-being needs to be considered and incorporated as an integral part of the product vision.

As discussed in Chapter 1, the machine learning layer takes input from the Big Data analytics layer. This concept can be visualized in multiple ways. For example, machine learning technologies may be part of the data analytics layer or they can be incorporated into the separate layer dedicated to machine learning. However, segregation, or division of the concerns, has multiple benefits, as it equips an enterprise to tune the technical architecture to synchronize with their requirements and needs. This fulfills the overall motive to present an architecture that's decoupled and extendable.

From a platform perspective, a machine learning technology stack can be divided into multiple layers. Each layer in turn is supposed to perform and coordinate some tasks. The main layers and associated technologies are described here:

- Connector layer

- Storage layer

- Processing layer

- Model and runtime layer

- Presentation and application layer

The Connector Layer

This layer collects data from applications and other data sources available in the cloud or from on-premise systems. This opens the gates to get data from enterprise systems, including ERP, CRM, HR, marketing automation, business intelligence, procurement, and financial systems or from the IoT devices. For example, say an enterprise uses multiple sources to gather and process data from systems provided by the vendors, including Salesforce, Oracle, NetSuite, Workday, Birst, Concur, and Coupa. That data would be pulled and passed to further layers through this layer. Technologies, like BigML from Informatica or tools like Kafka, MQTT, or even REST (a few are discussed in the Big Data section), would be used here. There are tons of offerings available from multiple vendors in this area and they all have pros and cons. It would be very difficult to summarize all the technologies available in this space into one chapter. However, some important ones are described in the next sections. Let's start with the new kid on the block—Logic Apps from Microsoft.

Logic Apps

Logic Apps is a hosted piece of integration logic in the Microsoft Azure cloud-based platform. It does hosting on Azure in a similar way as would be achieved for any web applications by other online/offline means. It also provides the facility to build the logic by creating a trigger followed by a series of actions similar to creating a workflow. The advantage of Logic Apps is that Microsoft provided many connectors that enable applications/products to connect quickly through various protocols. It enables applications to connect to a wide range of applications as well. Logic Apps runs on the cloud, so hosting, scalability, availability, and management are not bottlenecks.

Apache Flume

Apache Flume is used for efficiently and effectively gathering, combining, and moving large amounts of streaming data. The data may be comprised of application logs or sensor and machine generated data on a Hadoop distributed filesystem. It works in a distributed manner. Flume enjoys a robust and flexible architecture based on streaming data flows. It has excellent fault tolerance, failover, and data recovery capabilities.

MQTT

MQTT is a binary messaging transport protocol. It follows the OASIS standard and uses the client-server specific publish and subscribe model. It is an open, simple, and easy to implement messaging transport protocol. The best part of MQTT are its lightweight features. Therefore, it becomes a perfect option for IoT-based devises. For IoT devices, the HTTP protocol is too bulky. MQTT is designed with minimal protocol overhead. Thus, it has become a perfect option for machine-to-machine (M2M) and IoT-based applications/devices/objects. MQTT is also good at utilizing low network bandwidth and inherited most of the characteristics of the TCP transport. For MQTT, a TCP stack is the bare minimum.

Apache Kafka

Kafka is a high-quantity distributed messaging system. It is an excellent fault-tolerant tool that stores and processes streams of records as they occur. It is generally used for building real-time streaming applications that require transformation or quick reaction time on the data. It runs as a cluster on servers. The servers may be one or a combination of servers.

The Kafka "organizations" organize records into multiple categories, known as topics. Each record consists of a key/value pair and a timestamp. Consumers in Kafka are processes that subscribe to topics and in turn process the feed of published messages. Kafka runs as a cluster comprised of one or more servers, each of which is called a broker.

Kafka get its work done through four main APIs:

- *Producer*: Allows an application to publish a stream record to one or more Kafka topics.

- *Consumer*: Allows an application to subscribe to one or more topics and process the stream of records produced by them.

- *Streams*: Makes an application work as a stream processor. It does this by absorbing a stream of input data or records from one or multiple topics (depending on the design and architecture) and in turn produces an output stream to one or several output topics. Basically, it transforms the input streams to output streams.

- *Connector*: Generally used for construction and running reusable producers and consumers for the other uses. Kafka basically provides the ability to connect to topics for producers and consumers who already use applications or data systems/sources. For example, if a connector works on a relational database, it must gather and capture changes that happen to a table.

Apache Sqoop

Apache Sqoop is used to transfer data between unstructured data sources to a relational database system. It can also be used to transfer data to mainframe systems. It transforms the data using technologies like Hadoop MapReduce. Also, it provides functionality to export the data back into the RDBMS.

The Storage Layer

Most of the details and technologies related to this layer were discussed in the IoT and Big Data technology stack section. However, if you want to know about those technologies, you can refer to the specific details in those sections.

The Processing Layer

Most of the details and technologies related to this layer were discussed in the IoT and Big Data technology stack section. However, if you want to know about those technologies, you can refer to the specific details in those sections. Many technologies are discussed in the Big Data analytics section. On top of that, other data processing and analytics tools and techniques are available. Covering all of them is not possible, but a brief discussion follows.

The Model and Runtime Layer

This layer contains, facilitates, and uses frameworks, tools, and runtime systems that manage the entire lifecycle of the machine learning models. Machine learning models must be trained, validated, and monitored before deploying them into production. This requires many steps in order to operationalize a model's lifecycle. Managing a machine learning model in a systematic way is a challenging task. It involves lots of complexity and depends on factors like monitoring, retraining, and redeployment.

The next sections discuss some of the relevant technologies in this layer.

Apache Mahout

Mahout is a scalable machine learning library from Apache. It uses the MapReduce paradigm. When combined with other Hadoop technologies, it can be used as an inexpensive solution to solve machine learning problems. It is implemented on top of Apache Hadoop. Mahout serves as an excellent tool for finding meaningful patterns by running on the underlying data set. Once Big Data is stored on HDFS, Mahout runs automatically on them and extracts meaningful patterns from the diverse data sets. Apache Mahout converts Big Data into information and then into knowledge in faster and more efficient ways. Mahout performs all the important machine learning core activities, including the following:

- *Collaborative filtering*: Used to provide product recommendations by mining user behavior. Technically, collaborative filtering (CF) is a technique that uses user information such as ratings, clicks, and purchases to provide recommendations specific to the site users. The uses of collaborative filtering (CF) vary, including recommending consumer items such as music and movies based on design and targeting audiences of a particular business.

- *Clustering and classification*: Performs clustering activities. For example, it takes items from a particular group (web pages, newspaper articles, emails, and phone calls) and organizes them into similar collection

313

sets (web pages of same type, emails of similar type, and so on). Also, it can organize and reorganize things from a particular class and categorize them into naturally occurring groups. Organizing items into groups belonging to same cluster that are similar to each other is very helpful. Clustering and classification techniques are useful for acquiring knowledge from existing groups.

- *Item set mining*: This activity is about analyzing items in a group (e.g., items in a shopping cart or terms in a query session) and then identifying which items typically appear together.

Mahout supports multiple algorithms. A few of them are listed here:

- Clustering: K-means and Fuzzy K-means

- Classification: SVM and Random forests

- Recommenders

- Pattern mining

- Regression analysis

Amazon's Deep Scalable Sparse Tensor Network Engine (DSSTNE)

This is an open-source software library for training and deploying recommendation models. DSSTNE has been used at Amazon to produce custom-made and individualized product endorsements for customers. It is intended for production deployment of real-world applications that need to stress speed and scale over investigational elasticity. It is also capable of extending deep learning beyond speech, language understanding, and object recognition. It takes deep learning to areas like search and recommendations.

Google TensorFlow

Google initially developed TensorFlow to create its own machine learning systems. Later, they released the framework for general and commercial use. It is open-source software. Google wants to use TensorFlow in their existing and upcoming projects like next generation of Gmail, video intelligence, and image and speech recognition applications. As of now, it is retrieved through Python or C++ interfaces. Therefore, knowing how to code in Python or C++ is necessary in order to use TensorFlow.

Microsoft Cognitive Toolkit

This tool allows users to make neural networks portrayed in focused graphs. While principally made for speech recognition technology, it is now used as a general machine learning and cognitive toolkit that supports image, text, and RNN training. It also allows users to infer the intelligence in enormous data sets through deep learning without compromised scaling, speed, and accuracy with commercial-grade value and compatibility. It does all this with the help of programming languages and algorithms that users already use or are familiar with.

It is constructed with sophisticated algorithms to work consistently with huge data sets. Skype, Cortana, Bing, Xbox, and industry-leading data scientists now use the Microsoft Cognitive Toolkit to create high-quality artificial intelligence applications and products. The Microsoft Cognitive Toolkit also provides the greatest communicative, easy-to-use architecture. It allows working with familiar languages and networks. For example, users can use languages like C++ and Python to play with MCT (Microsoft Cognitive Toolkit). It also permits users to modify any of the built-in training algorithms, or to use their own customized versions.

Microsoft M.NET

Without leaving the .NET ecosystem, ML.NET enables you to build unique ML models in C# or F#. You can simply include machine learning into your web, mobile, desktop, gaming, and IoT products with the help of ML.NET because it enables you to reuse all the knowledge, skills, code, and libraries you already have as a .NET developer. To make creating custom ML Models incredibly simple, ML.NET provides Model Builder (a straightforward UI tool) and ML.NET CLI. These tools use Automated ML (AutoML), a state-of-the-art innovation that streamlines the creation of the top-performing models for your machine learning scenario.

All you need to do to begin developing a model is load your data; the rest is handled by AutoML. TensorFlow, ONNX, Infer.NET, and other well-known machine learning frameworks can all be used with ML.NET to access even more machine learning scenarios, including image classification, object identification, and more. ML.NET successfully trained a sentiment analysis model with 95 percent accuracy using a 9GB set of Amazon review data. Due to memory issues, other well-known machine learning frameworks were unable to process the data set. To allow all the frameworks to finish training, 10 percent of the data set was used for training, and ML.NET showed the highest speed and accuracy. Similar outcomes in other machine learning contexts, such as click-through rate predictions, were discovered during the performance review.

Apart from these offerings, multiple others exist and a few of them are covered in Chapter 3.

Other Solutions

There are multiple vendors and companies that provide machine learning solutions. For example, there is an offering from Spark in the form of the MLLib machine learning library and Azure ML from Microsoft. A few offerings overlap or borrow technologies from each other in order to provide good solutions to a wider audience. For example, Mahout and MLLib both have a common execution engine. However, Mahout focuses on machine learning and has a rich set of algorithms, while MLLib only adopts some mature and essential algorithms. Google's TensorFlow, Nervana Systems Neon, and IBM's deep learning platform, Caffe, Torch, and Theano are some of the existing technical offerings from vendors in regard to machine learning. However, the list does not end here and is increasing day by day.

A number of startups and established software companies have been developing their own machine learning frameworks and applications. For example, Microsoft came up with Distributed Machine Learning Toolkit and Intel offers the Trusted Analytics Platform. Netflix, Pandora, Spotify, and Snapchat also provide machine learning-centric products. A few lesser known startups—including Teradeep, Enlitic, Ersatz Labs, Clarifai, MetaMind, and Skymind—provide lots of innovative features in their machine learning-based products. The following section discusses the comparative study of some of the frameworks centered on machine learning.

The Presentation and Application Layer

The details about this layer are covered in the previous section. Refer to the appropriate section for further details.

Real-Life Scenarios

Video Analytics

This is used to analyze streaming video feeds received from cameras. It makes real-time analysis available about the activities of people, objects, and things. It can help recognize the activities or change around any boundary in real time. Smart video analytics is capable of catalog alerts,

317

notifications, and other actions across cameras and sensors. Therefore, a complete set of characteristics can be indexed covering every incident. One of the main reasons for using this technology is the area of emotion recognition, where video analytics is used to analyze emotions in real time. It also found its application in one of the most happening areas of self-driving automobiles.

Digital Adoption and Client Engagement

As mentioned, banks can use machine learning analytics to build stronger client relationships. Especially in situations when correlating different data points about client relationships and trading history analysis is required. The solution will also cater to the requirements of personalized client offerings and provide the global view of the customer. This case study highlights the use of specific technologies at each level of customer engagement application. This technology stack for the application takes care of multiple use cases at the same time, such as client behavior mapping and analysis, targeted advertainment recommendations, and so on.

Automated Intelligent Machine Learning-Based Email and Chat Management System

A machine learning application interprets and understands incoming emails and chats to understand customers and provide relevant responses. This can help agents provide quick, effective, and efficient customer service. This overall process of providing thoughtful results is based on the solid foundation of technology and sentiment analysis. The machine learning solution automatically separates and categorizes the incoming emails and chats. Here are the basic steps:

1. Automatically separate and categorize incoming emails and chats.

2. Analyze the email and chats based on context in order to understand intent and emotions imbedded in them.

3. After analysis, provide insights and give recommendations.

4. Take feedback and utilize that to further improve the system.

The smart machine learning targeted automation of email and chat management helps advisors deal with the back and forth with clients and provide them more time for other purposes.

Other Use Cases

- Machine learning-based forecasting systems anticipate power requirements, especially peaks and troughs in real time. They adjust the system accordingly to maximize the use of the available power grid. These same techniques can be used to maximize the use of intermittent renewable power.

- Facial recognition techniques incorporated in the software, along with machine learning, natural language processing, and deep learning, enable virtual agents and physical agents to provide context-based information. Depending on your mood, situation, culture, and geographical conditions, the virtual agent can adjust the greeting style. They can "anticipate" orders and provide personalized directions and guidelines.

- Computer vision and deep and machine learning identify items brought by customers in the retail store. Depending on the context, they can add more relevant data available through the sensors. After that, analysis happens on a machine learning-based system, which allows non-stop checkout and automatic payments.

- Interactive screens and household devices enabled with computer vision and machine learning technologies can identify/recognize goods and suggest complementary products that match the customer's lifestyle.

Role of Cloud Computing in the Machine Learning Technology Stack

Cloud computing has affected businesses in a big way in recent times. Nearly all functions in enterprise IT are influenced by the cloud computing paradigm. From development and testing to resiliency and backup, the IT ecosystem of cloud computing appears everywhere. It established itself as a new paradigm of building and managing applications. Cloud computing not only affects everyone in the IT department, but also affects the enterprise as a whole. Having said that, the reality is that not everything has been migrated to the cloud. On-premise systems and infrastructures are here to stay. In coming times, the mix and match of cloud and on-premise infrastructure is a reality. A machine learning or Big Data analytics solution will be developed, developed, tested, and validated on these hybrid models. Vendors like Google, IBM, and Microsoft offer excellent products and services in the cloud computing space. They provide end-to-end solutions to achieve almost anything on the cloud, from small retail applications to high performance machine learning and cognitive computing solutions.

Worldwide companies have either started or are starting to implement and use distributed technology platforms like Hadoop and Mahout in cloud-based environments to fulfill machine learning-specific needs. They are doing this to run increasingly advanced experiments and business logic on larger data sets. Technical teams are constrained by the explicit maximum amount of available on-premise resources (e.g., compute, disk, memory, and network). This situation is the by-product of dynamically changing data sets and requirements. Therefore, if they use the on-premise infrastructure, they are limited either by their computer's components or by the available resources of the cluster.

These limitations affect the productivity of project teams in many ways, including loss of productivity, lower accuracy, wasted resources, and limitations of capacity planning. Data is the raw quantifiable resource for the product of the cloud and machine learning. Data sizes are increasing at the rate of tenfold every five years. Using this rolling flow to attain a modest advantage is powering the growth of Big Data analytics and machine learning techniques.

Cloud and machine learning analytics (Big Data analytics and machine learning) are two topics that have almost merged in recent times. The cloud permits enterprises to subcontract maintenance and hosting of their business applications. Also, they are doing the same with their IT infrastructure. This saves lots of money because they are paying on a "use" basis and not investing in procuring, maintaining, and scaling the infrastructure. This has led to dramatic decreases of prices, ease of scale, and higher readiness or availability. However, to achieve the benefits and robustness of the cloud, companies have to migrate their data to the cloud service provider's data center. In the initial days of the cloud, there was an issue with data security. But the systems and overall cloud ecosystem have matured enough that this is not an issue any more. The cost benefits and ease of use lead companies to provision the machine learning and Big Data technology stack on the cloud. With the help of the cloud-based provisioned technology stacks, they can store and perform analytics on huge volumes of data. This permits them to generate deeper insights (including cognitive and anticipative cognitive insight) on the data. A machine learning technology stack can be hosted privately, as a hybrid cloud, preoperatory, or as a public cloud.

The Cognitive Computing Technology Stack

Cognitive computing systems gather and process structured and unstructured data in a natural way with the help of natural language processing (NLP) technologies. They take the input from the analytics and machine learning-enabled APS and then reason, learn, and generate contextual patterns and associations. This capability of cognitive computing allows humans to connect the dots faster and in smarter ways and to make more informed decisions and drive better outcomes.

It is feasible to develop apps around Generative AI technologies like Azure OpenAI thanks to tools like Semantic Kernel, TypeChat, and LangChain. This is due to the fact that they let you impose limitations on the underlying large language model (LLM), employing it as a tool for creating and using natural language interfaces.

A deep neural network predicts the subsequent syllable in a string of tokens that come after your initial query in an LLM, which is a tool for exploring a semantic space. The LLM can exceed its inputs when a prompt is open-ended, creating material that may look logical but is in reality total gibberish.

Because LLM findings are just another facet of a well-known technology, you also tend to believe them more than search engine results. When massive language models are trained on trustworthy data from websites like Wikipedia, Stack Overflow, and Reddit, all that is gained is the ability to produce text that follows the same patterns as content in those sources. On occasion, the result could be accurate, but it might also be wrong.

How can you ensure that your consumers receive logical and accurate answers to their questions while guarding against erroneous and ludicrous output from your massive language models?

The LLM has to be restricted so that it can produce text from a much smaller collection of data. The new LLM-based development stack from Microsoft fills that need. It offers the required tools to control the model and stop it from making mistakes.

A LLM can be restricted by using a program like TypeChat to compel a certain output format or by employing an orchestration pipeline like Semantic Kernel to deal with additional reliable data sources, effectively "grounding" the model in a well-known semantic space. Here, the LLM can do its best function—summarizing a built prompt and producing text based on that prompt—without experiencing overruns (or at the very least, with a much decreased likelihood of doing so).

The basis of this last strategy is what Microsoft refers to as "semantic memory." In order to offer factual output from an LLM, semantic memory performs a vector search to produce a prompt. A vector search locates stored material that matches the initial user question, a vector database controls the context for the initial prompt, and the LLM creates text based on that data. This strategy is used by Microsoft's Bing Chat, which constructs responses using Bing's search database and native vector search capabilities.

Vector databases and vector search are the tools for creating practical, solid LLM-based applications thanks to semantic memory. A increasing variety of open-source vector databases are available, or you can add vector indexes to well-known SQL and NoSQL databases. One new competitor that stands out as being very helpful enhances Azure Cognitive Search by giving your data a vector index and additional APIs for searching that index.

Cognitive Computing vs Machine Learning

Cognitive computing APSs are different from typical machine learning APSs in the following ways:

- Cognitive computing is based on context-driven dynamic algorithms. Typically, it is excellent at automating pattern discovery and matching understanding knowledge. For example, researchers at the University of Boston developed a cognitive computing-based algorithm that enables robots to ask intelligent questions if they are confused while they are trying to get the best available objects. They can quantify the "want" of the user. When the certainty of the "want" is high, they supply the desired object, whereas if it is not that certain, the robot makes a best guess about what the person wants and asks relevant questions, such as "this one?" for confirmation.

- Cognitive computing APSs can reason and learn instantly based on data in a dynamic fashion. In a nutshell, they are typically good at making sense of things. For example, scientists at the University of Rutgers developed a system for a smartphone when the user wants to be interrupted or left alone. The phone can predict the user's approachability to smartphone disruption by gathering, analyzing, and processing the user's personality trails.

- Cognitive systems can infer, hypothesize, adapt, and improve over time and with data without explicit programming.

- They can interact with humans in a natural language, like English.

Machine learning is about creating intelligent APSs and machines. However, the industry is slowly moving away from developing merely intelligent devices and APSs. They are looking and thinking about intuitive APSs and machines that are more like humans. Technology companies and researchers across the industries, as well as research labs, are developing decision-making APSs and devices that will make decisions on the users' behalf based on data and other types of natural inputs. Cognitive computing can achieve this. This is a big motivation for companies to innovate and develop solutions that resemble the human brain.

The cognitive computing technology stack is defined in multiple ways (most of the layers have been discussed in previous sections). The basic characteristics of a cognitive computing system is that it must be able to make sense of enormous volumes of data, apply reasoning, provide context-based insights, and continuously learn while interacting with people, machines, or other systems. Based on these characteristics, it can be broadly divided into three layers:

- *Data processing layer*: At this layer, huge data sets are processed to facilitate intelligent human support and enable smart business decisions. At this layer, technologies related to hyperscale computing, high performance searches, and natural language processing come into the picture.

- *Deduction and machine learning layer*: At this layer, the machine simulates human thinking processes in an automated way. Here, technologies like neural networks, statistical modeling, and machine and deep learning come into the picture.

- *Sensory perception layer*: This layer enables and simulates sensory feelings generally associated with a living organism (usually humans). Sensations such as touch, sight, test, and smell are simulated. Also, emotion simulation happens here.

If you want to generalize this discussion and visualize these layers, you have to consider the other version of the explanation, described next.

- *Data gathering layer*: This layer gathers data from all the available sources, such as structured, unstructured, and semi-structured data. Technologies involvers include AppLogic.

- *Data preparation, extraction, and conversion layer*:
  Here, the raw data is prepared in a usable format by
  extracting it from data stores and converting it to the
  desired format. The technology includes ETL-based
  systems like Informatica.

- *Data processing layer*: The converted data is processed
  here. The technology involved includes Hive, Spark,
  and other processing technologies.

- *Analytics, machine learning, and cognitive layer*:
  Insight is generated by applying multiple analytics and
  machine learning technologies. Technologies involved
  are Apache Mahout, Microsoft Azure, and so on. Also,
  multiple types of analytics, including descriptive,
  predictive, prescriptive, and cognitive analytics, are
  performed here.

- *Presentation and application layer*: This layer presents
  the insight to the decision-makers in a usable way so
  they can make business critical decisions. This layer
  also contains applications that use context-based
  information. IBM Watson's user interface and Microsoft
  Cortana are examples. All the graphs and BI tools falls
  under this "logical" layer.

In a cognitive computing technology stack, data flows in the following
order: Data gathering layer ➤ Data preparation, extraction, and conversion
layer ➤ Data processing layer ➤ Analytics, machine learning and cognitive
layer ➤ Presentation and application layer.

The data stars its journey from the data gathering layer in raw format
in the cognitive computing technical stack and, by the time it reaches the
presentation and application layer, it becomes gold. Decision-makers

use this information through multiple BI tools to make business-critical decisions. Also, the applications that exist in this "logical" layer are useful for decision-makers and individuals alike.

Use Cases

Smart Assistance

With the help of cognitive computing, smart digital assistants and knowledge-management activities can provide enormous benefits. For example, the content separation and dynamic content arrangement with analytics permit the business to produce leads using a dashboard and comprehensive reports of unidentified user access. This is accomplished by monitoring segmented research reporting and contextual regulatory reporting and rating, which in turn results in better employee efficiency.

Innovative Monetization

A cloud-based cognitive solution that manages images and videos with smart enterprise federated keyword search and smart learning management system is very helpful in getting a business advantage. For example, it could enable the business to create a single administration console with forward-thinking image processing and document organization proficiencies. Also, it could provide bulk upload and download capabilities to exploit better-quality cross-sell/up-sell opportunities.

A Case of Anticipative Computing

Anticipation, machine learning, and artificial intelligence are closely related concepts. Anticipative cognitive computing refers to the area that deals with the prediction of the future, not just based on historical data but also on behavior, specific gestures, body movement, walking patterns, gait, and other biometric data before making any decisions in an automated fashion. It signifies the data and corrects it based on the feedback received from all the available sources.

The combination of anticipative cognitive computing and predictive analytics is the future. Users not only want to know what the best course of action is, but they also want to know what to do next. Anticipative cognitive computing answers both of these questions. Anticipation is based on the predictive model of the system. Visualize the game of cricket and imagine a wicketkeeper behind the wickets. A fast bowler is bowling, now the wicket keeper would move in the direction by anticipating that the ball is "going out to the wicket" or "coming toward the wicket" to gather the ball. It's a responsive action. Now imagine the same situation during the "super over" in T20 match of cricket. The wicketkeeper would dive in a direction to gather the ball by anticipating the bowler's and batsman's foot movement, eye movement, and past data about the specific player. This is a practical example of anticipation.

Cognitive systems are not very responsive in nature but are anticipative and predictive along with behavioral characters. If a bot, for example, is powered with the ability of anticipation, it could technically read, comprehend, and understand a person's facial expressions and gestures against some elementary queries and then come up with suggestions and recommendations. It is worth taking a look at a few important aspects of anticipative cognitive computing.

The key stages of cognitive anticipation are as follows:

- Stage 1: Gesture capturing

- Stage 2: Emotion recognition

- Stage 3: Face recognition

- Stage 4: Social networking data analytics

- Stage 5: Real-time integration and analysis of the previous stage with the help of Big Data analytics and machine learning technologies

- Stage 6: Anticipate the behavior

Anticipative cognitive computing is the mix of the following: Psychology + Neuroscience + Linguistics + Artificial Intelligence + Social Science.

Cognitive anticipation evolved in this order:

1. Descriptive computing

2. Predictive computing

3. Perceptive computing

4. Cognitive computing

5. Anticipative computing

The Cloud Computing Technology Stack

The cloud computing technology stack is discussed in detail in Chapter 1. However, for completeness, I provide a brief snapshot of it from the machine learning perspective. Cloud computing is the biggest enabler of the revolution in the field of machine learning because it is capable of solving two main roadblocks—the availability of low-cost computing resources on the go and access to massive volumes of data. All machine learning systems need these two to be operational. Here is the main layer of cloud computing.

- *Infrastructure-as-a-Service layer*: It makes the infrastructure available, which contains hardware, networking, and storage solutions.

- *Platform-as-a-Service layer*: It makes platforms available in the cloud infrastructure. Platforms like operating systems, databases, and middleware fall in this offering.

- *Machine Learning-as-a-Service*: At this layer, machine learning-based technologies are available in a pay-as-you-go mode. Therefore, using and leveraging their benefits is easy for anyone, including individuals and enterprises. Technologies such as Big Data analytics, speech recognition, computer vision, and natural language processing are available.

- *Software-as-a-Service*: Finally, at this layer, software is offered as a service, which uses the underlying technologies of all stacked layers. Software like ERP, CRM, mobile games, video, and FinTech exist in this space.

Audio and Video Links

- Microsoft Cognitive service: (3392) How to build apps using Microsoft Azure Cognitive services on YouTube

- Getting started with Azure Cognitive Services: (3392) Getting started with Azure Cognitive Services - YouTube

The Latest Research

- The new iPhone has augmented reality. Having a 3D camera allows the device to measure how far things are away from it. This is one of the basic and mandatory steps for placing computer graphics in the real world so that they can integrate with each other seamlessly.

- Researchers at the Georgia Institute of Technology have come up with innovative ways of controlling smartphones. They used LG and Sony smart watches for their experiments. Researchers showed that smartphones are "controlled" using swipes of the watchband, skin taps, and breaths. Using a combination of microphone and machine learning systems, a newly developed technique called "whoosh" can identify and recognize blowing, exhaling, shushing, sipping, and puffing in an independent manner. If users hush on their smart watches to calm an incoming call, that means they are not interested in taking the call. If they have to take a call, they blow on the phone twice to accept it.

- Snapchat developed smart glasses called Spectacles and at the moment they are in the final stages of research. This glass contains a camera in the frame and users can capture videos and upload them on Snapchat. Spectacles record 10 seconds of circular video of 115 with built-in 115 degrees of lens. The captured videos are automatically transferred to the local machine as well to the cloud.

- The dating app called Hinge comes with a personal assistant, which will message you with the most appropriate dates. The VA is called Audrey.

Summary

This chapter explained in detail the technology stacks available for IoT, Big Data analytics, machine learning, and cognitive computing. It provided a glimpse at all the main technologies available for these stacks. It also discussed this technology in current business scenarios.

Mind Map

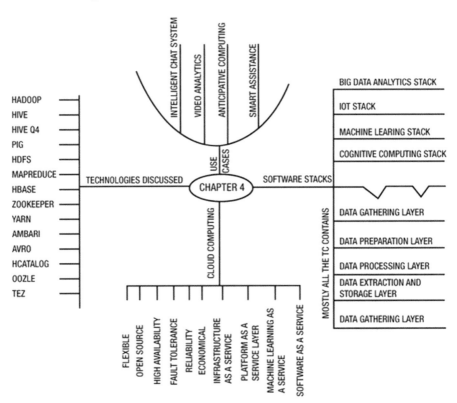

CHAPTER 5

Industrial Applications of Machine Learning

Dr. Patanjali Kashyap[a*]

ᵃ Bangalore, Karnataka, India

Abstract

Machine learning is set to unleash the next wave of digital disruption. Enterprises are preparing for it. The companies who adopted it early are benefitting from it. Technologies like robotics and autonomous vehicles, computer vision, natural language processing, virtual agents, deep learning, and machine learning are the technologies of the future. The new generation of machine learning applications are based on digitization. In most cases, sectors that adopted digitization are leading the machine learning space as well. Also, they are predicted to drive growth. Machine learning is likely to quicken the changes in market share, revenue, and profit pools. All of these are trademarks of digitally disrupted sectors, products, and applications.

© Dr. Patanjali Kashyap 2024
P. Kashyap, *Machine Learning for Decision Makers*,
https://doi.org/10.1007/978-1-4842-9801-5_5

There are many ways to classify machine learning technologies, but it is problematic to draft a list that is mutually exclusive and collectively exhaustive. The reason for this is that humans generally fuse and match multiple technologies to produce resolutions for separate problems. These formations every now and then are treated as autonomous technologies, sometimes as subcategories of supplementary technologies, and sometimes as applications. A few frameworks group machine learning technologies by fundamental functionality, such as text, speech, or image recognition, and others group them by commercial applications such as commerce or cybersecurity. Therefore, sector-by-sector adoption of machine learning is highly uneven, at least at the moment. This trend in the acceptance of technology is not new; we have encountered this behavior in companies accepting social technologies. This suggests that, at least in the coming future, machine learning deployment is expected to fast-track at the digital frontier. The end result is the increasing the gap among adopters and stragglers across enterprise, sectors, and physical regions.

A conventional statistic in IT literature is that big companies typically are early adopters of innovative technology, while smaller companies are generally unenthusiastic to be the first movers. This digital divide exists in the machine learning space as well. Bigger companies have very advanced rates of acceptance and responsiveness related to machine learning adoption. Industries, applications, and products in the big companies, especially those that have bigger strengths in terms of employee count, are more likely to adopt machine learning technologies than smaller companies. One of the reasons is that bigger companies generally have access to additional and better-structured data. Further they have staff with the appropriate technical skills required to comprehend the business case for machine learning investment and to effectively involve dealers. Larger companies also have an additional benefit to do fixed-cost investment, which is generally required for machine learning implementation. Because it initially needs a superior base of prices and revenue, it tends to generate higher returns. Commercial drivers also differ between sectors, industries, applications, and products. Businesses more likely to adopt machine learning technologies are those with multifaceted processes and varied geography. Their actions are motivated by prediction, fast and precise decision making, and custom-made customers.

This chapter discusses the business implications of machine learning. Machine learning impacts commerce and economics in a unique way. It changes the way we plan, act, and do things. The data-centered machine learning and analytics-based economics is booming. I call it the "data economy." This economy is different from the traditional economy, which is based on land, labor, machine, and industries. It is also different from the knowledge-based economy. This economy is based on data and its intelligent use. It affects all walks of life, and all types of individuals, groups, societies, and countries—ultimately the whole world.

Data, Machine Learning, and Analytics

There has been an exponential growth in data in recent times. It has fueled analytics and machine learning-based industries, technologies, and services. Traditional industries like manufacturing, healthcare, and retail are adopting the best part of machine learning and analytics at super-fast speed. At the same time, relatively new industries like cloud-based customer care are fundamentally using machine learning as the base of their business models. However, analytics and machine learning do not confine themselves to business, industries, and enterprises. On the border level, government policies and world politics are also impacted by it. For example, before establishing a "smart city," governments must perform a lot of data crunching and data-based technological assessments. To create people-friendly policies or to prevent crime, data analytics and insight generation is slowly become mandatory for government agencies. In the near future, all policies, social welfare activities, and infrastructure developments will be guided by Big Data (see Figure 5-1).

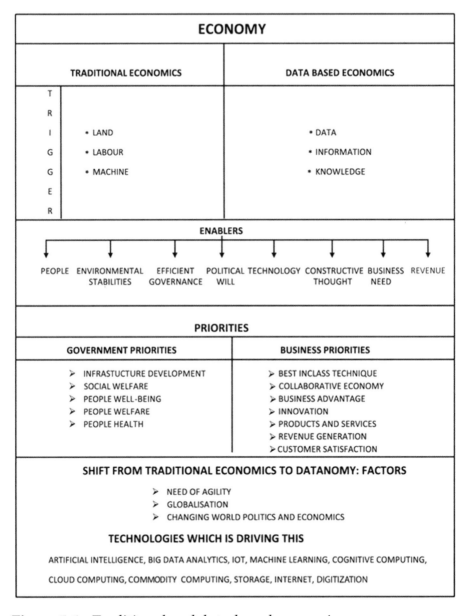

Figure 5-1. *Traditional and data-based economics*

There has been a clear shift in most of the world's governance and business ecosystems. Data-based decision making is not an elite and niche capability, it is the reality and it is here to stay. States, subcontinents, and governments are using machine learning analytics to raise the lifestyle of their population. Business houses, enterprises, and companies are using this for acquiring market share and are improving their profit margins and revenue. Data is changing the DNA and RNA of economics.

The plan of this chapter is to provide you with an integrative summary of the functioning, workings, and future of industries in the context of machine learning. The chapter also investigates the benefits of applying machine learning to the core business model and covers its impact on wider perspectives like government policy making. It also presents relevant use cases specific to these particular industries. The chapter discusses a new term, "data economy." The chapter tries to establish a case for how data can play a critical and central role in the economics of a countries, businesses, and enterprises.

What Is Machine Learning Analytics?

The scope of analytics is very wide and it's a multidisciplinary science (in fact, it is often called data science). It contains lots of good elements from several fields, ranging from mathematics to psychology to visual science. Therefore, it requires people who are good at logic and imagination. People who are capable of using both parts of their brains are more successful in analytics. Overall, machine learning analytics includes machine learning, plus other types of analytics (see Figure 5-2).

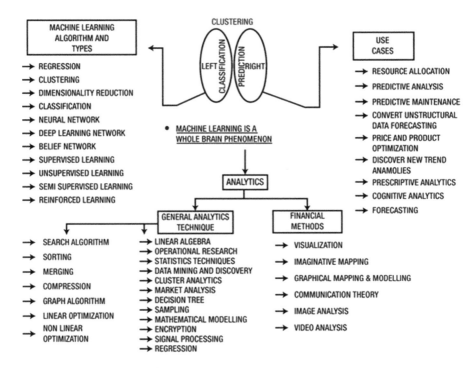

Figure 5-2. *A conceptual view of machine learning analytics*

The Need for Machine Learning Analytics

Machine learning analytics is the need of the hour; there are lots of market and business factors demanding it. For example, there is continuous change in the dynamics of the global economy, increasing cost of knowledge workers, and consistent pressure from clients to reduce overall costs. These are forcing companies to look for innovative ways to address these issues. However, implementing machine learning analytics in the space where you want it to function is not an easy task. There are existing forces that oppose it.

Eventually, organizations have to use information technology (Big Data or not) to enhance their analytics efficiency as they transition to provide value-based service/products to their customers. Moreover, with machine learning based on predictive analytics, companies can produce better outcomes, encounter fewer compliance and legal issues, and reduce unnecessary operational burdens. This enables companies to bring higher levels of satisfaction to their customers at a lower cost. In a nutshell, if machine learning analytics are applied correctly, the following benefits can be achieved.

- Improved and dynamic organization strategy based on data

- Improved customer and stakeholder engagement

- Improved and transparent data-based governance

- Improved service delivery model

- Improved fact and data-based outcome measurement

- Improved competency

- Less fraud loss

- Optimal pricing, which contributes to profitability

- Increased marketing ROI

- Less credit loss

Challenges Associated with Machine Learning Analytics

Here are some of the main challenges that organizations encounter during the preparation and implementation stages of machine learning analytics:

- Integrating different forms of data together in the uniform way.

- Managing the tremendous volume of data, which organizations receive from heterogeneous sources.

- Integration and interoperability of technologies.

- Refining and defining the need of the data across the organization.

- Cultural shift and resistance to change.

- Lack of appropriate talent.

- Lack of a uniform data model.

- Lack of security models/frameworks/standards.

- Appropriate infrastructures.

- Lack of compliance standards.

- Defining appropriate metrics to measure effectiveness of implementations.

However, with the proper explanation, reasoning, and education to the effected parties, these "resisting forces" can be reduced or removed. The complications of realizing improved business results, regulatory compliance, and strategic goals means that organizations need to become more proactive in their customer care. Present technologies have been permitting solution providers to perform data analytics across dissimilar systems running databases, data warehouses, and structured or unstructured data sets, without affecting regular daily operations or accessing available data. There are organizations who have already implemented analytics, while others are in a more advanced phase in the process.

Business Drivers of Machine Learning Analytics

Organizations always have motivation to cash in on market potential and earn profits. However, achieving that goal is not a cakewalk. Earning profit and becoming a leader is driven by multiple factors. This includes social, political, and environmental factors. The most important factors are price, revenue, effectiveness, and efficiency drivers. Here are some important drivers that organizations need to consider to excel in the market.

Cost and revenue drivers:

- Achieve effective pricing for the proved service and products

- Minimize losses

- Obtain efficiency and utilize capacity to its fullest

- Get market share

- Establish the brand

- Get a spike in demand

Efficiency and effectiveness drivers:

- Demand and supply forecast accuracy

- Inventory management

Organizations are betting on machine learning analytics because they understand that, in the data-driven world, they can achieve success by using them.

Industries, Domains, and Machine Learning Analytics

Machine learning-based analytics can potentially be applicable across all industries and domains. The following sections discuss a few areas already using machine learning-based analytics as a solution.

Machine Learning-Based Manufacturing Analytics

The manufacturing industry is known for its strict process orientation and documentation, procedural compliance, process matrices, risk and quality frameworks, and detailed reporting. There has been a boom in the field of technologies, especially in the areas of digitization, manufacturing organizations/enterprises, and supplemental production and technical logs with information from telemetry, sensors, and other machine-generated data. They are using machine learning, IoT, cloud computing, and data science techniques to help their clients. A silent revolution is happening that is turning data into a valuable tool for multiple types of uses, including profitability and productivity. Its uses include chemical, meteorological, automobile, and lots of other areas of manufacturing. Historically, the manufacturing industry has not been very enthusiastic about adopting machine learning technologies in comparison to other industries like finance, customer service, and healthcare. However, widespread success of machine learning analytics across industries has motivated leaders to adopt it.

Challenges in Implementing Machine Learning in the Manufacturing Industry

- Lack of appropriate infrastructure and sense of applying machine learning to the business problem.

- Lack of appropriate and quality data.

- Data standardization

- Lack of commitment to apply machine learning across an organization due to lack of adequate knowledge and clarity of business requirements

- Lack of data culture and mindset in the organization so that machine learning implementation can cater to day-to-day work.

- Lack of appropriate talent having sound knowledge of machine learning.

- The integration of legacy systems. Manufacturing organizations are traditionally using old and legacy systems. Introducing new systems and technologies and integrating them into the existing technical process ecosystem is a challenge.

- A unified data model. Unifying different data models and making them share data with each other is a challenge. However, with the advent of new business and process models like analytical operations (on the lines of DevOps), this will be resolved.

- Security challenges. Scattered control systems that are connected and linked to each other via networking, especially through the Internet, is excellent for quickly responding to changing situations and scenarios. However, it potentially exposes the systems to illegal, unauthorized, and unsolicited access by hackers who could damage the system or cause outages. IoT devices connect to each other and to the network though gateways, which potentially allow control and access of systems, machineries, and equipment from anywhere. The use of smart software and systems can mitigate this risk efficiently.

The Case of SCADA and PLC

A system called Supervisory Control and Data Acquisition (SCADA) tries to monitor and manage field equipment at off-site locations. SCADA systems are essential because they gather and process real-time data, which maintains efficiency. SCADA is a centralized system that keeps an eye on and manages the whole region.

PLCs and SCADAs vary in that PLCs are hardware-based while SCADAs are software-based. Both fall into the category of "control systems," although SCADA has more capabilities than PLC thanks to a number of components.

SCADA systems are commonly used to monitor and manage crucial processes and machinery in sectors including oil and gas, electricity production, water treatment, and manufacturing. However, in order to get the most out of SCADA systems in terms of performance and efficiency, you need to use data analysis and automation technologies that help you streamline processes, cut costs, boost quality, and increase safety.

Tools for Data Analysis

Software programs, known as data analysis tools, can assist you in gathering, processing, visualizing, and interpreting data from your SCADA system. You may do predictive and prescriptive analytics as well as find patterns, trends, anomalies, and correlations in your data with the use of data analysis tools. You may learn a lot about the operation of your SCADA system, including its effectiveness, productivity, and energy use, by employing data analysis tools.

SCADA systems are commonly used to monitor and manage crucial processes and machinery in sectors including oil and gas, electricity production, water treatment, and manufacturing. However, in order to get the most out of SCADA systems in terms of performance and efficiency, you need to use data analysis and automation technologies that help you streamline processes, cut costs, boost quality, and increase safety.

Automated Tools

You can automate processes, workflows, and operations in your SCADA system with the use of automation technologies. You can decrease manual intervention, human error, and operational hazards, and improve consistency, accuracy, and speed with the use of automation solutions. The functions of your SCADA system, such as data collecting, transmission, storage, backup, recovery, and data security, can then be made more efficient. Automation tools can also be used to put adaptive, feedback, feedforward, cascade, and other sophisticated control systems into practice.

Integration of Data Analysis and Automation

You can increase the effectiveness and performance of your SCADA system by combining data analysis and automation solutions. You can build a feedback loop that enables your SCADA system to learn from data, adapt to changing conditions, and carry out appropriate actions by combining data analysis and automation technologies. As an example, data analysis tools can be used to track and anticipate the supply and demand of energy in a power grid, and automation technologies can be used to modify the generation and distribution of electricity as necessary. By doing so, you can balance the load, cut down on losses, and save money.

Benefits of Data Analysis and Automation

Your SCADA system's performance and efficiency can benefit from data analysis and automation technologies in a variety of ways, including better decision-making, higher performance, lower costs, and increased safety. For instance, by delivering accurate, timely, and pertinent information and recommendations, data analysis and automation solutions can enhance your decision-making process. Additionally, they save costs by minimizing waste, rework, and defects by optimizing the parameters, settings, and variables that influence the output and quality of your processes and equipment. By averting dangers, risks, and occurrences that can endanger people, the environment, or equipment, they can also improve safety.

Drivers of Machine Learning Analytics in the Manufacturing Industry

Mixing Big Data analytics and IoT technologies and techniques with machine learning can benefit organizations and manufacturers. The capability to analyze and predict failure before it occurs will be a useful feature of machine learning and some manufacturing companies are already utilizing it to minimize production loss, as well as risk and financial loss. Timely prediction leads to achieving higher levels of efficiency and effectiveness in production and planning. There are hundreds of applications and use cases of machine learning techniques found in the manufacturing industry.

One of the important uses of machine learning analytics is to provide power to its users to track demands in real-time and predict fluctuations. This helps organizations optimize their demand and respond in a timely manner. This actually increases efficiencies in managing demand and supply in a balanced way. Ultimately, these will trigger minimization of cost, scrap, and redundancies. Machine learning analytics can be applied to multiple areas of manufacturing, starting from production planning to output optimization. Here are a few drivers of the adoption of machine learning analytics.

- Effective and efficient production and operation management

- Plant optimization

- Effective demand forecast

- Accurate and proactive error detection

- Efficient performance management

- Better predictive maintenance and interoperability

- Prediction of equipment failures

- Meaningful pattern reorganization

- Increased revenue and profitability

- Increased employee motivation

- Staying relevant and ahead in the market through technology adoption

Machine Learning-Based Analytics: Applications in the Manufacturing Industry

Machine learning analytics can potentially be applicable to all levels of manufacturing, starting with reductions in cost to improving efficiencies. Here are some uses:

- *Machinery monitoring and prediction*: Continuous monitoring of the machinery/equipment and prediction of its health and condition. With the help of machine learning analytics, all information regarding equipment and machinery is collected and benchmarked. This in turn compares machines, lines, and plants to drive continuous improvement.

- *Forecasting, demand, and marketing management through predictive analytics*: These features of machine learning help manufacturing organizations find appropriate launch times of specific machinery based on market demand. Also, they make specific marketing plans. Machine learning can also be used as an effective campaign tool for manufacturing organizations.

- *Intelligent quality assurance*: With the use of machine learning analytics, continuous monitoring in real time will become a reality. It will become very important for monitoring sold or in-process products. This makes performing quality checks easy and effective. If the product is faulty, it's more likely this will be identified early on. Therefore, machine learning contributes to reducing the need for testing by gathering, identifying, and alerting quality issues well before the damage done. Machine learning-based analytics increases the efficiencies and effectiveness of the machinery/equipment/products by improving overall quality.

- *Energy consumption optimization*: With the help of real-time tracking, and powered by prediction capabilities, modern machine learning equipment is capable of capturing demand fluctuations and forecasting energy consumption patterns. These insights are used to utilize energy consumption.

- *Predicting parts failure with the right analytical model*: A popular statistical method for forecasting behavior is predictive modeling. Data-mining technology called predictive modeling solutions creates a model by analyzing past and present data and using it to forecast future results. Examples include employing bagged decision trees to forecast a borrower's credit score or neural networks to determine which winery a glass of wine came from. Curve and surface fitting, time-series regression, and machine learning techniques are frequently used in predictive modeling.

Composite analytical models add an exploratory
step prior to applying statistical distributions to
predict failures. The amount of data to be explored
is vast, and it involves identifying relationships
between various data elements, as well as identifying
similarly performing devices, common causes of
failures from data, and so on. Techniques, such as
association analysis and decision trees, robustly
aid in performing such analyses. This in turn helps
reduce maintenance costs, increases product
success rate, and ensures customer satisfaction

- *To get a deeper understanding of root causes*: To resolve
complex plant issues by finding the true root cause.
Therefore, frequently appearing problems/issue would
not affect the productivity and efficiency. What-if
scenario analysis and simulations are two ways of
doing this. When they are paired with machine learning
analytics, they provide great results.

Other Uses of Machine Learning Analytics in the Manufacturing Industry

Machine learning is used in the manufacturing industry on multiple levels.
Therefore, its uses cases also exist at all the levels, ranging from equipment
maintenance to predicting and forecasting future occurrences. Here are
some of the events that are captured.

- Manufacturing process optimization and
improvements

- Supply and value chain optimization

- Reduction of research and development costs by
predicting outcomes based on data

- Intelligent and smart meters and grid management

- Predicting asset failure

- Using historical data, trends, and manufacturing-specific algorithms to proactively manage potential asset failures

- Reducing downtime. Insight into the most frequent downtime reasons helps focus on the downtime that hurts the business most

- Increase capacity utilization of the machines/systems. Real-time asset utilization and downtime smart statistics allow organizations to maximize the usage of the right assets at the right time

- Excellent at monitoring regulatory information, birth certificates, and tracking and tracing equipment

- Helps maintain comprehensive and accurate information about products

- Real-time manufacturing yield optimization

Machine Learning-Based Finance and Banking Analytics

The financial markets are always very dynamic, evolving, and ready to adopt changes. This industry always welcomes technologies and new systems that are effective in analyzing market behavior, sentiment, and attitudes of financial professionals. Recently a new financial paradigm has emerged, in which the psychological features considered by the advocates of behavioral finance and the quantitative techniques favored by the practitioners of established neoclassical finance are brought together.

Machine learning analytics is an excellent way to analyze, merge, and use behavioral aspects with the quantitative aspects of finance. Machine learning analytics have thousands of applications in the finance and banking industries. Proficient and intelligent mobile banking apps, smart chatbots, and search engines are examples of a few. Maintaining and gathering high volumes of customer data, keeping accurate historical records, and understanding the quantitative/number-based nature of the financial world are the triggers for machine learning implementations in finance and banking.

Challenges of Implementing Machine Learning Analytics in Bank and Financial Institutions

Machine learning analytics implementation involves strategic, financial, process-oriented, and technical aspects. Therefore, the path of implementation is not rosy and some really serious challenges occur. Here are some of the challenges to this industry when implementing machine learning analytics:

- *Forecasting errors*: Manual forecasting brings error.

- *Handling uncertainty*: Data exists in isolation and correlating, analyzing, and getting insight out of it is the biggest challenge.

- *Unified view of data*: Facts, figures, and numbers come from various areas and from different systems within the organization and exist in various forms. Combining these statistics presents a massive challenge.

- *Collaboration and communication*: Integrating inputs received from multiple sources, analyzing them, and communicating results or output in the format that is understood and makes sense for decision-makers is another big challenge.

- *Real-time results*: Everyone wants to be updated in real time with the available information. Providing desired information instantly when required is a massive challenge.

- *Data security*: Most of the data exists on a cloud infrastructure and sometimes on a public cloud due to multiple unknown reasons. Thus, there is an increased risk of data manipulation.

Drivers of Machine Learning Analytics for Financial Institutions

The driver for extensive use/implementation of machine learning analytical techniques is to come up with perfect solutions for customers. The industry is aggressively looking for the solution/product that contains excellent value propositions. To create this, they are integrating the best elements of different products, customer behavioral data, marketing strategies, available financial inputs, geographical details, and diverse channels analytics. However, this also leads to one of the biggest challenges for banking and financial institutions. Designing new products and services that target appropriate customers by the effective use of data science is crucial. Therefore, banks are using machine learning analytical techniques to come up with flexible and integrated processes for understanding the customer better. They do this by analyzing their buying habits and getting insight about the engagement channels. This is important for banks to sell their products in effective and optimized ways. Applying machine learning to personalized product offerings is key to the success of the next generation of banking.

- *Improving business strategies*: With the help of data-based dynamic modeling through machine learning, financial institutions can create more profitable and customer-centric strategies. To remain competitive in the market is one of the biggest drivers. Data is the soul of the interruptions happening in the boardroom and is documented and recognized as a critical business strength. Decision-makers should know what data they now have access to and where they can get more data appropriate to their enterprise's future achievement. Google, Amazon, Netflix, and Facebook are the most commonly used examples of companies that created strategies around data and disrupted the market in a big way. They essentially transformed their culture and shifted from a traditional business operating way to a data- and innovation-based operation. This started paying off and now most of their income is based on smart and intelligent use of data. They extract insight from the enormous quantities of data their customers generate on a daily basis by using their services and in turn use that data to create profitable strategies.

- *Making data usable*: One important capability will be making data usable that is not available in a relational format or that cannot be analyzed with traditional methodologies. So much of the data being produced today is "flat data," which means it has no relational structure. An estimated 90 percent of data is flat. Making this data usable requires new approaches that can efficiently handle large volumes of different types of data—for example, the NoSQL and Hadoop technologies.

- *Robust risk management*: Financial institutions are the prime targets of hackers, attackers, and frauds. Therefore, robust risk management is mandatory.

Machine learning analytics are one way to achieve this, by using automatic anomaly detection techniques and implementing other algorithmic approaches.

- *Better marketing*: Techniques like customer segmentations, campaign managements, and lead generation help financial institutions perform better in this capacity.

- *Channel execution*: Providing net available best offers to the customers potentially increases the profitability and sales performance of an organization. Hence, this is also a prime driver for the implementation of machine learning-based analytics.

- *Excel in customer experience management*: In changing times, engaging customers by providing them with instant information in real time is one of the biggest challenges. With the advent of virtual agents (chatbots), suggesting the next-best action based on their demand, behaviors, and financial status helps create customer loyalty. Therefore, it is one of the drivers for implementing machine learning analytics.

- *Customer insight*: Getting an edge in the market though sentiment, social media, and customer profitability analyses are important drivers for financial institutions.

Machine Learning-Based Analytics: Applications in Financial Institutions

Machine learning-based analytics plays a crucial role in the financial and banking ecosystem. Its application is widespread and multidimensional and includes fraud detection, loan approvals, handling risks, and securing online transitions.

- *Defaulting loan identification and prediction*: Machine learning is used by the financial giants to predict bad loans. The reason is simple, as learning algorithms are easily trainable on customer data, if applied correctly. For example, algorithm-based models can use data related to customer ages, jobs, marital status, financial status, and historical and current loan payments to generate insights. The data is collected and analyzed by the system. After that, processing happens. This flow of execution determines facts about the customer's financial behavior by finding the answers of questions, such as, has the customer paid their loan on time or have they defaulted, how is their online behavior, have they ever been involved in any type of financial fraud or other type of fraud, and so on.

- *Good decision making*: Machine learning analytics potentially automates end-to-end processes from data gathering to generation of actionable insight to suggesting the best action from the available options. Predictive, perceptive, and cognitive insight goes way beyond just providing the idea of "what to do" to "when to do it" to "how to do it."

- *Fraud detection*: Financial frauds are a major area of concern for financial intuitions. Machine learning systems can identify unique activities or behaviors and detect anomalies and flag them. Typically, the machine learning fraud detection solutions can analyze available historical transaction data with an algorithm-based model that identifies fraudulent patterns in the transactions and activities performed by the customer. However, the challenge is to train systems to detect false-positive situations. False-positives happen when legitimate transactions are identified as risks and are flagged.

- *Trading algorithm*: In the background of currently prevailing market conditions, algorithm-based trading is becoming popular. The concepts of algorithmic trading are multi-faceted and are relevant in all financial markets across the globe. They cover almost all the important areas like equities, fixed income, and currencies. Machine learning analytics is finding its role in making algorithms for profitable trading decisions. Algorithmic trading, alternatively known as high-frequency trading, helps automate or create systems that are smart enough to find useful patters in the massive data sets to get profitable decisions related to trading decisions. Machine learning analytics are extremely efficient in getting patterns through tools to extract any hidden insight of market trends. Machine learning trading systems generally make millions of trades in a day, and financial institutions become technical in nature in recent times.

- *Customer service*: Finance-specific chatbots are becoming popular as they provide answers to customers. These chatbots are also known as virtual assistants. They communicate to the customers in a natural language like English. They contain smart and effective natural language processing engines and tons of data of finance-specific customer interactions. Chatbots are not only confined to the banking and customer service sectors; they are used in a lot of other industries as well. (For details, refer to the chatbot section of this chapter.)

- *Sentiment analysis*: This is emerging as one of the
  more important soft technology tools and, with time,
  it will establish itself as one of the important factors/
  technologies to handle business intelligence and
  performance evaluation of organizations, markets,
  and commodities in effective ways. Sentiments
  captured on the basis of news of the prices of different
  commodity futures are used to make profitable
  sentiment-based trading strategies. News and opinions
  are very important in the financial domain, as market
  dynamics are heavily dependent on them. Structured
  and unstructured data is analyzed, processed, and
  presented to give valuable insights to the respective
  stakeholders. For example, to improve the performance
  of traders and marketers, sentiment mining is
  applicable to text mining of news, microblogs, and
  online search results. During the process of sentiment
  analysis, huge quantities of data are purified and
  information is extracted out of that. This information in
  turn is applied to make an actionable roadmap. From a
  financial perspective, sentiment analysis finds its role
  in trading, fund management, portfolio development,
  share dynamics crunching, and in risk assessment and
  control.

- *Recommendations of financial and insurance products
  and services*: Financial companies/institutions, banks,
  and insurance organizations have now started using
  robo-advisors to recommend products and services
  to their customers on a frequent basis. Even for the
  areas like suggesting portfolio changes, switching from
  one service to another based on the current financial

status, and behavioral situations, companies are
using machine learning technologies. In the next few
years, these features will become more reliable and
the customers will take them more seriously, as they
believe in e-commerce product recommendation sites,
like Flipkart.

Other Uses of Machine Learning Analytics in Financial Institutions

Machine learning analytics can potentially be applicable to all levels
of banking and finance, starting with reduction in costs to improving
efficiencies. Here are some uses:

- Comprehend and analyze the financial performance of
  an organization in automated way.

- Help manage and maintain the value of physical and
  virtual properties of an organization based on data.

- Smartly manage the investments of a company.

- Forecast and predict the variations in the market on
  the solid foundation of data-based decisions, which
  intensifies the functionalities of information systems.
  When these forecasts are paired with the data-based
  culture, the results come in the form of groomed
  business processes and profits.

- Machine learning analytics is the key technology for
  sharpening compliance and regulatory requirements.
  It is used for trade scrutiny, which identifies unusual
  trading patterns and behavior.

- Customer segmentation is another area where machine learning is very useful. The vision of banks and financial institutions change from product-centric operations to customer-centric businesses. Therefore, machine learning analytics are implemented to realize this vision by crunching data and detecting useful information.

- Enterprises are using machine learning analytics for personalized marketing. Financial institutions provide personalized products to customers with the help of analytics. Also, it is used to create a credit risk valuation of a customer or property. This provides insight to financial institutions to understand whether to go ahead with a deal/transaction.

- For better risk management. For example, to provide real-time warnings (if a risk threshold is exceeded). Another example is to find new, complex interactions in the financial system and do advance risk modeling.

- To increase sales and revenue in banking, because it helps them identify the churn-related risk early and implement renegotiation strategies accordingly.

- For optimization of skilled labor. This helps financial institutions use the available skills in an optimized way and reduce the operational costs across the organization, including frontend and backend.

- Optimization of branch and ATM centers.

- Routes calls appropriately to the call centers based on customer preference, which they get from analysis of multi-model/multi-channel data (social media, mobile, and web). This ultimately helps them increase customer satisfaction and reduce overall costs of the operation.

- The idea of the financial market is broad and includes a variety of markets, including the stock, commodities, cryptocurrency, and foreign exchange markets. Financial time-series are produced in the financial markets by tracking the price of an asset over a predetermined period of time at regular intervals. All financial time-series are stochastic and variable, even if they have varied value ranges depending on the market. Financial time-series are divided into tick-level, minute, hourly, daily, weekly, monthly, and so on. time-series based on the time interval between the data points. For the purpose of creating successful securities-trading techniques that have the potential to generate sizable returns, financial time-series forecasting—also referred to as price prediction—must be performed.

- Researchers have created a number of forecasting techniques for financial time-series. The most widely used techniques for analyzing and predicting the behavior of financial markets include classical statistical techniques like the autoregressive integrated moving average (ARIMA) model, exponential smoothing (ES) model, and generalized autoregressive conditional heteroscedasticity (GARCH) model. Machine learning techniques have become the best approaches for predicting problems in recent years, thanks to the quick rise in computer power and the accessibility of enormous amounts of data via the

Internet. Numerous machine learning models, such as neural networks (NNs), support vector regression (SVR), and random forests, have shown remarkable accuracy in forecasting financial time-series, and are becoming more widely used in commercial applications.

Machine Learning-Based Healthcare Analytics

The healthcare industry affects us all. New and innovative technologies are changing the way traditional healthcare establishments work. In just a few years, it moved from a doctor-specific to a technology-enabled industry, as technologies, including analytics, now play a crucial role in managing the health of the patient population. Machine learning analytics is an excellent way to improve treatment outcomes and results while keeping costs under control. Machine learning and deep learning paired with artificial intelligence are giving new meaning and directions to healthcare by transforming it. For example, deep learning algorithms teach computers to read medical images, by integrating imaging database with algorithms and models that will automatically notice and identify doctors about issues. Accurate imaging diagnoses help millions of people receive appropriate medication in a timely manner. Therefore, this contributes to saving millions of lives.

This change is adopted by doctors as well because it enhances their ability to deal with life threatening challenges, like cancer, AIDS, and so on. With the help of all the information available, systems try to find patterns and correlations in the available data points and compare them to the relevant data sets (see Figure 5-3). This complete process is done in a few minutes and it ends by suggesting appropriate treatments to the doctor.

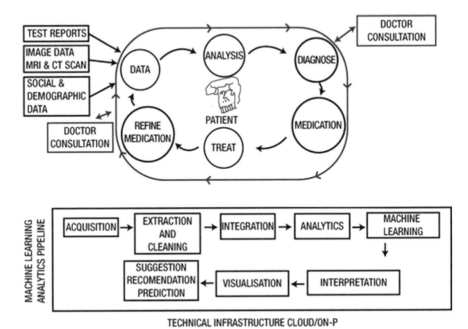

Figure 5-3. *Working with healthcare analytics*

The suggestion provided by the machine learning systems in turn could be customized by doctors, as per your need and personalized health conditions. Sounds like fiction, but it's not. Watson and Baby Watson (a cognitive computing system) from IBM are already doing something similar to this. Also, a company called AiCure's artificial intelligence-based platform can confirm that a patient took the desired dose of medicine using facial recognition technologies. Additionally, it provides real-time ingestion confirmation and automatic medicine identification. AiCure is a clinically validated platform that works on the smartphones. AiCure is very popular among drug companies running clinical trials, where taking medication on time is crucial.

Challenges in Implementing Machine Learning Analytics in the Healthcare Sector

Machine learning analytics can potentially be applicable to all levels of healthcare, starting with reduction in costs to improving efficiencies. However, it has its own challenges, especially in a traditionally disorganized sector like this. Here are a few challenges that exist in healthcare machine learning analytics:

- *Lack of centralized information*: A centralized database of information in a healthcare organization is required for keeping records of patients. This helps healthcare organizations manage their data in a better way. An Enterprise Master Patient Index (EMPI) is a database used for this purpose in healthcare organizations. It preserves consistent, correct, and up-to-date health, demographic, and vital therapeutic data about patients. The database is built by collecting and storing the data that a particular patient generates by visiting several departments of healthcare institutions, and it could be social, personal, and other forms of data. Typically, a patient is assigned a unique identifier that is used to refer/identify them across the enterprise. The EMPI is useful only if it helps identify patient records uniquely across all data sets. The real challenge is to implement this consistently. This is not done everywhere, due to multiple reasons, such as incorrect technical implementation, lack of integration of new systems with legacy systems, and so on.

- *Different format*: Medical and clinical data contain codes that are different from the prevailing coding schemes. The coding schemes are used for clinical purposes are generally, CPT, ICD9, ICD10, and

NDC. These codes contain non-standard coding schemes, so they require translation in order to have a common dictionary for data analysis.

- *Unstructured data*: Data sources from healthcare systems are mostly unstructured (80 percent) and are available in flat file formats like HL7, and they need to be de-serialized before they are useful. Once these files are de-serialized, they must be converted for the clinical processing pipeline. Also, data is normally split across multiple flat files with millions of rows. Therefore, there is a need for robust, effective, and efficient Extract-Transform-Load (ETL) processes.

Healthcare organizations are keeping patient health records and health information for record and analyses purposes in their digital data store (sometimes in the traditional way as well). Obviously, this data contains sensitive content. Therefore, information protection is key. Just imagine if there is a data breach on information that contains patient information. Life-threatening data must be as protected as possible. Machine learning analytics are important weapons to safeguard information. Machine learning algorithms/systems/solutions are capable of identifying unusual behavior on the network or in the data store. This happens when someone who is not authorized to access the data tries to manipulate or steal it.

Global privacy laws mandate the protection of three main categories of personal data: Personally Identifiable Information (PII), Payment Card Industry (PCI) data, and Protected Health Information (PHI). Any health that has one of the 18 components listed by HIPAA is considered to be protected health information (PHI). Data utilized in research that is not deemed PHI and is thus exempt from the HIPAA Privacy and Security Rules is referred to as Personally Identifiable Information (PII). The Health Insurance Portability and Accountability Act (HIPAA) is a collection of legal requirements designed to safeguard patient information from healthcare facilities, insurance providers, and hospitals.

PII includes any information that, alone or in conjunction with other information, might be used to identify a person. Face photographs are PII data by nature. Sometimes information is considered PII because, when paired with additional subject information, it may be used to identify the subject. It is because the subcategories of PHI and PCI are so sensitive that there is a need to regulate them. This is why there is a distinction between PII, PCI, and PHI in the United States. When major credit card firms created an independent group to establish rules safeguarding PCI that are mandated contractually on organizations handling PCI, the private sector took the initiative to fix the PCI problem.

You may decide which steps you need to take to adhere to the relevant laws or industry standards surrounding PII, PCI, and PHI if you have insight into the data that exists inside your organization and where it is stored. AI can assist in making that decision by locating several entities of PII, PHI, and PCI in unstructured data across many languages. The time it takes to identify and categorize your data may be reduced using the most recent developments in machine learning, which will also make compliance easier. For instance, the creative business called Private AI carries out this activity.

Drivers of Machine Learning Analytics in the Healthcare Industry

Machine learning analytics id critical at predicting and forecasting adverse conditions. The forecast, the notification/alert received by the healthcare professional, and the relative of patient enable them to take proactive preventive measures for the benefit of the patient. Therefore, the outcome and results of the cure and prevention of diseases or the health condition of the subject improve. Further, it can be applied in dynamic evaluation of current policies and protocols related to healthcare to come up with new or modified ones. The patient information is usually available through several channels and sources, so analysis of the data becomes comparatively easy. Here are some important sources of information about the patient. Correlating this information provides hidden insights about patients, which will greatly enhance treatment.

- Scan reports

- Fitness trackers

- IoT devices

- Gene sequencing

- Drug research

- Clinical trials

- Geographical records

- Cultural information

- Social media

- Treatment records

- Other patient related records (like doctor/nurse conversations related to a specific patient)

All these factors drive analytics in the field of healthcare. Applying machine learning analytics helps multiple stakeholders at the same time, which includes but is not limited to patients and their relatives, insurance companies, doctors, and so on.

Machine Learning Based Analytics: Applications in the Healthcare Industry

Machine learning analytics can potentially be applicable to all levels of healthcare, starting with reduction in costs to improving efficiencies. Here are some of the applications:

- *Imaging analytics*: Machine learning analytics can be used to automatically process and diagnose patients based on their basic medical imaging data, by training computers to automatically read, process, and diagnose medical imaging data. For example, Zebra Medical Vision, a machine learning analytics company, has a clinical research platform that provides next-generation imaging analytics services to the healthcare industry. Its imaging analytics technology helps institutions identify patients at risk for a particular disease. This enables healthcare professionals to provide preventative treatment roadmaps to improve patient care. Their platform, called the "Zebra platform," has already started contributing to the medical community by generating imaging insights that have been validated using millions of cases. Their algorithms work in the fields of bone health, cardiovascular analysis, and liver and lung indications.

- *Drug development*: One of the challenges of the development of drugs is proper testing. Drugs under development may contain nascent chemicals whose side-effects are not known. Therefore, they need to be tasted on real subjects before being rolled out to the public. However, availability of subjects is a challenge for the drug companies due to multiple reasons, like threat of life and ethical issues. Machine learning analytics provide very handy solutions with the use of predictive modeling. They accurately forecast what effect drugs will have on individual patients with specific reactions from specific medical conditions. For example, Life Extension and Insilco Medicine together developed anti-aging technologies based on artificial intelligence, to find nutraceuticals (pharmaceutical-grade and standardized nutrient) that mimic the tissue-specific transcriptional response (when the cell regulates the conversion of DNA to RNA) of many known interventions and pathways associated with health and longevity. This in turn provides actual human tissue simulation, which would be helpful in testing the drug.

- *Compliance*: Machine learning is excellent in finding patterns. Therefore, companies are using machine learning to detect patterns to stop unidentified access and legal implementation of access control of patients' medical records and histories in clinics and hospitals. For example, Protenus, a health data protection startup, is building a system that's intelligent enough to determine when patient data and records are accessed inappropriately. Their product helps health systems understand the purpose of how and why medical records are accessed.

- *Real-time monitoring and care of patients*: Traditional medicine, in association with smart IoT-enabled sensors, opens up new possibilities and avenues for medical science and healthcare. Machine learning, analytics, and IoT help real-time collection and seamless aggregation of disease and medical data. Medicine is operating as part of a larger ecosystem of connected devices, sensors, and technologies. The sensory data extracted or captured from patients is transmitted through a network to cloud infrastructure. Machine learning analytics then gets real-time insight from that data. The use of sensors in medical science and healthcare is not new. Thermometers, blood pressure monitors, and urine and pregnancy analysis strips are sensors that have been used in the field for a long time. However, these sensors are dumb, and incorporating intelligence into these devices through the use of machine learning analytics is a new phenomenon that benefits the industry and its patients.

- *Decision support for critical diseases*: For infectious diseases, machine learning-based dynamic models are very effective. The model created by the use of algorithms like Markov Decision Process (MDP) and optimized by reinforced learning can generate patterns. Doctors then have better data points to treat diseases. This strategy can be helpful in making effective decisions quickly.

- *Effective use of unstructured documents*: Diseases develop chronologically. Patients have restricted information about the exact time that a condition related to disease progresses or regresses. Hence, regular checkups and other forms of data gathered by patients are helpful. But the challenge is that they are available in unstructured formats (prescriptions, scan reports, test reports, etc.). However, if they are interpreted correctly and efficiently, they can clarify chronological pathways of disease. They can do that by performing analytics on aggregated Big Data sets. Machine learning analytics comes to the rescue by effectively decoding and getting insight from the data set. Once the data is analyzed, it can even predict what types of diseases a patient might encounter in the future. For example, based on the abdominal ultrasound reports paired with the liver function and kidney function test reports, machine learning-enabled systems can predict the chance of a patient developing kidney disease and even when that might happen. The physician can use those insights to answer patients' questions as well.

- *Linking historical and current data to get health insights*: The analysis of the data of all the events, treatments, behavioral aspects and wellness trends helps to properly diagnose diseases. The analysis of historical prescription information in association with the latest wellness data gives a real picture of a patient's health. Also, algorithmic pattern extraction and machine learning analysis reveal patient groups that are not identified for a particular disease, but their medical journey shows that they may suffer from or are suffering from a specific disease.

- *Conducting effective clinical trials using intelligent analytics*: Analytics is now used by drug companies to analyze the impact of integrating enclosure and prohibition conditions of the patient before selecting them for a particular clinical trial.

- *Treatment and drug market sizing*: This is the analysis of the current condition of products in the market by considering the factors like their use, switch-over, provider types, and on/off label prescribing patterns to understand the potential market size. Based on the results of the analysis, opportunities can be identified.

- *Remote healthcare*: Machine learning solutions analyze patient health remotely via mobile devices or other portable devices and then compare it in real time with the relevant medical records, forecast health conditions, and suggest a fitness routine or caution of probable illness.

- *Smart diagnosis devices*: Using machine learning and other artificial intelligence technologies to do simple medical tests like blood sugar tests, blood pressure monitoring, and identifying levels of "fever" without human intervention or assistance. This helps doctors, nurses, and other medical support staff do more important work instead of doing routine activities related to patients.

- *Accurate diagnostics*: Machine learning-powered analytical tools identify and categorize diseases quicker and with superior accurateness, using historical medical data and patient archives.

- *Identifying public-health intimidations and the utmost at-risk patients*: Primary healthcare workers will have information about precautionary actions that include medical services and lifestyle and environmental factors such as nutrition, workout history, and pollution avoidance. Also, hospital officers will be well armed to predict spikes in admissions in smart ways that are not available today. They will be able to better track the occurrence of infectious viruses. Moreover, combined with personal medical records, weather data, and geographical, cultural, and other information, this will help the machine learning tool make intelligent guesses about how many people will need hospitalization.

Other Uses of Machine Learning Analytics in the Healthcare Industry

- Predict the lifetime value of the patient.

- Predict the risk of churn of diseased customers.

- Track behavioral changes of the patient to provide suitable medication.

- Create effective emergency systems based on data received from wearables.

- Analyze severity of disease in real time.

- Analyze performance of doctor in real time and suggest appropriate improvement inputs.

- Improve and track wellness of elderly persons through personalized messaging, alerts, and sensor-based observations.

- Predict the area with the highest need in a hospital.

- Better manage drugs and their timely movement through automated tracking.

- Predict the admission rate of people and patients in the wellness center and hospitals.

- Optimize staffing and allocation of resources.

- Identify, predict, and forecast fraud, theft, anomalies, and waste by the analysis of heterogeneous available data (clinical/operational/administrative).

- Diagnose diseases before they actually occur with the help of accurate analysis of biopsy, tests, scans, and MRIs.

- Fast DNA analysis and mapping.

- Reduce research and development costs for drug testing, development, and marketing.

- Optimize and develop accurate drug launch strategies based on past and present data.

- Innovate and discover new uses of drugs.

- Optimize pricing strategies for drug portfolios.

- Provide invaluable information to medical insurance companies.

- Give a much more accurate idea of the PSSP (Patient Specific Survival Prediction).

- Assist radiologists in discovering unusual indications.

- Help physicians in understanding the risk profile of their patients.

- Improve genomic analysis.

- Enhance hospital processes, employee timetables, and accounting by using medical and environmental factors to predict patient actions and illness possibilities.

- Smart communication kiosks catalogue patients and direct them to suitable doctors, improving their involvement and reducing waiting time.

Unique Applications of VR in Healthcare

Machine learning integrated virtual reality has found its applications in a magnitude of sectors and industries, including gaming, manufacturing, interior design, customer support, banking, finance, and fashion. Apple is working on many apps and technologies that would change the healthcare industry. A brief summary of these products follows:

- The Apple Vision Pro is a mixed-reality headset that shows immersive information that's fully virtual layered on the actual environment. It's important to note, however, that the headgear is not transparent. You just see digital images.

- New Vision is a mental health function that monitors a person's emotional state of mind. It's new to Apple's Health app and makes its debut on the Watch with the Mindfulness app. Users provide answers to a series of straightforward questions using a sliding scale, and Apple analyzes aggregated health data to draw conclusions and links. It can carry out clinical depression and anxiety assessments that physicians might use to treat more severe disorders.

- Apple is tackling two causes of myopia, namely pediatric myopia, by addressing both sunshine and screen distance through a new vision. An ambient light sensor in the Apple Watch monitors and motivates the wearer to spend the recommended 80 to 120 minutes each day. Additionally, because Apple's major business is screen-based, it uses the FaceID sensor on iPhones to detect excessive device closeness, reducing the number of hours Americans spend hooked to their screens.

- Fitness+ members will have to wait for their VR exercises, even if Apple did unveil its much anticipated $3.5K headset. The full-body workout is cumbersome, because the first-generation Vision Pro requires constant power, whether from an outlet or an extra battery pack that charges in two hours.

Here is a link to an article that is an excellent read for decision-makers: `http://economictimes.indiatimes.com/small-biz/ security-tech/technology/a-virtual-revolution-in-the-head/ articleshow/57932219.cms`.

Machine Learning-Based Marketing Analytics

Marketing is all about adaptation. New-generation marketers are using social technologies to measure and understand customers. Web analytics technologies empower organizations to track people across the web and understand their browsing behaviors. Advancements in understanding and tracking technologies are the by-product of intelligent machine learning technologies. Machine learning analytics helps marketing in multiple ways. For example, in the areas of personalized messaging and product recommendations, the potential is huge. This transforms customers from mere site visitors of a specific site to an engaged customer of that site or business. Customers can relate to the company because it seems like that business cares about him. The result of successful, highly-relevant marketing is increased customer loyalty, engagement, and spending.

Machine learning-based analytics enables marketing organizations to collect, analyze, and process a huge volume of data flowing from diverse sources (e.g., purchase behavior, website visit flow, mobile app usage, and responses to previous campaigns). Implementing marketing machine learning analytics bridges the gap between data, information, and analytics. Machine learning-based analytics provide organizations with the power to use data to their competitive advantage by generating insight out of that. Data science, data mining, predictive modeling, "what if" analysis, simulations, new generation of smart statistics, and text analytics can all identify meaningful patterns and correlations in the data. The generated insight anticipates changing conditions and assesses the attractiveness of various courses of action.

Challenges of Machine Learning Analytics in Marketing

Some of the big marketing analytics challenges are mentioned here (most of them are self-explanatory or explained earlier in the chapter, hence they are discussed in more detail there):

- Integration of data

- Finding the right talent and support from top

- Competition in the industry

- Threat of substitute products

- Determining which kinds of customers exist for the products/group of products

- Implementing segmentation and optimization of the products/services for specific segments

- Failing to focus on a specific business initiative due to wrong or inappropriate utilization of data

- Investing in tools that produce little or no revenue

- Failing to operationalize findings

You can overcome these challenges by following these steps.

1. Identify and clarify the problem area that you want to solve.

2. Collect, store, process, and analyze the data necessary to solve the problem.

3. Establish what information is available and what is not available in the process to solve the problem.

4. Acquire the information that is not available.

5. Select the appropriate tools, technologies, and strategies required to solve the problem based on the available information and knowledge.

6. Solve the problem.

Drivers of Machine Learning Analytics for Marketing

Today's business is fueled by data. Technologies like Big Data, cloud based delivery models, and machine learning are driving data-driven marketing and sales. Thus, predictive analytics garners an incredible amount of attention. Early adopters of machine learning analytics are appreciating noticeable return on investment. Machine learning and scoring technologies are used to identify and prioritize financial records, leads, contacts, and clients at specific points in the marketing and sales pipeline. To take advantage and increase return on investment, marketing organizations are looking to machine learning analytics as a new, non-negotiable component of their marketing technology stacks. Different economic sectors are significantly impacted by macroeconomic variables, like interest rates, inflation, and GDP growth as well as microeconomic variables, like supply and demand, taxes, and regulations. Other examples of microeconomic variables include pricing, individual investment, market share of the company, demand quantity, consumption, produced quantity, budget, and cost of inputs. In contrast, macroeconomic models use both endogenous and exogenous factors. The identities or the stochastic equations can both be used to explain endogenous variables. The model does not provide an explanation for exogenous factors. From the perspective of the model, they are assumed to exist.

In addition to providing information about the status of the economy, macroeconomic indicators like output growth, inflation rate, and interest rate are crucial in determining the best monetary and fiscal policies. Macroeconomic forecasting is crucial for central bankers, policymakers, and academics, because it serves as a predictor of the economy's potential for future growth. In reality, the formulation of economic policy depends on precise predictions of the state of the economy. In addition, forecasting plays a critical role in households, enterprises, and financial investors' decision-making processes.

Despite the advantages of precisely predicting macroeconomic variables, updating conventional models has proven difficult over the past 20 years. Furthermore, the literature has mainly ignored the development of Big Data in economics and machine learning. You can do a lot with the help of Big Data and machine learning tools. For instance:

- Macroeconomic variable forecasting using machine learning techniques

- Making financial variable predictions using machine learning techniques

- A comparison of the predicting abilities of ML tools with conventional econometric techniques

- Analysis of the ML model specification and new developments in Big Data-based macroeconomic forecasting

Here are a few of the marketing drivers for machine learning analytics:

- Improve customer retention

- Target the most suitable customers for the product/ business

- Lead generation

- Sales development

- Opportunity management

- Consolidate social media strategies

- Engage customers in real time

- Visualize success across the enterprise

- Treat data as a strategic asset

- Identify the next-best action for the customers to engage them

Machine Learning Based Analytics: Applications in Marketing Analytics

Marketing is a very dynamic and adoptive field. Customers understand the product, service, or strategies through marketing campaigns. Some applications are explained here:

- *Customer segmentation*: Customer segmentation models are efficient at mining small, similar groups of customers containing the same behaviors and preferences. Successful customer segmentation adds value.

- *Customer churn prediction*: This is done by determining patterns in the available data set produced by customers who churned in the past. Learning analytics enabled systems can accurately predict which customers are at a high risk of churning. This churn prevention can equip markets with actions to retain and engage high-risk customers. Therefore, if marketers become successful in doing so, they can contribute in increasing revenues.

- *Customer lifetime value predication*: With the combination of machine learning and customer relationship management (CRM), businesses can predict the customer lifetime value (LTV). LTV is used to segment customers and to measure their contribution in the increasing or decreasing future value of a business by predicting growth and associativity.

- *Customer value maximization*: With the implementation of customer value maximization techniques and the actions suggested by it, the business can encourage customers to surge the occurrence and expand their transactions. It also increases the duration the customer remains active and associated with a business.

- *Customer behavior modeling*: Customer behavior modeling is used to determine communal behaviors and patterns observed among specific groups of customers. Likewise, it is used to predict how similar customers will perform under similar conditions or situations. Customer behavior models are constructed by data mining customer data. In the customer behavior model, each model is designed to respond to one question or query at one point in time. For example, a specific customer model could be applied to predict how a specific group of customers will react to a particular marketing action. This will provide the necessary insight to make a good decision.

- *Digital marketing*: Machine learning analytics allow digital marketers to predict, classify, and segregate customers at the point of entry, and individualize content to maximize business outcomes. Ultimately, due to this effort, customers are affected in a positive way. The advertising and offers they see become more relevant and customized to their needs.

- *Ranking customers*: One of the important uses of machine learning analytics is to rank customers based on the business value. This will help the company customize their product/services based on the value of the customers. For example, e-commerce companies customize and personalize page designs, offers, posts, and content dynamically based on the rank of customer with the help of machine learning algorithms, which can assess the expected value of each visitor.

- *Virtual assistance*: Used to provide support to all levels and are becoming smarter and smarter. For example, chatbots can now decipher the semantic resemblance among two replies. Also, they suggest responses that are dissimilar not only in phrasing but in their fundamental meaning as well.

- *Making user-generated content valuable*: For example, Yelp uses user uploaded photos to create semantic data about individual photographers.

- *Improving customer service*: Smartly identify useful data sets from the sea of data and generate insight to provide excellent customer service. Also, machine learning algorithms find deep insights hidden in data about customers. Moreover, they turn them into a data asset by finding the answers of the questions like what to offer, when to offer it, and to whom.

Jargon Buster

Market sizing: Market size analytics is about providing insight regarding market potential for your products and services, such as how large the market is for a particular product. It also provides information about the growth prospects of the product. Market size analytics is important for understanding the size and forecast of the potential market for a product. It is essential to know where your products are in their lifecycle and whether you are competing in a growing market or a declining market.

Other Uses of Machine Learning Analytics in Marketing

Machine learning analytics can be applied to multiple areas to enjoy business and competitive advantages. Here are some use cases:

- Design marketing strategies based on the prediction of in-store customer traffic.

- Review customer behavioral analytics for payment security. With the help of anomaly detection techniques, malpractices can be identified in real time even in very high-volume data/transactions/ communications.

- Create, analyze, and optimize real-time operational metrics.

- Identify and analyze root causes.

- Design futuristic data-based business and operational key performance indicators.

- Forecast and predict real-time data-based sales. Models can be developed for forecasting and predicting customer churn, credit risk, or train/bus/flight delay.

- Predict the success of fundraising campaigns. For example, it reports the success or failure of a particular fundraising campaign based on metadata.

- Predict suitable selling and buying time, make effective product recommendations, and classify best customers for the business.

- Prevent data breaches.

- Perform social semantics.

- Perform speech and language recognition.

Audio and Video

An interesting series of videos that provide insights about the role of machines in online advertising campaigns. This includes the role of digital media in changing times and more. See the following:

- (223) How Is Artificial Intelligence Is Transforming Advertising | Storyboard18 | CNBC TV18, on YouTube

- How the generative A.I. boom could forever change online advertising (cnbc.com)

Machine Learning-Based Analytics in the Retail Industry

Machine learning is changing the retail industry in a constructive way. It is allowing retailers to identify critical action areas that are hidden under the sea of unused data and opportunities. It is also providing them with the power of consuming and analyzing data that they thought beyond the processing capabilities of human ability (at least manually). These analytics enable retailers to predict the future with the help of customer churn analytics and to make useful decisions. Due to the advancement in data capturing and storage technologies, mountains of data are available related to products, prices, sales, performance, consumer behavior, logistic details, and so on. Organizations are using this information to decode consumers' purchases and financial DNA.

Challenges in Implementing Machine Learning Analytics in the Retail Industry

As the retail industry is growing, its associated challenges are increasing. The challenges are multidimensional and impact the people, processes, and technologies. The discussion in this chapter is confined to machine learning based analytics challenges. Here are some of the critical ones:

- *Right data*: Gathering quality data is one of the biggest challenges.

- *Data oriented management*: Once you get the data, its management is critical. Most of the data that organizations get is heterogeneous in nature and typically comes from multiple sources.

- *Technical expertise*: There is a huge scarcity of the right talent. Finding people for roles like data scientists, data engineers, and technology managers, who specialize in managing machine learning or analytics project, is difficult.

- *Integration*: In most cases the decision of implementing machine learning-based analytics in organizations is taken as the new initiative. However, if some new startups are opened, then the story is different. But in both cases, integrating multiple systems and technologies is far more important. Therefore, the right strategies, talent, and expertise are required at all levels. This enables organizations to reduce the discrepancies among "isolated" systems and empower the smooth flow of data among core business applications.

All projects are unique and need solutions as per situation, requirements, and demand. Hence, the challenges are also different. However, there are some guidelines that definitely help in coping with difficult situations and creating appropriate strategies. Here are some of the best practices/guidelines. These are presented in the "retail industry" context, but are applicable in almost all other industries:

- Incorporate information technology in the DNA of the organization.

- Be Agile and translate the vision to reality quickly through pilots.

- Ensure that the data is of good quality before it moves forward to sophisticated systems or is filtered in a proper and intelligent way by the effective use of the available tools. Also, create easy data access polices.

- Reuse existing process, processes, technologies, and people skills. Cross-train people whenever required.

- Before trying to understanding the problem, ask the right questions and document the opinions.

- Build effective and efficient teams that understand and interpret the problem. Also, work toward putting the right people in the right places.

- Select the technologies based on your needs, not based on hype.

- Produce insights that can be put into action easily and effectively.

Drivers of Machine Learning Analytics in the Retail Industry

- Provide a reliable, tailored, customized product mix and good pricing to customers and increase sales.

- Excel in the market.

- "My first" approach to become a differentiator in the market and offer innovative products for differentiating customer experiences.

- Increase customer loyalty by understanding behavior and shopping patterns.

- Use targeted marketing campaigns based on the customers' characteristics and psychology.

- Reduce cost by improving inventory, value, and supply chain management.

- Increase conversion rate of customers who come to know about the product and services through multiple channels.

- Manual data analysis is becoming absolute now. Because even the most experienced retailers are finding it difficult to get value from existing data through the use traditional technologies like databases, spreadsheets, and old warehousing techniques. There are multiple reasons for this, including the high volume of data, requirements of on-demand analytics, and dynamic change in infrastructure capabilities. However, with machine learning analytics, the retail industry can ensure that every single bit of data is analyzed and provides effective insights to them.

Machine Learning Analytics Based Analytics: Applications in the Retail Industry

The retail industry was one of the earliest adopters of machine learning analytics. It helped adopters excel in the market and have competitive advantages over competitors. Here are some of applications in the retail industry:

- *Pricing*: Machine learning analytics enable retailers to manage the price of their products in real time by comparing and considering competitors' prices. A smart algorithm based on the predictive pricing model can crunch all forms of data and provide accurate information in real time. For example, it can analyze sales data and dynamically optimize prices for a particular point in time.

- *Inventory management*: Smart, efficient, and effective inventory management are the keys to success. Whereas inefficient management leads to a loss in business. In sales for example, predictions made on inaccurate past data give inaccurate demand projections and create the wrong demand for certain items, whereas predictions done on an appropriate mix of historical and real-time data help generate the right demand of items and ultimately help move inventory. Retailers can use predictive analytics to decide what to store and where to store it, based on sensitivity and environmental and regional differences in preferences, weather, and customers.

- *Recommendation engines*: To recommend appropriate and most suitable products to the customers, e-commerce companies are using recommendation engines. However, this is not only limited to e-commerce companies; traditional retail industry uses them as well.

- *Smart revenue forecasting*: The retail industry is using machine learning analytics for accurate forecasts based on the buying habits of customers.

Other Uses of Retail Machine Learning Analytics

- Optimize in-store product variety based on customer demand to maximize sales.

- Provide next-best and personalized offers to the customers based on the their data.

- Real-time data-driven stock optimization through dynamic inventory management.

- Predict and forecast hyperrational sales, demand, supply, and other relevant business insights using real-time data.

- Analyze, predict, and innovate market sizing and potential.

- Optimize spend.

- Optimize market mix through process optimization.

- Enhance capabilities to understand customer through sentiment, emotions, review, video, and voice analytics.

- Predict, forecast, and decide which products to transport to relevant and most suitable stores based on demographics, customer perception, and other data inputs.

- Optimize in-store product placements based on customer data, so the possibility of getting attention increases.

- Optimize advertisements in real time based on customer preferences to increase sales and customer loyalty.

Customer Machine Learning Analytics

Customer analytics provide power to companies to predict and anticipate what they do for their customers, which customers are at risk of churning, how to add customers to their business, which customers are loyal to their business, and which are not. Also, machine learning analytics helps organizations properly segment customers so that they can implement the best business plan to retain and acquire customers. It also finds answers to questions like which high-value customers are at risk or which offer should we make to a particular customer segment.

When a huge quantity of data is available, applying machine learning-based analytics to customer data is essential to making appropriate business decisions. However, the success of machine learning-based analytics depends on having the right strategies, quality data, plans, and implementations of proper solutions.

Customer data is readily available to organizations, as they are smart at collecting data from multiple sources. However, availability and storage of the data is useless, unless some intelligent processing and analytics happen. Hence, organization focus needs to shift to extracting "insight" from the mountain of the data instead of collecting it. By applying machine learning techniques, organizations can understand their customers more intimately, and they can make the company's products and service more relevant to the customer.

To attach, associate, and build intimate customer relationships, Big Data and machine learning technologies play a critical role. They took central stage in the organizational journey to make customer-centric business strategies. However, the basic principle of customer satisfaction— that every customer is different and they need to be treated differently—is still relevant. This is important because every individual carries a different intensity of emotions, habits, and preferences. Analytics paired with machine learning play an excellent role by categorizing and segmenting customers into different groups and treating them uniquely. The most important goal of a successful segmentation is to achieve optimization.

Challenges in Implementing Customer Machine Learning Analytics

There are some challenges to implementing machine learning analytics in the customer space. Here are some of them:

- *Top-level leadership vision and support for analytics strategies*: While implementing customer analytics, top-level leadership support of the analytics vision is required. It requires big changes across organizational policies, frameworks, and thought process. For example, customer-collected data resides in multiple heterogeneous systems, with lots of people/groups accessing and using the data. Strong leadership, vision, and support ensure that the analytics strategy is properly implemented and aligned across the entire organization. This ensures that everyone in the organization moves the same direction and has clarity about how data will be gathered, analyzed, processed, and used to achieve business results.

- *Selecting the right data*: To make the customer analytics effort successful, the first step is selecting the appropriate data for the organization. It is a resource-intensive effort but it is critical and worth the investment. In an era when a lot of competition exists, clear data strategies and roadmaps need to be defined and created. If a gap exists, it will then be filled on time. This will allow organizations to effectively transform data into insights and then into wisdom.

- *Infrastructure readiness*: Machine learning analytics projects are different from general software or hardware projects. Thus, their need, requirements, and demands are different. Building the infrastructure may require additional investments and leadership must be willingly able to accept it.

- *Right resourcing*: Choosing the right resource that will convert the organization's vision, strategies, and thoughts to actionable steps is very important. However, finding the right resource and talent is difficult, as customer analytics is a multi-disciplinary field. Determining which data set is important and relevant is very important to success, and finding so-called data scientists who have these capabilities is difficult. Developing business-oriented (with the knowledge of sociology, business, psychology) scientists is essential, as they provide the business with a competitive edge.

- *To create data culture within the organization*: This is very important. The data culture means that everyone in the organization has a mindset to respect the data. The organization on the whole and the employee must understand the significance of the data. All the groups, especially the data-intensive analytics groups, must be integrated. There must be availability of tools that help them integrate the data and communicate seamlessly. All the lines of business must collaborate and share data though a uniform platform. Even the non-technical user should have opportunity to work with the data. In a nutshell, a data-aware enterprises invest in tools at all the levels that allow business people to use data to drive decisions.

Drivers of Customer Machine Learning Analytics

Data from machine learning analytics needs to be presented in the form of actionable steps and must be simple enough to be put into action. However, only knowing what to do is not sufficient. The decisions must be available in a format that allows involved parties to understand it. The final decision to take action is up to the decision-makers, such as the CIO, CEO, and product managers. Hence, the action steps need be clear and accurate. Only then will decision-makers have confidence in implementing the steps in real-life scenarios. Decisions like providing or suggesting appropriate products or services to a particular individual or group or innovating something unique for customers on the basis of behavioral data analytics to the customer need a careful approach. Any decision that is taken on the basis of all these parameters is crucial. Failure or success of any decision typically impacts the business and the branding of the company. Hence, properly testing and retesting data-based decisions is critical before taking any action.

- To understand customers better
- To improve products and services
- To create new revenue streams
- To improve the detection and prevention of fraud

Other Uses of Customer Machine Learning Analytics

Machine learning analytics finds its uses in the customer support/service space at its fullest. Here are some examples.

- Sentiment analysis
- Next-best offer analytics
- Customer churn analytics

- Predict customer wallet share

- Perpetual customer loyalty

- Customer experience and sales analytics

- Virtual customer care assistance

- Identification and management of best customers

- Customer retention

- Cross-channel behavior tracking

- Access of minute transactional data

- Fast onboarding of the customer

- Quality of service

- Mapping of the full view of the customers. There are multiple channels available that enterprises are using to get data about customers. With the use of kiosks, call centers, mobile, partners, e-commerce, and social media channels, data can be gathered and used to get a full view of the customer.

- More proactive and effective organizations. Machine learning-based marketing analytics helps organizations predict customer and market behavior. Accordingly, they make strategies to respond proactively and appropriately.

- Personalize customer marketing and engagements. Machine learning-based marketing analytics enable organizations to predict the probability of a customer reply to dissimilar offers. Hence, they are better prepared and know their customers.

Machine Learning Analytics in Real Life

- Google came up with the new voice recognition technology and incorporated it into its handset. Apple's Siri and Microsoft's Cortana are other examples.

- Google Gmail spam detection and email tagging are both based on machine learning.

- E-commerce companies are using machine learning to predict which products customers might return.

- Extracting insights from the user comments to understand the customer better and to understand the rating system better.

- Answering complex queries from customers in an automated way.

- Fraud and duplicate detection, for instance, automatically identifying if someone is using a duplicate image instead of an original one for authorization.

- Assessing the quality of the customer rating.

- Recommending and forecasting repeat purchases.

- Product classifications.

- Apple iPhone uses machine learning analytics to extract the background sound from the talker's voice.

- Apple iPhone's virtual keyboard technology uses machine learning analytics to determine the tap area of each key.

- Microsoft, Android, and iOS spelling-correction technologies use machine learning analytics.

- To identify faces in iPhoto apps and in Facebook social media sites.

- IBM Watson uses it for cancer diagnoses. Many other companies are using it to detect disease on the basis of scans and MRIs.

Machine Learning Analytics in Other Industries

Machine learning analytics has been applied to many industries/domains, ranging from fashion to aerodynamics. The following sections describe some of industries/areas where it is used.

Video Games

Although it's not yet extensively used by gaming companies, it has started showing its presence there. For instance, gesture recognition in Microsoft Kinect is one example of its mainstream use.

Disaster and Hazards Management

Machine learning has found a role in controlling and predicting natural digesters, such as geological, biological, hydrological, and climatic problems. By analyzing and processing geophysical and biological data, it provides insight to control them or at least to take proactive measures. The integration of IoT, Big Data, and cloud computing help organizations and governments as follows:

- Monitor hazards

- Anticipate the intensity of disaster risk

- Track effects of calamities and monitor recovery efforts

- Control the disaster exposures

- Detect earthquakes, floods, and hurricanes, as well as forecast future occurrences of such hazards with the help of sensors and analytics

Transportation

Transportation companies are using machine learning in a big way to make accurate predictions in real time. A few of its uses are listed here:

- Choose optimum/most profitable networks for transport services

- Predictions of future incidents/timely feedback about transport systems

- Vehicle delay analysis

- Mode choice and trip assignments

- Travel pattern behaviors of various modes, including time, location, and demand

- Track congestion and save driver's time and headaches

Hospitality

In this field, machine learning analytics are applied in very mature ways. Many companies are using a wide variety of machine learning techniques to solve their respective issues. They collect huge volumes of data in different forms, including video, audio, and web data. They use this data for areas like customer segmentation, loyalty information, dynamic pricing, and allocation of the resources (rooms), customer profiling, site selection, room availability forecasting, customer relationship management, menu engineering, personalized marketing website optimization, providing the right room at the right rate, and even investment management. Moreover, machine learning analytics are used to provide customer value and improve hotel operations.

Aviation

Machine learning analytics have been adopted by the aerospace industry in efficient ways. Traditionally, airplanes have used sensors to collect data. This is integrated within the plane's systems to gather information during the flight. That data/information is used to monitor the health of the airplane and its maintenance schedules. Now, machine learning analytics can more diligently predict weather conditions and identify faulty parts before they fail, making the overall system safer.

Fitness

Many health and fitness companies are using machine learning in their fitness products to get a better understanding of their users. Atlas devices, for instance, detect which type of exercise the user is doing based on their gestures and movements. There is a wealth of devices available that gather sleep patterns and diet choices, monitor heart rate, and check sugar level, all to offer recommendations toward healthier lifestyles. Fitbit is one company that provides a range of the devices. Apple, Microsoft, and Samsung all have their own variants, which are incorporated into their devices/software.

Fashion

The fashion industry has social and economic impact across the world. This industry uses machine learning technologies to their fullest to provide value to their customers. Technologies like data mining, knowledge discovery, deep learning, computer vision, and natural language understanding with structured and unstructured fashion are transforming the way this industry works. Luxury fashion houses are re-creating physical in-store experiences for their virtual channels. Many technology startups are also providing trending, forecasting, and styling services to the fashion industry.

Oil and Gas

Oil and gas is traditionally a data-intensive industry and generates tremendous amounts of data during oil and gas exploration. Machine learning analytics, with IoT and Big Data technologies, are used to process data related to operational activities—monitoring, pressure points, mud properties, hardness of the surface, seismic waves, and temperature. This ultimately helps the algorithms understand exactly what's going on downhole in that specific well. This data is investigated in an automatic way to understand the current situations related to exploration. Further, non-optimal events such as kicks, blowouts, and wellhead failures are analyzed. Potentially, an algorithm's capabilities of understanding what contributes to non-optimal events are identified. Recommendations can be performed. Oil and gas companies also use machine learning algorithms to develop better models for drilling, maintenance of tools, and so on.

Advertising

Online advertising is using advanced machine learning technologies to handle issues like how to select the right viewers for an ad, how to price an ad, or how to measure the effectiveness of advertising. The two broad categories of advertising and search and display are very popular on machine learning analytics.

Entertainment

While creating a trailer for the horror movie *Morgan*, machine learning techniques and experimental APIs of IBM's Watson platform were used extensively. The producer and directors of the film wanted to show the viewer something different. They, in collaboration with IBM, took Watson to film school. There, the system-analyzed hundreds of existing horror movie trailers. They incorporated the insight generated out of that research. The program selected the ten most intense moments in the film. Finally, a human editor created the finished trailer using those clips selected by the Watson.

Agriculture

The agriculture industry uses machine learning analytics and IoT to provide benefits to farmers. For example, Caterpillar Inc. uses sensors on its machines for farming uses. The machine provides insight on the quality of the soil and suggests which crop is best for that type of condition.

Telecommunications

One of the most important criteria for success in the telecommunications sector is to reduce customer churn. Customers switch service providers on a frequent basis and in unpredictable ways. With the help of machine learning analytics, analysis of structured and unstructured data becomes easy. Therefore, companies can precisely predict and forecast which customers are at risk of leaving. This insight helps them to reduce churn. Measures like marketing personalization and customer experience measurement, guided by machine learning, help manage and engage customers.

Insurance

Machine learning analytics helps insurers review analyses and process all forms of data, including pictures, videos, and audio. The insight generated is used to improve compliance and prevent inappropriate selling of products and services. The other benefits include:

- Product personalization and endorsement through machine learning analytics of customer data.

- Risk classification on the basis of analytics on heterogeneous data sources, like social media, click streams, and web.

- Faster claims processing through automated image classification (deep learning algorithms).

- Customer churns forecasting in real time.

- Fast and accurate insurance fraud identification and detections.

- Increased revenue and profitability.

A Curious Case of Bots and Chatbots: A Journey from Physicality to Mindfulness

The company Touchkin came up with the happiness buddy called Wysa. It is an emotional wellness and well-being machine learning-based chatbot. This chatbot comes in the form of a loveable, cute, and "caring" penguin that can talk to users about their feelings and try to understand them. Once the inputs are collected from the user, it guides the user by providing personalized mindfulness meditation based suggestions, or recommending appropriate exercises based on the specific need of the user. The penguin chatbot was designed and developed to understand a person's emotions and mood. It efficiently tracks the emotional state of the user. Therefore, it can motivate the user through the appropriate and most suitable mechanism of suggestions. It also equipped with the general features of the fitness apps like capability to track sleeping patterns through mobile phones. For completeness, the chatbot provides weekly reports with an overall summary of the wellness to the users. These reports provide insight as to how they were doing the entire week.

At present, chatbots are quite underutilized but they will definitely go far beyond texting purposes. New generations of machine learning-enabled smart and intelligent chatbots are coming. They will be used to build relationships with the stakeholder and take this exciting relationship to the next level. As the interface evolves over time, the interactivity will also improve. Personalized and individualized bots will be used to make long-term connections with stakeholders, users, and customers and help enterprises establish their brand. In the next few years, the convergence of technologies around bots will be revolutionary. The way we consume and process information will change. Interactive voice response (IVR) technology, cognitive computing, and machine learning technologies will bring new ways of consuming information for the bots.

The uses of bots are enormous. For example, they will become very useful for combating loneliness, such as when no one is available to talk to an elderly person or parents do not have time to talk to their children. Bots can come to the rescue.

One of the uses of bots in the recent news was to help visa applicants. A bot called Visabot, developed by Andrey Zinoviev and Artem Goldman, can help applicants with the process of procuring a U.S. visa. Initially, it was tested with B-2 tourist visas and O-1 visas applications. It works in a very natural way, by starting with questions about nationality and the purpose of the visit. Once the information is gathered, it is processed and then suggests the appropriate visa type to the specific user. After that, it suggest the relevant documents and fills out the forms. Once the forms are filled it out, it checks for their correctness and order. Just imagine how much time, effort, and unnecessary headache Visabot could same someone. People like it and the data itself shows this. As of this writing, Visabots have been used by 40,000 people (February/March 20117). Use is spread out over the globe, including the Middle East, Europe, Latin America, India, and China. Hence, it is natural that its promoters are planning to extend its reach and have ambitious plans around this. In the coming time, you will see Visabots that process H-1B to help a wider audience.

By analyzing the projections of the market demand of bots, tons of enterprises, including service providers, are betting on Internet robots/ chatbots to use have conversations with customers. One school of thought says that a rise in the demand for automated robots and chatbots puts many low-level jobs at risk. Particularly, the information technology-enabled services sector will be impacted with this rise of chatbots. Another thought, however, says that bots can actually create more jobs, especially high-end jobs. In reality, bots will bring momentum to dynamically changing markets and improve the efficiency of existing processes. It will definitely affect jobs at the lower level of the pyramid.

An Indian private sector bank called HDFC came up with the chatbot called Eva to handle customer chats. It has an excellent ability to scale up its capabilities based on demand. So, when more demand comes, it uses the technique of concurrent chats ,which roughly handles 150 customers at a time. Eva is a machine learning-based, web-based chatbot software designed to simulate conversation with humans. It is employed by the HDFC bank to help customers and visitors who are looking for the best products and service online.

One reason for the popularity of these bots (95 percent of bots in use are chatbots) in the businesses community is that they are easy to integrate into existing communication platforms. Voice bots (speaking bots) may take more time to become operational because of technological challenges like understanding different languages, accents, tone, and emotions associated with voice. All over the world, software-based enterprises, research organizations, and labs are trying hard to create bots that are close to humans, especially in terms of understanding and mimicking them. The ultimate vision and philosophy behind chatbots is that they serve as a communicative and collaborative gateway. This is the reason that private banks, telecom companies, and service providers, travel companies, e-commerce portals, private insurers, and drug manufacturers are betting big on bots.

Bots are being adopted across geographies within organizations. Gone are the days when only developing countries and the big enterprises were looking for a solution to their problems. Due to their potential and usability, bots went beyond the boundaries of helping developed countries. For example, Asian companies are adopting bots at a higher rate than their peers in Europe and the United States. Enterprise/companies based out of Asia, like China and India, are the biggest buyers of chatbots. The major reason for this is the proliferation of mobile phones and other portable devices. It enables easy "installation" of bots. Also, bots are cost effective in the long term and their return on investment is good compared to traditional investments and cost-cutting methodologies. For example, establishing a dedicated customer care center is more expensive and challenging than finding the right bot. To serve and handle customers' needs on a daily basis is very expensive. Also, day-to-day tasks are routine, boring, and monotonous and employees are generally not very engaged in this type of work. Hence, it makes more business sense to employ bots to perform routine and monotonous work. If this strategy is implemented correctly, it will save significantly on operational costs. Multiple research showcases that in performing monotonous tasks, "machines" are more efficient and able to serve a wider population (in this case, customers) at a time.

How Bots Work

A bot (an Internet robot) is a software-based application that executes automated scripts (written in some programming language) on the web/ Internet. Bots are used to perform simple and structurally repetitive tasks. They perform them at a much higher rate in comparison to humans. For example, humans are not good at executing concurrent tasks and they therefore find it difficult to answer multiple questions/queries at the same time. However, a single bot can easily handle multiple queries (concurrently) from numerous customers in any format (voice, chat, or email) effectively and efficiently. A typical bot does this with the help of automated scripts, which are typically executed on servers and provide responses based on data manipulation and input provided by the users. Data is plugged into data stores and resides on extra-large capacity servers on the cloud infrastructure. To provide an answer to the user, the bot communicates with knowledge banks.

Once the chatbot receives the customer queries, it reads and tries to understand and interpret them. Based on its understanding, it looks into the knowledgebase (in layman's language, an intelligent data store/ database) to find the answers. Once the chatbot gets the answer, it provides a suitable response to the user/customer. Hence, over the time knowledgebase become wider with having more content in it. Updating the data often helps the bots answer complex user queries. The smartness and efficiencies of bots are dependent on the quality of the data stored in the knowledgebase.

With the help of evolving technologies, frameworks, and APIs, chatbots are being customized to bring a "human touch" to their responses. For example, Watson cognitive APIs and Microsoft cognitive API both have capabilities to incorporate vision, picture, and emotions. In order to connect better with the customer, companies do not want just mere mechanical bots. They want bots that sound human and are sensitive to cultural and language difference. Therefore, they incorporate cultural information into the bots, which is one of the biggest challenges. Over time, with the help of knowledgebases and machine learning technologies, the bots can learn and process local sensibilities and are more context aware. Hence, their responses become more appropriate. To become more human-like, bots needs to understand informal terms and phrases. For example, they need to learn some slang or local greetings, so their conversations have an human element to them.

Data orientation, machine learning, and artificial intelligence technologies are the basics. To get the maximum from a bot, the company has to collect and store quality data. The variety of heterogeneous data makes the bot intelligent, smart, more intuitive, and better equipped to have a human-like conversation. Businesses are using bots to improve internal efficiency as well. For example, customer care executives use bots effectively to answer the queries of the customers. Bots can help executives offer suitable solutions to customers and establish a meaningful, effective, and efficient dialogue with them.

Usability of Bots

In order to do the holistic mapping of customers to understand them better, companies are feeding customers' behavioral data into bots. On the basis of those bots, they can understand and capture behavioral patterns of the customers. Therefore, they can find the "odd" information regarding the behavioral changes of the customers. This capability of the bot is a quantum step to prevent fraud by anomaly detection.

New generations of chatbots can measure and predict customer mood, sense wider emotions, and predict thoughts on the basis of a typed language. For example, if someone types "WHY YOU DID NOT PROVIDE ME THE INFORMATION UNTIL NOW!!!" to a bot, the bot will predict that the user is angry and automatically go to alert mode, as the statement contains uppercase letters and exclamation marks. It replies with something like this, "It looks like you are not in a good mood today. I will connect you to a customer care executive, who will help you." This is not an alien thought, as bots already contain these features and functionality.

Bot-based advisory services, like "Robot Advisory" financial services (investment advice), have become popular across the globe. In India, companies like FundsIndia.com, Scripbox, and MyUniverse are some of the popular robot advisory platforms that are creating momentum. Advisory bots are one of the area where bots have done significantly well. These bots help customers make correct investment decisions. These programs provide information after factoring in lots of technical parameters. The best part is, unlike human investment advisors, bots are not guided by emotions, prejudice, or greed.

Telecom companies are also using bots to accomplish their day-to-day operations and to provide customer services. Telecom companies are running trials to put their bots on various communication and collaboration platforms. Industries that have more business-to-customer interactions tend to invest more in the implementation of bots. Hence, across the globe there is an increasing number of e-commerce startups. Travel firms and insurance companies are using bots to fulfill their customers' needs.

Bots and Job Loss

There is an increasing fear of bots taking over the jobs of human beings. Industries and services like BPO (business process outsourcing) and voice process-based call centers may be impacted due to the monotonous nature of their work. Businesses and enterprises employ bots to reduce their operation costs and protect/increase profit margins. Businesses use bots for lower level transitional and operational work; therefore, they need fewer workers. In the BPO industries, chatbots can allow enterprises to work more efficiently and efficiently by minimizing repetitive work for agents (call centers). If they are used properly, they can reduce wait times. They can even reduce the average customer-handle time by suggesting responses while the agent is speaking with the customer, leading to quicker resolutions. Most of this type of work is repetitive and can be automated and handled though bots. So, at this level, there is a definite possibility that bots may obviate routine jobs performed by less skilled workers. The reason is straightforward— bots are best at monotonous and routine work. However, advanced bot technology will definitely boost more high-value jobs where human intelligence is required. Bots will not replace humans in the foreseeable future. When they do, the idea is that humans will have other high-value, high-paying jobs.

Summary

This chapter discussed machine learning analytics in detail. It broadly discussed the uses, applications, challenges, and use cases of machine learning analytics in areas like manufacturing, retail, marketing, sales, banking, and finance. Apart from that, the chapter briefly discussed the role of machine learning analytics in important sectors like video gaming, agriculture, disaster management, oil and gas, fashion, hospitality, travel, and aviation. Today, almost all industries need agility in their functions and operations. Machine learning itself is a very agile and iterative field of study. The chapter included a section on the Agile software methodology. A brief comparison of Agile and waterfall methodologies was also included.

Mind Map

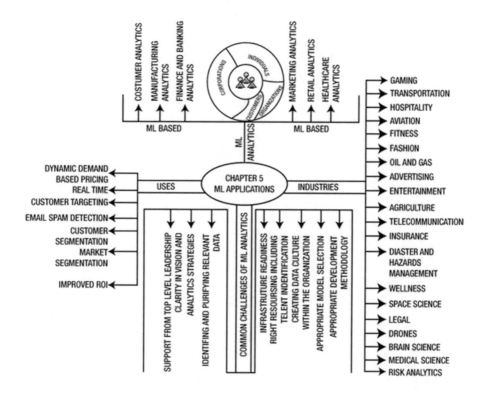

CHAPTER 6

I Am the Future: Machine Learning in Action

Dr. Patanjali Kashyap[a*]

[a] Bangalore, Karnataka, India

As the acceptance of fresh or renewed technologies like machine learning and artificial intelligence gain momentum, companies are revisiting their understanding of their business requirements. In order to recognize the business functions that will lead to the highest value, decision-makers have shown a readiness to invest in new technologies. During this journey, most of them discover that these technologies have huge value and potential. They also learn that, without disruption, their businesses will fail.

Disruption is the newest slogan of the changing and innovating business of today, and for good reason. It is shaping new directions. Enterprises are watching disruptive technologies to empower new development prospects and to be pertinent in the viable market. Enterprises are also looking to become more efficient and effective

© Dr. Patanjali Kashyap 2024
P. Kashyap, *Machine Learning for Decision Makers,*
https://doi.org/10.1007/978-1-4842-9801-5_6

through the flawless ride of technology, but, in the short term, they are confronting challenges in applying them seamlessly. These challenges are mainly due to:

- Higher price of investment

- Skill gaps in maintaining technology

- Quickness in incorporating novel technology

- Digitizing has exciting prospects but offers greater risks

- Worldwide legal and regulation changes

Vendors started offering off-the-shelf technology solutions to these issues. Multiple companies and vendors are offering solutions that are trial and tested. Also, if someone wants to develop something that suits their specific needs, customizable variants are available as well. This chapter deals with a few of them. However, you have to take care before deciding on any one solution. Here are some pitfalls to be aware of:

- Machine learning must be treated as business led rather than IT led. This strategy is helpful in developing robust partnerships with IT, cyber security, risk, HR, and other enterprise functions.

- Emphasis must be given to business cases and preparation before pilots.

- Categorize the accurate processes so the technology can produce value.

- Focus must be on amplifying employee potential and innovative priorities.

- Focus must be on empowering everyone to do fewer manual tasks rather than looking to cut costs.

In a nutshell, machine learning exists in nearly all environments. It may be incorporated into industrial robots, intelligent applications, and other products. Its form, shape, size, uses, and utilities change based on demand and uses. While adopting the technology, factors like size, capital, and availability of other resource matter, but in the longer run, the technology itself is guided by innovation. That means acceleration happens in a natural way.

Adopting anything early, especially technology, makes a difference. This chapter discusses the uniqueness of machine learning solutions and their widespread range. This discussion ranges from voice assistance technologies to cognitive technologies. It also takes a deep look at the driverless car, VR technologies, and brain-computer interfaces. There are multiple offering from vendors in the machine learning space in the form of readily available platforms, but decision-makers are often not aware of them. This chapter discusses SAP's Leonardo and Salesforce's Einstein as examples.

State of the Art Examples

Companies like Apple use machine and deep learning to track and detect fraud on the Apple Store and to get feedback about their products from testers and users. They extract insight from thousands of reports in an automated way. Apple also uses these technologies to establish whether an Apple device user is exercising or simply resting.

Facebook uses machine and deep learning to recognize faces and locations from users' photos. Through machine learning technologies, Apple devices can determine whether you will become fat in the next few weeks or remain thin. Your apps can quickly compile snapshots and videos you took into a mini-movie at the touch of a button. The Apple provided apps and devices will remember where you parked your car and provide information about that, all in real time. They give you reminders from your appointments based on the content of your emails. They provide real-time suggestions while you are typing, and so on.

Siri

The natural way Siri responds to queries after understanding them is one of the features that makes Siri so popular. Siri does this with the help of the deep learning technology. Deep learning is the field of study that facilitates machine learning to perform human-like tasks in smart and intelligent ways. Machine learning techniques level out sounds of individual words, which makes Siri sound like an actual person. Siri is capable of the following:

- Speech recognition capabilities: Converting human speech to text

- Excellence in natural language understanding: Interpreting what a human says

- Prefect execution: After understanding the question, fulfilling a query or request

- Excellence in response: Replying to the request

Siri uses machine learning techniques such as deep neural networks, convolutional neural networks, long short-term memory units, gated recurrent units, and n-grams in association with deep learning technologies to cut error rate by a factor of two in all the languages it supports. Also, it detects the voice of the user and spells out the user's name and password instead of typing them. Here is the basic working procedure of Siri:

1. You input/ask Siri a question, such as "Who won the 1983 Cricket World Cup?".

2. The phone app translates the speech to a format that Siri understands (binary code). Typically, it does that by collecting the analog speech and converting it to an audio file.

3. Once the speech is converted, it will send the data to the Apple servers. Once the data is submitted to the Apple servers, an appropriate response is generated there. Siri does not process the data locally (on the phone); it does this on the Apple cloud. Therefore, if you do not have an Internet connection, you face problems communicating with Siri.

4. The server returns the response. The data is processed on the server with the use of natural language processing. An appropriate response is returned to your device through the servers and Siri converts it into text and speech.

5. Siri responds to you. "India won the 1983 Cricket World Cup." The text will flash on-screen, and at the same time the speech is played back, provided the audio feedback option is on.

Alexa

Natural language processing (NLP), a method of turning voice into words, sounds, and thoughts, is the foundation upon which Alexa is constructed.

- Amazon captures your speech. Because deciphering sounds requires a lot of processing power, an audio recording of your voice is transferred to Amazon's servers for more thorough analysis.

- Your "orders" are divided by Amazon into distinct sounds. The words that most closely match the combination of individual sounds are then discovered by consulting a database of word pronunciations.

- Then it highlights key phrases so that you can understand the tasks and perform the necessary duties. For instance, Alexa might open the sports app if it detected the words "sport" or "basketball."

- Your gadget receives the data from Amazon's servers and Alexa can start speaking.

Signal processing is the first step, which offers Alexa as many opportunities as possible to understand the audio by enhancing the signal. One of the biggest issues in far-field audio is signal processing.

The goal is to enhance the target signal, which entails being able to recognize and reduce background noise. Seven microphones are used to detect roughly where the signal is originating from so that the gadget may focus on it. Acoustic echo cancellation can eliminate any extraneous signals, leaving just the crucial signal.

Wake word detection determines if the user has said "Alexa" or another word that switches the gadget on. This is necessary to reduce misleading positive and negative results, which might result in erroneous purchases and irate consumers. This is quite challenging since it calls for distinguishing between different pronunciations while using the device's limited CPU power.

In the event that the wake word is picked up, the signal is then transferred to cloud-based voice recognition software, which translates the audio to text. The output space is enormous since it considers every word in the English language, and the cloud is the only technology that can scale well in this situation. The fact that so many people listen to music on Echo and that there are more musicians than there are words further complicates matters.

Alexa will examine the user's voice characteristics, such as frequency and pitch, and provide you with feature values so you can convert the audio to text. Given the input data and the model, which is divided into two halves, a decoder will calculate what word sequence is most likely.

The first of these components is the prior, which without considering features, provides the most likely sequence based on a large quantity of previously published text. The second is the acoustic model, which is taught using deep learning by examining pairs of audio and text. These are merged, and dynamic coding—which needs to take place in real time—is applied.

Google Assistant

Google originally unveiled Google Assistant, a voice-activated virtual assistant, during the 2016 I/O conference in California. The Google Assistant offers contextual information and carries out tasks like making a restaurant reservation or sending a message on behalf of the user, much like Amazon's Alexa, Apple's Siri, and Microsoft's Cortana. If they choose not to utilize voice input, smartphone users can also text their requests to Google Assistant.

In order to comprehend what the user is saying, provide suggestions, or take action on that input, Google Assistant uses AI technologies, including machine learning and natural language processing. The cornerstone of Google's "AI-first" approach is Google Assistant.

Google produced Google Now, a digital assistant program, before Google Assistant. And even while Google Now is still theoretically in use, there are some minor variations between the two systems. While Google Assistant is only available on a select few products, such as Google Allo and some smartphones, Google Now functions in apps on Android and iOS. Since then, Google Now has been phased away and its features have been incorporated into Google's other products.

The purpose of Google Assistant is to "build a personal Google for each and every user." The link between all of Google's essential software and hardware products is provided by Google Assistant.

More than its features or capabilities, Google Assistant is significant for what it signals for Google's approach to consumer goods in the future. As mentioned, Google thinks that the tech industry will go from mobile to AI in the same way that it did from web to mobile.

Smartphone makers must compete on what they can provide through next-generation software and AI as hardware becomes increasingly commoditized. Additionally, an ecosystem of goods and gadgets that share access to AI must be developed. Google Assistant is a built-in feature of many Android phones, but it also functions in the Allo smart chat app and is an integral component of the Google Home smart speakers.

IBM Watson

IBM called it more than artificial intelligence and they coined the term "cognitive computer" for one of the most talked-about products of the recent times, known as Watson. Watson uses natural language processing capabilities, machine learning, and the vast quantities of data fed into it to directly to precisely answer questions posed in everyday human diction in seconds.

Watson is one of the most powerful artificial intelligence computing systems. It learns from the environment in three ways:

- One form of its learning is reading. For example, to enhance its knowledge of cancer, it "read" more than several million pages from a variety of sources.

- Another way it learns is by answering questions or in the "teach phase." For instance, in the cancer project, doctors put questions to Watson, and then tweak the responses if Watson's answer was not perfectly accurate.

- Lastly, it learns by doing, or from its own mistakes. It finds new patterns about the work, similar to what humans do.

Watson at a very high-level view looks like this:

- A huge amount of unstructured and semi-structured data that is publicly available is feed into the Watson database.

- The questions are put to Watson in the form of text or through voice commands.

- The questions are used as a search query to search the database. The is similar to how searches happen on Google or Bing.

- The search results plus the question are further used to get supporting evidence from the available knowledgebase.

- Each search result used to answer the question forms a hypothesis. In turn, the hypothesis is assessed on the retrieved evidence. Thereafter, the answer is scored on many dimensions.

- The high-dimension scored answers are ranked by a built-in algorithm.

- If Watson is confident enough with its final answer, it flashes or says the answer to the user.

Watson is a highly sophisticated and complicated system. Almost all the steps mentioned here involve a complicated net of machine learning algorithms that run on a parallel platform to provide the answer as soon as possible to the user.

Humans make mistakes and are not perfect. Also, with the availability to digital devices/media to the mass, information is flowing from all the sources. For example, the amount of available medical information doubles every five years. Every day around 130 research papers are published on oncology. However, physicians and other medical professional don't have enough time to update themselves on most of the latest advances, which can result in poor diagnoses. For instance, in the United States, it is projected that one out of five diagnoses were incorrect or incomplete. Also, approximately 1.5 million medicine mistakes are made every year.

Watson can potentially increase the correctness of diagnoses, advance the excellence of patient care, and reduce the cost of patient treatment. Many companies have started using Watson for their own benefits. For example, Wellpoint, one of the leading medical insurers in the United States, is using Watson to improve the accuracy and rapidity of insurance approval and authorization.

Capgemini, a European software service company, is using Watson to improve their services and bring efficiency to the organization. In India, the Manipal group of hospitals is using Watson to assist doctors and provide healthcare benefits to their customers/patients. The hospital recently started offering the service to patients and a medical test report from Watson comes at no additional cost. IBM Watson is also helping farmers understand when to fertilize and how much fertilizer to use for the optimal crop. They can get assistance from Watson on the basis of crop yield, weather patterns, and soil moisture to figure out what is really going on. This is relevant if we consider the reports that clearly show how thin the average profit margin of a farmer is. The decision of how much fertilizer to use can make or break profit for an entire year.

Microsoft Cortana

"Cortana is designed to help you get things done. Ready on day one to provide answers and complete basic tasks, Cortana learns over time to become more useful every day. Count on Cortana to stay on top of reminders and work across your devices. Cortana is great at reminders and helping you keep your commitments. She can remind you to do things based on time, places or even people. You can also add a photo to your reminder as an easy visual cue."

https://www.microsoft.com/en-in/windows/cortana

Microsoft has always been good at sensing market potential. They realized that analytics and machine learning were here to stay. Therefore, to cater to the market need, they came up with a machine learning-based analytics suite known as The Cortana Analytics Suite. Machine learning is the foundation of Cortana. Its unique instant, unlimited data storage and real-time processing capabilities in coordination with perceptual intelligence helps it realize the vision of "transforming data into intelligent action."

Cortana helps you forget less and become more productive. Cortana is the best at reminders and delivers them at the right time and place. Cortana is excellent in helping users organize their tasks by sending emails, arranging events, and searching on devices, the cloud, or the network. Cortana's way of search is called the *multistep search,* and it layers query upon query to accomplish complex tasks by voice alone. Cortana assistance uses analytic suites while making decisions about user queries. Therefore, a holistic view of the innerworkings would help users understand the complete picture (see Figure 6-1).

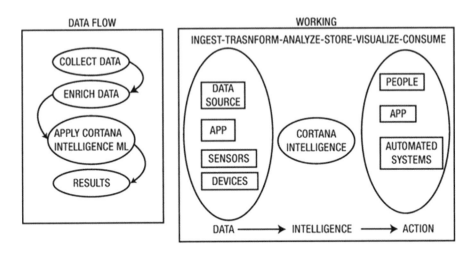

Figure 6-1. *How Cortana works*

Cortana provides a heads up to users when there's something important waiting that needs their attention. In a nutshell, Cortana is a voice-activated search engine, or an "interactive personal assistant." It falls under the same category as Apple's Siri and Google Now. On Microsoft devices, it effectively integrates with Bing searches to capture usage behavior. On the basis of that, it suggests things of interest to the users. Therefore, it makes the computing experience better and smoother.

Cortana continuously learns from the user's habits and interests. Also, alongside regular web searches for information, Cortana acts as a primary way to discover and search for information on the Windows 10 environment/ecosystem. One of the exciting features of Cortana is its capability to create activities based on actions, something similar to the popular web service IFTTT. For example, saying "Remind me the next time I call my son that we need to talk about Simba" will create a reminder that is activated when you next go to call your son or he calls you. No doubt it is a very powerful feature.

Cortana took some great ideas from Apple's Siri and Google's in-house product and incorporated them. However, the challenge from Microsoft is to leverage Xbox, Windows, and other products to incorporate Cortana everywhere. The road for Cortana to reach everywhere is not that difficult and challenging because, with Windows 10, Kinect, Azure, and MS Office products, Microsoft is everywhere. A few highlights of Cortana are mentioned here:

- Sends out emails and texts.

- Makes calls based on the user's contacts.

- Keeps track of the calendar events.

- Sets alarms.

- Provides timely reminders.

- Launches applications on the user's behalf.

- Searches content on the Internet based on the user's commands.

- Types conversions.

- Modifies settings as per the user's needs.

- Checks out movies and flight times and provides appropriate notifications as and when required.

- Gets directions for the user based on their needs.

It seems that that there is a lot of similarity between Cortana and Siri, because both provide voice-based assistance. However, there is a thin line between them—Cortana works as a personal assistant and provides the assistant based on the context, whereas Siri is voice command executer.

Cortana is closer to your thought process and understands your personal context. For example, when you ask questions of Cortana, it looks for connections among available historical data. It makes connections between your history of questions and provides answers that are relevant to your given scenario and context. When you ask a question of Siri, she provides the best available answer based on the data available on Apple's cloud data store.

Connected Cars

Connected cars use telemetrics, mechanics, electronics, machine learning, and artificial intelligence technologies in a holistic and integrated way to interact with the surroundings to provide better service, safety, entertainment, and connected life experiences. The connected car branches out into several areas of consumer suitability, such as all-in-one urban mobility, assisted driving, driverless cars, and car-sharing.

According to analysts and multiple reports, the connected car market is expected to exceed $40 billion by 2025. The evolution and growth of the connected car must be seen as a natural extension of the consumer selection process.

Connected cars are preferred by individuals for multiple reasons, including the strong urge to avoid issues like road congestion and driving stress. They also provide better mobility for seniors and differently-abled citizens. Customers are willing to spend money on connected cars because they want the same experience and connectivity while they are driving the car as they enjoy in life. Enterprises are conceptualizing and building solutions to address current and future challenges. However, these solutions obviously require a sound understanding of manufacturing, telematics, and in-vehicle systems. On top of technical and domain expertise, practical knowledge of consumer psychology also plays an important role in the overall solution design.

There are many solutions to vehicle-to–infrastructure communications (V2I) and vehicle-to-vehicle communications. These technology-led services enable cars to frequently exchange data/information with the surroundings they interact with and pass through. Benefits are not one directional, because multiple industries and sectors benefit from this evolution as well. Industries like insurance, banking, finance, retail, and agriculture are now in a better position to collect and process customer data and use it for their purposes. For example, insurance companies can now get more accurate data about car health. This enables them to develop more customized and personalized products for their customers.

Highlights of the Connected Car System

- Get directions in real time

- Accurate and connected mapping system.

- On-demand entertainment.

- Dynamic real-time route information.

- Accident alerts.

- Reduced carbon footprint.

- Optimal speed assistance.

- Car breakdown warnings.

- Automatic call for assistance in case of an accident.

- Maintenance notification.

- Optimize insurance; pay only for uses.

- Vehicle lifecycle management.

- Driver performance analysis and suggestions.

Driverless Cars

Traffic accidents happens mostly due to driver errors and carelessness. The demand for more entertainment features, cell phone integration, and music in cars are distractions that make drivers less attentive and more prone to error, which leads to more accidents.

However, these are not the only culprits. Other catalysts of accidents include increased traffic and haphazard and bumpy road systems (especially in developing countries). These distractions and complications are not going away, so who will focus and concentrate on the driver's behalf? Well... technologies are here to do this for you. You sit and enjoy music and entertain yourself and the technology drives the car for you. This is the ultimate promise of the driverless car. The promise of delivering driverless cars/trucks is coming to the masses in an iterative, phased manner. For example, features like self-parking and pre-safe systems have already been realized by some automakers.

The driverless car has gained a lot of traction in recent times. However, the concept itself is not new. The idea of a driverless vehicle has existed for a long time. It has always been part of the James Bond and Bat Man movies. The cars that work and operate automatically with intelligence have always fascinated people. However, it is no more imagination than it is reality now.

In the 1980s, anti-lock brakes (ABS) could be thought as the first step toward this idea. Anti-lock brakes prevent brakes from locking up during quick, hard presses. The car does this in an automatic way, with the help of speed sensors associated with the wheels. Auto manufacturers used these sensors to take the next step and make the car driverless by incorporating something called "traction and stability control." These systems are improvements to ABS. These sensors enable the wheels to detect when a car might skid (dangerously) or roll over and signal to the ABS and engine management to keep the car on track. As these systems are intelligent, they apply the brakes at the right time and increase or decrease intensity to individual wheels as needed. This smart technique is obviously better than applying breaks to all four wheels in a panic situation.

Many auto manufacturers are working toward driverless cars. Google is leading these initiatives. Their prototypes are heavily based on this technology. Google calls it the Chauffeur system. They use LIDAR, which stands for "light detection and ranging." Lidar inherited the concepts from radar and sonar, but it is more accurate. It charts out points in space by using 64 rotating laser beams. It takes more than a million measurements per second. In turn, on the basis of that, it forms a 3D model through the incorporated machinery, which locates things within accuracy levels of centimeters.

By using preloaded maps, the car can accurately locate traffic lights, crosswalks, telephone poles, shops, and bumpers. LIDAR identifies moving objects too, like humans. On top of LIDAR, it also has regular radar, an intelligent camera, and GPS to precisely locate obstacles and objects in its way. Cars are advancing every day, but the driver role will not be completely automated. Driverless cars still need drivers to take over sometimes. For example, pulling the car out of or in to the garage or driveway or managing tricky highway exchanges. Trucks, helicopters, and bikes are also in transition and, in the near future, all will ride or fly automatically and be driverless by an enabling technology called machine learning.

Google is not the only player in the automated and driverless car market. Manufacturers like Tesla, Mercedes Benz, and Audi are working on automated cars as well. For instance, BMW plans to roll out a Level 5 autonomous car. This means that the vehicle will be capable of handling any driving related situation by its own intelligence, without any human intervention. At the moment, most of the auto manufacturers are working on Level 4 cars. Apple recently submitted a plan to train operators of self-driving cars to California regulators and got permission. This clearly showcases their positive intention toward self-driving cars. The driver-assistance levels are defined as follows:

- Level 1: Most functions are still controlled by the driver. However, a few explicit functions are handled by the car, such as acceleration. The Level 1 car is intelligent enough to keep an instructed or set speed, slow down automatically to avoid other cars, and stay in its defined lane. But it is not able to handle any disastrous conditions and in adverse situations the driver has to take full control.

- Level 2: At this level, drivers are disengaged from the actual "basic" operation of the car. For example, the driver could leave their hand off of the steering wheel or foot off pedal at the same time. However, the driver of the car is expected to be ready to take control of the vehicle in complex, adverse situations.

- Level 3: Cars can make decisions based on data. Drivers are still compulsory in the car, but their responsibilities have changed. Their intervention is required only due to "safety-critical functions," which involves highly complex traffic or disastrous environmental conditions. Level 3 cars are not currently available on the market. However, a few prototypes are in the final stages. For example, Audi's prototype A7 can fulfill some of the expectations at this level. These cars don't just stay in their lane and away from other cars; they also make decisions.

- Level 4: This is a fully autonomous car. Level 4 cars are intended to take care of almost all security and life-threatening driving situations. They can monitor and analyze the road. The drivers are nonessential.

- Level 5: This refers to a fully-autonomous system that has equal driving capabilities of human drivers. The act like real "human" drivers in every driving situation. Google and Tesla are targeting this level of car. Ideally, the car at this level could go anywhere without a driver. They don't need monitoring, a steering wheel, or pedals.

Machine and Human Brain Interfaces

A company called Neuralink, which is backed by Elon Musk, is working on linking the human brain to a machine interface. They are planning to come up with the micro-sized device to help people with brain injuries communicate better. Riding on the artificial intelligence and machine learning technologies, the company is creating systems that help humans implant "neural links" into their brain in order to communicate.

This is based on the idea that the brain compresses concepts into low data flow activities like speech. Likewise, if two brains could perform uncompressed direct conceptual communication through interfaces, a communication channel would need to be established. With their technologies, Neuralink would do that. Neuralink is attempting to merge biological intelligence and digital intelligence. If this concept is realized by Neuralink, it will ultimately help humans take a leap with quick developments in AI. The initiative is to realize mixing AI with human awareness.

Neuralink would fundamentally allow humans to use AI as a supplementary ability on top of their senses. For example, to use our sense of selves or other higher in-brain thought faculties for constrictive purposes. It would be possible to connect high bandwidth directly into the brain and assimilate cloud-based AI computing with our brains in a way that's indistinguishable from our core selves.

A machine or device that reads the human mind by observing and analyzing brain waves is something that lots of other companies and research laboratories are working on. For instance, Japanese scientists at the Toyohashi University of Technology have developed a system with a 90 percent success rate when trying to recognize numbers from 0 to 9 and a 61 percent success rate for syllables in Japanese. The scientists also claim that these devices are easy to operate and can be controlled through a mobile app. In a nutshell, an electroencephalogram (EEG) is used to track human brain waves while people spoke. Brain wave patterns were then matched to syllables and numbers using machine learning. The participants then spoke the numbers and the system guessed in real time based on the real-time readings of an electroencephalogram (EEG) brain scan. The researchers are now going one step further to develop a so-called "brain-computer interface" that would identify and recognize words that would be thought and not uttered by humans. This could be achieved through a device with fewer electrodes and a connected smartphone in as soon as five years.

Virtual, Immersive, Augmented Reality

SLAM (Simultaneous Localizations and Mapping) is one of the ways to generate a map using a robot or unmanned vehicle that directs that environment while using the plan or map it produces. It generally refers to the problem of trying to simultaneously localize sensors with environments. The majority of SLAM systems are based on tracking a set of "points" through successive camera frames. These camera frames or tracks are used by the systems to identify and locate the "points" on a 3D position. With the assumed map of the environment, SLAM alternates between tracking and mapping and calculates the *pose* (position and rotation). Once the pose is found, it corrects the map and then again estimates the pose. This keeps happening in the loop until the mappings are accurate.

Due to markerless AR (augmented reality), it is possible to apply AR to solve bigger problems. For instance, it can be implemented to plan and design homes, furniture, and offices, and visualize data in interesting formats. The algorithms for markerless AR go hand in hand with machine learning algorithms. The algorithms play their role while analyzing varying sets of parameters, such as camera position, environment mapping, and visual content. This relates to position and environments. However, due to the dynamic conditions of developing and implementing an algorithm, delivering a markerless AR experience is a complex task.

Mixed Reality

The next big thing in computing after mainframes, PCs, and smartphones is mixed reality. For consumers and businesses, mixed reality is becoming more popular. By providing intuitive interactions with data in our living areas and with our friends, it frees us from experiences that are confined to screens. On their mobile devices, hundreds of millions of Internet users have had mixed reality experiences. The most popular mixed reality options available on social media right now are mobile AR. People might not even be aware that the Instagram AR filters employ mixed reality events. With gorgeous holographic representations of humans, highly detailed holographic 3D models, and the real environment around them, Windows Mixed Reality elevates all these user experiences.

Combining the physical and digital realms allows for more natural and intuitive 3D interactions between people, machines, and their surroundings. The development of computer vision, graphics processing, display technologies, input methods, and cloud computing are the foundation of this new world. Paul Milgram and Fumio Kishino first used the phrase "mixed reality" in their 1994 study, "A Taxonomy of Mixed reality Visual Displays." In their study, they looked at the taxonomy of visual displays as well as the idea of a continuum of virtuality. Since then, mixed reality has been used for more than just displays, such as:

- Environmental knowledge, including spatial mapping and anchors.

- Human comprehension: vocal input, eye tracking, and hand tracking.

- Spatial audio.

- Positioning and locations in both real worlds and digital worlds.

- Working together on 3D assets in mixed reality environments.

Different Mixed Reality Algorithms

1. *Calibration*: To construct MR applications, set MR devices are typically utilized.

2. *Model of space and simulation*: This algorithm ensures that the amount of space needed for simulation is accurate. Space modeling and simulation are typically divided into two categories:

   - *Object recognition*: This method identifies actual objects in the real world so that virtual replicas of those objects can be made to construct the MR environment.

   - *Object tracking*: This method aids in keeping track of the physical objects so that the virtual objects can be positioned in accordance with its movement.

The Metaverse

The metaverse is an evolving 3D digital environment that enables lifelike personal and professional encounters online by utilizing virtual reality, augmented reality, and other cutting-edge Internet and semiconductor technologies.

In order to merge and broaden the application of bitcoin, AI, augmented reality (AR), VR, spatial computing, and other digital technologies, this symbolizes a convergence of these technologies. Furthermore, the "enterprise metaverse" might come together in a way that opens up even more possibilities, going beyond its current use as a platform for online communication.

The metaverse will essentially have three characteristics: real-time interactivity, a sense of immersion, and user agency.

Additionally, the following will be part of the complete metaverse vision in the end:

- Seamless integration between platforms and devices

- Continuous interaction between thousands of users

- Use cases that go far beyond gaming

The metaverse is not about running from reality. It is instead about embracing and augmenting reality with virtual content and experiences that can make things more fulfilling and make us feel more connected to our loved ones, more productive at work, and happier.

The current metaverse is made up of ten layers, which are broken down into four categories: platforms, hardware and infrastructure, enablers, and content and experiences. Here are some examples of each.

Information and experiences:

- User-, creator-, and developer-created content improves metaverse experiences

- Virtual spaces where people can gather, talk, and create; software connected to certain metaverse use cases, such as education or events

- Platforms designed for 3D experiences that facilitate finding and accessing information, experiences, and apps

Infrastructure and Hardware of the Metaverse

Supporting infrastructure for the metaverse includes cloud computing, semiconductors, networks, and other technologies. Through devices, operating systems, and accessories, people communicate with the metaverse.

Enablers: For the metaverse to function properly, security, privacy, and governance are crucial.

What new technology developments will propel the growth of the metaverse?

Rapid technical advancements promise to open up future metaverse experiences and interoperability between realities, just as blockchain has energized the decentralized creative economy. Users will be able to process vast worlds on mobile devices once 5G is fully implemented. Other developments that will aid the growth of the metaverse include the following:

- Backend engines will dismantle obstacles to creativity, allowing a wider audience to produce cutting-edge experiences and games. The transition from 2D Internet environments to fully immersive experiences will be easier as a result.

- Edge computing will supply the metaverse with the computational power it needs to function. By allowing data to be collected, stored, and processed locally rather than in the cloud, edge computing helps to address issues with bandwidth and latency.

The physical and virtual worlds will come together through hardware gadgets. In 2021, Meta released 10 million Oculus Quest 2 headgear, and additional gadgets like gloves and bodysuits are also catching on.

On top of infrastructure, metaverse apps are powered by software development.

It's critical to remember that the current technology is insufficient to fully exploit the metaverse's potential. Infrastructure improvements will be needed in the computation, network, and interface hardware.

Startup Case Study: Absentia

Absentia was founded with the mindset of coming up with the first virtual reality operating system. Again, as college dropouts are often behind great ideas, Absentia is not an exception. Three computer science dropouts from BITS Pilani on the Goa campus conceptualized and founded it. The aim was to develop an artificial intelligence engine that would generate interactive content for games, with a faster rate and with negligible human intervention. Absentia started in early 2015, and from then the company has integrated a virtual reality technology with digital video content. They developed their own headset, similar to the Oculus Rift virtual reality system. At the moment, the company is working on an artificial intelligence product called Norah AI. Norah AI is basically a bot that can develop game designs and constructions based on the simple instructions given to it. The instructions or commands can be machine-generated stories, interchanges, characters, weapons, and various game scenes based on text or graphic inputs.

It could be specifically helpful to the individual who does not have coding capabilities. They can communicate with Norah AI based on text-based input. For example, commands like "Create a fat man with a moustache" would trigger the functioning of Norah AI and the character is made. The bot will help generate up to 80 percent of the game design and construction within a span of two or three hours. This is a huge improvement in automated content design and could potentially decrease game creation time to approximately 15 days. Norah AI would be able to generate a novel set of collaborating contents for colonnade games, casual games, puzzles, animations, and graphics. Technically, the Norah AI interactive engine platform and framework consists of a huge neural network. The interplay of the neural network behind the scenes enables interactive content designers to create games, GIFs, and simulations in less time.

Facebook is betting big on these technologies. They are making a camera as the first AR platform. Their Camera Effects platform would potentially transform smartphone cameras into the AR platform. It might mean that artists and developers can develop effects through the Facebook camera. The Facebook platform contains two creative tools—Frame Studio and AR Studio. They enable Facebook users to create camera effects, which range from simple frame generation to interactive AR experiences. This platform will allow artists and designers to connect art with data to bring AR into commonplace life through the Facebook camera.

Traditionally, machine learning has not been a part of artwork. However, in changing times, it is extending its reach to areas like art. The Facebook extension to AR, VR, and markerless AR is one example of this. Also, recently 29 printings were created by a neural network architecture-based Google computer and were auctioned in San Francisco with an $8,000 winning bid. The computers learned from example data before creating the artwork. The computers were fed a large number of images over time, which enabled them to recognize visual patterns (Source: `https://news.artnet.com/market/google-inceptionism-art-sells-big-439352`). Samsung, also working on enriching immersive video quality, claims that their recent Gear 360 product enables shooting 4K 360-degree video content. For more information, see the pictures and content available at `https://en.wikipedia.org/wiki/Projection_augmented_model`.

Google Home and Amazon Alexa

Google Assistant is a voice-controlled digital assistant. It runs on a variety of devices, including phones, Google Home, and smart TVs. It gives users context-aware help. Google Assistant has slowly started appearing on Android phones and a few other IoT-based devices like Android

Wear-based smart watches. Google Assistance is integrated into Google Allo (integrated chat apps) as well. However, the Google Home device is the only smart speaker to feature Google Assistant.

Amazon Alexa (AI assistant speakers) is built on the Echo, and is made available to any third-party licensee that's associated with the Echo family of products. Amazon is making effort to integrate it with cars, washing machines, and with other devices. Amazon's connected home speaker has gained in recent times as it positioned Alexa in a very good way and loaded it with a magnitude of features. Alexa includes more than 3,000 voice-driven capabilities. While consumers might not be aware of how to use a smart home, they can use voice commands with the assistant to turn on lights, play certain songs, record a television program, or perform any other number of tasks.

Google recently announced that the smart speaker would provide recipes for cooking over 5 million types of dishes in step by step instruction format. It will read out the recipes for you. You simply need to locate the recipes through Google assistance and then press the button to "send to Google home" to shuttle the instructions to your speaker. Alexa, Google Home, and Google Assistance are the by-products of machine learning technology. Machine learning sits at the core of these devices/ technologies.

Google Now

Google Now and Google Assistant are two separate things. Google Now enables users to quickly search the Internet and do a collection of tasks such as schedule events and alarms, adjust device's volume based on a voice commend, and post information to social media by using natural-sounding voice commands.

Google Now is a good choice when users want to search the Internet on a mobile device without lifting it up to use it, something similar to Siri and Cortana. One of the excellent features of Google Now is its hands-free accessibility from the lock screen, which is enabled by a simple voice command—"OK, Google." Google Now enables you to search the Internet and access information in your personal Google accounts. It is not context-aware and does not connect to or know the user, whereas Google Assistant is context-aware and actually "knows" you. This is the main difference between them. Both use machine learning technology to its fullest and incorporate some of the best ingredients of it.

Google Now is not platform specific and works with the Google Android and iOS, whereas Google Assistant is targeted at Google's Allo chat app. Google Assistant is integrated into Google Home and Google's Pixel phones. Theoretically, Google Now works on the iOS and Android seamlessly, but practically its hardware-controlling capabilities are limited on the iOS.

Brain Waves and Conciseness Computing

Facebook is working on a technology that enables users to type with the help of their brain. Facebook is in the process of creating a system that would type 100 words per minute by converting brain signals (scientists have already achieved eight words typing/texting through brain waves). The system will not include any type of transplant into the user's body, and it's done only by "monitoring" the brain.

Facebook is collaborating with several universities and academia. As per their briefing, the system will provide users with the capability to interact (text to) with friends without talking on the phone. For example, you could send an email just by thinking of the content. The technology may not require thinking in the terms of letters to frame the sentence, but just by thinking about the content, the text would be typed. Apart from this research, Facebook is also working to make it possible so people can hear through their skin. These research findings were shared at the Facebook developer conference.

Machine Learning Platforms and Solutions

This section covers two of the more common machine learning platforms—SAP Leonardo and Salesforce Einstein.

SAP Leonardo

Leonardo is a digital innovation system that contains multiple technologies, including machine learning, blockchain, data intelligence, Big Data, IoT, and analytics to enable business competitiveness. It is helping companies innovate on business models and processes and change the way people work. SAP Leonardo connects things with people and processes through data. It delivers an extremely ground-breaking IoT and machine learning-based solution ecosystem that encompasses adaptive applications, products, and services, including Big Data management and connectivity, to enable the following:

- New business processes (for example, Industry 4.0)

- New business models (for example, cloud computing)

- New work environments

SAP Leonardo has an excellent innovation portfolio, which helps businesses provide services and build applications from things/objects/devices to outcomes. For example, in the manufacturing industry, it could provide the following benefits:

- *Live insights*: Provides information like condition monitoring, location tracking, environment, usage, and consumption patterns

- *Predictive analytics*: In real time, it analyzes equipment health, remaining lifetime, demand and supply forecast, and time of arrival

- *Optimize processes*: Lower maintenance cost, higher efficiency, reduced waste, fewer claims, faster response, and shorter cycles

- *New business models*: Usage-based pricing, product-as-a-service

SAP Leonardo works on the philosophy of "intelligently connecting people, things, and businesses."

One business problem where Leonardo does excellent work is with customer retention:

- Takes incoming dynamic data from various channels and builds an overview of the customer's journey

- Sorts, classifies, and routes events and then identifies critical events/churn indicators, including identification of customers who are about to churn

- Identifies customers who are about to churn and takes proactive steps to prevent customers from churning

Another area is service ticketing:

- *Categorize tickets*: Reads ticket content, determines the category, and automatically routes the ticket to the appropriate agent or department.

- *Suggest solutions*: Provides potential solutions to an agent.

- *Boost customer experience*: Improves resolution rate, time to resolution, and closure rate by automated intelligent workflow.

Some benefits that SAP Leonardo provides to business include:

- Increases revenue

- Reimagines processes

- Increases quality time at work

- Increases customer satisfaction

- Enables innovations

Salesforce Einstein

Salesforce Einstein does not fall under the category of a "general AI" solution offering, which typically targets human like insight and thoughtfulness. Instead, Einstein is an intelligence competency assembled into the Salesforce platform. It focuses on bringing smarter and more intelligent customer relationship management (CRM). It is intended to discover hidden insights, predict results, endorse actions, and automate tasks. Einstein focuses on helping users deliver seven outcomes related to artificial intelligence:

- Perception

- Notification

- Suggestions

- Automation

- Prediction

- Prevention

- Situation awareness

Salesforce termed its solution as the world's smartest CRM. It is able to incorporate extraordinary machine learning capabilities into applications. Therefore, any app can ideally deliver individualized experiences and predictive customer capabilities if it is integrated with Einstein. Salesforce Einstein is tuned to automatically discover appropriate insights, predict future results, and proactively recommend the best next steps.

Einstein is developed on the top of the Salesforce platform, so it can help anyone create machine learning powered apps. Einstein offers multiple features, a few of which are mentioned next. They are available through the Salesforce cloud offering and are further categorized into sales cloud, service cloud, community cloud, marketing cloud app cloud, commerce cloud, and analytical cloud.

- *Einstein Supervisor Insights*: Empower managers with real-time, omnichannel insights and AI-powered analytics to efficiently manage service operations at scale.

- *Einstein Opportunity Insights*: Know which opportunities are most or least likely to close and why.

- *Einstein Account Insights*: Always know what's impacting your customers' companies.

- *Einstein Activity Capture*: Automatically log customer engagements and spend more time selling.

- *Einstein Email*: Provide tailored content for each customer email.

- *Einstein Recommendations*: Serve up personalized recommendations to every shopper.

- *Einstein Commerce Insights*: Transform customer data into actionable merchandising insights.

- *Einstein Experts*: Help members find certified experts on the topics that matter most to them.

- *Einstein Trending Posts*: Intelligently display the most interesting discussions in your company.

- *Einstein Social Insights*: Gain deeper insight into your customers by analyzing social conversations.

- *Einstein Segmentation*: Build the best audience for every campaign.

- *Einstein Journey Insights*: Uncover the optimal sequence of events to optimize every journey.

- *Einstein Data Discovery*: Automatically analyze millions of data combinations in minutes.

Salesforce Einstein is available through Salesforce clouds. Some innovative and new features powered by excellence and elegance of Salesforce Einstein come with an additional charge. However, the basic feature exist as a part of standard Salesforce license and editions.

Security and Machine Learning

In the next ten years, the amount of data in the world is projected to reach a mammoth 163 Zettabytes. A report from Seagate claims that, of all this data, most of it is created by enterprises of all kinds, including some critical sectors like finance, banking, and insurance. To visualize this growth of data, imagine watching the entire Netflix catalog 489 times.

Verizon recently collected data from 65 organizations across the world and analyzed it on 42,068 incidents and 1,935 breaches. The findings are surprising; it clearly indicates that phishing attacks, malware installation, and financially motivated breaches are on the rise. Ransomware saw a 50 percent increase as well.

The burning question is how organizations control all this and get rid of it. The answers lie in Big Data and machine learning analytics, because they have the capability to find anomalies in the data. These technologies can analyze huge mountains of data automatically and provide alerts to the respective teams in the organization before something bad happens. It could detect malware installation, phishing through email, or malicious machine learning-enabled systems, and then heal the system automatically.

The Indian Software Industry and Machine Learning

The Indian software services industry is worth $146 billion, which has been achieved in the last two decades, mainly by helping their global clients by managing their technology requirements. However, commoditized back-office maintenance work is not lucrative any more, and comes under strong pricing pressures. Indian IT giants like TCS, Infosys, Tech Mahindra, and Wipro Ltd are feeling this pressure and they are looking at building new platforms and services to retain their profit margin and serve their customers better.

Platforms like Infosys Nia, Mana, Wipro's Homels, and Tech Mahindra's TACTiX are machine learning-based products that are the by-products of this mindset. Typically, these platforms integrate machine learning with deep knowledge of an organization and their existing knowledgebase. IT companies are betting on their automation platform to bring differentiation. For instance, Wipro recently launched HOLMES, TCS make their presence by launching Ignio, and Tech Mahindra by TACTiX (they are calling it an integrated automation platform). However, the basic motive is the same—help clients automate their projects by improving efficiency and effectiveness. Fundamentally these platforms would help automate back-office work and support jobs.

Machine learning is all about finding deep insight and value for the user, if you see it from business perspective. These deep insights essentially lead organizations to the discovery of a new frontier of opportunities to enhance, simplify, and mechanize complex business processes. Now, customers demand that machine learning and AI be incorporated into their service and products. Therefore, almost all the major Indian IT companies are coming up with products to cater to the demand and need for machine learning/artificial intelligence. It may be in the form of platforms, services, and products. However, the basic principle remains the same. In turn, systems use the knowledgebase to automate repetitive business and IT processes. This equips enterprises to use their human resources to solve higher-value stakeholder problems that require creativity, passion, and imagination.

The target business and customers are also different for these products. For example, Ignio is not meant to compete with Watson. It is an artificial intelligence powered product that recognizes, diagnoses, analyzes, and learns from issues in the IT infrastructure/support. In turn, it automates basic technology work. Also, this product helps TCS use its talented human resources in an effective way by assigning them valuable and intelligence/creativity intensive work and releasing them from the monotonous and repetitive work. Watson, on the other hand, was created with the value driver to help clients across multiple industries make sense of large sets of unstructured, structured, and semi-structured data sets.

Tech Mahindra's machine learning enabled product AQT is used to drive intelligent automation use cases using technologies. The platform integrates RPA (robotic process automation), autonomics, natural language processing, machine learning, and predictive analytics. Again, the intent is to address the needs of customers. For example, their automation framework AQT (Automation, Quality, Time) consolidates all their existing automation platforms, practices, and tools. AQT is used by Tech Mahindra to holistically deliver increased business efficiencies to their stakeholders. Practically, AQT brings many benefits to the customers and helps deliver faster and better results, because of its excellent implementation of intelligent automation and automation thinking. Also, AQT makes Mahindra's value chain efficient because it impacts their processes, quality, user experience, time to market, and cost to deliver in a positive manner.

Infosys Nia (new artificial intelligence) is an artificial intelligence and machine learning platform. It is seamlessly integrated with the previous AI platform called MANA. This increases the scope of the first-generation AI platform beyond IT universalization and optimization. It enables clients to bring AI to their core business and achieve transformation. Infosys clients used Infosys Nia to power their organizational knowledge, produce deep insights, and determine opportunities to enhance, simplify, and automate complex business processes.

Use Cases for These Products

Incident management and the way to automation: A top food supplier wanted real-time visibility into product guides, costs, and pricing information in their customer order assignment system. Also, they needed a Sarbanes-Oxley-compliant user process. With the help of Nia, Infosys provided a "zero touch" automation resolution for provisioning and de-provisioning access. It also provided a solution that would take care of automated synchronization of data across multiple enterprise systems.

Highlights of this solution:

- 24 percent decrease of incidents across all groups, leading to a 16 percent decrease in overall IT support efforts

- 70 percent improvement in turnaround time in compliance-related audit reporting and failure resolution for data requests

- 6 percent service needs and 11 percent incident solutions were automated

Level 3 automation and way to automation: Level 3 support professionals realize that application enrichments and issue fixes are the most important talents in an IT enterprise. However, these talents take up a substantial percentage of their time (60-80 percent) in monotonous manual activities. For example, performing root-cause analysis, impact analysis, and test plan creation and testing. This triggers low employee productivity and extended lead periods when doing change requests and bug fixes.

Infosys Nia solves this problem in an innovative way by ingesting source code, historical incident tickets, and other documentation. It creates a knowledge model of the source code that maps across all the available modules. Then natural language processing, text analytics, and machine learning techniques are applied to accomplish bug localization, root-cause identification, and impact analysis, and test plan generation in an automated way.

Highlights of the solution:

- Improved employee competences

- Amplified employee productivity and utilization

- Shorter regular handle period of the tickets

- Shorter mean period of resolution of tickets

Source: Use cases inspired by the content available on the websites of Infosys and Tech Mahindra.

Quantum Machine Learning

Quantum physics is field of study that deals with atoms and their interplay at the microscopic level. Atoms contain electrons, protons, and neutrons. New near-term quantum devices can advantageously resolve computationally inflexible problems in simulation, optimization, and machine learning.

Quantum machine learning (QML) is a subdivision of quantum information science that tries to solve entire machine learning problems with the help of quantum algorithms. These algorithms/methods and models run on quantum computers. These algorithms may include nearest neighbor algorithms, neural networks, and Bayesian networks. A quantum computer is dependent on an atom's state. Quantum computers explore a feature of quantum machines called *superposition,* which fuels ultra-fast parallel computation and simulations.

On a silicon chip on which classical computers are based, data is rendered in two states—0 or 1. Whereas on a quantum computer (QC), data exists in both the states simultaneously. The quantum computer's basic processing unit is called a *qubit.* It has the special quality of acquiring two states at the same time. Hence, its processing speed grows exponentially.

Quantum mechanics offers provocative predictions to improve machine learning. It offers benefits like decreased computational difficulty to enhanced generalization performance. For instance, quantum boosted algorithms for principal component analysis, quantum support vector machines, and quantum Boltzmann machines enjoy benefits of both fields together. Development is happening at a superfast speed. Chinese scientists have already built the world's first quantum machine at the Shanghai Institute of Advanced Studies. In the near future, QCs will be outperforming their classical peers. QCs can potentially solve large-scale computation problems with ease. Therefore, due to the enormous potential of QC, Europe and the United States are collaborating on the research related to this. Companies like Google, Microsoft, and IBM are working on QC.

Practical Innovations

Here are some examples of practical innovations:

- *Augmented reality Shiseido's virtual makeup glass*: It gathers a photograph of your face and lets you examine different appearances and colors. There are many other companies working on similar ideas with their own versions, such as American Apparel's color-changing app.

- *Cross-merchant location-based offers*: Visa and Gap have teamed up to run a trial of a location-based marketing capability that triggers offers to frequent shoppers when cardholders swipe their card within the vicinity of a Gap.

- *In-store gamification*: Target 9 has announced a game that children can play when shopping with parents called Bullseye Playground. The game, played on a handheld device, discloses "Easter Eggs" unseen in the store.

- *Remote/machine ordering*: Amazon8 Dash is a button that a client places in the kitchen, bath, laundry, or anywhere a customer stores recurrently obtained products. When running low, the client pushes the button and the item is added to the customer's online shopping cart. The client then obtains an notification on their handheld device to order the product.

- Machine learning helps forecast before epidemics happen: AIME uses Big Data and machine learning algorithms to pinpoint the geolocation of dengue fever outbreaks three months before they occur.

- *Ross Intelligence*: Created on top of IBM's Watson, it usages natural language processing to answer legal questions.

- *Player XP*: Uses machine learning technologies to get productive feedback in mobile video game reviews.

- *Pefin*: A machine learning-based financial consultant that analyzes more than two million data points to deliver decisions.

- *Chile-based NotCo*: Replicates the taste and texture of animal food products using machine learning technologies, biochemistry, and plant science. They use machine algorithms to create nutritious vegetarian meals.

Machine Learning Adoption Scorecard

There are multiple platform/tools and products available, so it is a good idea to look at the adoption strategies. From a consumer perspective, machine learning adoption strategies are very important. Because if they do not strategize their adoption and proceed in a planned way, consumers might end up paying more for less effective solutions/products. Adoption strategies are multifaceted, which means price, planning, and need must be evaluated. It is worth mentioning here that the "consumer" may be an organization/enterprise or an individual.

Because the cloud infrastructure is readily available, it makes sense to use cloud-based analytics and machine learning solutions. There are many reasons to do this, including reduction of cost to 100 percent availability of infrastructures and services. However, not all applications and services can be adapted to cloud-based machine learning. Every available cloud analytics service need not be adopted by every consumer. They need to be evaluated first. The evaluation of adoption strategies is a combination of subjective and objective analysis.

Table 6-1 shows an assessment questionnaire for ten key areas under consideration. Each area is assessed and an objective score is obtained. You can use this template for assessments. The cumulative score gives an indication as to the suitability of cloud-based machine learning/analytics adoption. The template is self-explanatory and simple, so that a quick assessment can be done by the decision-makers even with moderate knowledge of the application/product/service that is being considered for cloud adoption.

When evaluating a project for cloud adoption, users need to perform a subjective analysis to determine the proportional weight that each of these key areas possesses. However, those types of details are not covered here. Multiply the raw scores by the weight you apply to each area, in order to arrive at a total score that meets your specific needs. The cumulative score will give you an indication of the suitability for adoption.

Note that this method is not conclusive in any way, but it may act as a good starting point for machine learning-based cloud adoption assessment. There are many other considerations that come into play depending on the technology, business, industry verticals, and so on.

Table 6-1. *Ten Key Areas for the Consideration and Evaluation Questionnaire of Cloud Adoption*

SI #	Key Areas	Details	Legend for Score (Use the Guidelines to Calculate the Score)
1	Business area	What is your primary area of business? Technology or service? If you are in the service industry or a startup, it may be advisable to focus your attention to service areas and embrace cloud analytics as an enabler for business.	1 Technical service offerings 2 3 4 5 Non-technical service provider
2	Criticality of the application	How critical is your application/ service? Before moving mission-critical and business-critical applications to the cloud, think twice. Also, on-premises solutions are a good option. However, due to the ease of use, reduced cost, and less overhead burden if you want to move to the cloud-based analytical solution, start with a less critical service.	1 Mission critical 2 3 4 5 Non-business critical

(continued)

Table 6-1. (*continued*)

SI #	Key Areas	Details	Legend for Score (Use the Guidelines to Calculate the Score)
3	Frequency of use	How often do you use the application? How many users use the application? Less frequent applications are preferable for cloud analytical adoption.	1 Very frequently used with a large user base 2 3 4 5 Less frequently used with a small user base
4	Customization	Are your customization needs high? Do you need highly customized interfaces? The cloud vendor may not be able to cater to highly customized needs.	1 Very high customization needs 2 3 4 5 No customization needs and can operate OOB
5	Compliance needs	Does your application require special compliance (apart from standard cloud compliances provided by vendor, such as FISMA)? Special compliance may include compliance standards for secondary, federal, government, and governing body policies.	1 Mandatory special compliance required from statutory bodies 2 3 4 5 No special compliance required

(*continued*)

Table 6-1. (*continued*)

SI #	Key Areas	Details	Legend for Score (Use the Guidelines to Calculate the Score)
6	Integration requirements	Does the application need to be closely integrated with other applications in the organization? Heavy integration poses a challenge for cloud analytical adoption.	1 Strong integration required with other systems and processes 2 3 4 5 No integration needs
7	Costing/expense planning	How do you want your expense to be allocated? Do you prefer a low recurring expense over a one-time large investment? If so, cloud adoption may be the preferred option.	1 Willingness to pay for one time, huge investment 2 3 4 5 Prefer low and recurring types of expenses

(*continued*)

Table 6-1. (*continued*)

SI #	Key Areas	Details	Legend for Score (Use the Guidelines to Calculate the Score)
8	Privacy needs	How stringent are your privacy needs/policies of sharing/storing data outside the corporate network? Some industry verticals and lines of business may have stringent needs that prevent cloud adoption.	1 Strong privacy needs 2 3 4 5 Low privacy needs
9	Performance service level agreements	How stringent are your performance SLA needs? If you have a strict SLA for service delivery to your customers, cloud deployment may not be able to help you. Inherent issues of Internet connectivity may provide hindrance to high performance SLA adherence.	1 Stringent performance SLAs, extremely low downtime tolerance, and very low response lags 2 3 4 5 Relaxed performance SLAs

(*continued*)

Table 6-1. (*continued*)

SI #	Key Areas	Details	Legend for Score (Use the Guidelines to Calculate the Score)
10	Infrastructure requirements and availability	Is your infrastructure requirement high? Do you already have underutilized infrastructure available? If yes, you can use the same to deploy your application/ software instead of adopting the cloud.	1 Large infrastructure is required and underutilized infrastructure is available 2 3 Existing infrastructure can be streamlined to be made available 4 5 Large infrastructure is required, but none is available and needs to be procured
		Total Score for Adoption	**> 40 Suitable** **20-40 Moderate** **< 20 Not Suitable**

Summary

This chapter covered lots of important information about the machine learning products, services, and applications that are offered and popular in the market. The chapter contained a detailed discussion about some established products and centered on machine learning, such as Siri, IBM Watson, Microsoft Cortana, and connected and driverless cars. It also presented a primer about some of the existing startups that are popularizing new ideas. The chapter concluded by looking at quantum machine learning, which is the ultimate direction of the technology in next ten years.

Mind Map

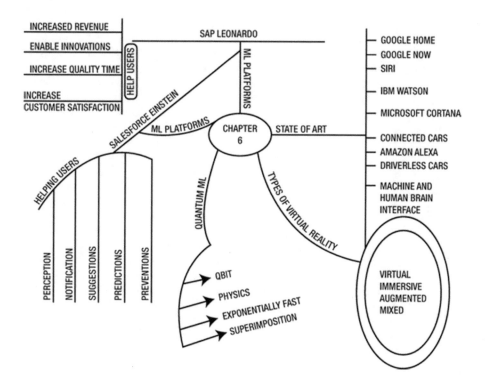

CHAPTER 7

Innovation, KPIs, Best Practices, and More for Machine Learning

Dr. Patanjali Kashyap[a*]

[a] Bangalore, Karnataka, India

Abstract

This chapter highlights how the traditional business model is changing and a new model is taking its place in mainstream industries and markets. It also provides a brief premier about how traditional IT vendors are adopting a new mindset and betting on the thought partnership way of working instead of the order and deliver model. The ranges from setting the context of the transformational state of the current IT vendor to their adoption strategies to new and evolving technologies like microservices and blockchain.

The chapter provides a view of how the process of thought partnership plays its role in the overall changing scenario. It also covers risk, compliances, best practices, and KPIs in the context of the machine learning ecosystem and provides some insight about how the technologies

© Dr. Patanjali Kashyap 2024
P. Kashyap, *Machine Learning for Decision Makers,*
https://doi.org/10.1007/978-1-4842-9801-5_7

will potentially transform the feature state of the industry, the domains, and ultimately the world. Guidelines for identifying some KPIs across the domains and technologies are also provided in the chapter.

The chapter also highlights the process of innovation and the importance of building culture around it. This discussion is relevant because ultimately it is innovation that fuels a simple, average-performing organization to the best performing organization. Especially in the last couple of decades, it is innovation that powered organizations to excel. For example, Google's driverless car, Amazon's cloud services, and Tesla's mission to create reusable rockets established them in the market of the future.

IT, Machine Learning, Vendors, Clients, and Changing Times

Information Technology (IT) forms a major part of the core strategic investments for all the growth-oriented institutions in this ultra-modern era of accelerated growth and dynamic decision making. Therefore, companies are increasingly banking on innovation, technology, and agility for their fast-tracked growth and success. Organizations with double-digit growth typically bet on their unique offerings, higher productivity, or niche area of expertise and often keep pure innovation in the back seat until the competition catches up with them and forces them to dedicate a good percentage of their revenue toward innovation.

Organizations utilize this time to clean up their cash surplus or achieve a desired level of size to grab the attention of their prospective and current customers. Organizations that have crossed all these hurdles and established themselves have a tougher path to sustained growth. Hence, they look forward to doing something new and put innovation in driving seat. They invest heavily on innovative technologies like machine leaning, Big Data, IoT, and on bringing novelty in product/service offerings, business processes, and customer management.

The same trend is seen in major and minor processes that are well established, having led to the organization's success until it's time to cope with the changing times. The concept is simple. Any delay or failure in innovation will lead to a hasty death of the organization. Cut-throat competition with ever increasing alternatives to the customers and users force these organizations to innovate.

Innovation and automation become the growth enabler for these organizations and there are multiple reasons for this. These parameters become growth enablers because innovative technologies like machine learning and Big Data need new mindsets for the traditional technologies (mainframes). Moreover, these are linked to profitability, growth, and productivity. Innovation is no more a luxury than a necessity. However, innovation involves cost and time. Therefore, commitment from the top management regarding its implementation and building culture around it are very important. Some important line items are mentioned here:

- Ensure all innovative ideas have an equal opportunity—being neutral to the source.

- Establish a mature culture and an ability to encourage, monitor, and develop ideas. Tap innovation from multiple sources.

- Develop the ability to spot, assess, mentor, and incubate ideas with business value. Implement the proper process for it.

- Develop a framework and team that can make early investment decisions on new ideas.

- Involve employees/partners in an engaged exercise. Organizations have to encourage them to tap their ideation potential.

- Form a robust and sustainable platform for employees/partners to receive rewards/recognition for their ideas.

In the wake of such intense competition, organizations look for avenues to innovate in every possible opportunity. They ask and desire their employees, management, vendors, business partners, channel partners, and other stakeholders to help them innovate. They willingly take help or support stakeholders to innovate in their respective areas. Because IT and innovative technologies are the growth accelerators, organizations assign the highest priority to innovation in IT. Routine delivery excellence, cost reduction, productivity benefits, and the "take orders and deliver" approach are now expected by all IT vendors by default. Any company proposing value only through these so-called default benefits will be referred to as an IT vendor, whereas organizations (especially large ones) are looking for IT vendors who can showcase benefits that are superior in scope, wider in thinking, and bolder in approach, with clear articulation of business value in measurable terms.

These organizations are referred to as IT partners and these are the ones who will earn more, obtain larger projects, and get greater respect from the market. IT companies have to continuously revisit their approach toward partnering with clients and bringing in superior thought processes to cater to the knowledge and innovation needs of the market. These companies have to transform themselves into "thought partners."

The result of this comes as the co-creation of the products and services. Co-creation is about continuous collaboration where the client and partner work together to create excellence in terms of services and products. For instance, vendors generally have good a setup for R&D and testing centers of new generation technologies. Also, they run centers of excellence and thought leadership initiatives, whereas clients are domain-centric. Therefore, clients can take these services or areas of expertise and create outstanding services and products in close collaboration with vendors. This strategy enables vendors and partners/clients/stakeholders to test APS in real time and provide instant feedback to vendors. Continuous collaboration is the backbone of this idea. Also, the same strategies can be used as a feedback mechanism and continue until the finished APS (application, product, and service) is delivered appropriately to the stakeholders.

Organizations will have a wide range of enhancements, upgrades, implementations, and other strategically important initiatives going on in parallel, apart from regular technical tasks. Taking all these parallel activities to a successful closure with clear ROI measurement will require a huge amount of skilled resources and management time. In most cases, these initiatives are traditionally broken into smaller chunks of work and handed over to multiple vendors, leading to unwarranted coordination issues, non-compliance issues, and cost and time escalations. Although this model has advantages in terms of reduced dependency on a single vendor, availability of multiple sets of skilled labor and risk distribution, a larger partner can single-handedly provide all these advantages using their expertise and prowess.

Clients have to choose their partners very carefully by examining their abilities to a perfect mix of high-end IT/business consulting and a wide range of rudimentary IT services. This is a huge upgrade for emerging IT service companies because they have a steep challenge of offering high-end consulting services along with their regular services, which they have to acquire. This model is different for the existing model that has existed for years. However, it is the need of the hour because to get excellence, clients want that brilliance to be incorporated into the DNA of their work culture.

This desire to achieve superiority and acquire excellence brings the need for automation, automation of automation, and smart and intelligent applications that assist the organization in managing their tasks with fewer human resources. It helps them implement efficiency and effectiveness with reduced costs, increased profitability, and increased ROI. Machine learning and its associated technologies fit appropriately in this pursuit. Moreover, if the solution around the machine learning ecosystem is created and implemented, there is no need to overdistribute the work. Some routine and repetitive tasks can easily be performed by the machine learning-enabled smart solutions. However, for highly technical requirements, there is still a need for an intelligent workforce and robust infrastructure readiness, as well as other factors for which vendors may be one option.

Building a machine learning solution focuses on a technical, process, people, and governance based approach. Therefore, appropriate cautions need to be taken. This requires a proper evaluation of existing processes, metrics, design considerations, and measurements. Also, before, during, and after implementation of the machine learning solution, some standard guideline needs to be followed. Otherwise, the overall effort will be in vain.

These guidelines include risk management, making sure of funding, compliance alignment, and many other factors. Here are some of the prerequisites of machine learning solutions and strategies:

- Design the machine learning implementation process (from the idea generation stage to the rapid prototyping stage).

- Design the machine learning project and organization governance structure, which includes the roles and responsibilities of the people involved.

- Bring together the design enablers.

- Support the implementation of the machine learning solution and program management.

- Enable the incubation of ideas with a rapid prototyping factory.

Designing Key Performance Indicators (KPIs) for Machine Learning Analytics-Based Domains

KPIs are measurable and computable metrics generally matched to enterprise goals and objectives. There are the various key process points that influence the overall performance of an organization and the projects. Performance measures help ensure that what the process delivers is aligned to a set of business objectives and meets the stakeholder's expectations. Therefore, the KPIs should be designed to measure individual contributor, project, and department level activities. They must be aligned to each other. The KPIs should be identified and defined with respect to business drivers and benchmarks. These KPIs should be continuously monitored to track the service performance.

Eventually, these performance parameters can be aggregated to business performance parameters. While defining KPIs, the five Ws—Who, What, When, Where, and Why (and How)—serve as a guide to achieve efficiency. Designing KPIs for measuring machine learning-based projects/individual contribution/organizational capabilities or unit performance is always a big challenge. However, the following guidelines help. It is always good to start by answering these questions:

- Who is the user?

- What is the business going to deliver?

- When do the stakeholders need the solution?

- Where and for which purpose do stakeholders need the solution?

- Why do the stakeholders need this?

- How can the business optimize the process and technology?

A performance measurement mechanism plays an important role in helping an organization measure the performance and formulate a future strategy. It is also helpful in keeping track of current performance status. Also, performance measurement is critical in projects like Big Data and machine learning due to the magnitude of factors like heavy investment requirements, time to market, and customer experience. Periodic performance measurement of business and operations is a key task. It is critical for simple reasons.

For example, unless performance monitoring and measurement is done, it is impossible to introduce improvement or control measures. There are several statistical techniques and methods used by enterprises to measure performance against the set KPIs from time to time. The main objective behind measuring the performance is to:

- Understand how well the business, projects, and operations are performing against the set parameters

- Combine data points in one place to see the bigger picture

- Set targets for improving performance on an ongoing basis

- Do proactive planning and forecasting to stay ahead of competitors

The process of defining key KPIs and performance measurement also helps enterprises and decision-makers prepare charters and formulate strategies for expansion and growth. A mandatory criteria for the success of any KPI or performance management system is that it must be realistic. It should not be theoretical in nature because, if it happens that way, it is impossible to measure and report metrics and KPIs that are not related to a given process/operation. Here are the few points related to KPIs and the metrics measurement framework that you should take into consideration to execute your KPIs effectively:

- Any contractual obligations that may have been agreed on with the customers and vendors

- Measures important from a people, process, and technology standpoint

- Measures that top management will want to see, for example, revenue growth, year on year profitability, and so on

The KPI and ML Teams

After you understand the KPIs, you have to extend them further to get a sense of ultimately who is responsible for implementing them. You also need to know how to measure their productivity, because then you have the opportunity to further fine-tune them. Let's look at some of the important KPIs from this perspective.

Top KPIs for your team's data analytics:

- The number of monthly insights produced

- The proportion of decision-makers who routinely utilize analytics

- The precision with which the analytics team makes forecasts

- How quickly the analytics team can produce results

Top KPIs for your team of data engineers:

- The proportion of time that systems and data pipelines are available

- The monthly frequency of mistakes and occurrences

- The turnaround time for resolving mishaps and problems

- The rate of automated production deployments' success

- The monthly delivery of new features or updates

Top KPIs for your team of data scientists:

- How many models are created each month

- The precision of data science models' predictions

- How many businesses issues data science has resolved

Monitoring the KPIs

Designing and implementing the KPIs are fine, but it is important to know and understand how these KPIs are performing. Therefore, it is important to know which KPIs you need to monitor for ML.

The following KPIs are for monitoring ML:

- Training

- Accuracy

- Number of rows and columns

- Time

- Variable Importance

- Scoring

- Iteration data-validation

- Prediction

- Data health summary

- Accuracy summary

- Data error rate

- Cache hit rate

- Monitoring

- The number of models in the production stage

- Where the models run

- How long have they have been in business

- Whether the models were validated and approved

- Who approved the models

- The tests that were run

- Whether the results are reliable/accurate

- Whether the compliance and regulatory requirements are being satisfied

- Whether the models are performing within the threshold

- The ROI for the models

Designing Effective KPIs Using a Balanced Scorecard

There are multiple ways by which KPIs and metrics are defined. One effective way to define them is using the balance scorecard method. The balanced scorecard principles are helpful when defining KPIs and an overall performance management system. In a nutshell, balanced scorecard (BSC) is a strategic development, planning, forecasting, and management scheme that enterprises and organizations use to:

- Communicate what they are trying to achieve

- Align the day-to-day routine and regular work that everybody is undertaking with a strategy

- Prioritize and order projects, products, and services

- Measure and monitor growth and improvements toward strategic goals

The balanced scorecard technique is not only about measuring performance against the determined KPIs, but it also helps organizations develop or revise its strategies efficiently. Here are the basic steps in KPI definition that need to be followed:

- *Start with stakeholders, including customers*: Prioritize the customer expectations critical to quality.

- *Top-down view*: Start from the service and decompose it further to the lowest levels involved. This provides a comprehensive view.

- *Establish key, consistent metrics*: This provides insight into which metrics are required on the dashboard.

- *Determine a baseline*: Identifying current status is required because it provides insight into the key indicators in the current processes.

- *Benchmark processes*: Determine who is doing the same or similar things better.

- *Set goals*: Define the new parameter to be achieved.

Some of the key attributes that should be kept in mind while defining KPIs and metrics for any process are as follows:

- *Relevance and validity*: Selecting relevant KPIs for a given process is one of the key aspects. Unless relevant KPIs have been identified, the purpose of performance reporting will not be served.

- *Controllability*: The KPIs should be defined in such a manner that they can be measured and controlled. This is important because the overall effectiveness of a process and its operations are largely dependent on this.

- *Completeness*: KPIs should be quantitative to the extent possible. Performance metrics should be complete in nature because it will be difficult to measure performance unless the key KPIs have been agreed on by all concerned parties. This completeness will ultimately leads to higher accuracy and yields the desired results.

- *Logic/consistency*: KPIs and metrics should be defined using mathematical formulae. There should a logic that helps in the measurement and the overall performance validation process.

Preparation

The following broad points should also be taken care of before the KPI and metric definition exercise commences:

- How will the KPIs create value for the current and future customers/business.

- Whether the KPIs will help in measuring performance of operational processes and IT systems and help in deriving the conclusions for business performance.

- There should be deep dive sessions to develop, discuss, and formulate the strategy for developing the performance management system, including KPI and metrics definitions.

- Communication is a very important aspect that plays a pivotal role during this exercise. The defined and agreed on strategy should be socialized with the concerned parties so that all the parties are on the same page.

- While formulating the KPIs, it is also important to take into account role of any third parties or other internal teams that may be directly or indirectly involved in delivering a part of the service.

- Even before the KPIs are introduced, it is important to distribute them to all the concerned parties. Improving the business is everyone's prerogative as well as responsibility.

Measurement Categories

Here are some important categories of measurements in the context of the balance scorecard method:

- Financial
  - Sales and Service
  - Cost of Service
  - Return on Net Assets
  - Operating Margins
  - Ratio of Margin to Revenue—Service Offering Profitability
  - Ratio of Operating Expenses to Capital Expenditures
  - Ratio of Operating Expenses to Revenue
- Customer Experience
  - Customer Satisfaction
  - Product Quality
  - Usability
  - Accuracy
  - Availability
  - Security
  - Service Quality
  - Timeliness

- – Preferred Access: The channels and touchpoints available to customers such as real people, the web, and the storefront

- – Pricing Flexibility

- Internal Business Operations

  - – Process Reengineering

  - – Unit Cost

  - – Time

  - – Defects

  - – Capacity vs demand

  - – Simplicity

  - – Process Flexibility and Automation

  - – Resource Utilization

- Learning and Growth

  - – Retention

  - – Workforce Diversity

  - – Training Hours

  - – Expenditures

  - – Performance Reviews

  - – Employee Satisfaction

Benefits of KPIs

Here are some benefits of using KPIs:

- *Continuous improvement*: Through an efficient performance management system, efficiently tracking the processes, people, and technologies becomes a reality. Also, the customer experience and end user's perception about rendered services can be tracked very closely.

- *Business planning and budget/revenue forecasting*: Performance measurement enables organizations to introspectively look at their performance on a periodic basis and make meaningful conclusions, revise their budgets, and adjust revenue forecasts from time to time. This can also be used by demand and planning teams for future business planning.

- *Competitive edge*: It becomes easy to compare the performance with rivals in the market and continuously upgrade in order to stay ahead of the competition.

- *People management*: Employees play an important role in the success and growth of an organization. In current times, it has become a practice to link bonuses and performance pay-outs with employee performance KPIs. This also motivates employees to perform to the best of their abilities.

- *Regulatory and standards compliance*: Many customers want the vendor to comply with certain industry standards. A performance management system that's aligned to industry standards and best practices will help comply with regulatory standards.

KPIs help judge, measure, and improve the performance criteria of an organization and they flow down to all the departments. Machine learning and Big Data could be technically domain-agnostic. It is applicable in all the domains, either it retail, manufacturing, fashion or any other field of interest. This section discussed this in detail. However, it is good to look at an example that practically shows how this works. The following section describes a case of selling KPIs in the retail industry.

Some Important KPIs from Specific Organization and Industry Perspectives

KPIs can be designed to measure almost anything. This discussion is mainly based on machine learning. This section includes some important KPIs that provide measurable benefits to an organization that can be used to generate revenue. Other KPIs measure important aspects of global phenomena related to the machine learning industry perspective. This helps companies evaluate the relevance and impact of machine learning across their sectors.

Organization/Enterprise Specific Machine Learning KPIs

- Percentage of projects in a specific organization using machine learning technologies.

- Percentage of machine learning-specific technology used in an organization. For example, how many projects across the organizations are using Mahout or MS Azure ML.

- How many products, services, and applications in the organization are built using machine learning and how many of them are new. Also, how many are enhancement projects.

- What is the ratio of success of the machine learning projects in the organization.

- What is the percentage of machine learning-based project staff efficiency versus non-machine learning-based project staff efficacy and effectiveness.

Industry-Specific KPIs

- Percentage of firms using machine learning and associated technologies in the fields of retail, hospitality, healthcare, education, and so on.

- Percentage of organizations using machine learning in customer services, sales and marketing, finance, banking, and insurance and operations.

- Percentage of firms using the cloud, Big Data analytics, cognitive computing, and machine learning.

Stock and Customer Analytics KPIs

Objectives: Reduce costs, eliminate the unnecessary expense of stock-outs and overstocks, understand important customers to target, encourage loyalty, and make powerful, rapid decisions.

Retailers face huge challenges in keeping track of goods in real time and synchronizing them with in-stock locations by supplying the goods optimally. Being in constant touch with all stakeholders, logistics, and connectivity is the key to responding to consumer demand quickly. Keeping track of seasonal trends and fashion styles ensures that customers get the right products at the right time. Stock analysis will improve inventory-related decisions. Machine learning-based analytics can enable quick shipments by evaluating top-selling products in real time. Predictive analytics can help companies make quick decisions by analyzing data for seasonal sell-through, canceling shipments for bottom-selling products, and communicating more effectively with vendors.

Here's a list of stock analytics:

- Department Contribution

- Hot Item Report

- In Stock Percent

- Inventory Turns

- Lineal Feet

- Mark Down Percent

- Pull-Through

- Reallocations

- Seasonal Buying

- Sell-Through

- Weeks of Supply

Here are some customer analytics:

- Behavior Profiling

- Preference Modeling

- Affinity Tracking

- Attachment Rates

- Basket-Register Correlation

- Brand Switching

- Customer Loyalty

- Demographic Baskets

- In-Basket Price

- Items per Basket

- Revenue Contribution

Differences Between KPIs and Metrics

It's vital to differentiate between KPIs and metrics. KPIs can be thought of as metrics that collectively provide a report card. Metrics are simply a summary of an activity. A healthcare analogy makes it clearer, whereby KPIs provide the details of the overall health of a person, whereas metrics include measuring temperature or shortness of breath of a patient. KPIs are like hidden variables in programming languages, which store value in the background.

Risk, Compliances, and Machine Learning

History is full of the instances where organizations fail due to fraud and non-compliance. This is a global phenomenon. For instance, Enron in the United States, Satyam in India, and South Korean President Park's frauds. Fraud can be done at any level and by anyone. It may happen in the form misleading accounting practices or submitting wrong proof of investments by an employee in the organization to some army weapons deal of government officials.

Ultimately, all these practices take away shareholder's wealth. This also leads to adulteration of manpower and potentially ruins careers. These incidents trigger modifications to the current regulatory policies and lead to the introduction of new acts, such as the Sarbanes-Oxley Act, to put more control in place. A report from the Association of Certified Fraud Examiners (ACFE) projected that up to five percent of an enterprise's profits vanish due to fraud.

Regardless of tighter regulations over the past few years, money laundering and financial scandals occur on a continuous basis. A projection from the Financial Action Task Force said that over one trillion dollars is laundered yearly. In recent times, financial services industries have fallen under increased examination. Therefore, banks have been instructed to implement full measures to avoid financial corruptions. Watchdogs progressively need bigger oversight from institutions, including closer monitoring for anti-money laundering initiatives and implementations. Most of these fraudulent actions go undetected. Detection of fraud has become more challenging in the current world because the amount of data that machines generate is enormous. With the changing times in the era of technology, fraudsters are always one step ahead. Therefore, connecting the dots using old-style techniques is useless.

Older technologies for detecting money laundering use business rules, neural networks, and statistical approaches. Pattern-recognition techniques are also used to detect fraudulent behaviors. To generate meaningful insight, these technologies require a massive amount of historical data. As the nature of fraud could be classified in the broader categories, large repositories of confirmed fraudulent behavior are available and are used to train these supervised technologies (the label/output is known). However, with money laundering there is no labeled data to learn from. Also, apart from the lack of historical data, each money laundering case is exclusive. Rule-based systems apply the same logic to every entity because they do not have ability to learn in real time.

Therefore, depending on the older approaches of detection, money laundering results in low positive rates of success. Also, deploying legacy models often requires costly hardware and databases. Even on top of that, the resulting solutions are unable to provide real-time performance.

New generation anomaly detection techniques—enabled by Big Data analytics, IoT, and machine learning—are changing the way risk, audit, and compliance functions work. These technologies are very useful in the intellectual property theft, workforce compliance, fraudulent employee claims, accounts payable, and insurance claims processing areas. The implementation of machine learning based-systems provides substantial improvements in proficiency and the capability to recognize high-risk and distrustful transactions quicker than before. Also, it enables employees and staff such as the back-office and audit teams to focus on other important tasks. They can be more productive in coming up with ideas that ultimately help in investigation and unraveling new fraudulent schemes.

Historical data related to money laundering is not readily available and is generally rare and unreliable. Therefore, it is crucial to use unsupervised machine learning techniques to extract insight from the data without any previous knowledge of what to look for. Technically, unsupervised learning uses progressive clustering, connection analysis, associative learning, and other techniques to enable customers to track transaction unpredictability, entity interactions, and behavioral changes.

However, to use unsupervised learning to its fullest to detect money laundering, companies must gather and integrate data from multiple sources. Only then will data be consumed by the system correctly. Once this is implemented optimally, tracking individuals and the money/assets laundered becomes easy. Some essential data elements to monitor are as follows:

- Inflow and outflow

- Links between entities and accounts

- Account activity, such as speed, volume, and anonymity

- Reactivation of inactive accounts

- Deposit mix

- Transactional activities in alarm areas

- Use of multiple accounts and account types

Detecting money laundering activities is a complex task, so it's important to apply a technology that potentially tracks the actions of each individual or person or groups involved and links them. With the help of machine learning, virtual reality, and artificial intelligence technology, it is easier to analyze the behavior of each specific entity (card holder, merchant, account, computer, etc.) and their activities over time and generate a comprehensive view of anyone who might attempt money landing.

Organizations execute the machine learning based-project. They take care of a lot of activities. Broadly, those activities are on the organizational and project levels. From a typical mid-level manager project, specific activities are very important. From the organizational perspective, as well for the flawless execution of projects, timely identification of risks is critical. The ultimate vision is to get a sense of realization through the projects.

One major concern for technology managers and teams is to execute the projects with minimum or no risk. This is not easy, due to the complexity of the risk portfolios and their multi-dimensional nature. Hence, proper identification, analysis, planning, assessment, and responses are key to minimizing this risk.

Risk and Risk Management Processes for Machine Learning Projects

Risk is here to stay. Therefore, attaching the appropriate mitigation plan to any identified risks is important. Identifying risk early and keeping track of it throughout a project's lifecycle is important. Identifying, analyzing, and implementing risk is always a challenge. Machine learning can potentially automate this overall process. It starts happening in pockets. However, manual risk management has its own importance (at least as of now). Therefore, the following sections discuss risk management in more detail. Figure 7-1 shows the overall risk-management process.

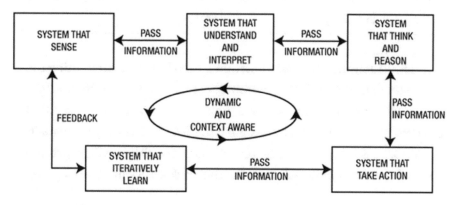

Figure 7-1. *Risk management process*

Risk Identification

Risks can be of multiple types and they can be identified by any member of the team or any person in the organization. Having risk-free environments/projects/organizations is everyone's responsibility. However, this chapter confines its discussion to project risk (see Table 7-1).

Table 7-1. *Types of Risk*

Project Product	People	Process	Management	Financial
Integration	Training	Quality	Customer/vendor/ partner relationship	Compliance
Scalability	Availability	Manageability	Cooperation	Confidential
Usability	Training	Quality	Schedule and cost	Legal
Performance	Adoption	Traceability	Financial	Schedule and cost
Security	Technical knowledge	Measurability	Management process	Value realization

If risk is identified by a team member, then before documenting the risk, the team member should communicate this issue with their lead to ensure that the situation fits the definition of project risk. If the risk is validated, an owner should be assigned to the risk. The owner is usually a person who is interested in the resolution of the risk or will be primarily impacted if the risk materializes. After that, risk assessment takes place.

Risk Assessment

An assessment of the overall threat must be done based on the probability of the threat occurring and the severity of the impact (if it occurs). This is estimated using this formula:

Risk Exposure (RE) = Probability x Impact

Once this assessment is complete, a risk response plan is developed.

Risk Response Plan

This is a plan, or course of action, to be implemented prior to the risk occurring. This eliminates or reduces the probability of the risk occurring or reduces the impact (if the risk occurs). You must determine the strategy to mitigate the risk and develop a clearly defined set of steps. Here are the main activities:

- Identifying potential risk responses
- Selecting the risk response
- Adding the risk responses to a risk log
- Assigning ownership
- Assigning due dates

Monitoring and Controlling Risks

Monitoring and controlling risk are done during this phase. Consider these tasks that help monitor and control risk:

- Monitoring residual risks. These are risks that remain after implementation of mitigation plans.
- Ensuring the execution of risk plans.
- Evaluating the effectiveness of the risk responses.
- Reevaluating the risks.
- Holding status meetings.

After you have an understanding of the risk framework, you should consider it in teams of data privacy, model leaks, and data bias.

The term "privacy" encompasses a wide spectrum in the technology industry. The two categories of "user control" and "data protection" may be used to summarize the existing methods to privacy and machine learning. Therefore, under the "user control" part, a user's rights may be established by knowing who is collecting what information, why, and for how long, among other factors. These models need massive data sets to learn from in order to achieve reasonable levels of accuracy. But the information you provide them is highly private and sensitive. Therefore, it's imperative that you figure out how to unleash the potential of ML while maintaining data privacy.

When your training data contain details about the goal but the same data won't be accessible when the model is used for prediction, this is known as data leakage (or leaking). Due to this, the model performs well on the training set (and probably the validation data as well), but it will perform badly in actual use.

In other words, leakage makes a model appear correct until you start using it to make judgements, at which point it becomes wildly wrong. In many data science applications, data leakage can be a multi-million dollar error. It may be avoided by carefully separating training from validation data. Pipelines can be used to carry out this separation. Similar to that, using prudence, good judgement, and data research can locate target leakage. Target leakage occurs when your predictors include data that will not be available at the time you make predictions. It is important to think about target leakage in terms of the timing or chronological order that data becomes available, not merely whether a feature makes good predictions.

When a collection of data is unreliable and does not accurately reflect the full population, data bias develops. It is a serious issue because it may cause partial replies and distorted results, which will result in inequity. So it's critical to spot them early and steer clear of them.

Once you identify the biases, you have to avoid them:

- Finding alternative data sets that do the same thing but are less biased is one method to achieve this.

- Machine learning reproduces human mental processes and, as a result, biases. As a result, reducing human biases when collecting data is another wise move.

- Additionally, plenty of benchmarks measure discriminating signals. The algorithm has a clause that automatically recognizes certain situations.

Fine, now, let's look at the best practices of ML.

Best Practices for Machine Learning

Best practices are very important in the context of machine learning. Machine learning is a very specialized field. Therefore, it needs technical expertise, process excellence, and proper and timely application of the appropriate methodologies and framework. Hence, the best practices become critical and take central stage. Here are some important best practices:

- Identify your need and understand the business requirements.

- Be specific about your requirements and tune them with your needs.

- Keep your development approach simple.

- Identify a reliable source of data. Gather the desired data and make it noise free.

- Normalize your data before using algorithms.

- Identify the appropriate language, framework, and libraries as per your needs.

- Define strategies to train models, including hardware infrastructure and licensing.

- Define execution strategies like implementation of parallelism and iterations.

- Test infrastructure and software independently and then in combination. This enables holistic testing.

- Design and create an appropriate model. Also, do not forget to ensemble such models.

- Start with an independent model to help with testing.

- Train multiple, single-threaded models in parallel.

- Make your code portable and try to be environmentally independent. Using a cloud environment is the best way to achieve this.

- Iterate your model to purify and make it accurate based on changes to the underlying data.

- Measure the outlet between the models.

- Business problems change over time, so keep the model in tune with the requirements. Monitor models for decreasing accuracy.

- Keep track of predictions and forecasts.

Evolving Technologies and Machine Learning

There are many changes happening in the field of machine learning with rapid speed. Therefore, it is natural that multiple supporting technologies will evolve around it to make it better and more efficient. However, machine learning alone is not the driving factor for these technologies to come into the mainstream. The cloud, Big Data, IoT, and cognitive computing are also the driving factors. It is always good to be using the latest technological advancements. Consider these upcoming technologies:

- *Serverless computing*: According to the serverless computing concept, you can develop, build, and run applications and services without the headache of infrastructure management. In the serverless environment (cloud infrastructure), applications can still run on servers, but all the server management is done by the vendors or cloud service providers. Amazon is a pioneer of serverless architecture. Amazon Web Service (AWS) implements serverless computing through AWS Lambda. AWS Lambda runs the users' code without provisioning or managing servers. Lambda provides with you facility to virtually run any type of application or backend service and it takes care of everything required to run and scale (up and down) your code with high availability. The advantages of going serverless are many:

- – *No servers to manage*: No infrastructure management headache for the users, and they can just concentrate on functionality. It is one of the reasons that the serverless paradigm is also known as function as a service (FaaS).

- – *Automatic scaling*: Depending on the requirements of the application, application scaling happens by getting an application trigger (for example, an event).

- – *Pay per user pricing*: If you use the services for ten seconds, you pay for ten seconds.

- *Blockchain*: The blockchain is a distributed database that maintains a continuously growing list of ordered records called blocks. Each block contains a timestamp and a link to a previous block. By design, blockchains are inherently resistant to modification of the data. Once it's recorded, the data in a block cannot be altered retroactively. By the use of a peer-to-peer network and a distributed timestamping server, a blockchain database accomplishes autonomously. Blockchains by concept can be defined as "open, distributed ledgers that can record transactions between two parties efficiently and in a verifiable and permanent way." The ledger itself can also be programmed to trigger transactions automatically.

- *Bitcoin*: Digital money and payment system. Roughly, this is open-source software. This means that no individual, enterprise, or nation maintains this network similarly as no one preserves the Internet. This is peer-to-peer system where individuals can execute transactions directly without an in-between system or person like a bank, a credit card organization, or a clearinghouse. Transactions in bitcoins are tested by a net of nodes and logged in a public distributed ledger, known as a blockchain. It is also known as the currency of the blockchain.

- *Microservices*: A tier-based architecture that tells you to divide your code into multiple tiers so that you have clear segregation of code. Hence its execution and management is easy. For example, in three-tier architecture you divide your core in to three tiers— presentation, business logic, and data—and achieve cleanness and separation. Even after dividing your code into different tiers, the tiers are still dependent on each other for passing, processing, consolidating, and presenting holistic information. Microservices provide a mechanism to cater to this problem, as you divide your application on the basis of functionality and develop and deploy the tiers in one self-sufficient module, so that they work independently. If the project has customer, invoice, CRM, SCM, and user interface modules, you must break each service into an independently deployable module. Each module must contain its own maintenance, monitoring, application servers, and database. Therefore, with microservices, there is no concept of a centralized database, as each module is self-sufficient and contains its own database.

Summary

This chapter discussed the technical relationship among vendors, clients, and organizations. It also highlighted the importance of innovation in the context of machine learning, IoT, and cognitive computing. After a brief discussion of KPIs, risk and compliance were discussed. Finally, the chapter included an overview of the best practices related to machine learning and explained some insights into the evolving technologies around machine learning, including serverless architectures, blockchains, and microservices.

Mind Map

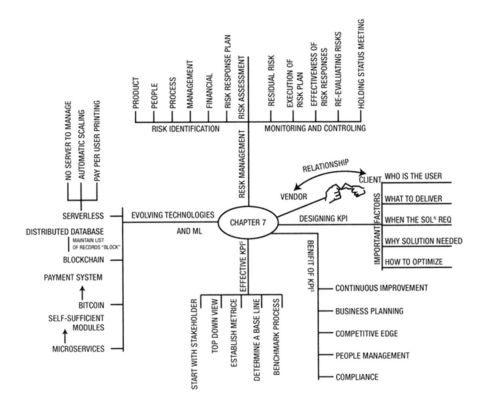

CHAPTER 8

Do Not Forget Me: The Human Side of Machine Learning

Dr. Patanjali Kashyap[a*]

[a] Bangalore, Karnataka, India

This chapter is the master of all the chapters but it does not discuss machine learning or its related issues. How does a chapter in a book about machine learning that does not discuss the technology become the master of all the chapters? The plain and simple answer is that this chapter considers the people who realize machine learning on the ground level. This chapter considers the people who strategize about machine learning implementation and its future in the organization. This chapter is important because it covers how to manage machine learning projects and train the human resources who are involved in the overall process.

In a nutshell, this chapter discusses the following issues:

- Why are social and emotional intelligence important for machine learning teams?

- What basic qualities should team members have to better plan and execute projects?

© Dr. Patanjali Kashyap 2024
P. Kashyap, *Machine Learning for Decision Makers,*
https://doi.org/10.1007/978-1-4842-9801-5_8

- What are the lean Project management principles? Why are they required in machine learning projects?

- How will innovative technologies like gamification enhance the productivity of the team and why are they required?

- How do you achieve optimal performance and commitment from the team members in a machine learning project?

- What are the techniques for thought and innovative leadership and why are they required in machine learning projects?

Economy, Workplace, Knowledge, You, and Technology

The workforce is comprised of humans and their complex social, moral, emotional, behavioral, and psychological interactions. High technical skills do not automatically generate high performance unless the team's members are committed, motivated, and enjoy their work. It is also important that they handle stress and conflicts and communicate and collaborate in the workplace.

Alignment of employee values, skills, competencies, and goals with the organization, clients/vendors, and the philosophy of technical methodologies is needed to achieve excellence. In fact, many academic and professional viewpoints have recognized the significant contribution of being aware of and managing emotions (*emotional intelligence,* EI) in the workplace. The ability to navigate and facilitate social relationships (*social intelligence,* SI), and the ability to apply universal principles to one's values and actions (*moral intelligence,* MI) generally lead to success in the workplace. This way, organizational efficiency and effectiveness can be achieved. In highly technical teams, implementing these innovative motivational methodologies has become very important.

In the current knowledge-based economy, many have noted the shift of corporate market value creation toward intangible assets. As early as 1995, the IT, medical care, communications, and education industries, whose primary value-adds are from intellectual and information processes, counted for 79 percent of all U.S. jobs and 76 percent of all U.S. GNP (Quinn, Anderson, & Finkelstein, 1996).

There is an enormous potential to expand intellectual assets. By using employee potential the right way, and by using employee minds to the fullest, you can maximize employee potential. Knowledge, critical reasoning, and emotional, moral, and social competencies—as well as spirituality—are all involved in the creative and technical processes. Most companies know the technical skills and knowledge they require in their employees, but are unclear as to the emotional, social, moral, and spiritual intelligence required.

Numerous results have established that these measures are more important than IQ. Daniel Goleman and Danah Zohar, in their landmark books (*Emotional Intelligence: Why It Matters More Than IQ* and *SQ: The Root of All Intelligence*), explained in detail the importance of these competences and skills in the workplace. With the changing times, companies started realizing that honing emotional, social, moral, and spiritual dimensions of a resource/talent is important for optimal performance.

Machine learning and its associated technologies are highly technical, so they need creativity and an innovative approach. Therefore, a knowledge worker who can use their intellectual as well as psychological capability together has a better chance at success than one who only has very good mathematical skills. For instance, a data scientist who is excellent at problem solving but not good in articulating, presenting, and creatively linking the analysis to the bigger picture is probably not a good pick for an organization. Therefore, organizations, and in turn projects, need many people who are good at mathematics, logic, and problem solving, and at the same time, they must possess good communication and social skills.

Likewise, a bank deals with account holders whose financial data is available in their databases. In this typical case, misuses of this data are possible because ultimately a small set of employees have access to it Hence, moral values and ethics come into the picture. Technologies and processes are here to help, but only to an extent. Finally, the manager who is dealing with this is most important. If the employees are morally strong, all this is taken care of automatically.

Spiritual intelligence is basically about understanding one's core potential and desires. It is about finding one's true sense, value, and meaning in life. It forces one to ask fundamental questions like, why am I doing this. What is the purpose? Am I the right fit for this? The answers to these questions are very important, especially in specialized fields like machine leaning. If someone is not fit for a particular role and does not want to do the job, it will hamper everyone. The negativity spreads in all directions, starting from the individual to the team to the organization. The end result of this can be disastrous, including project failure.

Half-hearted efforts lead to inefficient and ineffective work. In turn, poor quality deliverables are delivered to the customers, which affects the organization's branding and capabilities of revenue generation and profitability. Also, in the upcoming era of machine learning, where the tasks and activities are being automated quickly and machine learning enabled APS are becoming main stream, these skills help the employees and the organization. These tasks can be automated, but automating emotional and social skills is definitely not easy, if impossible.

The latest research (McKinsey & Company: MGI-A-future-that-works_ Full-report.pdf) shows that people with excellent interpersonal skills, social intelligence, and vocational interests may be less likely to be affected by job automation of and hence are less likely to lose their jobs. These are unique human skills that lead to flexibility and commitment.

In conclusion, the organization that's betting on highly technical projects needs to be careful in selecting their people resources. They have to select highly self-motivated people with a mix of technical and psychological qualities. This is possible only if they consider people with qualities like high EQ, SQ, and MQ, all apart from IQ. The good news is that these qualities can be taught. They are not "fixed," like IQ. They can be learned with the help of appropriate training and a positive environment.

Jargon Buster

- *Emotional Intelligence (EI) and quotient:* The capability to find, practice, appreciate, and accomplish one's own emotions in constructive ways to release stress, communicate effectively, empathize with others, overcome challenges, and resolve conflicts. This skill also enables a person to identify and appreciate what others are feeling emotionally. This is mostly a nonverbal process that affects thinking and influences how well people connect with others. Emotional quotient (EQ) is way of measuring EI in any form. Measurement may happen in multiple ways. One way of doing it is to circulate a questionnaire.

- *Moral Intelligence (MI):* The ability to appreciate right from wrong in a rational and empathic way. It is the ability to have solid ethical beliefs and to act on them positively. It enables a person to behave in the correct and honorable way. Moral Intelligence (MQ) is way of measuring a person's MI in any form. Measurement may happen in multiple ways. For example, one way of doing it is to circulate a questionnaire.

- *Social Intelligence (Social I)*: The aptitude to connect with others and to encourage them to collaborate with you positively. It is also called "people skills," but SI is more than just that. Social intelligence is about mindfulness of the situations and awareness of the social forces at work. This competency enables people to be aware of communication styles, strategies, policies, and practices that help them attain desired objectives in the context of dealing with others and with society. Social intelligence provides insight and awareness. Social quotient (Social Q) is way of measuring a person's SI in any form. One way of measuring it is to circulate a questionnaire.

- *Spiritual Intelligence (SI)*: The intelligence with which people address and solve problems of meaning and value, the intelligence with which they can place their actions and their lives in a wider, richer, meaning-giving context, and the intelligence with which people can assess that one course of action or one life-path is more meaningful than another. SQ is the necessary foundation for the effective functioning of both IQ and EQ. It is the "ultimate intelligence" (Zohar & Marshall 2000, pp 3-4). Spiritual quotient (SQ) is way of measuring one's spiritual intelligence in any form. One way of measuring it is to circulate a questionnaire.

Key Characteristics of Intellectual Assets

The key characteristics of the corporate climate that foster intellectual assets creation are discussed in this section. This is relevant at the organizational level, as well as the unit and team level.

Bottom-Up Innovation

The importance of innovation in today's businesses cannot be overstated. Knowledge creation has been proposed in two types—by combining elements previously unconnected (incremental) or by developing novel ways of combining previously associated elements. Because intellectual assets are generated from each level of the organization, innovation also needs to happen in a bottom-up fashion. Employees throughout the organization contribute improvements and novel ideas, perfecting operation details at all levels (incremental). This adds up to big, transforming ideas. It rests on two enabling factors—an innovative organizational culture and creative individuals.

Teamwork and Knowledge Sharing

As stated, creation of new knowledge depends on combining different ideas and knowledge. Therefore, the more exchange there is between different parties, the broader expertise and experiences can be brought into the creative process. In fact, knowledge grows exponentially when shared. Sharing and collaboration within the team, between partners, and through external knowledgebases can all accelerate growth. However, since the end product is intangible, the effectiveness and feasibility of sharing relies heavily on high moral standards, social relationships, and mechanisms to protect intellectual property and information security.

Adaptability to Change

Most of the benefit of knowledge-based organizations derives from constantly creating market needs and following up on changing demand promptly. As a famous example in the electronic devices industry, innovative leaders like Apple created an ever-expanding market for smartphones in a matter of a few years. Others in the industry cannot survive without adapting to the new demand by providing their own alternatives or something more innovative. To continue producing value, the organization must detect and adapt to the latest external market changes, be flexible and act promptly while maintaining quality during internal change, and be able to manage the enormous pressure brought with each change.

Customer Focus

The quality of the product is no longer the only concern of customers for today's knowledge-based business. The whole service experience is at play. Whether it is identifying and serving the future need of the customer, a supreme communication experience, or even the social responsibility and integrity demonstrated in the organization's conduct, these all can generate vast amounts of intangible assets. Only through providing an outstanding customer service experience will the corporation attain a unique identity and reputation, build trusting relationships, and thus win a competitive advantage.

Spirituality

Researchers and experts in the subject have recognized that employees need to find meaning and purpose in the workplace. This can no longer be underestimated (Danah Zohar and Ian Marshall: *SQ: Spiritual Intelligence, the Ultimate Intelligence*). Here, spirituality refers to the harmony between one's self and one's spiritual pursuits, knowledge, and social/natural environment. Employees get motivation and inspiration to create when they're connected to and allowed freedom of their authentic selves and can integrate knowledge from different perspectives. High spirituality of the organization is also shown to have a positive impact on the customer's experience, when employees perceive their work as a way to contribute to higher purposes for the community or society.

Key Performance Drivers of Individuals

What is required of each employee to form the desired corporate climate analyzed in the previous section? Six performance drivers for individuals can be summarized from understanding each aspect of the corporate climate, as shown in Figure 8-1.

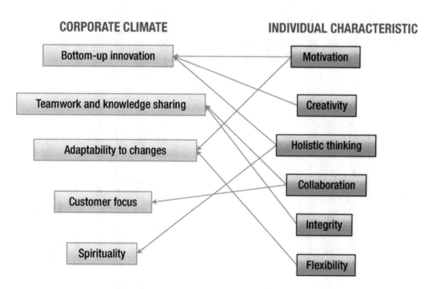

Figure 8-1. *Key performance drivers of individuals*

Measuring Intelligence

The performance drivers for individuals listed in Figure 8-1 are complex skillsets that require integration of one's emotional, moral, social, and spiritual competencies. Table 8-1 shows how these psychological competencies work together to enable the desired motivation, flexibility, integrity, creativity collaboration, and holistic thinking skills.

Table 8-1. *Emotional, Moral, Social, and Spiritual Competencies for Personal Performance Drivers*

Competency Metrics	Motivation	Integrity	Collaboration	Creativity	Flexibility	Holistic Thinking
Emotional competencies	Confidence, emotional awareness, emotional management, sustained motivation, endurance, drive for achievement	Emotion and impulse control, confidence in one's values and principles	Healthy self-regard, optimism, impulse control	Optimism, emotional management, confidence	Stress management, emotion and impulse control, stable self-esteem	Emotional awareness
Social competencies	Motivating/managing others' emotions	Empathy, understanding complex social relationships	Empathy, situational radar, resolving conflicts, change catalyst, moving others toward oneself, responsiveness, authenticity, sincerity	Self-expression, influencing others	Building bonds, effective communication, situational radar, resolving conflicts	Empathy, situational radar

Moral competencies	Responsibility, self-control	Moral judgment, standing up against injustice, keeping promises	Respect, tolerance	Social responsibility	Tolerance	Social responsibility, applying universal principles to personal actions
Spiritual competencies	Self-understanding, access to deep values and will, inner harmony, purpose seeking	Intrinsic drive to serve and give, access of deep values of self, meaning seeking and being led by a vision	Embracing diversity, love, and unity with people	Spontaneity and energy, seeking truth, curiosity, flexibility of perspectives	Time-management, flexibility of perspectives	Seeing the fundamental and essence, love and unity with nature/universe

503

The goal and motivation of the organization to develop employees' emotional, moral, social, and spiritual competencies is to generate intellectual assets (see Figure 8-2). This figure presents a view of the final objective of capturing intelligence and then measuring it. It is targeted to employees to improve their overall performance and then provide a competitive advantage to the organization by tuning the organizational objective, the corporate climate.

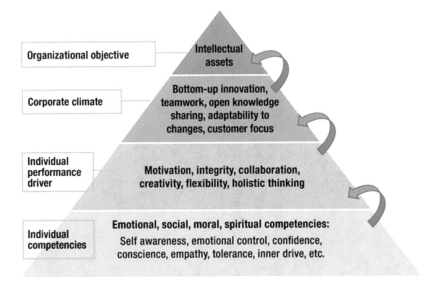

Figure 8-2. *The hierarchy from employee emotional, moral, social, and spiritual competencies*

Measurement is important. EI, SI, and MI are subjective in nature. It is not like 2+2 = 4. Therefore, defining key performance parameters for these competencies is one criteria for success. There are multiple ways to measure the performance of the resources, based on the competencies and parameters explained in Tables 8-2 to 8-5. For example, one way to measure them is to create a questionnaire. Questionnaires contain specific questions with weights associated with each question.

Table 8-2. *Highlights of the Key Performance Parameters for EI*

Key Emotional Intelligence Performance Parameters

Emotional Self-Awareness	Emotion Management	Self-Attitude	Motivation
• Aware of the emotion being experienced • Understand how the emotion is linked to one's thoughts and behaviors • Understand how the emotion is related to one's values and goals • Insight as to the environmental factors that triggered the emotion	• Impulse control • Controlling negative emotions: distress, jealousy, etc. • Intentionally eliciting and sustaining feelings when needed • Mental adaptability to changes • Stress management • Optimism	• Confidence in individual values and principles • Trust in individual abilities and judgment • Self-regard: not inferior/superior to others • Stability of self-esteem • Take environmental factors into consideration: expertise and familiarity in the field	• Need for achievement • Drive for self-improvement • Sustain motivation/endurance • Take environmental factors into consideration: management, team, commitment/interest in this particular project/team/field

Table 8-3. *Highlights of the Key Performance Parameters for MI*

Key Moral Intelligence Performance Parameters

Integrity	Responsibility	Respect	Tolerance
• Act consistently with universal principles, values, and beliefs • Tell the truth • Stand up against injustice, corruption, etc. • Keep promises	• Committed to carrying out assigned work • Take responsibility for results of decisions and conduct, especially mistakes • Embrace responsibility for the welfare of the team/ organization • Social responsibility	• Respect and take interest in others' feelings, work, culture, and welfare • Treat others courteously • Not harm others • Treat others fairly	• Handle constructive criticism well • Tolerate disagreeing opinions • Tolerate different abilities and personalities • Forgive others' mistakes

Table 8-4. *Highlights of the Key Performance Parameters for Spiritual Intelligence*

Key Spiritual Intelligence Performance Parameters			
Integration of Self	**Integration of Knowledge**	**Love and Unity**	**Some Additional SQ Qualities**
• Access of deep values and will of self • Holistic: understanding/ evaluation of self's tendencies, abilities, and position in relation to the world • Purpose seeking and vision-led inner harmony of will and reality • Compassion: having the quality of "feeling-with" and deep empathy • Celebration of diversity: valuing other people for their differences, not despite them • Positive use of adversity: learning and growing from mistakes, setbacks, and suffering	• Seeking truth and being curious • Seeing the fundamental and essence • Flexibility of perspectives • Time management • Ability to reframe: standing back from a situation or problem and seeing the bigger picture or the wider context	• With people and nature/universe • Intrinsic drive to serve and give • Empathy • Competitiveness • Humility: having the sense of being a player in a larger drama, of one's true place in the world • Tendency to ask fundamental "why" questions: needing to understand things and get to the bottom of them	• Self-awareness: knowing what one believes in and values and what deeply motivates one • Spontaneity: living in and being responsive to the moment • Being vision- and value-led: acting from principles and deep beliefs and living accordingly • Holism: seeing larger patterns, relationships, and connections; having a sense of belonging • Field independence: standing against the crowd and having one's own convictions • Sense of vocation: feeling called upon to serve, to give something back

Table 8-5. *Highlights of the Key Performance Parameters for Social Intelligence*

Key Social Intelligence Performance Parameters			
Empathy	Effective Communication	Influencing Others	Positive Psychology
• Interest in others' concerns and feelings. Understand other's feelings, concerns, and perspectives • Able to reconcile conflicting opinions by incorporating other's needs and feelings • Knowledge of rules and norms in human relationships • Self-positioning and understanding (general and in specific situations)	• Assertiveness • Provision of feedback • Authenticity, sincerity • Express own feelings • Show sympathy • Good listening skills	• Impression management • Move others toward you • Change catalyst • Motivating/ managing others' emotions • Building bonds	Numerous research has proven that positive emotions are linked with improved well-being, extended life, and better well-being, whereas, long-lasting anger, anxiety, and aggression increase the risk of generating heart illness and other emotional disorders. Individuals respond to these feelings with elevated blood pressure and thickening of blood vessels. However, it not easy to uphold a healthy, positive emotional state all the time. One reason for this is that individuals generally miscalculate what would make them joyful and gratified. Positive psychology is a branch of psychology that studies the positive aspects of human behavior and can be extended to organizations. It connects the influence of pleasure and mindfulness to the inner strength of an individual. Practices of it enable individuals to find well-being and happiness.

- Judge other's personality
- Understand complex social relationships
- Devise strategies that are most likely to be successful in the current social situations

There are multiple ways to assess and improve happiness, including self-assessment tests and exercises that help to maximize the positive emotion in one's life. Machine learning project teams are going through stress because they are dealing with the challenge of a large data volumes and tight delivery lines. Therefore, organizations must enable their employees with these skills to cope with these situations in the better way

Finally, all the weight is added and a composite score is achieved. Those scores indicate which areas need improvement and where is the employee is performing fine. In the area where the resource needs improvement, a training plan is typically attached and appropriate training is given. Another approach is to provide performance coaching to fine-tune the resource. The same exercise is repeated for all the competencies:

- Assessment:

  - Understanding strengths and weaknesses of self and others

  - Orientation workshop on EI, MI, social intelligence, and spiritual intelligence

  - Discussing and sharing with the team

- Goal alignment

  - Introspection: Aligning actual self with ideal self and team goals

  - Team discussion about shared values and goal alignment

  - Input to tracking system

- Action plan

  - Suggestion of new behavior

  - Recording of action plan

  - Sharing on forum

- Implementation

  - Pairing up to practice new behavior

  - Finding and building coaching relationships

  - Tracking progress

Holistic intelligence and competencies presented in this section are not limited to "only" improvement of the team members. Its applications and scope are very wide. Figure 8-3 presents an integrative and comprehensive view of emotional, social, moral, and spiritual intelligence and shows that these competencies are applicable to almost all areas, including finance, customer satisfaction, internal process, and employee learning and growth. All these areas are actually part of the balance scorecard methodology, which is one of the ways to measure the performance of the organization and its employees. However, it can be extended to measure virtually anything, including the performance of one's life activities.

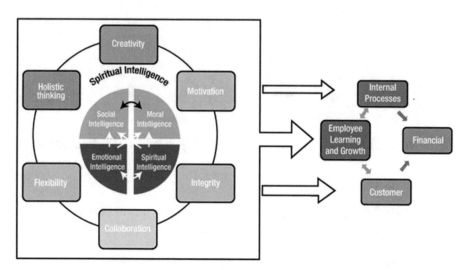

Figure 8-3. *Holistic and comprehensive view of emotional, social, moral, and spiritual intelligence, and their diverse application areas*

Benefits of the Intelligence Competencies

Equipping individuals with these competencies is helpful at all levels of an organization. They provide benefits to individuals, project teams, and organizations. Figure 8-4 provides a snapshot of these benefits.

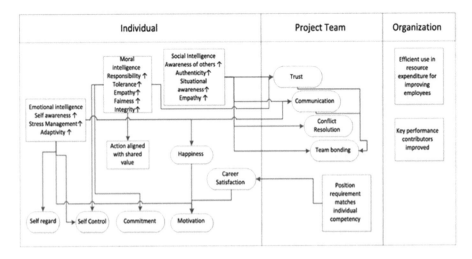

Figure 8-4. *Benefits provided by the multiple types of intelligence*

Some thoughts:

- EI, Social I, MI, and SI have a meaningful impact on the performance of human resources.

- Increased EI, Social I, MI, and SI correlate with profitability via customer satisfaction.

- EI, Social I, MI, and SI can inculcate service quality, which improves customer satisfaction.

- These competencies can be used for improving team performance and human behavior in totality in all the dimensions, including intellectual capabilities.

- Theory and practice of management science, human resource development, organizational behavior, and industrial psychology can be integrated with these competencies and could be applied to the team through the proper use of appropriate methodologies and frameworks.

- These competencies can be integrated with gamification, storytelling (automated and manual), and concept comics. In turn, these can be used to improve efficiency and effectiveness of software development and support teams.

Gamification

Gamification is the process of making game science work in non-game contexts to derive desired behaviors. Smart gamification taps into innate human motivators.

Some highlights of gamification:

- Organizations find it difficult to engage their workforce, engage their customers, and provide users with a good experience with service transactions. It is estimated that this issue costs enterprises billions of dollars annually. The good news is that gamification can help, due to its unique approach to human psychology.

- Garter reports are indicating that global organizations are using gamification and successfully deriving business value from it.

Comics and Gamification

Comics are used by enterprises to promote their products and services, either directly (as a form of advertising and marketing), or through product placement in a comic strip. Organizations can also use comics to clarify how to use an application/product/service, because they are easy to use and understand and most importantly engage both hemispheres of the brain. Therefore, user engagement is better compared to text-based explanations. The latest research has established the importance of visuals during interactions or communications (Scott & Vargas, 2007, p. 342); this research mentions that cartons convey more detail, analogous to "writing in more detail." Many enterprises have started using comics to educate employees about internal procedures and processes. Also, they use them to explain technical details in a more engaging way. Hence, gamification and comics can be used to achieve employee motivation, customer loyalty, and service improvement. They can also be used to manage projects better.

Corporate Storytelling

Telling stories for entertainment, engagement, education, and enlightenment is not a new concept. With corporate storytelling, the philosophies are similar to old-style stories. However, you are utilizing stories to encourage an application/product/service or to promote a brand. Stories generally appear in the form of text. However, to tell a good story about an enterprise/organization/company, video can also be used. Stories can be automated or appear manually. The form of the story depends on the need and availability of the infrastructure, budget, and other resources.

Building an Efficient ML Team in Relation to EQ, SQ, MQ, and Social Q

MQ, SQ, and other types of intelligences discussed in this chapter are helpful in building a world-class machine learning team. World-class technical teams require courage, persistence, and the ability to deal with ambiguity. Also, giving a freehand to the team members is one of the mandatory criteria for an effective and efficient team.

Consider this general criteria to build a great team from a machine learning perspective:

- Senior executives participate in setting up the team.

- Senior management offers continuous support.

- Team goals are aligned with the vision and mission of the organization.

- The machine learning team must be a mix of business and technology specialists, because requirements and business needs must be understood before the technical implementation.

- The team must be able to work in cross-functional environments and situations.

- The team has freedom to develop its own working style and create internal roles.

- The team has clear guidelines about how to measure the success of the team and its team members.

- Team members and leaders must be selected on the basis of diversity, knowledge, and competencies.

- The team must be a mix of people who are newly hired from outside the organization and who are already working on the team. That gives the team different perspectives.

- Continuous learning, effective knowledge management, and development environments must be included.

- Proper communication processes and infrastructure availability must be priorities.

- There must be proper reward and recognition mechanisms for the team, leader, manager, and individual team members. Value addition must be appreciated at all the levels.

- There must be repetitive, timely, and effective feedback and performance evaluation mechanisms.

- There must be proper training for evolving technologies, team skills, problem solving, and decision making.

- The well-being and health frameworks must align with the team members.

- There must be a clearly defined RASCI matrix. A RASCI matrix is a tabular representation of Responsible, Accountable, Supportive, Consulted, and Informed attributes of roles in the team/organization/project.

- The team must know how to communicate visually. They must communicate their insights from the data to the stakeholders through graphs, infographics, animation, and reports. Mere raw facts are of no use in business.

- Team members must have curious minds and be able to answer the how, what, and why of a problem.

- In a nutshell, the team and therefore the team members must process mathematical, statistical, computational, programming, data management, and positive psychological, communication, and change management skills.

In an organization, a team has multiple dimensions and includes multiple roles. It is good to discuss a few important roles and their qualities. A few roles—like organizational leadership, decision making, and data scientists—must use both hemispheres of the brain. Therefore, Figure 8-5 shows how these skills and roles fit from a brain science point of view. The following sections discuss the key roles on each team.

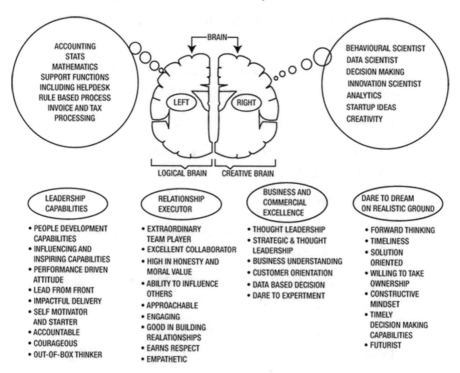

Figure 8-5. *Brain science*

Team Leader

A good team leader must:

- Be aligned with the business perspective and issues.

- Be aware of the organizational level frameworks, processes, and the goals of the company.

- Be aligned and updated with the technical, process, and people issues that the team is facing and be able to solve them.

- Have good leadership and intermediate managerial skills.

- Have good project management skills.

- Have good problem solving, conflict resolution, and team management skills.

- Have good collaboration and communication skills (including inter- and intrapersonal skills).

- Be passionate, creative, and innovative.

- Be self-motivated and good with time management and administrative work.

- Know the business.

- Be able to lead and guide a multi-disciplinary team of technical experts.

- Be good at statistical analytics techniques and with mathematical concepts.

- Be experienced in the Agile software development methodologies, like Scrum and extreme programming.

Technology Manager

A good technology leader must:

- Have excellent communication skills.

- Lead with transparency and honesty.

- Support employees with clear direction and remove any roadblocks.

- Embrace technology.

- Motivate with positive feedback and recognition.

- Be an expert in the field.

- Mediate with productivity and calmness.

- Promote cross-level and cross-functional collaboration.

- Create a productive and lively work environment.

- Trust their employees.

- Be experienced in machine learning projects and able to distinguish between normal technical projects and machine learning projects.

Team Members

A good team member must:

- Be technically excellent in their work.

- Have multi-task management skills.

- Be capable of doing individual as well as group decision making and be good at conflict management.

- Be open about taking feedback.

- Be good at planning and organizing.

- Be good problem-solvers and have analytical and mathematical skills.

- Have good collaboration and communication skills.

- Be able to take initiative.

- Be flexible.

- Be passionate about data crunching

- Be good at adopting concepts.

- Be good at handling unstructured data and analyzing it.

- Have knowledge of high computing and multithread programming models.

- Have knowledge of Agile software development methodologies.

Organizational Leader

A good organizational leader must:

- Have good social, moral, ethical, and emotional intelligence skills.

- Be a visionary who is committed and has the ability to inspire others.

- Be honest and self-aware.

- Be good at making decisions.

- Take actions with responsibilities.

- Be productive, innovative, and thoughtful at work.

- Have the ability to simplify things and communicate/present information in an understandable way.

- Have a positive outlook toward work, life, and self.

- Be realistic at work.

- Have clear thinking and good judgment skills.

- Be aware and considerate and show sensitivity.

- Be able to lead by example.

- Have a desire for excellence and for getting things done.

- Have excellent coaching and motivational skills.

- Be a good listener and strong executor.

- Have an excellent understanding of business, process, and people skills.

The Differences Between a Leader and a Manager

A world-class team is built on the directions and guidelines provided by the leader and, on the ground level, it is managed by the project/development/support/technology managers. There are occasions when people are confused with the line of separation between these roles and mistakenly think these are the same role and use them interchangeably. However, there is huge difference between these two roles:

- The manager administers, whereas the leader innovates and encourages.

- The manager always implements and continues with the status quo; the leader however always develops.

- The manager focuses on systems, processes, and structure; the leader focuses on people and their enablement.

- The manager relies on control; the leader inspires trust.

- The manager has a short-range view and believes in getting things done; the leader has a long-range perspective.

- The manager has their eye always on the bottom line; the leader's eye is on the horizon.

- The manager copies; the leader creates.

- The manager accepts the status quo; the leader challenges it.

- The manager is the classic good soldier; the leader is their own persona.

- The manager does things right; the leader does the right thing.

How to Build a Data Culture for Machine Learning

Machine learning projects are technical in nature. However, the behavioral aspects of the involved stakeholders also play an important role. The most important aspects in machine learning-based projects and organizations is the data. Therefore, it is expected that data-based culture will be developed within the project and company alike. Classic examples of this are Amazon and Netflix, which are pioneers in their field. Here are some guidelines for building and training a data-based culture in an organization:

- Train your team (almost everyone) on data dynamics, datanomics (data-based economy), and statistics. Provide a refresher course on these issues to the stakeholders.

- Provide knowledge of domain, information flow, data flow, storage capabilities, and external and internal data sources to the stakeholders.

- Establish and educate stakeholders about the importance of data inside and outside of the organization.

- Explain technology to relevant people in deep and to loosely coupled people at the 200-foot level. This must include the architecture.

- Be involved in the projects.

- Provide proper reward and recognition to your people.

- Encourage research, innovation, and thought leadership at all levels.

- Incorporate knowledge sharing sessions into the DNA of the organization.

- Create a culture of shared success celebration that brings people together.

- Teams must not be bothered about the organizational policy and changes. Essentially, they should be free from the organizational bureaucracy and hierarchy.

- Equip the teams with the latest technologies and tools. Give them challenging work and encourage them to solve the issues.

- Encourage teams to publish their work on internal and external forums, including attending conferences, filling patents, and writing whitepapers.

In addition to these general distinguishing qualities, the following points are some "must have" characteristics of machine learning teams and team members.

- They must process data science skills, be good at statistical, numerical, problem solving, analysis, data crunching, and modeling techniques, and have a process research and innovative mindset.

- They must be exposed to handling large volumes of data, and have knowledge of diverse sources of data and gathering techniques.

- They must have knowledge of tools, frameworks, and libraries related to machine learning.

- They must have knowledge of the business process, company specific policies, and business jargon.

- They must have an excellent capability to present complex ideas in easy ways to the lay audiences with the help of data visualization tools.

- They must be flexible, adaptable, innovative, and self-motivating.

A team is a complex entity, as it revolves around humans. Therefore, managing a team is always a challenge and satisfying its need for organization is a big responsibility. Every team member wants to excel. They always want to perform better if the surrounding environment supports them. They have some questions. If the proper answers are provided, it will motivate them to work better. The following section contains a list of questions that every team member wants to be answered. If these questions are answered in the proper way, that brings transparency across the board.

Questions for Bringing Transparency to the Team and Enterprise

What business challenge is the team supposed to solve? Who selects the team leader? How is the team related to other organizational units? Who assigns work to a team member? What are the roles and responsibilities of the team members and the team leader? What are the roles and job descriptions of the team members and the team leader? What are the selection criteria of the team members and leader? What are the technologies, tools, and programming languages that the team members and leader need? How will individuals allocate their time to the team versus their other functional responsibilities? Who measures the overall team member performance and what are the metrics for that? What is the appraisal cycle for the team members and leader? What is the optimal size of the team? Who establishes the team's priorities? Who manages the team boarders with the other areas in the organization? What authority and responsibilities are implied by the dotted line reporting structure? How will cross-functional and cross-cultural conflicts and priorities be resolved?

What process help teams improve productivity, efficiency, and effectiveness? How can the team improve internal and external communications? How often should the team meet and in what format should they share the minutes of meetings? What are the locations the teams reside on? How can they meet if face-to-face meetings are not an option? What are the technical means of communication and collaboration (video conferences)? What reports does the team have to produce and who is the audience? What processes can be used to help team members evolve and improve continuously? What is the team value?

How is the team motivated? How can team loyalty be increased? How should team results and individual performance be measured? Who evaluates the team members and what is the criteria? How is individual and team performance linked to the company's performance and to salary? What training programs exist to develop skills?

Ultimately, the goal is to align team members with the higher value and with the vision of the organization. After processing the skills and competencies mentioned here, the individuals and the groups become highly effective in delivering and creating high-quality products and in dealing with team dynamics. They achieve individual and organizational effectiveness. Figure 8-6 depicts this process.

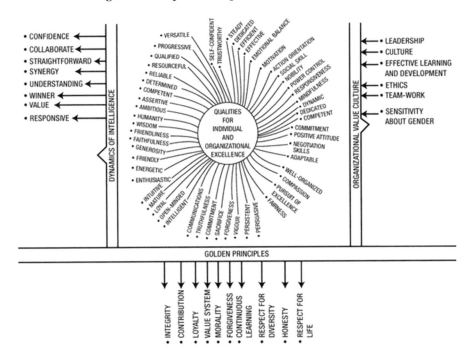

Figure 8-6. *Achieving effectiveness*

Machine Learning-Specific Roles and Responsibilities

A good and successful project needs a mix of technical and behavioral capabilities at least at the talent level. Therefore, there are many other factors that need to be considered. Factors like business domain knowledge, challenging the status quo, and visual communication skills in a resource are equally important. A successful machine learning team contains some typical roles and naturally there are some responsibilities associated with those roles. After a wider discussion about generic roles and responsibilities, it is a good time to summarize the practical roles that exist in the world of machine learning.

This information helps the decision-makers/managers hire the best fit for their projects. This also helps organizations create and organize an effective team. The following sections examine some of these important roles.

Role 1: Deep Learning/Machine Learning Engineer

Typical designation: They are very innovative and always thinking. They are strong at solving problems, analyzing data, and programming.

Role and responsibilities associated with this designation:

- Collecting, analyzing, understanding, and interpreting the qualitative, mathematical, statistical, and quantitative aspects of data with established statistical theories, frameworks, libraries, and analytical methods.

- Able to develop innovative, intuitive, and customer-oriented user interfaces.

- Serve data through APIs to data scientists (another designation). Data scientists in turn use them for queries.

- Develop useful insights from raw data and must have working experience with Big Data.

- Investigate, alter, and put data analytics and scientific prototypes to use.

- Develop and build plans and procedures for machine learning.

- Use test results for statistical analysis and model improvement.

- Look for easily available training data sets online.

- Ensure that models and ML systems are trained and updated as needed.

- Enhance and expand the present ML libraries and frameworks.

- Develop machine learning applications in line with user or client requirements.

- Look into, try out, and use the right ML tools and algorithms.

- Assess the potential for ML algorithms to solve problems and rank them according to success likelihood.

- More fully understand data through exploration and visualization, as well as identify differences in data distribution that could impact a model's performance when used in practical situations.

Skills and talents:

- Grasp of ML frameworks in practice.

- Recognize data models, data structures, and software architecture.

- A working knowledge of computer architecture.

- An understanding of calculus, linear algebra, and Bayesian statistics, as well as advanced mathematics and statistics.

- An ability to apply established algorithms in business-specific scenarios. Knowledge of ML-specific libraries.

- An ability to understand the strengths and weakness of different machine learning algorithms.

- Knowledge of predictive modeling, machine learning, and data mining techniques.

- An understanding of database technologies.

- Knowledge of machine learning friendly programming languages like, R, Python, C/C++, SQL, and NoSQL.

- An ability to do sentiment and what-if analyses.

- Knowledge of object-oriented programming, including multi-threaded and high-performance computing environments.

Psychological and behavioral skills:

- Calm and composed, innovative, and creative.

- Logical genius, emotional and social intelligence.

- Aptitude to comprehend business jargon across the enterprise.

The best way to find a machine learning engineer is to find a quality data engineer that you can groom in your organization. For that, you have to find a good engineer or developer and train them on the specific machine learning technology and techniques. Another way is find them through a job portal. If the organization is okay with hiring a freelancer engineer, they can be found via that mode as well.

Role 2: Data Scientist

Typical designation: Someone who is inquisitive, shares and analyzes data, and can spot trends. Also, they can identify anomalies and data associations. Data scientists are typically good at detecting data patterns and dependencies. Typically, they can balance research and business outcomes. They cross over multiple discipline such as statistics, mathematics, engineering, psychology, sociology, linguistics, and business management.

The roles and duties of a data scientist include gathering data from various sources, using machine learning tools to organize the data, processing, cleaning, and validating the data, looking for information and patterns in the data, developing prediction systems, clearly presenting the data, and making recommendations for strategies and solutions.

Role and responsibilities associated with this designation include these:

- Find useful data sources and automate the procedures for gathering them.

- Preprocess data, both organized and unstructured. Analyze vast volumes of data to find trends and patterns.

- Create machine learning algorithms and prediction models. By using ensemble modeling, combine models.

- Bring up strategies and solutions to corporate problems.

- Work together with the product development and engineering teams.

- Analyze, understand, and interpret the qualitative, mathematical, statistical, as well as quantitative aspects of data using established statistical theories and analytical methods.

- Solve business/data learning problems. Create ML solutions to achieve the organization's objectives.

- Clean existing raw data and build models to predict future happenings.

- Look at data from multiple angles and make sense out of it.

Skills and talents:

- Knowledge of distributed computing and data visualization.

- Capability to understand the strengths and weaknesses of different machine learning algorithms.

- Knowledge of predictive modeling, machine learning, and data mining techniques.

- Understanding of database technologies.

- Knowledge of machine learning friendly programming languages, such as R, Python, C/C++, SQL, and NoSQL.

- Knowledge of object-oriented programming, including multi-threaded and high-performance computing environments.

- Knowledge of data mining and data warehousing.

- Overall understanding of artificial intelligence, deep learning, and neural networks.

- Experience in high performance, natural language processing and distributed computing.

- Experience as a data scientist or data analyst with a track record.

- Data mining expertise.

- Knowledge of machine learning and operations research.

- Experience working with data frameworks like Hadoop and business intelligence tools like Tableau.

- A mind for analysis and business sense.

- Strong math abilities (such as algebra and statistics).

- Ability to fix issues.

- Excellent presentation and communication abilities.

- An advanced degree in data science or another quantitative discipline is desired; a BSc or BA in computer science, engineering, or a related field is required.

Behavioral and psychological skills:

- Calm and composed, innovative, and creative.

- Logical genius, equipped with emotional and social intelligence capabilities.

- Aptitude to comprehend business jargon.

- Ability to comprehend the corporate mission, vision, and strategy and the accompanying KPIs.

Quality data scientists are not easily available. Therefore, finding them is a difficult task. You can find experienced data scientists through job portals or by references. However, they are typically expensive. The other option is to hire them from academic institutions and universities. The perspective candidate must process an advanced degree in computer science, mathematics, and statistics. PhDs are preferable. Also, the candidates may be hired from fields like space science, bio-informatics, or neuro-science, where a lot of data crunching and analytical skills are necessary. Once these candidates are hired, training specific to machine learning and project requirement would be helpful.

Other Important Roles

Apart from these important roles, there are other roles on the machine learning teams and in organizations. A few of them are so unusual that you might never hear about them. The technical roles require more or less the same types of competencies. Therefore, this chapter will not discuss each and every role in detail. However, it good to look at them briefly.

Analytics Practice Leader	Data Architect	BI Analyst
IOT specialist	Data hygienist	BI solution architect
Machine learning coach	Data miner/statistician	Big Data researcher
Machine learning expert	Metadata administrator	Big Data solution architect
Information architect	Data modeler	Big Data visualization specialist
Hadoop developer/engineer	Visualization tool developers	Predictive analytics developer
Big Data loading specialist	Java developer	OLAP developer

(continued)

Analytics Practice Leader	Data Architect	BI Analyst
Algorithm expert	Machine learning researcher	Innovation lead
ETL architect and developer	Security and archival specialist	Change leader
Infrastructure specialist	Application developer	Experimental analysts
Project manager	Technology manager	Development manager

This list is not complete. However, it should give you a feel for the related roles that exist in the organization from a machine learning perspective. Along with these roles, there are lot of other "leadership and decision-maker" roles. Let's look at them as well.

CEO—Chief Executive Officer: The highest policymaking position in an enterprise. Their principal responsibilities comprise making business decisions. They are accountable for managing the complete operations and resources (including the funds) of an enterprise. They generally act as the main point of communication among the board of directors and corporate operations, including executives. Here are the main direct reports of the typical CEO.

- *CRO—Chief Risk Officer*: The highest level of authority regarding risk practices and policies creation related to the risks of the organization. This role defines and provides a roadmap for the implementation of the risk strategies at the enterprise level.

- *CFO—Chief Finance Officer*: The leader who provides and manages the financial roadmap and strategies of the organization. The CFO is responsible for the inside and outside the organization, especially to the stakeholders.

- *CMO—Chief Marketing Officer*: The highest level of authority regarding marketing practices and policies related to these marketing strategies. Defines and provides a roadmap for the implementation of the same at the enterprise level.

- *CIO—Chief Information Officer*: The highest level of authority regarding information technology practices and policies creation for the organization. Defines and provides a roadmap for the implementation of the IT strategies at the enterprise level.

- *CAO—Chief Analytics Officer*: The highest level of authority regarding business intelligence-related policies creation across the organization. Broadly takes care of analytics related activities, including Big Data and machine learning related strategies. Defines and provides a roadmap for the implementation of the same at the enterprise level.

- *COO—Chief Operating Officer*: The executive who creates operational strategies for the organization. The COO is tasked with the routine management and operation of the business. Responsible for making sure that business will run as usual.

- *CDO—Chief Data Officer*: The highest level of authority regarding data practices and policies creation related to the data. Defines, architects, and provides a roadmap for the implementation of the data strategies at the enterprise level. The CDO and CAO coordinate with each other on a regular basis to create strategies around the following:

  - Data security and privacy

  - Data architecture

- Data integration

- Data management

Again, there are no hard and fast rules that these roles "must" exist within an organization. Sometimes these roles merge into each other.

Lean Project Management and Machine Learning Projects

Software systems are, by their very nature, flexible and will change over time (except for many legacy systems which, by definition, are not very flexible). Integration with each of these domains therefore is not just a one-time activity; it's an ongoing activity. Lean principles applied to IT focus on the goal of delivering value to the customer with minimum possible resources and zero defects. Multiple types of waste can be reduced by using Lean tools and techniques, but it's a continuous process and not a one-time initiative. At a broader level, Lean might help IT partners support innovation, with skills to deliver IT-enabled capabilities quickly that drive top- and bottom-line growth for business.

The Lean IT process also tells companies how to improve efficiency and minimize waste in a knowledge-intensive industry and reduce unevenness to enhance process capability effectively. The basic idea of Lean is to give maximum value to the customers by minimizing waste. Simply put, Lean means creating more value with fewer resources with the ultimate goal to meet customer requirements perfectly through a value creation process that has zero waste.

Value is defined as any action or process that a customer is willing to pay for. The Lean idea originated from the manufacturing sector, and now has extended to many other domains. Today, Lean has deep rooted implementations in the IT sector, where it helps improve information processing capability, cost optimization, and IT process management, and provide higher IT value to core businesses.

Lean project management has become attractive to team leaders looking for fast results on critical turnaround assignments. Most project managers decide to "go Lean" when faced with budget cuts or other constraints. Tasked with eliminating waste from a project or a process, managers must discover how to make their teams more effective using fewer resources. Some project managers find themselves attracted to Lean project management, thinking that "eliminating waste" means shortening or abandoning the traditional project cycle.

In fact, Lean teams rely more heavily on the project cycle and on their organizational processes than traditional project teams. The idea is to eliminate extra effort and replace low-efficiency processes with better and more optimized ones by identifying and reducing waste. Lean project management can be summarized by seven principles:

- *Eliminate waste*: Anything that does not add value to the customer is considered waste.

- *Amplify learning*: The learning process can be sped up by involving all stakeholders in short and iterative feedback sessions. Less documentation/planning and more direct reviews of the action items in quick succession will amplify learning.

- *Decide as late as possible*: Lean suggests holding the decisions to be made by facts and not on the basis of assumptions and predictions. For that, sometimes decision making should be delayed if all the required facts and information are not available. Better results can be expected with an options-based approach with more available information in hand. Thus, certain crucial decisions are delayed until the customer understands their needs better. This reduces waste of resource, time, and effort in terms of rework and change request communicated after significant advancement in development. This minimizes the risk of failing delivery schedules and last-minute possibility of committing errors.

- *Deliver as fast as possible*: Delivery of items on time is most crucial in IT, quickly recognizing specific client requirements and environment by proper planning and distribution of work. The sooner the end product is delivered without considerable defects, the sooner feedback can be received and incorporated into the next iteration. Project scheduling must have the required buffer time to plan the delivery on time to ensure business continuity and testing of deliverables.

- *Empower the team*: There has been a traditional belief in most businesses about the decision-making in the organization, in that the managers tell the workers how to do their jobs. In a Lean technique, the roles are reversed, and the managers are taught how to listen to the developers so they can better explain what actions might be taken as well as provide suggestions for improvements. The Lean approach favors the aphorism "find good people and let them do their jobs," by encouraging progress, catching errors, and removing impediments, but not micro-managing. People need motivation and a higher purpose, with the assurance that the team might choose its own commitments.

- *Build integrity*: The customer needs to have an integrated and holistic experience of the system to identify the value delivered to them by any solution. How it is being advertised, delivered, deployed, and accessed, how smart the utility is, the price, and most importantly how well it solves problems. This is called *conceptual integrity*. It's important to understand how different components of the system work together as a whole to create value. Clients must have an integrated view of the system and for that solution team management should ensure smooth information flow. One big chunk of information shared after an interval raises confusion, smaller bits of information shared and analyzed on shorter intervals render a detailed understanding. In Agile software development, at the end of a phase, a more in-depth and integrated knowledgebase is created. This reduces repetition, isolation in understanding, and the gap between expectations and actuality. Building and sharing an integrated view of the system helps maintain the balance between flexibility, maintainability, efficiency, and responsiveness to the best possible extent.

- *Optimize the whole*: A system should have the clarity and a defined standardized structure so that, by decomposing the big tasks into smaller tasks, and by standardizing different stages of development, the root causes of defects can be found and eliminated. The big picture should be crystal clear to all the stakeholders.

How to Do the Right Resourcing and Find the Best Match

Before wrapping up, let's look at how machine learning teams can do right resourcing. Both the perspective organization and the potential candidate have to look at some important factors related to onboarding candidates. For example, candidates must process important characteristics like not being afraid of failure and taking ownership. Whereas organizations have to look at the cultural fit. Here are some important points to consider:

- *Make it right*: In any professional commitment, your attitude matters the most. There is no doubt that skills have their own importance, but attitude is more important. One important part of the right attitude is the ability to see things differently, because it gives you a different perspective. Machine learning projects need different perspectives all the time. They demand continued learning, trying new approaches, and flexibility. Therefore, attitude counts.

- *Change is the only constant*: To be successful at machine learning projects, you need to have a readiness to learn, the capability to acquire new thoughts, and the ability to change. In this technology space, change is the norm. No one can be an expert at everything. Therefore, willingness to adapt is key. Having intellectual and behavioral humility is key to having a learning attitude.

- *Welcoming culture*: Creating an appropriate culture of innovation is necessary, not only for companies that deal with machine learning. A paradigm shift is needed to create a data culture if it doesn't already exist. In the journey of adopting new thoughts, people have to accept change and motivate themselves to fit into the framework of the changing culture. One of the mantras of achieving this is that each individual can attain something great or at least keep trying to do so. High energy and enthusiasm are the other requirements for effective machine learning professionals. This culture fit becomes so important that companies have started testing this in prospective hires. For example, a company called Chumbak has a team of people who are explicitly skilled to administer a culture test. They conduct this test once the particular resource has cleared the rounds of technical and managerial interviews. One of the common questions they ask during their testing is, "If money were not an object, what would you be doing instead?". This panel of interviewers has veto power. If they are not convinced that the culture fits the candidate, they have the right to reject this person, even if the candidate is excellent from a technical perspective.

- *Owning it*: Finding problems by analysis and then completing the tasks with minimum intervention and within the timeline is the key. Therefore, this is one of the "must have" skills for the machine learning professional.

- *Love of failure*: Failure is a reality and is here to stay. How one copes with failure is very important. In machine learning projects, these "coping" skills are mandatory. There are times when you will try multiple things and wait for results. While success at previous roles is good, answers to questions like "When was the last time you failed?" make sense. Finding a candidate who does not repeat mistakes is excellent, because they know what they've done wrong and have learned from their mistakes.

DevOps

DevOps (a portmanteau of development and operations) is a software development method that bridges the gap between software developers and information technology (IT) professionals. It stresses the interdependence between software development and IT operations. DevOps seeks to establish communication channels between development and operations in software projects that increase the time and labor involved in delivering and maintaining software systems. It helps a company continually deliver highly stable features, faster and more often. As a result, a business asks more and more from its IT organizations, which in turn requires that the two traditionally separate teams work together to enable the business to deliver more features while continually ensuring the stability of its systems.

Development methodologies adopted across organizations follow a traditional approach, with separate departments for development, deployment activities, and QA. These activities do not integrate across departments. DevOps promotes a set of processes, methods for communication, collaboration, and integration between departments.

DevOps is about cultural change, therefore, it is useful for you to be aware of the concepts. It is all about bringing behavioral and technical aspects together. The chapter covered building data culture and an effective team at length, and DevOps is relevant in this aspect.

The Need for DevOps

Here are some reasons that DevOps is needed:

- Multi-platform requirements

- Just-in-time solutions for frequent delivery of software

- Code complexity and increasing application complexity

- Business requirements and frequency of releases

- Collaboration among teams and the gap between development and deployment processes

- To reduce frequent changes and shorten the gap for release planning

- Increasing compliance and control, including security, availability, and performance

- Requirements for consistent, fast delivery at reduced costs

The Benefits of DevOps

The benefits of DevOps are many:

- It accelerates software delivery.

- It eliminates wait times and delays in manual processes.

- It increases the capacity to innovate by reducing/ eliminating rework.

- It captures markets with time to value based on software innovation with improved success rates.

- It emphasizes fast and continuous iterations.

- It balances risk, cost, quality, and speed.

- It reduces the time to customer feedback.

- It optimizes risk management with delivery analytics.

Summary

This chapter dealt with the people aspects of machine learning. It explained some of the most important competences that a machine learning team needs to possess—emotional, social, moral, and spiritual intelligence. It also discussed ways to measure them. Apart from those concepts, the chapter discussed the basis of building great teams and the different roles associated with doing so. For example, it explained the basic characteristics of team leaders, team members, and technology managers. You can have a great team that's not managed properly. If so, that team is of no use.

This chapter also discussed Lean project management principles in brief. There are many new and evolving technologies associated with machine learning, including gamification and comics. This chapter took a quick look at those concepts as well.

Mind Map

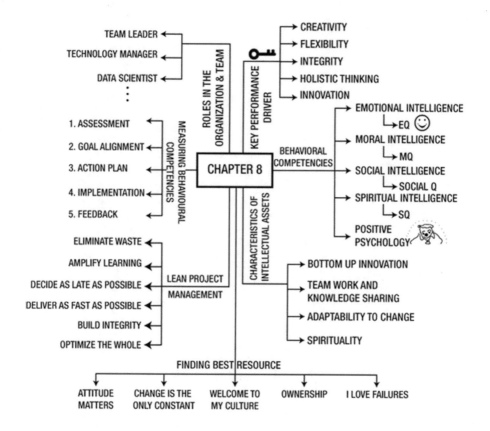

CHAPTER 9

Quantum Computers, Computing, and Machine Learning: A Review

Introduction

Quantum theory has perhaps had the greatest effect over logical advancement during the last 100 years. It introduced another line of logical ideas, anticipated incomprehensible circumstances, and affected a few spaces of present-day innovations. Over 50 years after its initiation, quantum theory was wed with software engineering, and the new subject of quantum calculation was conceived. Quantum computing combines two logical insurgencies of the last 100 years: quantum physical science and software engineering.

Data, represented by the 1s and 0s of traditional computers, must invariably be stored by some physical device, whether it is silicon or paper. Atoms, which are made up of nuclei and electrons, make up all matter. The interactions and temporal development of atoms are regulated by the

© Dr. Patanjali Kashyap 2024
P. Kashyap, *Machine Learning for Decision Makers,*
https://doi.org/10.1007/978-1-4842-9801-5_9

principles of quantum mechanics. The whole semiconductor industry, with its transistors and integrated circuits, and consequently the computer, could not have grown without our understanding of the solid-state from a quantum perspective and the band theory of metals, insulators, and semiconductors.

The transistor, the laser, and other inventions that sparked the computing revolution all have their theoretical roots in quantum physics. On an algorithmic level, however, modern computer equipment continues to use "classical" Boolean logic. Quantum computing is the development of hardware and software that, at the computational level, uses superposition and entanglement to process information instead of Boolean logic. Because everything is fundamentally quantum mechanical, it is possible to imagine information being stored on individual atoms or electrons. The Schrödinger equation, known as "Newton's Law" of quantum mechanics, governs how these minuscule particles evolve and interact instead of Newton's Laws of classical physics.

Quantum computing promises to significantly accelerate some tasks, such as optimization, sampling, searching, and quantum simulation. A lot of jobs in artificial intelligence and machine learning need the solution of challenging optimization issues or the execution of effective sampling, so quantum computing is also used in these fields. For computational issues in chemistry, material science, and machine learning, quantum algorithms offer a significant increase in speed. Molecular and material modeling, logistical optimization, financial modeling, cryptography, and pattern matching tasks, including deep learning artificial intelligence, are potential examples of tasks where quantum computers will outperform conventional computers. A traditional computer would need years to handle the same amount of data that quantum computing can handle in a matter of moments.

This chapter discusses quantum computers, computing, and quantum machine learning in brief. It introduces quantum computers and their relationship to machine learning and artificial intelligence. During this journey, you learn about several concepts, including superposition, interference, entanglement, and the tunnel effect.

Quantum Computers and Computing

Molecular and material modeling, logistical optimization, financial modeling, cryptography, and pattern matching tasks, including deep learning and artificial intelligence, are potential examples of tasks where quantum computers outperform conventional computers. A traditional computer would need years to handle the same amount of data that quantum computing can handle in a matter of moments. (Note: In this chapter, the terms classical computer/old-style computer/traditional computer are used interchangeably.)

In old-style computing, machines utilize paired code, a progression of 1s and 0s, to send and handle data. In quantum computers, a *qubit* (a quantum bit) empowers these tasks. Similarly, as a bit is the fundamental unit of data in an old-style computer, a qubit is the essential unit of data in a quantum computer. Where a bit can store either a 0 or a 1, a qubit can store a 0, a 1, both a 0 and 1, or a limitless number in the middle. There also can be numerous states simultaneously.

In quantum computers, a *state* is very important concept and is taken from quantum physics. A quantum state is a mathematical concept that represents the knowledge of a quantum system in quantum physics. The creation, development, and measurement of a quantum state is described by quantum mechanics. The outcome is a quantum mechanical forecast for the state's illustrative system.

Two qubits in a quantum computer can each represent one of four possible states (00, 01, 10, or 11). Qubits can simultaneously represent all four states due to superposition. That is comparable to running four standard computers simultaneously. A ten-qubit computer will have a superposition of slightly over a thousand states, while a 100-qubit machine—roughly the size of the greatest quantum computers today—has a mind-boggling 10^{30} states. With quantum computers, old-style computers won't disappear. For years to come, the model will be a cross-breed one. You will have an old-style computer where everything occurs and then use a quantum computer to handle specific directions. Then you'll obtain the outcome from the old-style computer.

The Wave of Quantum

The first wave of innovation was about steam power, the second was electricity, the third was high tech, and the fourth wave we are presently entering is physical science at the atomic level, like man-made intelligence, nano and biotechnology. At that point, we will see the fifth influx of innovation, which will be overwhelmed by physical science at the nuclear and sub-nuclear levels, that is, electron twist and photon polarization used to deal with data. A few centralized servers will be supplanted by quantum computers in the future, yet cell phones and workstations won't be swapped because of the need for a cooling foundation for the qubits.

Quantum mechanics is strange. Strange patterns that are extremely challenging to make conventionally can be produced by quantum systems. However, unlike classical systems, quantum systems may also learn and recognize old patterns. The reason they can accomplish this is because linear algebra is fundamental to both quantum physics and quantum computing. However, we can have states that represent vectors in a very high-dimensional vector space with a very tiny amount of quantum bits. Then, exponentially quicker than we can accomplish with conventional computers, linear algebra operations like Fourier transforms, eigenvector and eigenvalue discovery, and matrix inversion may be performed on quantum computers.

Fundamentals of Quantum Computing

An optimization problem in math and computer science is the problem of selecting the optimal answer out of all potential answers. Finding the ideal answer to a problem from an infinite number of choices is the essence of an optimization problem. A large-scale problem might take millions of years for traditional computers to configure and filter through all potential solutions. Using superposition and entanglement, quantum computers can simultaneously locate every potential variant and sort through a huge number of input variables in a remarkably short amount of time. Let's quickly see the important terminologies that are useful in understanding the concepts of quantum computers:

- *Entanglement:* The capability of quantum particles to attach their calculated outcomes to each other. Although a system of particles' quantum states cannot be characterized independently of one another, even though they are far apart, the particles are said to be entangled.

- *Superposition:* Occurs when two quantum states are combined and a third, legitimate, quantum state results. Superposition comprises the uncertainty of one particle being in numerous states. In quantum computing, superposition is explained as the aptitude of a quantum particle to be the amalgamation of all likely states.

- *Classic bit or bit*: A small amount in a transmission medium or via traditional electrical equipment.

- *Traditional logic gate*: Hardware components that can process and transmit bits, or "classical bits," and are found on an electrical circuit board or integrated circuit (chip).

- *The flip-flop:* A traditional logic gate that has the ability to send, alter, and store a single bit.

- *Register:* On a traditional computer, a parallel configuration of flip-flops that collectively represent a single number, often a 32-bit or 64-bit integer. A register may be simulated as a series of contiguous qubits by certain programming tools on quantum computers, but only for initialization and measurement rather than for full-fledged bit and arithmetic operations like on a conventional computer. In any case, a qubit is just a one-cycle register, in truth, with the capacities of superposition and entanglement.

- *Memory cell:* An addressable area in a memory chip or capacity medium that is fit for putting away a solitary digit, an old-style cycle.

- *Quantum data:* Data on a quantum computer. Dissimilar to a traditional piece, which is either a 0 or a 1, quantum data can be a 0 or a 1, or a superposition of both a 0 and a 1, or an entanglement with the quantum data of another qubit.

- *Qubit:* Ostensibly a quantum bit, which addresses quantum data, yet in addition an equipment gadget equipped for putting away that quantum data. It is what could be compared to both a bit and a flip-flop or memory cell that stores that data. On the whole, a qubit is an equipment gadget, free of what quantum data might be put in that gadget.

- *Quantum states*: There is a lot of talk about the concept that a quantum computer with n qubits can simultaneously display and process 2^n different and superimposed quantum states. A four-qubit machine has 16 states, an eight-qubit machine has 256 states, a 20-qubit machine has over a million states, and a machine with more than 32 qubits has more states than a four-qubit machine can count. The power of these qubits lies in their inherent ability to scale exponentially, so that a two-qubit machine performs four computations simultaneously, a three-qubit machine performs eight computations, and a four-qubit machine performs 16 computations simultaneously.

- *Instructions*: A solitary activity to be acted on by a computer. Applies to both old-style and quantum computers.

- *Quantum logic gate*: Guidance on a quantum computer. Not the slightest bit practically identical to an old-style rationale gate.

- *Schrodinger wave equation*: A mathematical statement that accounts for the electron's nature as a wave inside an atom when describing the energy and location of the electron in space and time.

- *Wave nature of matter*: The notion that objects are made up of particles that move in waves. Particles that are always in motion make up atoms and molecules. These waves may be thought of as oscillations or vibrations. This gives matter its existence as well as its characteristics.

- *Interference*: When two waves collide while moving across the same medium, wave interference is the result. The medium adopts a form as the result of the net of waves' interference effect of the two individual waves upon the particles of the medium.

- *Electromagnetic radiation*: Physics states that the wave nature of electromagnetic radiation causes the phenomenon known as *polarization*. Because sunlight travels through the vacuum to reach the Earth, it serves as an illustration of an electromagnetic wave. These waves are referred to as electromagnetic waves because an electric field interacts with a magnetic field. In its most basic form, polarization is the process of making non-polarized light polarized. Unpolarized light is the type of light in which particles vibrate in all possible planes.

- *Magnetic field*: The area in which the force of magnetism works around a magnetic substance or a moving electric charge. Moving electric charges and magnetic dipoles form a force field called a magnetic field that pulls on other adjacent moving charges and magnetic dipoles.

- *Electric field*: Each point in space has an electric field associated with it when a charge of any kind is present. The value of E, often known as the electric field strength, electric field intensity, or just the electric field, expresses the strength and direction of the electric field.

- *Radiation*: Energy that emanates from a source and moves through space at the speed of light. This energy has wave-like characteristics and is accompanied by an electric field and a magnetic field. The term "electromagnetic waves" can also be used to describe radiation.

- *Hilbert space*: A vector space having a natural inner product, or dot product, that offers a distance function, directly analogous to n-dimensional Euclidean space. It transforms into a full metric space under this distance function and serves as an illustration of what mathematicians refer to as a complete inner product space.

- *Euclidean space*: A space with a finite number of dimensions in which points are identified by coordinates (one for each dimension) and the distance between two points is determined by a distance formula. Euclidean space can be two-dimensional or three-dimensional.

- *Vector space*: A collection of vectors that have been added collectively and multiplied ("scaled") by numbers known as scalars. Also known as linear space.

- A dot product generalized into an inner product. This is a method of multiplying two vectors in a vector space; the offspring of this multiplication is a scalar. The magnitude of the two vectors and the cosine of the angle between them are combined to form the dot product of two vectors. Recall that there are two ways to multiply vectors.

- Dot product or the scalar product of vectors

- Cross product or a vector product of vectors

The only distinction between the two approaches is that the result of the first technique is a scalar value, while the result of the second technique is a vector.

Traditional Quantum Calculations

Computing has changed data handling. The processing and management of information has been revolutionized by computing. Humans have understood that information can be processed by physical systems since Charles Babbage's time, and more recently (e.g., via the work of Rolf Landauer) that information must be represented physically in order to be subject to physical rules. It's crucial to comprehend the computational constraints of the physical rules that apply to the information processing system. As a result of their adherence to classical physics, conventional computing equipment is referred to as "classical computers." Because proposed "quantum computers" are subject to the principles of quantum physics, their computing power differs significantly.

Fundamentally, quantum mechanics adds elements to classical mechanics that are missing. For instance, physical quantities are first "quantized," so they cannot be split. As an illustration, light is quantized; the basic unit of light is the photon, and it cannot be split into two photons. Furthermore, according to quantum physics, physical states must change over time in order to prevent the creation of independent copies of random, unknowable states. This serves as a safeguard against information copying in quantum cryptography. Additionally, quantum physics explains systems in terms of superpositions that permit the simultaneous processing of several distinct inputs, even if only one of them can be viewed at the conclusion of processing, and the result is typically of a probabilistic character. Finally, correlations in quantum mechanics are possible that are not feasible in conventional physics. Such correlations include what is called *entanglement.*

Logic Gates

Traditional computers are quite good in two ways. They can store numbers in memory and can perform basic mathematical operations (like adding and subtracting) on stored numbers. By combining the straightforward operations into a sequence known as an algorithm (multiplying, for instance, may be done as a series of additions), they can do more complicated tasks. Transistor switches—miniaturized copies of the switches you have on your wall to turn on and off the lights—perform both these tasks: storing and processing. Similar to how light may either be lit or unlit, a transistor can either be on or off.

We can use a transistor to store a number in either state: if it's on, it stores one (1); if it's off, it stores zero (0). A binary-based code may be used to record any number, letter, or symbol. For example, computers can store the uppercase letter A as 1000001 and the lowercase letter A as 01100001. A string of eight bits may contain 255 distinct characters (including the letters A–Z, a–z, numbers 0–9, and most symbols), each of which is represented by one of the binary digits (also known as *bits*), which are either zeros or ones.

The circuits known as *logic gates,* which are created by connecting many transistors together, are used by computers to do calculations. This is the computer version of what our brains would name addition, subtraction, or multiplication. Logic gates compare patterns of bits stored in temporary memory called *registers* and then change them into new patterns of bits. The algorithm that does a certain computation is represented physically by an electrical circuit made up of several logic gates, with the output from one gate flowing into the input of the next.

Because they rely on ordinary transistors, conventional computers have a problem. If you consider the incredible advancements achieved in electronics over the past few decades, this might not seem like an issue. The switch that the transistor, also known as the vacuum tube, replaced was roughly the size of a thumb when it was created in 1947. Modern microprocessors (single-chip computers) can now fit up to 30 billion transistors on a silicon chip the size of your fingernail! These integrated circuits, sometimes known as *chips*, are a remarkable achievement in miniaturization. The vast 30-ton predecessors of the current computer, which had 500 miles of cable and 18,000 vacuum tubes, are substantially identical to it.

The challenge of manipulating and decoding a binary bit and encoding it into a usable computing output hasn't changed despite computers becoming more portable and noticeably faster. Digital logic and bits are the foundation of the traditional computers that we use on a daily basis. Simply said, a bit is a thought or thing that may have one of two different values, often denoted by the numerals 0 or 1. Transistors, which may be charged (1) or uncharged (0), are frequently used in computers to represent this idea. A logic gate is a circuit that conducts operations on a set of bits that a computer has encoded as information. A given rule is simply applied to a bit via logic gates. An OR gate, for instance, inputs two bits and outputs a single value. The gate outputs 1 if any of the inputs is 1. If not, it returns 0. After the procedures are complete, the bits may be used to decode the information regarding the output. As long as the input and output information can be stored in bits, engineers can create circuits that do addition and subtraction, multiplication, and nearly any other operation that comes to mind.

Universal Computing Machine

Alan Turing, who is regarded as the founder of computer science, had the idea for what we now know as the *universal computing machine* in 1936. Turing proposed creating a read-write head that would move a tape, read the various states in each frame, and copy them in accordance with directions it received. He proposed this years before there were any actual computers in existence. The theoretical Turing machine and a laptop are not fundamentally different, despite what it may seem. The laptop's high rate of read-write frames per second makes it hard to tell whether it is truly calculating. These computations are carried out by transistors in traditional computers. The first transistor was created in 1947 by William Shockley, Walter Brattain, and John Bardeen. The word *transistor* is a mixture of "transfer" and "resistor." The multi-state frame that Turing envisioned is the transistor, a type of switch that is housed inside a piece of silicon. When the switch is turned on, electricity passes through the transistor; when it is turned off, no electricity passes. Thus, using transistors in computers is binary: the bit, or binary digit, is 1 if electricity flows through the transistor; the bit is 0 if no current flows through the transistor.

With transistors, the situation is scaling down. The more modest the transistors, the greater amount of them it is feasible to pack into the silicon cut, and the more perplexing the computations it can perform. It required an entire ten years to get from one transistor to an incorporated circuit of four transistors. After a decade, in 1965, it had become conceivable to pack 64 transistors onto a chip. At this stage, Gordon Moore anticipated that the number of transistors per silicon cut would keep on developing dramatically.

In this manner, we got the brilliant time of computers: the Intel 286, with 134,000 transistors in 1982; the 386, with 275,000 transistors, in 1985; the 486, with 1,180,235 transistors, in 1989; and the Pentium, with 3.1 million transistors, in 1993. Today, mankind is fabricating many billions of transistors each second. Your cell phone has around 2 to 4 billion transistors. As per an estimation made by the transistors expert Jim Convenient, starting from the principal semiconductor that was made in 1947, 2,913,276,327,576,980,000,000 transistors—that is 2.9 sextillion—have been produced, and inside a couple of years, there will be a greater number of transistors on the planet than every one of the cells in every one of the human bodies on the planet.

The number of transistors per inch on the coordinated circuit will increase twofold at regular intervals and this pattern will go on for no less than 20 years. This forecast was formed by Gordon Moore in 1965. Today, Moore's law actually applies. On the off chance that Moore's law is extrapolated innocently to the future, it is discovered that sometimes, each cycle of data ought to be encoded by an actual arrangement of subatomic size. On the off chance that we keep on scaling down semiconductors at the pace of Moore's law, we will have arrived at the phase of transistors the size of an atom.

The problem will emerge when the new advances permit the making of chips of around 5nm (nanometers). Current chips are dealing with 64-cycle designs coordinating beyond 700 million transistors and they can work at frequencies over 3GHz. For example, the third-age Intel Center (2012) developed from 32nm to 22nm wide, permitting duplication of the number of transistors per surface unit. A dual-core mobile variant of the Intel Core i3/i5/i7 has around 1.75 billion transistors for a die size of 101.83 mm². This works out at a thickness of 17.185 million transistors for each square millimeter. In addition, a bigger number of transistors implies that a given computer framework might do more and more quickly. In any case, following the contentions of Feynman (a physicist, who was a pioneer in quantum computers), there is an " essential limit " for this. The restrictions of the purported "tunnel effect."

It is a reality that smaller and smaller microchips are produced. The smaller the gadget, the quicker the computing process. We are unable to indefinitely reduce the size of the chips, nevertheless. There is a point at which they cease to function properly. When it gets to the nanometer scale, an unusual quantum phenomenon known as the "tunnel effect" causes electrons to escape from the channels where they normally flow. Due to the fact that electrons are quantum particles and exhibit wave-like activity, it is possible for some of them to escape from the confines of their surrounding space. This prevents the chip from functioning correctly.

Under these circumstances, because we are beyond the size of only a few tens of nanometers, conventional digital computing shouldn't be too far from its limitations. But where exactly is the limit? The extremely tiny world may have a significant role in the solution. In this regard, the different techniques currently in use to calculate the atomic radius yield values range from 0.5 to 5. The normal atom's size is on the order of angstroms (Å), but the size of the contemporary transistor is on the scale of nanometers (nm). But 10 Å equals 1nm.

Before constructing computers with quantum physics limitations in mind, you need to step up one order of magnitude! The laws of quantum physics, which govern tiny matter, differ greatly from the classical laws that govern the characteristics of ordinary logic gates. The process of miniaturization, which has contributed to the affordability and power of modern classical computers, has already advanced to the microscopic scales where quantum effects take place. Chip manufacturers frequently take considerable pains to suppress these quantum effects, but one can alternatively attempt to cooperate with them in order to facilitate further miniaturization.

Researchers have started looking at the possibility of these quantum behaviors for computation when the size of components in classical computers shrinks to the point where the behavior of the components is effectively controlled by quantum theory rather than classical theory. Surprisingly, it appears that a computer with all of its parts operating in a quantum manner is more potent than any conventional computer is capable of becoming. The study of quantum computing is motivated by the physical constraints placed on conventional computers and the potential for quantum computers to complete some valuable tasks more quickly than any classical computer.

Quantum Mechanics

The study of extremely tiny objects is known as quantum mechanics. On the level of atoms and subatomic particles, it describes how matter behaves and interacts with energy. Classical physics, in contrast, can only describe matter and energy on a scale that is relatable to the human experience, which includes how celestial things like the Moon behave. In a lot of contemporary research and technology, classical physics is still applied. However, as the 19th century came to a close, researchers found phenomena that classical physics could not account for in both the great (macro) and small (micro) worlds. Two significant revolutions in physics that changed the original scientific paradigm were sparked by the need to explain discrepancies between observable events and classical theory: the theory of relativity and quantum mechanics.

According to Newtonian physics, the world is made up of discrete things, similar to tennis balls or stone blocks. According to this theory, every action results in an equal and opposite response, and the cosmos is a vast machine made up of interlocking pieces. Unfortunately, the subatomic level is where the Newtonian universe collapses. Everything appears to be an ocean of interrelated possibilities at the quantum realm. Every particle is only a wave function that may exist everywhere at any moment. It can even exist in several locations at once. Swirling electrons can be both waves and particles at the same time because they occupy two places simultaneously.

Physicists have recently learned about a phenomenon known as *quantum entanglement*. Two particles that at first glance appear to be independent can act as one cohesive unit in an entangled system. The two entangled particles have similar spin velocities but in opposing directions if they are separated, according to theory. Twins in the quantum realm. Despite the seeming absurdity of these ideas, researchers have shown over the past

120 years that this field, known as quantum mechanics, is the one upon which our physical existence is based. It is among the most widely accepted scientific hypotheses today. Without it, among many other breakthroughs, we would not have such wonders as atomic clocks, computers, lasers, LEDs, global positioning systems, and magnetic resonance imaging.

Fundamental physics prior to the development of quantum mechanics was characterized by an odd dualism. We had electric and magnetic fields on the one hand, which were controlled by Maxwell's equations. The fields were continuous and covered the entire area. Atoms, on the other hand, were subject to Newtonian mechanics. The atoms were distinct, spatially constrained, and relatively tiny particles. The difference between light and matter—a subject that has captivated artists, mystics, and scientists for many ages—was at the center of this dualism. The fact that the dualistic understanding of matter has been replaced with a unified one is one of the wonders of quantum theory.

We discovered how to create atoms from electrons and fields from photons, among other primary particles. The mathematical framework used to explain photons and electrons is the same. They are particles in the sense that they have distinct, repeatable units that make up each one. The new quantum-mechanical type of "particle" can't, however, be tied down to a specific spot in space. Instead, a probability distribution provides the potential outcomes of measuring its location. The so-called wave function of that distribution is the square of a space-filling field.

Quantum mechanics, which includes quantum field theory, is a basic physics theory that represents nature at the tiniest scales, including atomic and subatomic levels. It is also referred to as quantum physics, quantum theory, the wave mechanical model, or matrix mechanics.

Max Planck presented the notion that energy and matter both exist in discrete units (which he named "quanta") to the German Physical Society in 1900, marking the beginning of the development of quantum theory. The following 30 years saw more research by other scientists, which resulted in the contemporary knowledge of quantum theory.

The fundamental components of quantum theory are as follows:

- Energy, similar to matter, comprises discrete units, as opposed to exclusively as a nonstop wave.

- Elementary particles of both energy and matter, contingent upon the conditions, can act like particles or waves.

- The movement of elementary particles is inherently random, and, thus, unpredictable. The synchronous measurement of two reciprocal qualities, like the position and force of an elementary particle, is inescapably flawed. The more precisely one value is measured, the more flawed the measurement of the other value will be.

Further Advancements of Quantum Theory

Niels Bohr proposed the Copenhagen interpretation of quantum theory, which states that a particle is anything that it is estimated to be (for instance, a wave or a particle) yet that it can't be expected to have explicit properties, or even to exist until it is measured. So, Bohr was saying that objective reality doesn't exist. This leads to something called *superposition,* which claims that while we do not know what the state of any object is, it is actually in all possible states simultaneously, as long as we don't look to check.

The *multiverse,* often known as the *many-worlds theory,* is the second interpretation of quantum theory. According to this theory, as soon as there is a possibility for anything to exist in any condition, that object's world transforms into an array of parallel universes with an identical number of possible states for that object in each universe. Additionally, there is a method for interaction between these worlds that allows for access to all potential states and their eventual manipulation in some fashion. Among the scientists who have favored the many-worlds idea were the late Stephen Hawking and the late Richard Feynman.

Nature is described at the ordinary (macroscopic) scale by classical physics, the description of physics that existed prior to the development of the theories of relativity and quantum mechanics. The majority of classical physics theories may be derived from quantum mechanics as a large-scale (macroscopic) approximation. With respect to energy, momentum, angular momentum, and other quantities of a bound system, quantum mechanics differs from classical physics in that these quantities are constrained to discrete values (quantization), objects exhibit wave-like and particle-like properties (wave-particle duality), and the uncertainty principle places restrictions on how accurately physical quantities can be predicted before being measured.

Gradually, theories to explain observations that could not be explained by classical physics—such as Max Planck's 1900 solution to the black-body radiation problem and Albert Einstein's 1905 paper explaining the photoelectric effect—led to the development of quantum mechanics. Midway through the 1920s, Erwin Schrödinger, Werner Heisenberg, Max Born, and others fundamentally rethought early quantum theory. The modern theory is expressed in a number of newly created mathematical formalisms. In one of them, the probability amplitude of a particle's energy, momentum, and other physical attributes are described by a mathematical function called the *wave function*. Because they represent behaviors quite different from those seen at larger sizes, many parts of quantum physics are paradoxical and might seem nonsensical. For instance, the uncertainty principle of quantum mechanics states that the more precisely one measurement is determined, such as a particle's location, the less precise must be a complementary measurement of the same particle, such as its speed. Another illustration is *entanglement*, whereby a measurement of any two-valued state of a particle (like light polarized up or down) made on either of two "entangled" particles that are very far apart causes a subsequent measurement on the other particle to always be the other of the two values (like oppositely polarized). A last model is *superfluidity*, in which a compartment of fluid helium, chilled to approach absolute zero in temperature suddenly streams (gradually) over the top of its holder, against the power of gravity.

The Structure Blocks of Quantum Mechanics

Quantum mechanics attempts to conquer the serious impediments to the legitimacy of traditional physical science, with the primary irregularity being the Board's radiation regulation. Einstein, Debye, Bohr, de Broglie, Compton, Heisenberg, Schrödinger, and Dirac, among others were the trailblazers in fostering the theory of quantum mechanics.

The essential structure blocks of quantum mechanics are as follows:

- *Quantization*: The physical quantities of a bound system, including energy, momentum, angular momentum, and others, are limited to discrete numbers.

- Objects are both waves and particles due to wave-particle duality.

- The Heisenberg principle states that the more precisely a particle's location is known, the less precisely its momentum can be computed, and vice versa. As a result, the accuracy of measuring a particle's physical properties has a basic limit.

- *Fragility*: When we measure a quantum system, we erase all past knowledge. The no-cloning theorem, which claims that it is impossible to produce an exact

duplicate of any random unknown quantum state,
arises from this.

Quantum field theories, which integrate quantum mechanics with other physics concepts to explain how things function in the actual world, are mostly based on Albert Einstein's special theory of relativity, which describes what occurs when objects move very quickly. Three different quantum field theories address three of the four fundamental forces that matter interacts with: the strong nuclear force, which explains the stability of the nucleus at the center of the atom; electromagnetism, which explains why atoms hold together; and the weak nuclear force, which explains why some atoms undergo radioactive decay.

Quantum Entanglement in Detail

Two electrons in a single system cannot be in the same state, according to the Pauli exclusion principle. The idea that two electrons might have both states "superimposed" on them is left open by nature. Nothing is certain until the waves that are overlaid collapse. According to the likelihood that is the square of the absolute value of the sum of the complex-valued amplitudes of the two superimposed waveforms, an electron appears someplace at that precise moment. There is already a lot of ambiguity about the issue. Entangled photons, or photons with two opposing states superimposed on each of them at the same event, can be conceptualized. Imagine that there are two states of photons that are identified by their respective colors: blue and red. Let the blue and red states together appear (in your mind) as a purple state. You can analyze a scenario in which a single atomic event results in the production of two photons. They may result from the stimulation of a crystal, which typically absorbs a photon of a certain frequency and produces two photons with a frequency that is half that of the original photon. The photons in this instance are related to one another because they both originated from the same atomic event. The photons end up in mixed states as a result of this configuration.

In this way, the two photons come out purple. In the event that the experimenter presently plays out some trial that decides if one of the photons is blue or red, that examination changes the photon required from one having a mix of blue and red qualities to a photon that has only one of those attributes. The matter that Einstein had with such an envisioned circumstance was that in the event that one of these photons had continued to bob between mirrors in a research center on the planet, and the other one had gone most of the way to the closest star when its twin was made to uncover itself as one or the other blue or red, that implied that the far-off photon currently needed to lose its purple status as well. In this way, at whatever point it very well may be explored after its twin had been estimated, it would essentially appear in the contrary state to anything that its twin had uncovered.

In attempting to show that quantum mechanics was not a complete theory, Einstein began with the theory's forecast that at least two particles that have communicated in the past can show up firmly corresponded when their different properties are subsequently estimated. He tried to make sense of this appearing communication in an old-style way, through their normal past, and ideally not by some "spooky action at a distance." The contention is worked out in a well-known paper by Einstein, Podolsky, and Rosen (1935; curtailed EPR), setting out what is currently called the EPR paradox. Expecting what is currently as a rule called neighborhood authenticity, the EPR paradox shows from quantum theory that a atom has both position and energy at the same time, while as per the Copenhagen interpretation, only one of those two properties really exists and just right now that it is being measured. EPR reasoned that quantum theory is fragmented in that it won't consider actual properties that dispassionately exist in nature. (Einstein, Podolsky, and Rosen 1935 is Einstein's most referred to distribution in physical science journals.)

Around the same time, Erwin Schrödinger utilized "entanglement " and proclaimed: "I would not call that one but rather the characteristic trait of quantum mechanics." But Irish physicist John Stewart Ringer hypothetically and tentatively refuted the "hidden variables" theory of Einstein, Podolsky, and Rosen. Now let's look at qubits and quantum computers.

Superposition and Entanglement in a Quantum Computer

The condition of *superposition*, which is important for performing computations, is challenging to accomplish and gigantically hard to keep up with. Physicists use laser and microwave shafts to put qubits in this functioning state and then utilize a variety of methods to protect them from the smallest temperature changes, clamors and electromagnetic waves. Current quantum computers are mistake-inclined because of the delicacy of the functioning condition, which scatters in a cycle called decoherence before most tasks can be executed. Quantum computations is not entirely settled by the number of qubits a machine can process all the while influence. Beginning with an unassuming two qubits accomplished in the main examinations in the last part of the 1990s, the most impressive quantum computer today, worked by Google, can utilize something like 72 qubits. To summarize the importance of qubit and superposition in the world of quantum computers, it is important to keep in mind the following points:

- Qubits, unlike bits in traditional computers, can be in a superposition of both 0 and 1

- A mind-boggling arrangement of qubits can be in numerous superpositions without a moment's delay. For example, model 5 qubits can be in a superposition of 32 states ($2^5 = 32$).

- Two entrapped qubits are associated with each other; data on one qubit will uncover data about the other obscure qubit.

Quantum Computing, Classical Computing, and Data Innovation

The area of information technology is where we may end up owing quantum mechanics the most. In order to build an ultra-powerful computer that can tackle issues that conventional computers cannot, researchers plan to apply quantum principles. These difficulties include enhancing cybersecurity, simulating chemical interactions, developing novel medications, and optimizing supply chains. These objectives may completely alter some areas of computing and unleash new technical possibilities. A few businesses have now released prototype quantum computers as a result of developments at universities and industry research centers, but there are still many unanswered questions regarding the hardware, software, and connections required for quantum technologies to realize their full potential.

Fundamentally, quantum mechanics adds elements to classical mechanics that are missing. Physical quantities are first "quantized," so they cannot be split. As an illustration, light is quantized; the basic unit of light is the photon, and it cannot be split into two photons. Furthermore, according to quantum physics, physical states must develop in such a way that it is impossible to create an independent duplicate of an arbitrary, unknowable state. This serves as a safeguard against information copying in quantum cryptography. Additionally, quantum physics explains systems in terms of superpositions that permit the simultaneous processing of several distinct inputs, even if only one of them can be viewed at the conclusion of processing, and the result is typically of a probabilistic character.

Finally, correlations in quantum mechanics are possible that are not feasible in conventional physics. One relationship is entanglement. However, many of these computations might not be possible to do effectively on traditional machinery. Imagine you wanted to comprehend something like a atom's chemical behavior. This behavior is dependent on how the atom's electrons, which are in a superposition of several classical states, behave. Entanglement, a quantum-mechanical phenomena, makes things more complicated because it causes each electron's quantum state to be dependent on the states of all the others. Even for extremely basic atoms, calculating these entangled states using traditional methods can turn into a nightmare of exponentially growing complexity.

To portray a straightforward particle with 300 atoms—penicillin—suppose you need 2^{300} exemplary semiconductors, which is more than the number of atoms in the universe. What's more, that is just to depict the particle at a specific second. To run it in a re-creation, you would need to fabricate more universes to supply all the material required. A quantum computer, on the other hand, can manage the interweaved destinies of the electrons under concentration by superposing and catching its own quantum bits. This empowers the computer to handle uncommon measures of data. Each qubit you add pairs the states and the framework can at the same time store: Two qubits can store four states, three qubits can store eight states, and so on.

Along these lines, you could require only 50 snared qubits to display quantum expresses that require dramatically numerous old-style bits—1.125 quadrillion to be precise—to encode. A quantum machine could in this way make the traditionally obstinate issue of reproducing huge quantum-mechanical frameworks manageable, or so it showed up. "Nature isn't traditional, darn it all, and if you need to make a reproduction of nature, you would do well to make it quantum mechanical," the physicist Richard Feynman broadly joked in 1981. "And by golly, it's a wonderful problem, because it doesn't look so easy."

Old-style computing depends, at its definitive level, on standards communicated by Boolean variable-based math, working with a (typically) seven-mode logic gate principle. However, it is feasible to exist with three modes (AND, NOT, and COPY). Data should be handled in a selective paired state anytime—that is, either 0 (off/misleading) or 1 (on/valid).

These numbers are binary digits, often known as *bits*. Computers include millions of transistors, each of which can only be in one state at any one time. There is a limit to how rapidly these devices can be made to switch states, even if the amount of time that each transistor has to remain in either 0 or 1 before flipping states is currently measured in billionths of a second. Smaller and quicker circuits push us closer to the physical limitations of materials and to the breaking point of classical physics. Beyond this, the quantum realm takes over, presenting opportunities that are as significant as the difficulties.

Contrarily, a two-mode logic gate that allows the quantum computer to convert 0 into a superposition of 0 and 1 (a logic gate that is not possible in classical computing) may be used to perform operations. A variety of elementary particles, including electrons and photons (but ions have also been successful in practice), can be utilized in a quantum computer, with either their charge or polarization serving as a representation of 0 and/or 1. The nature and behavior of each of these particles—known as a quantum bits, or qubits—form the cornerstone of quantum computing. The concepts of superposition and entanglement are the two most important components of quantum physics.

A qubit might be compared to an electron in a magnetic field. The spin of the electron can either be aligned with the field, known as a spin-up state, or it can be offset from the field, known as a spin-down state. A pulse of energy, such as that from a laser—let's suppose that you use one unit of laser energy—can be used to shift the electron's spin from one state to another. What if, however, you totally shield the particle from all outside forces while only applying half a unit of laser energy? The particle then moves into a superposition of states, where it acts as though it is simultaneously in both states, in accordance with quantum theory. Each qubit used might be superposed using both 0 and 1.

Particles (such as photons, electrons, or qubits) that have interacted at some time maintain a certain relationship and can be entangled with one another in pairs. You can infer the direction of the spin of an entangled particle's partner by observing the state of the entangled particle's spin, whether it is up or down. Even more astounding is the fact that the observed particle has no single spin orientation prior to measurement but is instead simultaneously in a spin-up and spin-down state as a result of the superposition phenomenon.

Qubits that are separated from each other by impossibly large distances can interact with one another instantly (and not just at the speed of light) because of quantum entanglement. No matter how far apart the associated particles are, as long as they are separated, they will stay entangled.

Quantum entanglement and superposition combined greatly increase computer power. A two-qubit register in a quantum computer may hold all four numbers concurrently because each qubit represents two values, in contrast to a two-bit register in a conventional computer, which can only store one of the four binary configurations (00, 01, 10, or 11) at any given moment. The additional capacity grows exponentially as qubits are added. Utilizing quantum-mechanical quirks like superposition and snare to carry out computations is known as quantum computing. Such computations, which may be carried out either hypothetically or in reality, are carried out on a quantum computer. At the present, there are primarily two methods to deal with operating a quantum computer: easy and computerized. Quantum logic entryways are used by computerized quantum computers to do computations. Qubits are used in both approaches. The worldview of sophisticated quantum computing offers incredibly advantageous features, including inclusivity, flexibility, and quantum mistake correction.

However, the real resources required to perform worthwhile error-rectified quantum computations are constrained.

The core logic of universal quantum computers is based on logical gates and functions similar to that of classical computers. As a result, universal quantum computers are very helpful for computing issues and expanding the present understanding of solutions. The most potent and widely applicable quantum computers are universal ones, but they are also the most challenging to construct. There are some estimates that put the number of qubits needed for a genuinely universal quantum computer at 1 million. Keep in mind that the number of qubits we can currently access is not even 128. The fundamental notion behind the universal quantum computer is that it can be used to quickly solve any enormously complicated task when directed at it.

Adiabatic computers are simple yet are more straightforward to deliver. These are more loose regarding qubit state steadiness. Subsequently, it is more straightforward to deliver thousands of qubits on adiabatic computers. Be that as it may, adiabatic computers can be utilized for restricted use cases like advancement issues.

We have now covered a good background for the foundations, structure, and basic workings of quantum computers. It is time to go into the world of quantum programming.

Quantum Programming

The potential for writing programs in an entirely new approach that quantum computing provides is maybe even more exciting than its sheer capability. With a quantum computer, for instance, a programming sequence along the lines of "take all the superpositions of all the prior computations"—something that is useless with a classical computer—would be possible, allowing for incredibly quick solutions to some mathematical problems, such as the factorization of large numbers.

So far, quantum programming has achieved two major breakthroughs. The first was made in 1994 by Peter Shor, who created a quantum algorithm capable of factoring big numbers quickly. It concentrates on a system that determines the periodicity of a lengthy number series using number theory. The other significant development was made by Lov Grover in 1996, who developed an extremely quick algorithm that has been shown to be the quickest available for searching through unstructured data sets. In contrast to searching in classical computing, which typically requires N searches, the technique is so efficient that it only needs, on average, around N square root (where N is the total number of elements) searches to discover the required result.

Some basic terms and terminologies related to quantum ecosystem and their mathematical notation will be useful for understanding quantum programming.

- *Linear algebra* (vectors and matrices): In quantum calculus, quantum states are represented by vectors, and quantum operations are linear transformations applied to these vectors.

- *Complex arithmetic*: The coefficients of the quantum state vectors are complex numbers. Without them, you might understand some of the basic concepts of quantum computing, but you won't get far before you need to integrate them into your quantum toolbox. You must learn complex arithmetic, which explains some of the basic math required to work with quantum computers.

- *Quantum computers are more probabilistic than strictly deterministic*: One of the great features of a classical computer based on the concept of the Turing machine is that it is strictly deterministic. You can mimic non-determinism, such as generating random numbers, but this is the exception rather than the norm.

Quantum computers, on the other hand, are inherently probabilistic rather than deterministic, much like the quantum mechanics on which quantum computers are based. This distinction requires a significant and radical rethink in the design of algorithms and code for a quantum computer. Rather than computing the answer to a problem as classical calculus would do, quantum calculus generates probabilities for any number of possible solutions. Analogous to a classical Turing machine, a quantum program can emulate determinism, but does not use the power of a quantum computer in this way.

- *Interrelation of qubits and superposition*: The usual bits you use in typical digital computers are 0 or 1. You can read them at any time, and unless there's a hardware failure, they won't change. Qubits are not like that. They have probabilities of 0 and 1, but until you measure them, they may be in an indeterminate state. This state, along with other state information allowing for further computational complexity, can be described as anywhere on the sphere (radius 1), reflecting both the probability of what's being measured as 0 and 1 (what is the North Pole and what is the South Pole).

- The Bloch sphere is used to represent the possible states of a single qubit. The state of a qubit is a combination of values along the three axes. This is called *stratification*. Some texts describe this property as "being in all possible states at the same time," while others believe that it is somewhat misleading (between 0 and 1) and that it is better to stick with

the probabilistic explanation. Either way, a quantum
computer can actually perform calculations on a qubit
while it's in.

Qubits usually begin their existence at 0, but they are frequently put
into an indeterminate state via a Hadamard Gate, which results in a qubit
that will read out as 0 half the time and 1 the other half. Other gates are
available to flip the state of a qubit by varying amounts and directions—
both relative to the 0 and 1 axes, and also a third axis that represents
phase and provides additional possibilities for representing information.
This third axis, which represents a phase, opens up more options for
encoding information. Your choice of quantum computer and toolbox will
determine the exact operations and gates that are available.

Groups of independent qubits are insufficient to deliver the enormous
advances promised by quantum computing; entanglement is where the
action is. When the quantum physics idea of entanglement is used, the
magic truly begins to happen. Qubit without entanglement was compared
by one industry insider as a "very expensive classical computer." No
matter how far away they are, entangled qubits instantaneously impact
one another when measured, according to what Einstein euphemistically
referred to as "spooky action at a distance." This is comparable to having
a logic gate linking every bit in memory to every other bit in conventional
computing. When contrasted to a conventional computer, which must
read and write from each constituent, you can begin to appreciate how
powerful that may be compared with a traditional computer needing
to read and write from each element of memory separately before
operating on it. As a result, there are multiple large potential gains from
entanglement.

The first is a significant rise in the amount of programming complexity
that can be used, at least for some sorts of issues. The modeling of
complicated molecules and materials, which are challenging to replicate
with traditional computers, is one that is generating a lot of enthusiasm. If

and when it is feasible to maintain a quantum state over great distances, there might be advancements in long-distance secure communications. Entanglement programming commonly begins with the CNOT gate, which flips a particle's state if its companion is read out as a 1. This resembles a conventional XOR gate in some ways, but it only works when a measurement is taken.

While traditional computers are capable of fully optimizing tiny systems, they can only make minor adjustments to huge systems like pricing and transit routes. This is a result of their running times, which rapidly increase as a function of issue size. An illustration is the placement of logic gates on an integrated circuit. Logic gates are placed on a chip's surface by chip design tools' optimizers with just enough room between them to accommodate the wire that specifies the chip's function. Better placement decreases chip size and costs while enhancing chip speed, because shorter lines transmit information more quickly.

Perfect optimization is not necessary, though; a chip could still be lucrative even if it is a few percent bigger than required. The idea behind traditional placement methods like simulated annealing is similar to how raindrops seek the lowest height by moving downward. Consider the water energy landscape across the United States. Almost anywhere water goes, it will eventually flow into an ocean. While low, the oceans are not as low as Death Valley. A chance raindrop would not likely fall into Death Valley's limited rainfall basin, which is surrounded by tall mountains.

Algorithmic Complexity

Quantum algorithms are good at solving a few specific complex problems. So, it is important to discuss that complexity.

Mathematicians divide problems into complex classes. Class P problems are simple for a typical computer. The time it takes to solve the problem increases with each polynomial, so 5 x 3 is an example of a polynomial problem. I can keep multiplying and my computation time scales linearly with the number of digits I add to the problem. There are also NP problems related to nondeterministic polynomial time. I'll give you 15 and you have to find the prime factors—5 times 3. Here the computation time increases exponentially if the problem is scaled linearly. NP complexity problems are difficult for classical computers. In principle, the problem can still be solved, but the computing time is becoming unrealistic. Complexity is the science of algorithms. The "universality" of Turing machines allows computer scientists to classify algorithms into different "classes of complexity." For example, multiplying two N x N matrices requires a number of operations that increase by N^3 with the size of the matrix. This can be analyzed in detail using a simple implementation of the algorithm on a Turing machine.

The important point about "universality" though, is that while you can multiply matrices a bit faster than a Turing machine, you can't change N^3's enlargement operation, regardless of the Pentium chip or special-purpose multiplication hardware of the chip you choose to use. Therefore, algorithms such as matrix multiplication, in which the running time and resources grow exponentially with the problem size, are considered "feasible" and belong to the P complexity class. Algorithms that increase time and resources exponentially with problem size are called "hard". This classification scheme has many subtleties: for example, the famous "travelling salesman problem" belongs to the NP complexity class (which you'll see shortly).

Computational complexity is a theory of efficient computing, in which "efficiency" is an asymptotic term referring to situations where the number of computational steps ("time") is at most a polynomial of the number of input bits. The complexity class P is the class of algorithms that can be run with a polynomial number of steps in the input size. The complexity class NP refers to non-deterministic polynomial time. Basically, they are questions where you can show that you can do the job in a polynomial number of operations of the size of the input, provided you get a polynomial "index" of the solution. An algorithmic problem A is NP-hard if the subprogram A to be solved solves every NP problem in a polynomial number of steps. An NP-complete problem is an NP-hard problem in NP. A useful analogy is to think of the gap between NP and P as similar to the gap between looking for proof of a theorem and checking whether the given proof of the theorem is correct. P and NP are the two lowest computational complex classes in PH's polynomial hierarchy, which is a countable sequence of these classes, and there is extensive theory of complexity classes outside of PH.

The P-NP problem is the most important unsolved problem in computer science. It asks if a problem whose resolution can be quickly verified can also be quickly resolved. That is, there is an algorithm that solves a problem that runs in polynomial time, so the running time of the task varies as a polynomial function depending on the size of the algorithm's input (as opposed to exponential time, for example). The general class of questions that some algorithms can answer in polynomial time is called "class P" or just "P." For some questions, there is no known way to quickly find the answer. However, if you get information that tells the answer, you can quickly verify the answer. The class of questions whose answers can be tested in polynomial time is called NP, which stands for "nondeterministic polynomial time." The answer to the question P=NP would determine whether problems verifiable in polynomial time can also be solved in polynomial time. Should it turn out that P≠NP, as is commonly believed, this would mean that there are problems in NP that are more difficult to compute than to verify—they cannot be solved in polynomial time, but the answer can be in polynomial time to be verified.

Our understanding of the world of computational complexity depends on a whole range of conjectures: P≠NP is the best known, and a stronger theory is that PH does not decay, that is, there is strict confinement between classes of computational complexity that defines the hierarchy of polynomials. The observations on computational complexity, while asymptotic, apply strongly to finite and small algorithmic tasks.

No optimization problem is NP-complete because only decision problems are in NP. Optimization problems can have associated decision problems in NP, and these associated decision problems can be NP-complete. For example, finding minimum size vertex coverage is an optimization problem, but determining whether there is at most k vertex coverage is a decision problem. This decision problem is NP-complete, but the optimization problem is not.

Quantum Gates

To introduce a quantum gate, I refer to the classical logic gates for comparison. The set of gates shown in Figure 9-1 provide a bit-manipulation tool. The simplest gate, NOT, has a one-bit input and the output is the inverse of the original state, H. If A is 0, it is converted to a 1 state as an output, and so on. The other ports have a two-bit input and handle depending on the inputs shown. Note that a gate is said to be universal and functionally complete if all the other sets of gates can only be constructed using some combination of that universal gate, as is the case with NAND or NOR gates (see Figure 9-1). With enough bits and a set of general-purpose logic gates, you have the tools to create any digital circuit.

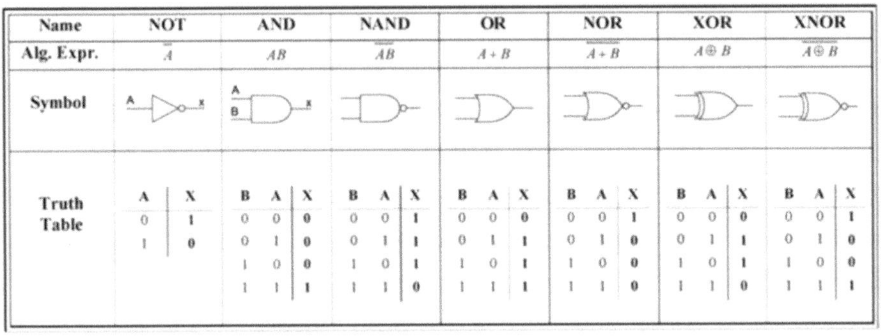

Logic Gates

Name	NOT		AND			NAND			OR			NOR			XOR			XNOR		
Alg. Expr.	$\overline{A}$		AB			$\overline{AB}$			$A+B$			$\overline{A+B}$			$A\oplus B$			$\overline{A\oplus B}$		
Symbol																				
Truth Table	A	X	B	A	X	B	A	X	B	A	X	B	A	X	B	A	X	B	A	X
	0	1	0	0	0	0	0	1	0	0	0	0	0	1	0	0	0	0	0	1
	1	0	0	1	0	0	1	1	0	1	1	0	1	0	0	1	1	0	1	0
			1	0	0	1	0	1	1	0	1	1	0	0	1	0	1	1	0	0
			1	1	1	1	1	0	1	1	1	1	1	0	1	1	0	1	1	1

Figure 9-1. *Conventional logic gates*

Note that most of these common logic gates are irreversible. A logic gate is said to be *invertible* if it is possible to reconstruct the gate's input bits by examining the outputs. So, to build an invertible digital circuit, you need a general-purpose gate with multiple output bits, such as B. Fredkin or Portes de Toffoli. All quantum gates are invertible because all quantum gates are uniform arrays.

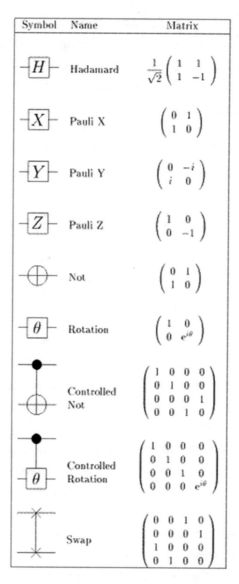

Figure 9-2. *A representative set of quantum gates for universal computing*

A quantum system can perform two types of operations: measurements and transformations of quantum states. Most quantum algorithms involve a sequence of quantum state transformations followed by measurement. Classical computers have sets of ports that are universal in the sense that any classical computation can be performed using sequences of these ports. Likewise, there are sets of primitive transformations of the quantum state, called *quantum gates* (see Figure 9-2), which are universal to quantum computing.

The Quantum Gate Is a Unitary Matrix

As physical devices will be used to construct quantum gates, they must adhere to the principles of quantum physics. No information is ever lost when moving between points in the past and the future, according to a pertinent law of physics. *Unitarity* is the term for this. Our quantum gates must also adhere to unitarity because they determine how we change between states. Second, note that qubits will be used with our quantum gates. Because qubits are actually simple vectors, quantum gates must somehow work with vectors. Keep in mind that a matrix is simply a linear modification of a vector!

Combining these two concepts, we consider quantum gates unitary matrices. Any square matrix of complex numbers that has its conjugate transposed value equal to its inverse is referred to as a *unitary matrix*. Just to refresh your memory, the conjugate transpose of a matrix is obtained by taking the conjugate of each element in the matrix and then the matrix's transpose (element ij element ji). The dagger, or, is commonly used to signify the conjugate transposition. The norm (or vector length) of unitary matrices is preserved, which is an important finding. Your qubit's probability may add up to something other than 1 if you permitted gates that altered the norm! That doesn't make sense, because the summation of all likelihoods must at all times equal 1.

Also, note that unitary matrices have an inverse by nature. This has the implication that you cannot "assign" qubits to random states. Imagine that you have a quantum gate that could "assign" values and, as a result, transform any vector of two complex numbers into a particular vector of two complex numbers in order to see why not. This quantum gate would have a unitary matrix as its underlying representation, and that matrix would have an inverse that could change a particular vector back into the state the qubit was in before the operation! However, there is no way to tell which state the qubit was in before the procedure. As a result, you are unable to "assign" qubits to any given state. A higher-level reason that we frequently consider quantum computing to be a type of reversible computing is the fact that all quantum gates are invertible. Last but not least, keep in mind that because quantum gates are unitary matrices, which are square by definition, they must include an equal number of input and output qubits (as square matrices translate n standard basis vectors into n columns)! The majority of logic gates, like the AND gate, which has two inputs and one output, operate somewhat differently from this.

Quantum Algorithms

Quantum algorithms can be described by a quantum circuit when the circuit model is adopted as a computational model. A quantum circuit is composed of qubits and gates operating on those qubits. All quantum gates are reversible, unitary operations and are represented by $2^n \times 2^n$ unitary matrices, where n is the number of qubits they act on. The most commonly used gates are single-qubit and two-qubit quantum gates and their corresponding matrix representations. Another essential operation in quantum circuits is measurement. There are two important properties of this measurement:

- The act of measuring collapses the quantum state to the state corresponding to the measurement result.

- This implies that with a single quantum measurement, you cannot read the superposed qubit state.

Therefore, the quantum state cannot be measured directly without losing the quantum state and thus the information stored. Finally, note that there are also universal sets of gates in quantum computing, and any quantum operation can be approximated by a finite sequence of gates from such a set.

The quantum gates change the state of qubits. For example, the Hadamard gate produces an equivalent superposition of two ground states. Without them, how different would your quantum computer be from a classical computer? In fact, it is these quantum gates that make quantum computers so powerful. A quantum computer can process several classical states in parallel. As the number of qubits increases, the number of dimensions increases exponentially! Try to solve a 50-qubit (or 2^{50} complex space) problem with a classical computer—it will literally take forever! Think of all the things you could have done during that time. Quantum computing is extremely powerful because it does what classical computers can't do: solves optimization problems by computing all the possibilities at once. A simple and basic example of two entangled qubits is known as the *Bell state*, and is represented by

$$\psi = (00>+11>)/\sqrt{2}$$

where, using the same probability derivative, we find that the probability of two qubits is 50 percent For example, 0.50 percent indicates the possibility of finding both qubits in state 1, and 0 percent indicates that qubits can be found in opposite states 01> or 10>. One way to prepare for the Bell state is to take two qubits, both initialized to 0>, and then apply a Hadamard gate to one and a CNOT gate. If you reach the Bell state and measure one of the qubits, you immediately know the state of the other. As in a classical computer, there is a set of quantum gates that makes it possible to simulate any reversible quantum circuit, that is, a universal set of quantum gates. This set of gates can be achieved with CNOTs and single-qubit unit gates, or alternatively with multi-qubit gates such as the quantum equivalent of a Fredkin gate.

Quantum Circuits

A *quantum circuit* (also called a quantum network or quantum gate array) generalizes the idea of classical circuit families by replacing the AND, OR, and NOT gates with elementary quantum gates. A quantum gate is a unit transformation of a small number (usually 1, 2, or 3) of qubits. The most important two-qubit gate you have seen is the NOT-controlled gate (CNOT). Adding another control register gives a three-qubit Toffoli gate, also called a Controlled-Controlled-not (CCNOT) gate. This negates the third bit of its input if the first two bits are 1. The Toffoli gate is important because it is complete for the classical reversible computation, that is, any classical computation can be implemented with a Toffoli gate circuit. It's easy to see that using auxiliary wires with fixed values, Toffoli can implement AND (set the third input wire to 0) and NOT (set the first and second input wires to 1). It is known that AND and NOT gates together are sufficient to implement a classic Boolean circuit. So, if we can apply (or simulate) Toffoli gates, we can reversibly implement any classic gate.

Computations

Mathematically, these elementary quantum gates can be assembled into larger unit operations using tensor products (when the gates are applied in parallel to different parts of the register) and simple matrix products (when the gates are applied sequentially). The basic element of memory in classical computers is a bit that can have two states—0 or 1. The computer (or circuit) has n bits and can perform specific logical operations on them.

For universal classical computations, a NOT gate operating on a single bit and an AND gate operating on two bits are sufficient. This means that calculations based on a different set of logic gates, each operating on a finite number of bits, can be replaced with calculations based only on NOTs and ANDs. Classical circuits with random bits lead to both practical and theoretically sound random algorithms.

Quantum computers allow the creation of probability distributions far beyond the capabilities of classical computers with access to random bits. A qubit is a piece of quantum memory. The state of a qubit can be described by a unit vector in a two-dimensional complex Hilbert space, H. For example, the basis of H can correspond to the two energy levels of a hydrogen atom, or to the horizontal and vertical polarization of a photon. Quantum mechanics allows a qubit to be in a superposition of basis vectors, described by any unit vector in H.

The memory of a quantum computer consists of n qubits. Let Hk be a 2D Hilbert space associated with the kth qubit. The state of the entire memory n qubit is described by the unit vector in the tensor product $H1 \otimes H2 \otimes \cdots \otimes Hn$. You can feed a qubit or two through gates representing unitary transformations acting on the corresponding two- or four-dimensional Hilbert spaces, and as far as classical computers go, there is a small gate list sufficient for universal quantum computing. Each step of the computational process consists of applying a uniform transformation to a large two-dimensional Hilbert space, that is, H. It applies a gate to one or two qubits, constrained by an identity transformation on all other qubits.

At the end of the calculation process, it is possible to measure the state of the whole computer and get a probability distribution on 0-1 vectors of length n.

A few words on the relationship of the mathematical model of quantum circuits to quantum physics: In quantum physics, states and their evolutions (the way they change over time) are governed by the Schrödinger equation. The solution of the Schrödinger equation can be described as a unit process in Hilbert space, and quantum computation processes, as just described, form a large class of such quantum expansions.

Quantum Registers vs Classical Registers

Registers are a type of computer memory used to quickly receive, store, and transfer data and instructions for immediate use by the CPU (Central Processing Unit). A processor register can hold an instruction, a memory address, or any data (such as a sequence of bits or unique characters). The register is a temporary storage area built into the CPU. Some registers are used internally and are not accessible outside the processor, while others are user accessible. Most modern processor architectures contain both types of registers. The number and size of the registers differ by processor architecture. Some processors have 8 registers, others 16, 32, or more. For many years, registers were 32-bit, but many are now 64-bit in size. The 64-bit register is necessary for a 64-bit processor because it allows the processor to access 64-bit memory addresses. A 64-bit register can also contain 64-bit instructions that cannot be loaded into a 32-bit register. Therefore, most programs written for 32-bit processors can run on 64-bit computers, while 64-bit programs are not backward compatible with 32-bit computers.

Figure 9-3 shows an example using the four-qubit register.

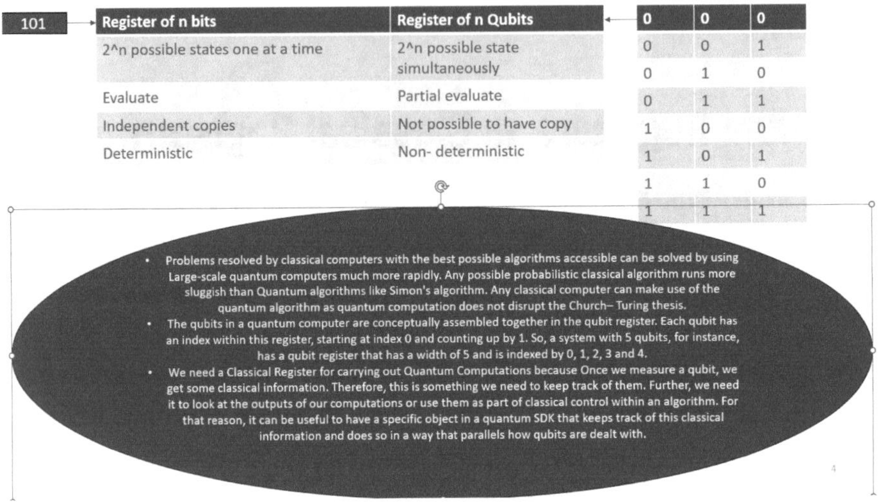

Register of n bits	Register of n Qubits	0	0	0
2^n possible states one at a time	2^n possible state simultaneously	0	0	1
		0	1	0
Evaluate	Partial evaluate	0	1	1
Independent copies	Not possible to have copy	1	0	0
Deterministic	Non- deterministic	1	0	1
		1	1	0
		1	1	1

- Problems resolved by classical computers with the best possible algorithms accessible can be solved by using Large-scale quantum computers much more rapidly. Any possible probabilistic classical algorithm runs more sluggish than Quantum algorithms like Simon's algorithm. Any classical computer can make use of the quantum algorithm as quantum computation does not disrupt the Church–Turing thesis.
- The qubits in a quantum computer are conceptually assembled together in the qubit register. Each qubit has an index within this register, starting at index 0 and counting up by 1. So, a system with 5 qubits, for instance, has a qubit register that has a width of 5 and is indexed by 0, 1, 2, 3 and 4.
- We need a Classical Register for carrying out Quantum Computations because Once we measure a qubit, we get some classical information. Therefore, this is something we need to keep track of them. Further, we need it to look at the outputs of our computations or use them as part of classical control within an algorithm. For that reason, it can be useful to have a specific object in a quantum SDK that keeps track of this classical information and does so in a way that parallels how qubits are dealt with.

Figure 9-3. *Detailed overview of the n-qubit register versus the n-bit register*

However, these two powers of *n* do not really correspond to the information storage capacity. This is the ability to overlay states, which is then applied to processing to highlight the combinations being sought according to the specified algorithm.

Quantum Computer Algorithms

Algorithms and code are not the same. Basically, many people, including experienced professionals, think of algorithms and code as the same thing, but that's just not true. As discussed earlier, an *algorithm* is a series of steps to solve a problem, perform a task, or perform a calculation. In mathematics and computer science, an algorithm is a finite sequence of well-defined instructions that can be implemented by a computer, usually to solve a class of problems or perform calculations. Rather, the algorithm represents a higher-level specification of how to achieve a desired function or goal, at a higher level than the raw code level. It can contain relatively detailed passages, but not as detailed as is required for a direct translation into machine language for a classical or quantum computer.

On the other hand, code is so detailed that it can be directly and completely translated into executable machine language instructions. Code is always expressed in a programming language and then compiled into executable code or into an intermediate form that can be interpreted as if it had been compiled into executable code.

Algorithms can sometimes be expressed in a form that superficially resembles code, or at least a code-like language, but they are usually expressed in more expressive linguistic forms. Code is often simple, repetitive, and uncritical. For example, code that displays a user interface validates input, performs a transaction, or calculates a value is usually easy to implement. Algorithms have different levels of complexity and can start as a research project or similar intensive effort. It should be noted that companies often use the term algorithm simply because it sounds good. As a result, the term has gradually lost its meaning and has increasingly become synonymous with code.

Main Classes of Quantum Algorithms

This section covers the different classes of quantam algorithms:

- *Search algorithms*: Search algorithms based on the algorithms of Deutsch-Jozsa, Simon, and Grover. These types of algorithms typically search for the equilibrium point of a complex system. For example, to train neural networks, to find the optimal path in networks, or to optimize processes.

- *Algorithms based on Quantum Fourier Transforms (QFT)*: Like Shor's integer factorization, which has sparked a debate among those wanting to build

quantum computers capable of cracking RSA-type
public security keys, and those who want to protect
digital communications with algorithms resistant to
fast integer factorization.

- *Quantum mechanism simulation algorithms*: These
  are used in particular to simulate the interactions
  between atoms in various molecular, inorganic, and
  organic structures. The development of new quantum
  algorithms is an active research area that has seen
  increasing growth in recent years. Many companies and
  research institutes are trying to develop new quantum
  algorithms that solve important computational
  problems better than classical algorithms.

Important Quantum Algorithms

The most important quantum algorithms developed so far are discussed in
the following sections.

Shor's Algorithm

This algorithm factors large numbers and solves the discrete logarithm
problem. This algorithm can crack most of the public key encryption
currently in use. Shor's algorithm uses the brilliant number theory
argument that the two prime factors p, q of a positive integer N = pq can be
found by taking the period of the function $f(x)=yx\bmod N$ for any y<N that
has no factors. N is not equal to 1.

Shor's result is by far the most spectacular example of quantum
acceleration of computations, although the factorization is believed to
apply only to NP and not to NP-completeness. To check whether *n* is
prime, a series of $\log_2 n$ polynomial steps must be followed (the binary

encoding of the natural number n requires $\log_2 n$ resources). But no one knows how to prime numbers in polynomial time, and the best classical algorithms we have for this problem are subexponentially algorithms. This is another open problem in computational complexity theory.

It is easy to find large prime numbers quickly and it is difficult to factor large composite numbers in a reasonable amount of time. The discovery that quantum computers can solve factors in polynomial time, therefore, had dramatic implications. The implementation of the algorithm on a physical machine would have economic as well as scientific consequences.

Grover's Algorithm

This algorithm searches in an unordered list. This is a general method that can be applied to many types of computational problems. Quantum computers offer polynomial acceleration for some problems. The best-known example of this is the search in quantum databases, which can be solved by the Grover algorithm with far fewer database queries than classical algorithms require. In this case, the advantage is not only verifiable but also optimal. The Grover algorithm offers the greatest possible probability of finding the desired article with any number of Oracle searches. Since then, many more examples of detectable quantum accelerations in query problems have been discovered, such as collision detection in two-to-one functions and NAND tree evaluation.

The running time of Grover's algorithm on a quantum computer scales as the square root of the number of entries (or items in the database), in contrast to the linear scaling of classical algorithms. A general class of problems to which Grover's algorithm can be applied is the Boolean satisfiability problem. In this case, the database on which the algorithm iterates contains all possible answers. An example (and possible) use for this is a password cracker that attempts to guess the password or secret key of an encrypted file or system.

Symmetric encryption is particularly vulnerable to this type of attack. Symmetric encryption uses a single key to encrypt and decrypt. If you encrypt a ZIP file and then decrypt it with the same key, you are using symmetric encryption. Symmetric encryption is also called "secret key" encryption because the key must be kept secret from third parties.

Quantum Approximate Optimization Algorithm (QAOA)

This is a general method for solving optimization problems in certain conditions. Many problems in finance, manufacturing, transportation, and so on, can be formulated as optimization problems, showing the potential implications of this algorithm.

An important parameter for the success of a quantum algorithm is its performance compared to classical algorithms. From a theoretical point of view, some computational problems turned out to be difficult to solve (or at least impossible to solve in a reasonable amount of time) with classical computers. Implementing a quantum algorithm to solve such a problem would be a great achievement. On a more practical level, a quantum algorithm will already be very successful if it performs better than a classical algorithm. This creates (healthy) competition between developers of classical and quantum algorithms. The bottom line is that advances in this area are already having a generally positive impact on the field even before the first demonstration of a quantum computer.

Translating Algorithms Into Programming Languages

You need quantum code libraries to achieve this. Nowadays countless libraries with functions, classes, modules, frameworks, and example programs are filled with classic calculations, so starting a new project does not mean starting from scratch. While it will take time to compete with the vast libraries of code accumulated over 80 years of classical computing, the need is clear. Open sources and project and source code repositories like GitHub will simplify this process.

More than 40 years ago, Microsoft took advantage of its microcomputer tools thanks to software made available on magnetic tape by the Digital Equipment Corporation User Society (DECUS). There is currently a small number of quantum code samples on GitHub, but we are still at the very early stages. These are very fragmentary examples and are not ready to be included in realistic programs. The fact that the quantum world lacks rich tools for structuring code, such as compiled functions, classes, modules, and formal libraries, makes it much more difficult to share code at a higher level than in stand-alone example programs.

With this background, let's look at the quantum computing programming language. The Quantum algorithms allow you to analyze data and propose simulations based on the data. These algorithms are written in a quantum programming language. Several quantum languages have been developed by scientists and technology companies. Here are some programming languages for quantum computers:

- *QISKit*: IBM's Quantum Information Software Kit is a comprehensive library for writing, simulating, and running quantum programs.

- *Q#*: Programming language included in the Microsoft Quantum SDK. The development kit includes a quantum simulator and algorithm libraries.

- *Cirq*: A quantum language developed by Google that uses a Python library to write circuits and run them in quantum computers and simulators.

- *Forest*: A development environment created by Rigetti Computing used to write and run quantum programs.

Because the qubit is the fundamental unit of the quantum computing paradigm, it's important to understand the what, why, and how of quantum programming, as well as the general structure of quantum computers.

Qubit Details

You now know that the qubit is the fundamental unit of a quantum computer. However, many candidates are being sought for the physical implementation of a quantum computer (as opposed to the physical system used to implement the qubits).

So far, "quantum computing" is used as a general term for all calculations that use quantum phenomena. In fact, there are many types of operational frameworks. Gate-based quantum logic computations are perhaps the best known. In it, qubits are prepared in their initial states and then, depending on the qubit type, subjected to a series of "gate operations" such as current pulses or lasers. Through these gates, qubits are stacked, entangled, and subjected to logical operations such as the AND, OR, and NOT gates of traditional computer science. Then the qubits are measured and a result is obtained.

Another framework uses a measurement-based computation, which starts with highly entangled qubits. Instead of manipulating the qubits, measurements are taken of individual qubits, leaving the single target qubit in a final state. Based on the result, further measurements are made on other qubits and finally, an answer is obtained.

The third structure is a topological computation where the qubits and operations are based on quasiparticles and their convolution operations. While nascent implementations of the topological components of quantum computers have yet to be demonstrated, the approach is interesting because these systems are theoretically shielded from noise that disrupts the coherence of other qubits.

596

Finally, there are the analogue quantum computers or quantum simulators invented by Feynman. Quantum simulators can be viewed as special quantum computers that can be programmed to model quantum systems. Thanks to this ability, they can, for example, answer questions about how superconductors work at high temperatures, the reactions of certain chemicals, or the design of materials with certain properties.

Here's a summary of some physical realizations of qubits:

- Superconducting quantum computing (qubits from the state of small superconducting circuits known as Josephson junctions)

- Quantum computer with trapped ions (qubits implemented by the internal state of trapped ions)

- Optical lattice (a qubit consisting of the internal states of neutral atoms trapped in an optical lattice)

- Spin-based quantum dot computer (e.g., Loss-DiVincenzo quantum computer), where qubits are determined by the spin states of trapped electrons

- Space-based quantum dot computer (qubits determined by the position of an electron in a double quantum dot)

- Paired quantum wire (a qubit implemented by a pair of quantum wires connected by point quantum contact)

- Nuclear Magnetic Resonance Quantum Computer (NMRQC) implemented using the nuclear magnetic resonance of molecules in solution, where qubits are provided by nuclear spins in the molecule in solution and probed with radio waves

- Semiconductor Kane NMR quantum computer (qubits made from the nuclear spin state of phosphorus donors in silicon)

- Quantum computation of electrons on helium (a qubit is the spin of an electron)

- Quantum cavity electrodynamics (CQED) (qubits provide the internal state of trapped atoms coupled to high finesse cavities)

- Molecular magnets (qubits determined by spin states)

- Fullerene-based ESR quantum computer (qubits based on the electron spin of atoms or molecules trapped in the fullerene)

- Linear optical quantum computer (qubits implemented by processing the states of different light modes using linear elements such as mirrors, beam splitters, and phase shifters)

- Diamond quantum computer (qubits made by electronic or nuclear rotation of empty nitrogen centers in diamonds)

- Quantum computers based on the Bose-Einstein condensate

- Transistor quantum computer (string quantum computer with electrostatic positive hole trap)

- Quantum computer based on inorganic crystals doped with rare earth ions (qubits implemented by the internal electronic state of dopants in optical fibers)

- Quantum computers based on metal-like carbon nanospheres

The large number of applicants shows that, despite rapid progress, the topic is still in its infancy. There is also great flexibility.

General Structure of a Quantum Computer System

Almost every part of the design is unusual because the quantum effect usually, but not always, needs components to operate close to absolute zero. The thermal mobility of the atoms in the computer's structure causes problems in quantum computer components when they run at normal temperatures. Quantum error correction must be used to eliminate the faults. However, without cooling the components to a temperature of a few thousandths of a degree above absolute zero (273.15 °C or 0 K), the rate at which errors accumulate makes this impractical. It is necessary to maintain the qubits (quantum bits) at a temperature of around 15 mK.

They need the assistance of traditional superconducting electronics based on Josephson junctions, which run at temperatures of 4 K, or about as hot as helium will boil. The user interacts with a traditional computer in the general design of a quantum computing system. A classical computer can transform a user's problem into a standard form for a quantum computer, such as QUBO (Quadratic Unconstrained Binary Optimization), or into a new form if a different quantum method is needed. After receiving information from the qubit measurements, a conventional computer creates control signals for the qubits in the cryogenic environment. Some classic electronics are placed in a cold environment to minimize heat transfer through the wiring via a cryogenic temperature gradient to the ambient temperature.

Quantum Software Example: Qiskit Aqua

It is important to see the types of quantum software in the market to understand the workings of quantum computers and their simulation. However, covering multiple programs is not possible due to multiple reasons, including space constraints. Therefore, I cover one program in detail, called Qiskit Aqua, which is a library and application for quantum algorithms.

Aqua includes cross-domain quantum algorithms and applications operating on Noisy Intermediate-Scale Quantum (NISQ) computers, and it sits atop the Qiskit ecosystem. An open-source library called Aqua was created with the intention of being modular and expandable on several levels. It was entirely developed in Python. This adaptability enables users with various degrees of experience and scientific interests to contribute to and expand Aqua across the stack.

Since the inclusion of Aqua, Qiskit has emerged as the sole scientific software framework for quantum computing that can translate domain-specific issue requirements from the highest level through circuit creation, compilation, and ultimately execution on IBM Q quantum hardware.

Input Generation

Currently, Aqua supports four applications in the fields of chemistry, artificial intelligence (AI), optimization, and finance, all of which have long been recognized as possible uses for quantum computing. The adaptable Aqua interfaces allow for the simple addition of new domains. At this level of application, Aqua enables the use of classical computing software as the frontend of quantum applications without the end user having to learn a new programming language. Behind the scenes, Aqua uses hybrid classical/quantum processes, in which some initial computation is done conventionally, the results of which are then mixed with configuration information unique to the task and converted into inputs for one or more quantum algorithms. The Terra component of Qiskit, which is in charge of creating, constructing, and running quantum circuits, serves as the foundation for the Aqua algorithms. The Aqua algorithms run on top of Terra, the element of Qiskit responsible for building, compiling, and executing quantum circuits on simulators or real quantum devices.

Quantum Algorithms on Aqua

Researchers specializing in quantum algorithms can experiment with numerous algorithms made accessible in Aqua. Numerous domain-independent methods, such as Grover's Search Algorithm, the VQE algorithm, the Quantum Approximate Optimization Algorithm (QAOA), and other Quantum Phase Estimation (QPE) techniques are among them. Additionally, there are accessible domain-specific methods for supervised learning, such as the Support Vector Machine (SVM) Quantum Kernel and Variational algorithms. By enhancing the Aqua Quantum Algorithm interface, researchers can add their own algorithms. Inverse Quantum Fourier Transforms (IQFTs), local and global optimizers, variational forms, starting states for variational-form initialization, oracles, feature maps, and extensions for binary-to-multiclass classification are just a few of the many supporting elements that help with these efforts. To facilitate the integration of new components, Aqua includes an automatic component-discovery mechanism that allows components to register themselves for dynamical loading at runtime.

User Experience

Utilizing classical computational software at the frontend of Aqua has unique advantages. Users at the top of the Aqua software stack are industry-domain experts, and are most likely very familiar with existing classical software specific to their own domains, such as the PySCF computational chemistry software driver used in the code. These practitioners are interested in experimenting with the potential benefits of quantum computing, but at the same time, they might be hesitant to learn the intricate details of the underlying quantum physics. Ideally, such practitioners would benefit from a workflow centered on the computational software they are comfortable with as the frontend, without having to learn a new quantum programming language or Application Programming Interface (API). Moreover, such researchers may have collected, over time, numerous problem configurations, corresponding to various experiments that are all tied to a specific classical computational package. Aqua has been designed from the outset to accept input files in the language of any classical computational package it interfaces, thus not requiring users experienced in a particular domain to learn a new quantum-specific language for the same task.

Functionality

Other quantum software libraries force a middle programming layer or API between the classical and quantum components of a hybrid program, but Aqua is special in that it can directly interface with classical computational software. This allows the computation of the intermediate data necessary to construct the quantum algorithm input to be performed at its highest level of precision without losing any functionality inherent in the underlying classical software.

Debugging a Quantum Program

On a classical computer, no professional programmer would ever consider doing without their debugger, yet on a quantum computer, such a tool isn't even conceivable. Quantum programs provide the following significant difficulties because it is not theoretically feasible to examine the quantum state (the wave function) of a qubit:

- You can't single step or set breakpoints in a quantum program, examine the quantum state, possibly even change the quantum state, and then continue execution.

- You can't examine the wave function of a quantum system or qubit—you can only measure or observe a single observable, which then causes the rest of the wave function to collapse.

- Quantum decoherence means that even if you could stop and study a state, you couldn't stop and think about it, because a quantum state tends to decay in a tiny fraction of a second—less than a ten-thousandth of a second. A second is 90 microseconds on a 50-qubit IBM quantum computer.

- Due to the fact that the quantum state tends to decay in a very small fraction of a second, or less than one 10,000th of a second, or 90 microseconds, on the 50-qubit IBM quantum computer, quantum decoherence means that even if you could halt and study the state, you could not pause and ponder about it.

You only need to run the quantum program all the way through to the end, and then look at the outcomes. Because debugging isn't a possibility, this effectively implies that quantum programmers need to be much, much, more cautious about developing proper, bug-free code. However, quantum simulators offer at least a portion of the answer.

Quantum Simulators and Computers

On current classical computers, simulations of smaller quantum computers and algorithms of equivalent complexity work well. Certainly, quantum simulators operate much more slowly, but this is not a concern for simpler algorithms. Running a quantum computation on a simulator has the largest advantage over using an expensive actual quantum computer.

There are now cloud-based quantum computing services, so you can queue up a program to be automatically executed when a quantum computer becomes available, but if your algorithm is relatively small and you need to do a lot of experimentation with many variations, that can be tedious, inconvenient, and ultimately expensive.

Another compelling argument in favor of a simulator is its hybrid way of operation. The efficiency benefit of executing directly on a genuine quantum computer could be completely eliminated if the hybrid algorithm is rapidly switching between classical code and quantum code. Not all companies offering cloud-based quantum computing services will give the hybrid mode of operation the same amount of support.

The removal of three of the main obstacles to developing quantum programs is a key benefit of quantum simulators:

- You are only able to measure or witness a single observable in a quantum system or qubit, which subsequently causes the remainder of the wave function to collapse.

- It is impossible to look at the probability amplitudes for qubit-based vectors.

- In a quantum program, it is not possible to run a single step, establish breakpoints, look at the quantum state, and then resume execution.

A quantum simulator can perform all three of these tasks because it mimics the physics of a quantum computer, preserving its complete state or at least a close approximation of it, including the wave functions for the qubits and the probability amplitudes for the ground states of individual qubits. The third drawback of a quantum simulator is that, while it can be near enough for many purposes, it is not a perfect duplicate of how a quantum computer operates. Although, at the time of writing, I am not aware of any quantum simulator that offers functions that adhere to all quantum requirements, such functions may theoretically be created.

In essence, quantum simulators, a hybrid mode of operation using a quantum computer as a coprocessor and quantum-inspired algorithms, would allow the quantum computing approach to evolve far more quickly than pure quantum hardware and algorithms currently being developed.

Quantum Computing, Artificial Intelligence and Machine Learning: The Basics

Computers discover data pattern patterns using machine learning. Utilizing quantum mechanical phenomena like superposition and entanglement to carry out computations is known as quantum computing. Such calculations are carried out using a quantum computer, which may be theoretically or practically realized. Therefore, quantum machine learning is the study of how quantum computers and other quantum information processors discover patterns in data that traditional machine learning algorithms are unable to discover.

Although the term artificial intelligence is now used quite loosely, it refers to the idea that robots will eventually be able to do activities that are indicative of human intellect. AI/machine learning may help analyze huge volumes of data quickly, as well as develop and analyze models and predict trends to reveal patterns that are difficult to understand. Machine learning is a simple technique to accomplish AI. Machine learning can be utilized in many different applications and is a faster approach to identifying and evaluating these patterns than using conventionally written algorithms, but artificial intelligence is where the world's attention is now focused. More quantum algorithms that significantly outperform classical ones are sought by quantum physicists. Some AI challenges seem like ideal candidates for the search for fresh issues that fit the bill. The AI community, on the other hand, thinks that quantum computing holds considerable promise for overcoming previously intractable issues. The construction of intelligent machines is a technological objective of artificial intelligence, as is the scientific goal of comprehending the intelligent conduct of people, animals, and robots.

Computational methods are generally used by AI researchers to accomplish their technical and scholarly objectives. To emphasize the essential role that computers play in artificial intelligence, "computational intelligence" is a more apt term for the subject than "artificial intelligence." We naturally wonder how this new computing method may assist us in achieving the objectives of artificial intelligence given the rapid growth of quantum computing.

It appears evident that using quantum computing in different AI systems to speed up the computing process will significantly advance the technological objective of AI. To tackle some AI issues more effectively than current ones, it is exceedingly difficult to create quantum algorithms. Furthermore, it is not yet obvious how quantum computing may be used to the development of artificial intelligence, a scientific aim. What is striking, though, is that rather than being focused on quantum computers, a sizable body of research is devoted to the application of quantum theory to artificial intelligence and vice versa. Two general types of research coming from the interplay between quantum theory and AI are:

- Using specific ideas from quantum theory to solve specific problems in AI.

- Conversely apply ideas developed in artificial intelligence to quantum theory.

From the current work, it seems that due to its intrinsic probabilistic nature, quantum theory joins more naturally to digital AI than to logical AI.

The Interface Between Machine Learning and Quantum Computing

Quantum computing may enable AI machine learning solutions to process their data sets exponentially faster than their traditional computing counterparts, although these ML/AI algorithms cannot be coded in the traditional sense. However, the intersection of these two areas goes even further and not only AI applications can benefit from it. There is an intersection where quantum computers implement machine learning algorithms and traditional machine learning methods are used to evaluate quantum computers. This area of research is growing so rapidly that it has spawned an entirely new field called *quantum machine learning* (QML). Recent work has yielded quantum algorithms that could serve as building blocks for machine learning programs, but the hardware and software challenges are still significant and the development of fully functional quantum computers is still a long way off.

There are four approaches to machine learning, classified according to whether the system under consideration is classical or quantum and whether the information processing device is classical or quantum, as shown in Figure 9-4.

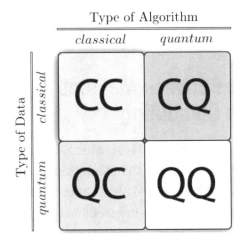

Figure 9-4. *Four approaches to combining quantum computing and machine learning*

Artificial Quantum Intelligence

The multidisciplinary topic of quantum artificial intelligence (QAI) focuses on developing quantum algorithms to enhance computing tasks in artificial intelligence, including branches like machine learning. When compared to traditional AI methods used in computer vision, natural language processing, and robotics, quantum computing is far more efficient because of the quantum mechanics phenomena of superposition and entanglement. The idea of quantum-enhanced AI algorithms as a whole is still being researched conceptually. Initial empirical research suggests that these ideas may be put into practice in the laboratory, under tightly controlled circumstances, building on recent theoretical recommendations.

Quantum Machine Learning (QML)

Quantum machine learning is a developing interdisciplinary research area at the intersection of quantum physics and machine learning. The most common use of this term denotes machine learning algorithms for classical data analysis executed on a quantum computer, that is, volume-assisted quantum machine learning. While machine learning algorithms are used to calculate huge amounts of data, quantum machine learning intelligently extends them by creating possibilities for the analysis of quantum states and systems. This includes hybrid methods that comprise both classical and quantum computing, where computationally tough routines are externalized onto a quantum device. With quantum devices, these procedures can be performed more complexly and faster.

In addition, quantum state analysis may be performed using quantum algorithms rather than conventional data. The phrase "quantum machine learning" is frequently used in contexts other than quantum computing to refer to traditional machine learning techniques used on data obtained from quantum experiments (i.e., the term includes a branch of research that examines methodological parallels and structures between some physical systems and learning), especially neural networks in systems. Examples include the ability to use certain mathematical and numerical methods from quantum physics to classical deep learning and vice versa. This last section looks at the more esoteric ideas in learning theory that are connected to quantum information and are frequently referred to as "quantum learning theory."

Machine Learning with Quantum Computers

Enhanced quantum machine learning refers to quantum algorithms that solve machine learning tasks while improving and often accelerating classic machine learning techniques. Such algorithms typically require that a specific set of classical data be encoded in a quantum computer to make it available for quantum information processing. Quantum information processing methods are then applied and the result of the quantum calculations is read off by measuring the quantum system. For example, the result of a qubit measurement reveals the result of a binary classification task. While many proposals for quantum machine learning algorithms are still purely theoretical and require testing a large general-purpose quantum computer, others have been implemented on small or dedicated quantum devices.

Quantum Neural Networks

Quantum neural networks (QNNs) are frequently used to refer to quantum counterparts or generalizations of classical neural networks. The phrase is used to describe a broad variety of techniques, such as the development and use of photonic neural networks, layered variational circuits, and quantum Ising-type models. Deutsch's notion of a quantum computing networks is frequently used to define quantum neural networks. In this approach, gates that are nonlinear and irreversible—differing from the Hamiltonian operator—are used to make predictions about the supplied data set. These gates produce certain oscillations and prevent the observation of particular phases. Quantum neural networks integrate conventional neurocomputing with the concepts of quantum information and quantum computation.

According to recent research, QNN can exponentially enhance a computer's processing capacity and degrees of freedom, which are both constrained by a classical computer's physical size. A quantum neural network has the ability to accelerate computing by reducing the amount of time, qubits, and steps required. The quantum mechanical wave function is analogous to the neuron in a neural network.

Limitations and discoveries of quantum deep learning:

- The key barriers preventing deep learning's transition to quantum computing. The lack of a working quantum computer to conduct experiments on was the initial barrier to the development of quantum neural networks.

- The inability to train quantum networks was the second barrier.

- The classical neuron/perceptron's nonlinear functions put it at odds with quantum qubits, which can only function with unity and linearity. This is the third issue.

Great discoveries changed these obstacles. Several companies have deployed quantum computers in the last year, including IBM, which has made its computers available to researchers free of charge on the Internet.

- A new algorithm solves this problem in two main phases: Simple Quantum Neural Network and Training Quantum Neural Network.

- This problem was solved with a new quantum perceptron using a special quantum circuit, the repeat-until-success (RUS) loop.

The use of quantum algorithms in artificial intelligence techniques will enhance machine learning capabilities. This will lead to improvements in development, for example, forecasting systems, and also in the financial sector. However, we will have to wait before we can start implementing these improvements. The computing power required to derive added value from the currently collected, unmanageable data and in particular to apply artificial intelligence techniques such as machine learning is constantly increasing.

As you know scientists have tried to find a way to speed up these processes by applying quantum computing algorithms to artificial intelligence techniques, giving birth to a new discipline called *quantum machine learning* (QML). Quantum machine learning may be more powerful than classical machine learning, at least for some models that are inherently difficult to learn with traditional computers. Machine learning and artificial intelligence technologies are two key research areas in the application of quantum computing algorithms.

Among the characteristics of this computer system is that it allows the simultaneous representation of several states, which is particularly useful when artificial intelligence techniques are used. Voice assistants, for example, could benefit greatly from this implementation, according to Intel, as quantum technology could exponentially improve their accuracy, increasing both their computing power and the amount of data they could process. Quantum computing increases the number of computational variables that machines can juggle and therefore allows them to provide answers faster, just like a human.

Quantum computing is suitable for addressing issues in a range of sectors because it can represent and handle a large number of states. On quantum algorithms, Intel has established various new research avenues. Their initial uses will be in areas like material sciences, where simulating minuscule molecules requires a lot of computational power. In the future, bigger machines will make it possible to create pharmaceuticals or optimize logistics, such as choosing the most practical path from among a variety of options. The majority of artificial intelligence applications in the industry now include "supervised learning," which is applied to tasks like picture identification and consumption forecasting.

Based on the various QML proposals that have already been made, it is likely that we will begin to see an acceleration in this area, which, in some cases, could be exponential. The field of non-supervised learning is a less-traveled route that has a lot of potential. Algorithms for dimensionality reduction are one example. These techniques are used to represent original data in a smaller space while maintaining the majority of its characteristics. The researcher says that at this stage, using quantum computing will be especially helpful for identifying specific global aspects in a data set.

Quantum Computing Applications

As technology advances, quantum computing could lead to significant advances in many fields, from chemistry and materials science to nuclear physics and machine learning. Key potential applications include:

- IT security

- Drug development

- Financial models

- Better batteries

- Better fertilizers

- Weather forecast and climate change

- Artificial intelligence

- Discovery of electronic materials

- Building a super catalyst

- Bioinformatics

- Photovoltaics

- Advanced calculations in physics

- Healthcare

- Safer airplanes

- Discovery of distant planets

- Optimization, planning, and logistics

- Genomics

- Molecular modeling

Quantum computing applications will be limited and focused because general-purpose quantum computing will most likely never come cheap. However, this technology has the potential to revolutionize some industries. Quantum computing could enable breakthroughs in:

- *Machine learning*: Improved machine learning with faster-structured prediction. Examples include Boltzmann machines, Boltzmann quantum machines, semi-supervised learning, unsupervised learning, and deep learning.

- *Artificial intelligence*: Faster calculations can improve the perception, understanding, and diagnosis of errors in binary classifiers/circuits.

- *Chemistry*: New fertilizers, catalysts, and battery chemicals will help improve resource use.

- *Biochemistry*: New drugs, adapted drugs, and maybe even hair conditioners.

- *Finance*: Quantum computers could enable faster and more complex Monte Carlo simulations; for example, trading, path optimization, market volatility, price optimization, and hedging strategies.

- *Healthcare*: DNA gene sequencing, for example, to optimize radiation treatment/brain tumor detection, can be performed in seconds instead of hours or weeks.

- *Materials*: Super durable materials, corrosion resistant paints, lubricants, and semiconductors.

- *IT*: Faster multidimensional search functions; for example, query optimization, mathematics, and simulations.

Cloud Quantum Computing

The future of computing is undoubtedly represented by quantum computers. They use the power of quantum physics to generate computational power, unlike traditional computers. The underlying technology of a real, functional quantum computer is still quite hazy, therefore it is still only a fantasy. You can create quantum cloud computing by giving users online access to a quantum computer. Cloud-based quantum computing involves the use of virtual quantum computers, simulators, or emulators. More people are considering using cloud services to have access to quantum computing. Quantum computing in the cloud refers to using quantum computers that are accessible to users through the Internet.

Cloud-based quantum computing is used in several contexts:

- Teachers can employ cloud-based quantum computing to build and evaluate quantum algorithms while also assisting students in understanding quantum physics.

- Among other things, researchers can test quantum information theories, do experiments, and compare designs using cloud-based quantum resources.

- To teach players quantum principles, game creators can design quantum games using cloud-based quantum resources.

Here are some existing quantum computing platforms in the cloud:

- Forest, a toolkit for quantum computing created by Rigetti Computing, provides development tools, a programming language, and illustrative algorithms.

- LIQUi|>, a software architecture and toolkit for quantum computing from Microsoft, comes with a programming language, illustrative scheduling and optimization methods, and quantum simulators. Microsoft's Q#, a quantum programming language for the.NET Framework, is seen as LIQUi|>'s replacement.

- The IBM Q Experience gives users access to HPC simulations and quantum hardware. These may be viewed graphically using the IBM Q Experience GUI or programmatically using the Python-based Qiskit framework. Both are built on the OpenQASM standard for quantum operation representation. A tutorial and online community are also available.

Some quantum simulators and devices include the following:

- Several transmon qubit processing units. Those with 5 and 16 qubits are available to the general population. On the IBM Q Network, there are gadgets with 20 qubits.

- A cloud-based simulator with 32 qubits. Qiskit also includes software for simulators that are hosted locally.

- The University of Bristol's Quantum in the Cloud, which is comprised of a four-qubit optical quantum system and a quantum simulator.

- Google's Quantum Playground, which includes a simulator with an easy-to-use interface, a programming language, and a 3D visualization of a quantum state.

- Tsinghua University's Quantum in the Cloud is a new four-qubit quantum cloud experience based on NMRCloudQ, or nuclear magnetic resonance.

- Quantum Inspire by Qutech offers access to QX, a backend for a quantum simulator. On Cartesius, the Dutch national supercomputer of SurfSara, up to 37 qubits may be simulated using 16 fat nodes, whereas up to 26 qubits can be simulated using a common cloud-based server. The Python-based Quantum Inspire SDK, which serves as a backend for the projectQ framework and the Qiskit framework, can be used to construct circuit-based quantum algorithms. A knowledge source containing user manuals and a few cQASM-written sample algorithms are offered by Quantum Inspire.

- Forge by QC Ware gives users access to D-Wave hardware and simulators from Google and IBM. A 30-day free trial of the software comes with one minute of quantum computing time.

Quantum Computing as a Service (QCaaS)

As with any new technology advancement, there is a chance that product development could lag behind the hype, which might have a detrimental effect on perceptions and investments. This is referred to as the *quantum winter* in the context of quantum computing. In addition to raising awareness and advancing society, media hype often raises irrational expectations about timing and capacity. Disillusionment is a harmful byproduct of this degree of hype because quantum computing calls for long-term, ongoing, targeted investment. Quantum computing is intriguing as an investment due to the buzz surrounding it. Consistent findings won't come about for at least five to ten years, and maybe much longer, given that the fundamental physics are still in the developing stage. As a result, any expenditures made in the search for quantum computing prospects must result in discoveries that can be commercialized.

In terms of logistics, maintaining quantum computers is challenging and calls for specialized settings that are chilled to 0.015 Kelvin. A dilution refrigerator insulated to 50,000 times less than the earth's magnetic field and a high vacuum to 10 billion times less than atmospheric pressure are required for the quantum processor. Additionally, it will require calibration on a regular basis. This is not practical for the majority of businesses. To reduce risk and control costs, Gartner advises organizations interested in quantum computing to use quantum computing as a service (QCaaS). Ninety-five percent of companies looking into quantum computing strategies are considering QCaaS.

Amazon Web Services (AWS) Runs Braket, A Quantum Computer as a Service

The e-commerce behemoth Amazon has slyly played all of its cards. This e-commerce giant's cloud computing platform collaborated with D-Wave, IonQ, and Rigetti to launch *Braket*, a brand-new quantum computing service, after realizing the potential of using quantum mechanics to create tools for information processing that are more powerful than classical computers. The preview launch of Braket, AWS's first-ever quantum computing service, was just made official. The phrase "Braket" is derived from "bra-ket notation," which is a typical quantum mechanics nomenclature for quantum states. Using a development environment to explore and build quantum algorithms, test them on virtual quantum computers, and run them on a variety of quantum hardware technologies, Amazon's Braket is a fully managed service that aids in the beginning stages of quantum computing.

How Amazon Braket Can Help

It can be expensive and cumbersome to obtain the quantum computing gear needed to run the algorithms and optimize designs. A new set of abilities are also needed for programming quantum computers to solve a problem. By offering a service that enables developers, researchers, and scientists to investigate, assess, and experiment with quantum computing, Amazon Braket aids in solving these challenges.

Users of this service can select from a range of quantum computers, such as ion trap computers from IonQ, quantum annealing superconductor computers from D-Wave, and gate-based superconductor computers from Rigetti. Additionally, users of Braket are given the option of creating custom quantum algorithms from scratch or selecting one of a number of pre-made algorithms. Amazon Braket offers a fully managed simulation service to assist in debugging and evaluating the implementation once the algorithm has been developed. The program can then be executed on any of the aforementioned quantum computers.

Furthermore, Amazon Braket assists in managing classical compute resources and creating low-latency links to quantum systems in order to make it simpler for customers to create a hybrid algorithm that combines both conventional and quantum workloads.

The Current State of Quantum Computing

NISQ devices, or noisy intermediate-scale quantum devices, are the norm nowadays. This indicates that even if there are 20–70 qubits involved, they are so useless that nothing beneficial can be done with them. The primary explanation for this is that they must work at a temperature of

15 mK because they are very sensitive to all sorts of noise. Additionally, any encounter with the outside world might result in the demise of the quantum state. The second reason is that you usually can't make two arbitrary qubits interact with each other, and this limits their computational power significantly. The third reason is that in order to be useful, these machines have to outcompete regular computers, which have at least a 50-year head start. Keep in mind that the "crappy" machines we are talking about are marvels of contemporary engineering, with dedicated teams of people working on refining this technology.

Summary

This chapter explained the history of quantum mechanics to quantum computers. It discussed different types of quantum gates that are available in typical quantum computers. It also discussed the interrelation of quantum computers, machine learning, and artificial intelligence. Further, you learned about quantum machine learning and the general architecture of quantum computers. Apart from this, you learned about different types of quantum algorithms and their complexity. Finally, the chapter touched on the base quantum cloud and the offering of Braket from Amazon.

CHAPTER 10

Let's Wrap Up: The Final Destination

Dr. Patanjali Kashyap[a*]

[a] Bangalore, Karnataka, India

You are now at the end of this book. It was a great journey for me and I enjoyed it a lot. There is a reason behind writing this book—machine learning and its associated technologies are vast, complex, and challenging. I like challenges, so I chose to write it. Presenting a purely mathematical subject without using mathematics is a challenge. However, I tried my best to present the facts lucidly and to create it an equation-free book. My goal is that it can be understandable to all.

The goal of this book was to provide an overview of the appropriate tools and techniques. Chapter 1 set the stage for machine learning and its associated technologies for business users. It also provided a brief explanation of technical details and business cases, and their importance in the present business ecosystem. The chapter discussed cloud, Big Data, Big Data analytics, machine learning, and cognitive computing in brief. In a nutshell, the chapter provided a holistic and integrative view of these technologies. The chapter explained how technologies work together to provide solutions to solve business challenges.

Knowing the flow of technologies is not enough to grasp the command of the subject matter, so Chapter 2 presented a thesis of basic practical machine learning concepts. At the same time, it discussed the evolution and history of ML in the context of artificial intelligence and brain science. The chapter provided a snapshot of concepts like the generalized machine learning architecture and discussed its associated components. It also showed users how to build a machine learning solution. It also presented details of business opportunities in the context of machine learning, which exist in the multiple areas of industries, domains, verticals, and horizontals. The chapter introduced some innovative models, which essentially provide a futuristic view on the possible opportunities and dimensions of machine learning and its associated technologies. In the process, the chapter provided a glimpse of tools, frameworks, libraries, languages, and APIs of the machine learning ecosystem. Machine learning is a highly mathematical and algorithm-based subject.

Chapter 3 discussed some important algorithms and their uses. It also provided guidelines for using algorithms and machine learning models in effective and efficient ways. While discussing the important aspects of algorithms, the chapter provided success stories associated with particular algorithms/models/techniques. In order to ensure that users are aware of vital machine learning-based trends and the impact on businesses in the current times, the chapter provided a brief overview of these topics. Almost every industry today needs agility in its functions and operations. Machine learning itself is an agile and innovative field of study. Therefore, a section on the Agile software methodology was provided in Chapter 3.

Chapter 4 explained in detail the technology stacks available for IoT, Big Data analytics, machine learning, and cognitive computing. It explained nearly all the main technologies available for the respective stacks. It also provided a perspective of technology in current business scenarios. However, that is the challenging task because of the complex nature and availability of multiple products. There is also a lot of overlap of products and services among the technologies, like machine learning, cloud, Big Data analytics, and cognitive computing. Hence, drawing a clear line between these technologies is difficult.

Chapter 5 built the house on the foundation that the previous chapters laid. It discussed machine learning analytics in detail. It broadly discussed the uses, applications, challenges, and use cases of machine learning analytics in multiple domains, such as manufacturing, retail, marketing, sales, banking, and finance. It provided a comprehensive view of the some of the important sectors of our time, such as video gaming, agriculture, disaster management, oil and gas, fashion, hospitality, travel, and aviation. It also briefly discussed the role of machine learning analytics.

It's important to see these concepts in action, which is where Chapter 6 came into play. Chapter 6 covered the "real action" of machine learning and its associated technologies. This chapter covered lots of important information on working on machine learning and associated technologies. Chapter 6 contained a detailed discussion about some of established products centered on machine learning, like Apple Siri, IBM Watson, Microsoft Crotona, and connected and driverless cars.

The IT industry is going through a transformation, there is absolutely no doubt about it. Numerous reports, trends, and projections indicate this fact. Hence, understanding the current business dynamics is important. Also, understanding the interplay of thoughts and business models between the vendors, clients, and partners is important. Hence, Chapter 7 provided transformational states of current IT vendors and their adoption strategies to new and evolving business models. This is based on the technologies like machine learning. This chapter provided a view of how the process of thought partnership will play a role in the overall scenario. It also covered risk, compliances, best practices, and KPI in the context of the machine learning ecosystem and provided some insight into how the technologies can potentially transform the future state of information technology and business.

Because people are the most important aspect of this compressive discussion, ideas need proper support from the people and stakeholders involved in the process. Also, shifting from traditional IT to data-driven IT requires a change in mindset. Therefore, Chapter 8 discussed the people aspects of organizations and enterprises. It discussed how an effective team is essential for the implementation of machine leaning projects and the ingredients required to build that team. This is done through the psychological and technical aspects of data culture in the organization, because that is mandatory criteria for a successful organization.

Most of the time we think and believe that our professional and personal lives are different and should not overlap. This is true in some ways, but with the condition that we are all humans, not machines, and therefore, we all carry emotions wherever we go. The workplace is not an exception. However, with the proper management of emotional, moral, and social intelligence of individuals, teams and in turn organizations can get exceptionally good results. The good news is these skills can be learned; they are not like your intelligent quotient, which remains mostly fixed throughout to one's life. So, if organizations facilitate their employees to hone their MQ, EQ, and SQ skills, they can achieve many benefits, such as better commitment, motivated workforces, and excellent team dynamics. Chapter 8 discussed the important aspects of people and organizational psychology—the cultural and behavioral part of organizations and enterprises.

There are certain critical skills that need to be honed that can potentially lead to excellence in four critical dimensions of human endeavors—physical, emotional, social, and spiritual:

- Complex problem-solving skills

- Critical thinking skills

- Design thinking

- Creativity and passion to excel

- People and talent management

- Communication, collaboration, coordination, and inter- and intrapersonal skills

- Emotional, social, moral, and spiritual intelligence

- Instant judgment and decision-making capabilities

- Service orientation

- Negotiation skills

- Cognitive flexibility

- Having the right attitude toward work

- Capabilities to apply mindfulness techniques to work, life, and so on

Chapter 9 discussed quantum computing and quantum machine learning. This will make you ready for the future. When the real shift happens, you will be able to deal with it. This chapter provided a premier of quantum physics and explained the fundamental concepts that are relevant from a quantum computer perspective. For example, it covered the details of entanglement, superposition, coherence, and decoherence and tried to explain them in simple words and examples so that a novice can understand them. These are the foundational concepts for quantum computers (QC), so clarity around these concepts will help you move toward the extraordinary world of QC.

Index

A

Absentia, 435, 436
Absolutdata, 216
Adiabatic computers, 574
Advancements, 157
Advertising, 113, 157, 158, 399
Advisory bots, 407
Agile
    description, 222
    development methodology, 222
    disadvantages, 225
    needs, 223, 224
    project development, 222
    SDLC, 224
    types, 223
    usage, 225
Agile fashion, 73
Agriculture industry, 400
AiCure's artificial intelligence-
        based platform, 362
AI-generated outputs, 243
AirBnB, 232
Alexa, 437
    acoustic model, 417
    Amazon, 415
    microphones, 416
    NLP, 415

orders, 415
output space, 416
signal processing, 416
sports app, 416
user's voice characteristics, 416
Algorithm, 557
    business support, 166
    definition, 166
    integrated ML, 166
    Jargon Buster, 168
    ML algorithm adoption, 167
    productivity and
        intelligence, 167
Algorithm-based models
    binary classification model, 133
    linear amalgamation, 134
    multinomial logistic
        regression, 134
Algorithm-based themes
        and trends
    connectivity-based
        economies, 233
    driverless cars, 231
    intelligent clothing, 231
    IoT's marriage, 234, 235
    IoT wearables, 232
    macro-level changes, 234

© Dr. Patanjali Kashyap 2024
P. Kashyap, *Machine Learning for Decision Makers*,
https://doi.org/10.1007/978-1-4842-9801-5

M

Printed in the United States
by Baker & Taylor Publisher Services